Rethinking Holocaust Justice

RETHINKING HOLOCAUST JUSTICE
ESSAYS ACROSS DISCIPLINES

Edited by
Norman J.W. Goda

berghahn
NEW YORK · OXFORD
www.berghahnbooks.com

First published in 2018 by
Berghahn Books
www.berghahnbooks.com

Library of Congress Cataloging-in-Publication Data

Names: Goda, Norman J. W., 1961– editor.
Title: Rethinking Holocaust justice : essays across disciplines / Norman J.W. Goda.
Description: New York : Berghahn Books, [2018] | Includes bibliographical
references and index.
Identifiers: LCCN 2017050537 (print) | LCCN 2017051078 (ebook) | ISBN
9781785336980 (eBook) | ISBN 9781785336973 (hardback : alk. paper)
Subjects: LCSH: War crime trials–Europe–History–20th century. | Holocaust,
Jewish (1939–1945)–Influence. | Holocaust, Jewish (1939–1945)–Reparations
Classification: LCC KZ1174.5 (ebook) | LCC KZ1174.5 .R48 2018 (print) | DDC
341.6/9–dc23
LC record available at https://lccn.loc.gov/2017050537

British Library Cataloguing in Publication Data

A catalogue record for this book is available from the British Library

ISBN 978-1-78533-697-3 hardback
ISBN 978-1-78920-514-5 paperback
ISBN 978-1-78533-698-0 ebook

חיים בן נחמן ושרה

לאה בת יעקב ואסתר

Contents

Figures

TABLES

Acknowledgments

This book of essays emerged from a set of meetings dealing with how scholars across disciplines might rethink the judicial reckoning of the Holocaust. My colleagues who have contributed essays and I are most pleased that the volume has appeared and we hope that it will be of interest to scholars across disciplines dealing with Holocaust justice and its broader meaning. Besides the colleagues represented in this book, with whom it was a joy to work, I have many others to thank.

Thanks to their keen interest in Holocaust studies, Norman and Irma Braman have been a steady support to the Center for Jewish Studies at the University of Florida. Their generosity made it possible for the Center to host the meetings and discussions from which the present volume emerged. My friend Jack Kugelmass, the Center's director, has also been an enthusiastic supporter of Holocaust-related projects at the Center in terms of research, teaching, and imaginative programming, so much so that the University of Florida has become an important hub under his stewardship for the interdisciplinary study of the Holocaust. Also very generous in this regard are Nan and David Rich and Gary and Niety Gerson, all steadfast friends of the Center.

Several of my colleagues have helped with the completion of this volume. Michael R. Marrus of the University of Toronto provided critical advice as did Devin Pendas of Boston University. I am indebted as well to the three readers commissioned by Berghahn Books who provided all of us with a careful and detailed reading and made invaluable suggestions for improvements. Marion Berghahn and Chris Chappell of Berghahn Books have been, as always, supportive, helpful and patient during the production process. Rebecca Rom-Frank did a fine job managing production, Ilana Brown provided careful copyediting, and J. Naomi Linzer patiently created a fine index for the volume.

In the end, though, there is my family. I thank my sons, Grant and Lucas, two lovers of learning who are on the verge of embarking on their own careers. And, of course, I thank my wife and best friend Gwyneth for her loving support and patience during this project and all of the others.

Gainesville, Florida
2017

Abbreviations

ABS	Archiv bezpečnostních složek (Security Services Archive, Prague)
AEKIR	Archiv der Evangelischen Kirche im Rheinland (Düsseldorf)
AMV	Archiv ministerstva vnitra (Archive of the Ministry of the Interior, Prague)
APT	Archiv Památníku Terezín (Archive of the Terezín Memorial)
BA	Bundesarchiv (Koblenz, Lichterfelde, Ludwigsburg)
BA-MA	Bundesarchiv-Militärarchiv (Freiburg)
BDA	Bundesdenkmalamt (Vienna)
BStU	Bundesbeauftragte für die Unterlagen des Staatssicherheitsdienstes der ehemaligen Deutschen Demokratischen Republik (Berlin)
CIA	Central Intelligence Agency
CHI	Concordia Historical Institute (St. Louis, MO)
CIC	US Army Counterintelligence Corps
CROWCASS	Central Registry of War Criminals and Security Suspects
DP	Displaced Person
EBA-F	Erzbistumsarchiv Freiburg im Breisgau
EBA-M	Erzbistumsarchiv München und Freising
EKD	Evangelische Kirche in Deutschland
ESLI	European Shoah Legacy Institute
FSIA	Foreign Sovereign Immunities Act

GAO   General Accounting Office (US)

GPU   Gosudarstvennoe politicheskoe upravlenie (State Political
               Directorate, USSR)

HDA-SBU   Haluzevyi derzhavnyi arkhiv Sluzhby Bezpeky Ukrainy
               (State Archive Branch of the State Security Service of
               Ukraine, Kyiv)

HURI   Harvard Ukrainian Research Institute

HVIRA   Holocaust Victim Insurance Relief Act

IMT   International Military Tribunal (Nuremberg)

INS   Immigration and Naturalization Service (US)

IPN   Instytut Pamięci Narodowej (Institute of National
               Remembrance, Warsaw)

IRO   International Refugee Organization

KGB   Komitet gosudarstvennoy bezopasnosti (Committee for
               State Security, USSR)

LAS   Landeskirchliches Archiv Stuttgart

LGfZRS   Landergesricht für Zivilrechtssachen (Vienna)

MoMA   Museum of Modern Art (New York)

NARA   National Archives and Records Administration (College
               Park, MD)

NATO   North Atlantic Treaty Organization

NCO   Non-commissioned officer

NCPW   National Council for the Prevention of War (US)

NKVD   Narodnyi Komissrariat Vnutrennykh Del (People's
               Commissariat of Internal Affairs, USSR)

OGPU   Ob"edinënnoe gosudarstvennoe politicheskoe upravlenie
               (Joint State Political Directorate, USSR)

OMGUS   Office of Military Government, United States

OSI   Office of Special Investigations

OSS   Office of Strategic Services

OUN   Organization of Ukrainian Nationalists

OUN(b)   Organization of Ukrainian Nationalists (Bandera branch)

OUN(z)   Organization of Ukrainian Nationalists Abroad

RFSSR   Russian Soviet Federative Socialist Republic

RG	Record Group
SB OUN	Sluzhba Bezpeky (Security Service, Organization of Ukrainian Nationalists)
SD	Sicherheitsdienst
SNCF	Société Nationale des Chemins de fer Français
SOAL	Státní okresní archiv Litoměřice (State Regional Archive Litoměřice)
SOAP	Státní okresní archiv Praha (State Regional Archive Prague)
SS	Schutzstaffel
SWA	Simon Wiesenthal Archiv (Vienna)
TGC	Tripartite Gold Commission
TWC	*Trials of War Criminals before the Nuremberg Military Tribunals under Control Council Law No. 10*
UPA	Ukrains'ka Povstans'ka Armiia (Ukrainian Insurgent Army)
URIA-HURI	Ukrainian Research Institute Archives, Harvard Ukrainian Research Institute
USHMM	United States Holocaust Memorial Museum (Washington, DC)
WHVA	Wirtschafts- und Verwaltungshauptamt (SS Economic and Administrative Main Office)
WJC	World Jewish Congress
WStLA	Wiener Stadt- und Landesarchiv
YVA	Yad Vashem Archives (Jerusalem)
ZCh OUN	Zakordonne Chastyny (Foreign Section, Organization of Ukrainian Nationalists)
ŽMP	Archiv Židovského Muzea (Archive of the Jewish Museum, Prague)
zpUHVR	Zakordonne predstavnytstvo Ukrains'koi Holovnoi Vyzvol'noi Rady (Foreign Representation of the Ukrainian Supreme Liberation Council)

Note on Editing

Place names have been spelled in accordance with current local practice (Kyiv instead of Kiev, Lviv instead of Lvov, Vilnius instead of Vilna), except in book titles where older, anglicized spellings appear. Place names with more universal anglicized spellings among scholars (Munich, Prague, Warsaw) have been spelled accordingly.

The term "antisemitism" is spelled in the text in accordance with current usage, save in book titles and direct quotes where the older spelling "anti-Semitism" is retained.

Introduction

Norman J.W. Goda

The examination of legal proceedings related to Nazi Germany's war and the Holocaust has expanded significantly in the past two decades. It was not always so. Though the Trial of the Major War Criminals at Nuremberg in 1945–1946 generated significant scholarly literature, most of it, at least in the trial's immediate aftermath, concerned legal scholars' judgments of the trial's efficacy from a strictly legalistic perspective. Was the four-power trial based on ex post facto law and thus problematic for that reason, or did it provide the best possible due process to the defendants under the circumstances?[1] Cold War political wrangling over the subsequent Allied trials in the western German occupation zones as well as the sentences that they pronounced generated a discourse that was far more critical of the trials than laudatory.[2] Historians, meanwhile, used the records assembled at Nuremberg as an entrée into other captured German records as they wrote initial studies of the Third Reich, these focusing mainly on foreign policy and wartime strategy, though also to some degree on the Final Solution to the Jewish Question.[3] But they did not historicize the trial, nor any of subsequent trials, as such. Studies that analyzed the postwar proceedings in and of themselves from a historical perspective developed only three decades after Nuremberg, and they focused mainly on the origins of the initial, groundbreaking trial.[4]

Matters changed in the 1990s for a number of reasons. The first was late- and post-Cold War interest among historians of Germany, and of other nations too, in *Vergangenheitsbewältigung*—the political, social, and intellectual attempt to confront, or to sidestep, the criminal wartime past. The degree to which postwar trials by the Allies, the Soviets, and the Germans themselves

1

were effective or ineffective in forcing such a confrontation was naturally a part of this kind of study.[5] A second reason was the reemergence of genocide in the 1990s in former-Yugoslavia and in Rwanda coupled with the decision by the United Nations to try even minor perpetrators based on the broad legal principles used at Nuremberg and in accordance with the UN's 1948 Genocide Convention. These developments not only brought a new interest in the social sciences concerning the question of genocide and other state crimes. They also, together with developments in South America and South Africa, brought interest in transitional justice, most notably the degree to which trials, but also truth commissions, could aid through their narratives in creating the conditions for acknowledgement of state-sponsored criminality and ultimately peace.[6]

But the third reason for expanded scholarly interest in postwar trials was the tremendous expansion of interest in the Holocaust in the late 1980s and 1990s. This interest went in several directions.[7] Using pretrial interrogation records and trial transcripts themselves, as well as captured German records held formerly by the Soviet Union, historians began to study the perpetrators in an effort to reconstruct the German decision-making process toward mass murder and also the mentality of killing.[8] Scholarly interest in disciplines other than history, meanwhile, turned to the difficulties of representing the Holocaust in everything from survivor testimony to literature to art and film, partly incorporating recent thinking on trauma and memory, partly revisiting German philosopher Theodor Adorno's famous dictum on the impossibility of balancing the aesthetics of art on the one hand, and the horror of Auschwitz on the other.[9] In the political arena, the issue of reparations re-emerged in the 1990s, partly in the form of renewed searches for looted assets and partly in the form of class-action lawsuits against international firms on behalf of still-living victims.[10] The general interest in everything from assets to the escape and reintegration of unpunished Nazi criminals even led to the declassification of millions of pages of intelligence and diplomatic records in the United States, and efforts in that direction in Germany.[11]

It should not be surprising in this broad context that historians also began to take up the theme of Holocaust trials and other postwar legal proceedings. They reexamined iconic trials such as the Trial of the Major War Criminals and the 1961 trial of Adolf Eichmann in Jerusalem, this time regarding the ways in which trials augmented our historical understanding of Nazi atrocities as well as the memories of the victims. Additional source materials from Nuremberg were published, ranging from pretrial interrogations of major Nazi perpetrators to psychiatric profiles of the same types of defendants.[12] Contemporary correspondence and memoirs of prosecutors also appeared in published form.[13] But scholars also began examining for the first time the lesser-known trials. These included the "subsequent" Nuremberg trials under the American Military Tribunal on which very little had been written,[14] and also the Dachau trials held under the auspices of US military commissions, which were virtually unstudied.[15] They also included the numerous trial programs carried out by the other Allied states.[16] Scholars also examined the administration of justice in the Federal Republic of Germany before and after the watershed 1958 formation of the Zentrale Stelle der Landesjustizverwaltung in Ludwigsburg, which assembled evidence against Nazi perpetrators, and also in the German Democratic Republic, which used trials primarily as a propaganda tool against West Germany.[17] Austria, which had its own unique issues with the Nazi past following revelations concerning Kurt Waldheim in 1985, has also come under scrutiny by historians there.[18] The postwar proceedings in the Soviet Union and Eastern Europe have also been partially analyzed.[19] Finally, there have been brief treatments of relatively obscure individual cases, often to make a larger point concerning the politics of justice in specific countries at specific times.[20] Even postwar Jewish honor courts have been examined for the first time.[21] Scholars are not close to examining each and every postwar trial, but their progress in the past fifteen years in considering the most important ones has been remarkable.

In pausing, we might ask what the new scholarship on trials, particularly from different academic disciplines, has achieved. Surely from the legal perspective, the new scholarship has provided a fuller, more contextualized picture of Nuremberg itself and the development of international criminal law since 1945. At the same time, scholarship on national trials in Germany, France, the Soviet Union, and elsewhere has told us more about ways in which nations have confronted the past, or obscured it further, through the creation of signature legal proceedings and their choice of subjects and specific defendants. The scholarship has also elucidated the effect of domestic and international politics on war crimes trials, set in particular against the corrosive backdrop of the Cold War.[22] The thinking on these issues is surely not complete. But for the most part our conceptions of the broader legal and political problems will probably not change dramatically with more research into those classes of trials on which we already have significant scholarship. The subsequent Nuremberg trials, for instance, were all based on Control Council Law Number 10 and all faced opposition in the US occupation zone in Germany. West German trials were all, until very recently, built on a narrow reading of the definition of murder in the German Penal Code, and the West German public in the 1960s was always ambivalent concerning trials of Nazi perpetrators in German courts. The circumstances of individual trials indeed remain interesting, of course, but our understanding of these particular issues is not likely to be altered much.

Yet the wider meaning of Holocaust justice moves beyond the effort to deliver justice itself, even amid contentious politics. It also carries within it a host of questions concerning individual testimony, national and international discourse, gender, symbolism, and other themes of broader interest to Holocaust scholars across disciplines. We may thus consider whether current approaches to Holocaust justice are in need of expansion. Currently scholars, historians in particular, are fond, for instance, of a one-trial approach that establishes a narrative of a chosen case in order to elaborate certain broader themes, ranging from justice to memory to the ways in which the trial succeeds or fails in providing true justice. But might broader, perhaps comparative approaches be potentially fruitful as well? Are there types of sources that we have not fully mined—including surrounding diplomatic and intelligence sources, pre-trial interrogations and affidavits, and literary and film representations—when considering the problem of the meaning of Holocaust justice? Are more obscure trials worth examining? How might we approach the issue of guilt and victimization in more than historical and legal terms? Do we take pre-trial and courtroom testimony for granted, ignoring the heavy weight of the trial itself? And what of the many cases, including very recent ones, where justice was delayed or never delivered at all?

The most expansive issue to consider may concern the almost aesthetic theme of Holocaust representation, and specifically the degree to which the enormity, the horror, and the uniqueness of the Holocaust has been adequately represented within the confines of the courtroom and in other types of legal proceedings.[23] In her famous, flawed, yet enduring consideration of the trial of Adolf Eichmann in Jerusalem in 1961, Hannah Arendt rejected the Israeli prosecution's choreography of the proceedings, which aimed at infusing meaning by using Eichmann in such a way as to represent the Holocaust's totality and its horror through a multilayered narrative that spanned the European continent and beyond. In particular, Arendt rejected the prosecution's use of over a hundred witnesses, most of whom gave eyewitness accounts of the horrors, but few of whom had any direct connection with Eichmann himself. The proper purpose of any trial, Arendt famously insisted in her epilogue, "is to render justice, and nothing else; even the noblest of ulterior purposes … can only detract from the law's main business." For Arendt, the Jerusalem proceedings became a "show trial" that detracted from their initial potential and ultimately their legacy.[24]

At the time, most legal scholars who considered the matter agreed with Arendt, at least on this particular principle if not with her assessment of

Eichmann himself. The reemergence of state-sponsored mass violence, however, helped to change minds decades later. We have moved toward some consensus that the narrative—or better said, the narratives—of an atrocity trial might be its most important aspect, surely more important than the necessarily insufficient punishment that the defendant receives. Legal scholar Mark Osiel, building on the then-unorthodox thinking of 1960s political theorist Judith Shklar, argues that notwithstanding the lack of agreement concerning trial procedure, the political trial that serves liberal ends in the wake of mass atrocity is desirable and even essential.[25] The courtroom properly becomes a "theater of ideas" where the broad questions of collective memory and national identity are engaged through sometimes competing narratives; this pedagogical impact means that, for Osiel, trials "should be unabashedly designed as monumental spectacles."[26]

This is not to say that the process has ever been easy, particularly with regard to the Holocaust itself. On the one hand, the law must be observed; justice must be served to the defendants. But the proceeding also must do justice to the historical events. This conundrum necessitates bending the boundaries of both law and history in order to produce a narrative of atrocity that reaches legal consensus. In his book *The Memory of Judgment* (2001), Lawrence Douglas wrestles with this problem and argues that the glass is more than half full. The Holocaust helped to create the legitimately "didactic trial" that not only weighs evidence and delivers a considered verdict, but which also carries a historical narrative for posterity. Meanwhile a "jurisprudence of atrocity" emerged. On the other hand, Douglas shows that the attempts to represent an unprecedented crime within the constraints of law and procedure is not without problems. Nuremberg, for instance, carried a new charge—"crimes against humanity"—which referred to the mistreatment and murder of civilians even in peacetime and even by their own government. But the tribunal's restrictive reading of this legal innovation necessitated a "tortured history," whereby the Holocaust, though discussed from different angles, became an ancillary part of the main and more sure-footed criminal charge, which focused on Germany's aggressive war.[27] Representation, though legitimately attempted, is never perfect.

This problem is endemic to all Holocaust proceedings, though the ways that it is confronted depends on the place and the time. Recent scholarship on the 1963–1965 Frankfurt Auschwitz Trial demonstrates how the determination of West German prosecutors to try Nazi criminals ran up against the Federal Republic of Germany's constitutional rejection of "crimes against humanity" as ex post facto law. Prosecutors had to charge Nazi criminals with the comparatively pedestrian crime of murder, which made for its own refracted history. The need to demonstrate a direct physical or administra-

tive connection between the defendant and specific crimes together with the
need to prove an internal "lust for killing" on the part of the defendant for
a murder charge to stick, meant that the most monstrous perpetrators were
convicted of murder while the more ordinary criminals, who could plausi-
bly deny depravity, were convicted of being accomplices at most.

In France, the signature trial of Klaus Barbie in 1987 had very different
problems of representation, these concerning the Holocaust's uniqueness, a
point of contention among scholars today.[28] The determination of former *ré-
sistants* to be included as victims under the rubric of "crimes against humanity" meant that the French courts' definition of these types of crimes was
recalibrated in such a way as to include Barbie's torture of resisters under
the same legal designation as his deportation of Jewish children, who were
murdered for being Jewish children. Worse, Barbie's lead attorney Jacques
Vergès deployed a postmodernist defense that denied the Holocaust's singular elements. The crimes of the Western world, for instance France's crimes
during the war in Algeria (1954–1962) and the killing of Palestinian Arabs
by Jewish irregulars at Deir Yassin (1948) were equal in the annals of atrocity, and in a sense even worse owing to what Vergès insisted was Western
"denial."[29] As another Barbie attorney, the Algerian Nabil Bouaïta, argued
to the court, "If you elevate the history of one people, automatically you
commit an injustice."[30]

Nor are criminal proceedings the only ones with such implications. Restitution cases in fact also bear issues of representation far beyond the issue
of monetary compensation. Michael R. Marrus has expressed skepticism in
this regard concerning 1990s restitution cases, wherein US class action lawsuits mainly reflected US lawyers' propensity to pursue the low hanging fruit
of vulnerable targets, namely European companies that do business in the
United States and can thus be sued. Latter day restitution moreover, plays
out in the newspapers, where inaccurate and even sensational allegations
can be made, and they are settled out of court with little public narrative
one way or the other.[31] On the other hand, the close reading of certain cases
can be revealing regardless of their flaws. The struggles of heirs to recover
family property, for instance, creates a close narrative for how the property
was plundered in the first place and the successes and failures of restitution
efforts with postwar authorities whether in occupied Germany, Western Europe, or the emerging communist bloc.

In the meantime, a most critical issue concerning Holocaust representation in criminal or restitution cases may be that of testimony. Holocaust
testimony in the broad sense—in the form of diaries, memoirs, videotaped
statements, fiction, and film—has been amply discussed both from the stand-
points of its collection after the war, the psychological impact of trauma

on testimony, and the factual efficacy of testimony as opposed to official documents. This goes for the testimonies of perpetrators and victims alike. Gitta Sereny showed in her lengthy interviews with Treblinka Kommandant Franz Stangl and Hitler's munitions minister Albert Speer that both men, even long after their verdicts were read, constructed layered narratives mitigating their guilt so that they could live with themselves.[32] But testimonies of perpetrators at trial are interesting too, coming as they do in full public view and under the pressure of cross-examination and the threat of punishment. Arendt legendarily evaluated Eichmann's testimony in a way that portrayed him as the reluctant cog that he argued himself to be, thus mistaking his essence.[33] Yet Eichmann's self-portrayal was interesting nonetheless, not least because his particular take on himself was less universal than we might think. In his trial before the American Military Tribunal in 1947 and 1948, Otto Ohlendorf, the first commander of Einsatzgruppe D, adopted a narrative whereby the murder of Jews in the USSR was an unimpeachable Führer order and whereby he had argued with Reinhard Heydrich on first receiving his assignment in the East. But he also characterized the mass murder of the Jews as a necessary security measure. "It is known from European history," he said under cross-examination, "that the Jews actually during all wars carried out espionage service on both sides." When questioned about murdering Jewish children, he added "the children were people who would grow up and ... would constitute a danger no smaller than that of the parents." And, referring to the Americans' difficulties with the Soviets in late 1947, he sought common ground. "[We] ... as the ones who were closer to Bolshevism than you in the States, much sooner came to realize [the danger] than you; and with this I agree ... with your statesmen in America at the moment."[34] Ohlendorf thus blamed superior orders and sought to immunize himself against carrying them out, but also embraced the orders on the grounds of military security while representing the preemptive killing of children as part of a community of interest shared with his prosecutors. It was a noteworthy performance. Yet for the most part we have studied neither pre-trial interrogations nor the trial testimonies of perpetrators in this way as explanatory statements that aimed at self-representation.[35]

Jewish Holocaust testimony in traditional forms carries its own methodological challenges depending on, among other things, when and how the testimony was given.[36] But, as is the case with perpetrators, we have not thought about Jewish testimony within the courtroom as much as we might. Facing the accused while feeling the weight of speaking for millions, all within a charged political atmosphere that includes journalists and possibly television cameras, all make for a different kind of burden. Thus the Vilna poet and resister Avrom Sutzkever felt what he called a "crushing respon-

sibility" when he testified at Nuremberg as part of the Soviet case against
the major war criminals. His testimony, he felt, was a unique instance; he
did not know that there would be a host of trials afterwards. The presence
in the dock of Alfred Rosenberg, the former minister for the eastern territories, added to the moment.[37] Sutzkever's opening, in which he stood silently
for some forty-five seconds, carries a poetic context tied to his sense of the
singular moment and his understanding that Jewish testimony was hardly
privileged at Nuremberg.[38] The Eichmann trial, Arendt's criticisms notwithstanding, legitimized Jewish courtroom testimony. Yet this did not make it
easy. Pinchas Freudiger, a former Orthodox member of Budapest's Jewish
Council, faced accusations of collaboration from the gallery; Joel Brand
still felt a heavy burden of guilt for the failure to realize Eichmann's blood-
for-trucks ruse with the Allies in 1944; Israeli novelist Yehiel Dinur (aka
Ka-Tzednik) collapsed on the stand as he faced apparitions from "the Planet
Auschwitz" and perhaps, as he also bore the weight of the Israeli questions
about resistance.[39] These, of course, are well-known testimonies. The larger
point is that many others await analysis within this context.

The present volume comprises essays by diverse scholars from several
disciplines ranging from law to history to religion to comparative literature
to art history. All have an interest in Holocaust proceedings, and all have
pressed past the chronological sequence of individual trials in order to examine postwar justice from different angles and perspectives, and in one
way or another, all focus on the broader issue of Holocaust representation
through the theme of justice. And while some have revisited well-studied
proceedings such as the Eichmann trial or the fate of Klaus Barbie in an effort to offer new angles of consideration, others have looked at understudied
or even very recent proceedings and have divined new ways to think about
postwar justice.

The volume's first section concerns innovative approaches to the problem of historic guilt. Eric Kligerman, a scholar of comparative literature,
reconsiders Hannah Arendt's *Eichmann in Jerusalem* not so much as a historical work, but as a work of literature in which Arendt's view of Eichmann
reflects the effect on Arendt's reading of Franz Kafka. Though Arendt was
surely incorrect concerning the criminal motivations of Eichmann personally, and thus the defining nature of his guilt, it is also true that her notion
of "the banality of evil," has been remarkably durable. The assessment of
Eichmann as a Kafkaesque character provides not only a new way to read
Arendt's reading of Eichmann's guilt; it also helps to explain why her image
of Eichmann ultimately carried such power. Katherina von Kellenbach is a
scholar of religious studies who has considered historic guilt from the inti-
mate standpoint of interfamily relations and from the standpoint of broader

rituals of purification. Her assessment of West German defendants in the 1960s, their limited reading of their own guilt, their definition of themselves as scapegoats for a broadly guilty nation, and the degree to which their trials could or could not have led to a more general purification, all provides a new reading on West German justice in the 1960s.

The second section of this volume concerns the narrative of testimony both from the perspective of victims and from that of major perpetrators. Historian Anna Hájková deconstructs Jewish testimony about the Terezín ghetto. She demonstrates first that trial testimony on ghettos as opposed to concentration camps is an understudied area. But she also examines how witnesses were chosen for different types of trials by Jewish and communist organs, how they testified differently at the trials of German perpetrators and those of Jewish "collaborators," how they defined their Jewishness depending on the circumstances of the trial, how certain language referencing resistance helped in having their stories accepted, how testimony changed as did political circumstances in Eastern Europe between the 1940s and 1970s, and how gendered language influenced narrative. Kerstin von Lingen, another historian, examines the testimony and the private conversations of major perpetrators, in particular Karl Wolff and Klaus Barbie. Using trial records and also closely guarded personal records, she further examines the issue of perpetrator narrative within the context of new scholarship on the seemingly oxymoronic principle of Nazi ethics. Here, the testimony emphasizes certain types of "honorable" killing, dissociating perpetrators from the murder of civilians while reassigning responsibility to superiors, all while deploying the time-bound ethical principles of honor and duty.

The volume's third section concerns judicial narratives in the controversial field of Ukrainian perpetrators. Historian Alexander Prusin's chapter concerns a practically unknown set of proceedings, the "second wave" of Soviet trials in the 1960s, which concentrated on Trawnikis, the specially trained Ukrainian SS (Schutzstaffel) guards who aided in extermination measures. Prusin places the proceedings partly in a propaganda context. As West Germany debated whether to extend the statute of limitations on murders committed under the Nazis, Moscow aimed to show that Nazi crimes would never be forgiven in the USSR. At the same time, Nikita Khrushchev sought to discredit the arbitrary judicial standards of the Stalin years. The result was a series of investigations and trials that one would not expect, not only in terms of careful collection of evidence, but in terms of emphasizing, even in the midst of the Soviet anti-Zionist/antisemitic campaign of the 1960s, the mass murder of Jews, in court if not in the newspapers. Per Anders Rudling examines the case of Mykola Lebed, the Ukrainian nationalist leader who for a time collaborated with the Nazis and whose guerilla organizations launched savage killings of Jews and Poles. After the war, Lebed forged a relationship with the CIA that lasted the entire length of the Cold War. Lebed's exposure by the *Village Voice* in the 1980s triggered fiery reactions in the Ukrainian émigré community concerning narratives of Ukrainian leaders' wartime pasts. Lawrence Douglas, a legal scholar, examines the saga of Ivan Demjanjuk, the Ukrainian Sobibór guard whose judicial saga in the United States, Israel, and Germany spanned more than four decades. Here Douglas looks at Demjanjuk's final chapter, his 2009 murder trial in Munich. In what turned out to be a landmark case rather than simply a judicial coda, the German court reinterpreted the murder statute to create more accurate judicial narratives of the extermination camps. Douglas thus shows a correction of previous German court narratives in Holocaust-related cases.

The fourth section includes new considerations on restitution and reparations by historian Regula Ludi, legal scholar Michael J. Bazyler, and art historian Sophie Lillie. Ludi provides an updated and essential theoretical basis for our understanding of reparations and restitution. It was not, she shows, an ancillary phenomenon based simply on monetary amounts of compensation. Its evolution, filtered through postwar European antifascist politics and scientific development in the field of psychological trauma, is at the very center of creating survivor narratives that brought differences between the Holocaust and other wartime brutalities such as political persecution into sharper relief. Bazyler provides a survey of the legal efforts at restitution since the 1990s, which he updates to include present-day efforts. Interestingly, he also points to narrative symbols in the litigation, especially as regards recent litigation about German, French, and Hungarian railroads. Though Bazyler concedes that civil litigation has distorted the narrative and even the public understanding of the Holocaust itself, he argues that this is a short-term problem; civil litigation, he says, has reintroduced law and history to one another, and has led to, among other things, new research on the business angles of genocide. Lillie examines in detail a very recent case of art restitution—that of Gustav Klimt's *Beethoven Frieze*. Here the Austrian state rejected the claims of the frieze's rightful owners, the heirs of the Jewish businessman Erich Lederer. The focus on a single masterwork's odyssey from its owners to the Nazi state to the Austrian state is interesting in its own right. It recreates the world of major private art collections in *fin-de-siècle* Vienna, Klimt's unorthodox place in it, the role of Jewish industrial families, and the rank opportunism of Vienna's museums in acquiring plundered works. But the Austrian decision not to restore the painting also demonstrates the shortcomings of restitution laws and the limits of state cooperation regardless of legitimate claims.

The final section deals with overall narratives concerning trials and trial programs themselves, and it circles back to interpretations of the Nuremberg and Dachau trials from the immediate postwar period to the present day. It is well known that the US trials had few German supporters. But by tracing the evolution of the hostile public relations campaign by the Catholic and Evangelical Churches in occupied Germany—a campaign that reached to Washington while questioning the motives of US prosecutors, especially the German-Jewish émigré Robert Kempner—JonDavid K. Wyneken examines how outside public pressure and a counter narrative of the trials was created. It is an instructive lesson for contemporary genocide trials. Tomaz Jardim, meanwhile, challenges present-day narratives about judicial proceedings after World War II. Nuremberg, he says, was actually the exception both in terms of the number of defendants and in terms of its commitment to due process. The military commission trials at Dachau, he says, were more the rule with lower level defendants and far more lax standards of evidence and procedure. For Jardim, the irony is that while Nuremberg fed into a tradition that led to the UN's International Criminal Court, the Dachau trials were part of a tradition that led to Guantanamo Bay.

As this introduction shows, this is not the first book of essays concerning the judicial reckoning with Nazism or with the adjudication of the Holocaust. There has been an effort, however, to collect viewpoints from a number of disciplinary perspectives and to suggest avenues that might augment future research approaches. We hope that our colleagues find the collection to be of interest and that it might help in future writing on the question of retribution.

Norman J.W. Goda received his Ph.D. in history from the University of North Carolina at Chapel Hill. He is the Norman and Irma Braman Professor of Holocaust Studies at the University of Florida. His publications include *Tales from Spandau: Nazi Criminals and the Cold War* (2006) and *US Intelligence and the Nazis* (2005), with Richard Breitman, Timothy Naftali, and Robert Wolfe. He is currently working on a new treatment of the 1987 trial of Klaus Barbie.

NOTES

1. Contrary legal opinions in Norman E. Tutorow, ed., *War Crimes, War Criminals, and War Crimes Trials: An Annotated Bibliography and Source Book* (New York, 1986).
2. Discussed in Frank Buscher, *The U.S. War Crimes Trial Program in Germany, 1946–1955* (Westport, CT, 1989); Tom Bower, *A Pledge Betrayed: America and Britain and*

the *Denazification of Post-War Germany* (New York, 1982); Ulrich Brochhagen, *Nach Nürnberg: Vergangenheitsbewältigung und Westintegration in der Ära Adenauer* (Hamburg, 1994); Thomas Alan Schwartz, "John McCloy and the Landsberg Cases," in *American Policy and the Reconstruction of West Germany, 1945–1955,* ed. Jeffry M. Diefendorf, Axel Frohn, and Hermann-Josef Rupieper (New York, 1993), 433–54.

3. On the use of captured records including those used at Nuremberg, see Robert Wolfe, ed., *Captured German and Related Records: A National Archives Conference: Papers and Proceedings of the Conference on Captured German and Related Records, November 12–13, 1968, The National Archives Building, Washington, D.C.* (Athens, OH, 1974). The initial two waves of scholarship on the Third Reich is lengthy, but see for example John W. Wheeler-Bennett, *The Nemesis of Power: The German Army in Politics, 1918–1945* (London, 1953); Gerhard L. Weinberg, *The Foreign Policy of Hitler's Germany,* 2 vols. (Chicago, 1970–1980); Raul Hilberg, *The Destruction of the European Jews* (New York, 1961), rev. ed., 3 vols., (New York, 1985).

4. Bradley F. Smith, *Reaching Judgment at Nuremberg* (New York, 1977); Bradley F. Smith, *The Road to Nuremberg* (New York, 1981); Bradley F. Smith, ed., *The American Road to Nuremberg: The Documentary Record, 1944–1945* (Stanford, CA, 1982).

5. See Charles Maier, *The Unmasterable Past: History, Holocaust, and German National Identity* (Cambridge, MA, 1988); Jeffrey Herf, *Divided Memory: The Nazi Past in the Two Germanys* (Cambridge, MA, 1996); Norbert Frei, *Vergangenheitspolitik: Die Anfänge der Bundesrepublik und die NS-Vergangenheit* (Munich, 1996). See also Henry Rousso, *Le syndrome de Vichy, de 1944 à nos jours* (Paris, 1987).

6. For early literature see, for example, Michael P. Scharf, *Balkan Justice: The Story Behind the First International War Crimes Trial Since Nuremberg* (Durham, NC, 1997); Gary Jonathan Bass, *Stay the Hand of Vengeance: The Politics of War Crimes Tribunals* (Princeton, NJ, 2000); Mark Osiel, *Mass Atrocity, Collective Memory, and the Law* (New Brunswick, NJ, 1997). The literature on transitional justice is massive, but see, for example, William Schabas, *Unimaginable Atrocities: Justice, Politics, and Rights at the War Crimes Tribunals* (New York, 2014); Hugo van der Merwe, Victoria Baxter, and Audrey R. Chapman, eds., *Assessing the Impact of Transitional Justice: Challenges for Empirical Research* (Washington, DC, 2009); *Journal of Genocide Research* 9, no. 2 (2007) [Special Issue: *Genocide and International Law*]. In general, on genocide studies, see Donald Bloxham and A. Dirk Moses, eds., *The Oxford Handbook of Genocide Studies* (New York, 2013).

7. The library of books produced on the Holocaust since the end of the Cold War is too lengthy to mention but for contemporary assessments see Michael R. Marrus, *The Holocaust in History* (Lebanon, NH, 1987) and the essays in Michael Berenbaum and Abraham J. Peck, eds., *The Holocaust and History: The Known, the Unknown, the Disputed, and the Reexamined* (Bloomington, IN, 1998). For more recent historiography, see Dan Stone, *Histories of the Holocaust* (New York, 2010).

8. For the use of different types of interrogation and trial records see, for example, Richard Breitman, *The Architect of Genocide: Himmler and the Final Solution* (New York, 1991); Christopher Browning, *Ordinary Men: Reserve Police Battalion 101 and the Final Solution in Poland* (New York, 1992). On the intersection of war crimes

investigations and historical research, see Erich Haberer, "History and Justice: Paradigms of the Prosecution of Nazi Crimes," *Holocaust and Genocide Studies* 19, no. 3 (2005): 487–519.

9. Thus also taking up earlier work by Lawrence Langer, *The Holocaust and the Literary Imagination* (New Haven, CT, 1975). See especially Saul Friedländer, ed., *Probing the Limits of Representation: Nazism and the "Final Solution"* (Cambridge, MA, 1992). Also Lawrence Langer, ed., *Art from the Ashes: A Holocaust Anthology* (New York, 1995); Neil Levi and Michael Rothberg, eds., *The Holocaust: Theoretical Readings* (New Brunswick, NJ, 2003); and the newer readings in Peter Hayes and John K. Roth, eds., *The Oxford Handbook of Holocaust Studies* (New York, 2010).

10. *The Eizenstat Report and Related Issues Concerning United States and Allied Efforts to Restore Gold and Other Assets Looted by Nazis during World War II: Hearing Before the Committee on Banking and Financial Services, House of Representatives, One Hundred Fifth Congress, First Session, June 25, 1997* (Washington, DC, 1997); Greg Bradsher, ed., *Holocaust-Era Assets: A Finding Aid to Records at the National Archives at College Park, Maryland* (Washington, DC, 1999). For a summary of the lawsuits, see Michael R. Marrus, *Some Measure of Justice: The Holocaust Era Restitution Campaign of the 1990s* (Madison, WI, 2009).

11. The initial study in the United States is Richard Breitman, Norman J.W. Goda, Timothy Naftali, Robert Wolfe, *US Intelligence and the Nazis* (New York, 2005); Richard Breitman and Norman J.W. Goda, *Hitler's Shadow: Nazi War Criminals, US Intelligence, and the Cold War* (Washington, DC, 2012). For Germany see Eckart Conze, Norbert Frei, Peter Hayes, Moshe Zimmermann, *Das Amt und die Vergangenheit: Deutsche Diplomaten im Dritten Reich und in der Bundesrepublik* (Munich, 2010). Studies based on declassified West German intelligence records include Martin Cüppers, *Walther Rauff–In deutschen Diensten: Vom Nazi Verbrecher zum BND-Spion* (Darmstadt, 2013); Peter Hammerschmidt, *Deckname Adler: Klaus Barbie und die westlichen Geheimdienste* (Frankfurt am Main, 2014). See also Daniel Stahl, *Nazi-Jagd: Südamerikas Diktaturen und die Ahndung von NS-Verbrechen* (Göttingen, 2013); Gerald Steinacher, *Nazis on the Run: How Hitler's Henchmen Fled Justice* (New York, 2011).

12. Richard Overy, ed., *Interrogations: The Nazi Elite in Allied Hands, 1945* (New York, 2001); Robert Gellately, ed., *The Nuremberg Interviews: An American Psychiatrist's Conversations with the Defendants and Witnesses* (New York, 2004).

13. Telford Taylor, *The Anatomy of the Nuremberg Trials: A Personal Memoir* (New York 1992); Christopher J. Dodd, ed., *Letters from Nuremberg: My Father's Narrative of a Quest for Justice* (New York, 2007); Joshua Greene, *Justice at Dachau: The Trials of An American Prosecutor* (New York, 2003); Drexel Sprecher, *Inside the Nuremberg Trial: A Prosecutor's Comprehensive Account*, 2 vols. (Lanham, MD, 1999); Benjamin B. Ferencz, *Mémoirs de Ben: Procureur à Nuremberg et avocat de la paix mondiale* (Paris, 2012). Excerpts from contemporary statements by those involved in Guénaël Mettraux, ed., *Perspectives on the Nuremberg Trial* (New York, 2008).

14. Gerd R. Ueberschär, ed., *Nationalsozialismus vor Gericht: Die alliierten Prozesse gegen Kriegsverbrecher und Soldaten 1943–1952* (Frankfurt am Main, 1999); Hilary Earl, *The Nuremberg SS-Einsatzgruppen Trial, 1945–1958: Atrocity, Law and History* (New

York, 2009); Valerie Hébert, *Hitler's Generals on Trial: The Last War Crimes Tribunal at Nuremberg* (Lawrence, KS, 2010); Ulf Schmidt, *Justice at Nuremberg: Leo Alexander and the Nazi Doctors' Trial* (New York, 2004); Paul Julian Weindling, *Nazi Medicine and the Nuremberg Trials: From Medical War Crimes to Informed Consent* (New York, 2004); Annete Weinke, *Die Nürnberger Prozesse* (Munich, 2006). Also Kevin Jon Heller, *The Nuremberg Military Tribunals and the Origins of International Criminal Law* (New York, 2011).

15. Patricia Heberer, "The American Military Commission Trials of 1945," in *Nazi Crimes and the Law,* ed. Nathan Stoltzfus and Henry Friedlander (New York, 2008), 43–62; Michael Bryant, "Punishing the Excess: Sadism, Bureaucratized Atrocity, and the U.S. Army Concentration Camp Trials, 1945–1947," in Stoltzfus and Friedlander, *Nazi Crimes and the Law,* 63–85; Lisa Yavnai, "U.S. Army War Crimes Trials in Germany, 1945–1947," in *Atrocities on Trial: Historical Perspectives on the Politics of Prosecuting War Crimes,* ed. Patricia Heberer and Jürgen Mattäus (Lincoln, NE, 2008), 49–74; Tomaz Jardim, *The Mauthausen Trial: American Military Justice in Germany* (Cambridge, MA, 2012).

16. For example, Donald Bloxham, *Genocide on Trial: War Crimes Trials and the Formation of Holocaust History and Memory* (New York, 2001); Claudia Moisel, *Frankreich und die deutschen Kriegsverbrecher: Politik und Praxis der Strafverfolgung* (Göttingen, 2004); Bernhard Brunner, *Der Frankreich-Komplex: Die nationalsozialistischen Verbrechen in Frankreich und die Justiz der Bundesrepublik Deutschland* (Göttingen, 2004); Richard J. Golsan, "Crimes-against-Humanity Trials in France and their Historical and Legal Contexts: A Retrospective Look," in Heberer and Matthäus, *Atrocities on Trial,* 247–62.

17. Dick de Mildt, *In the Name of the People: Perpetrators of Genocide in the Reflection of their Post-War Prosecution in West Germany: The "Euthanasia" and "Aktion Reinhard" Cases* (The Hague, 1996); Rebecca Wittmann, *Beyond Justice: The Auschwitz Trial* (Cambridge, MA, 2005); Devin O. Pendas, *The Frankfurt Auschwitz Trial, 1963–1965: Genocide, History, and the Limits of the Law* (New York, 2005); Annette Weinke, *Die Verfolgung von NS-Tätern im geteilten Deutschland: Vergangenheitsbewältigungen 1949–1969* (Paderborn, 2002). See also Henry Friedlander, "Nazi Crimes and the German Law," in Stoltzfus and Friedlander, *Nazi Crimes and the Law,* 15–33; Patrick Tobin, "Crossroads at Ulm: Postwar West Germany and the 1958 Ulm *Einsatzkommando* Trial," Ph.D. diss., University of North Carolina at Chapel Hill, 2013.

18. See the essays in Thomas Albrich, Winfried R. Garscha, and Martin F. Polaschek, eds., *Holocaust und Kriegsverbrechen vor Gericht: Der Fall Österreich* (Innsbruck, 2006).

19. Alexander V. Prusin, "'Fascist Criminals to the Gallows!': The Holocaust and Soviet War Crimes Trials, December 1945–January 1946," *Holocaust and Genocide Studies* 17, no. 1 (2003): 1–30; Alexander V. Prusin, "Poland's Nuremberg: The Seven Court Cases of the Supreme National Tribunal, 1946–1948," *Holocaust and Genocide Studies* 24, no. 1 (2010): 1–25; also Andreas Hilger, Ute Schmidt, and Mike Schmeitzner, eds., *Sowjetische Militärtribunale,* vol. 2: *Die Verurteilung deutscher Zivilisten, 1945–1955* (Cologne, 2003).

20. See, for example, Michael J. Bazyler and Frank M. Tuerkheimer, *Forgotten Trials*

of the Holocaust (New York, 2014) as well as the essays in Kevin Jon Heller and Gerry Simpson, eds., *The Hidden Histories of War Crimes Trials* (New York, 2013).

21. See the essays in Laura Jockusch and Gabriel N. Finder, eds., *Jewish Honor Courts: Revenge, Retribution and Reconciliation in Europe and Israel after the Holocaust* (Detroit, 2013); also Tuvia Friling, *A Jewish Kapo in Auschwitz: History, Memory, and the Politics of Survival* (Madison, WI, 2014).

22. See on these issues the excellent review article by Devin O. Pendas, "Seeking Justice, Finding Law: Nazi Trials in Postwar Europe," *Journal of Modern History* 81, no. 2 (2009): 347–68.

23. On this issue see also the essays in David Bankier and Dan Michman, eds., *Holocaust and Justice: Representation & Historiography of the Holocaust in Post-War Trials* (Jerusalem, 2010), and in Florent Brayard, ed., *Le génocide des Juifs entre procès et histoire 1943–2000* (Paris, 2000).

24. Hannah Arendt, *Eichmann in Jerusalem: A Report on the Banality of Evil,* rev. ed. (New York, 1977), 253, 266.

25. On Shklar's thinking, Judith N. Shklar, *Legalism* (Cambridge, MA, 1964); Andreas Hess, *The Political Theory of Judith N. Shklar: Exile from Exile* (New York, 2014), 64–71.

26. Osiel, *Mass Atrocity, Collective Memory, and the Law,* 2–3, 41–91. Leora Bilksy talks of "the new (international) political trial" that began with Eichmann and was revived in the 1990s. She also traces how testimonies were actually used in the court's judgment. See Leora Bilsky, "The Eichmann Trial and the Legacy of Jurisdiction," in *Politics in Dark Times: Encounters with Hannah Arendt,* ed. Selya Benhabib (New York, 2010), 198–218; Leora Bilsky, "The Eichmann Trial: Towards a Jurisprudence of Eyewitness Testimony of Atrocities," *Journal of International Criminal Justice* (2014): 1–31.

27. Lawrence Douglas, *The Memory of Judgment: Making Law and History in the Trials of the Holocaust* (New Haven, CT, 2001), 11–94; Lawrence Douglas, "The Didactic Trial: Filtering History and Memory into the Courtroom," in Bankier and Michmann, *Holocaust and Justice,* 11–22; Lawrence Douglas, "From IMT to NMT: The Emergence of a Jurisprudence of Atrocity," in *Reassessing the Nuremberg Military Tribunals: Transitional Justice, Trial Narratives, and Historiography,* ed. Kim C. Priemel and Alexa Stiller (New York, 2012), 276–95.

28. Dan Michman, "The Jewish Dimension of the Holocaust in Dire Straits? Current Challenges of Interpretation and Scope," in *Jewish Histories of the Holocaust: New Transnational Approaches,* ed. Norman J.W. Goda (New York, 2014), 17–38; Daniel Blatman, "Holocaust Scholarship: Toward a Post-Uniqueness Era," *Journal of Genocide Research* 17, no. 1 (March 2015), 21–43. See also "The Question of Genocide in Palestine, 1948: An Exchange between Martin Shaw and Omer Bartov," *Journal of Genocide Research* 12, no. 3–4 (2010), 243–59.

29. See the contemporary assessment in Alain Finkielkraut, *Remembering in Vain: The Klaus Barbie Trial and Crimes against Humanity* (New York, 1992).

30. See the Lyon newspaper *Le Progrès,* 2 July 1987.

31. Michael R. Marrus, *Some Measure of Justice,* points out that the cases of the 1990s provided but a fraction of the reparations payments covered by the West Ger-

man government after it gained independence. For reparation as a whole, see Constantin Goschler, *Wiedergutmachung: Westdeutschland und die Verfolgten des Nationalsozialismus 1945–1964* (Munich, 1992); Michael Bazyler, *Holocaust Justice: The Battle for Restitution in America's Courts* (New York, 2005); Regula Ludi, *Reparations for Nazi Victims in Postwar Europe* (New York, 2012). See also the essays in Norbert Frei and José Brunner, eds., *Die Praxis von Wiedergutmachung: Geschichte, Erfahrung und Wirkung in Deutschland und Israel* (Göttingen, 2009); Constantin Goschler and Jürgen Lillteicher, eds., *Arisierung und Restitution: Die Rückerstattung jüdischen Eigentums in Deutschland und Österreich nach 1945 und 1989* (Göttingen, 2002); Dan Diner and Gotthart Wunberg, eds., *Restitution and Memory: Material Restoration in Europe* (New York, 2007); Martin Dean, Constantin Goschler, and Philipp Ther, eds., *Robbery and Restitution: The Conflict over Jewish Property in Europe* (New York, 2007).

32. Gitta Sereny, *Into that Darkness: An Examination of Conscience* (New York, 1983); Gitta Sereny, *Albert Speer: His Battle with Truth* (New York, 1995).

33. David Cesarani, *Becoming Eichmann: Rethinking the Life, Crimes, and Trial of a "Desk Murderer"* (Cambridge, MA, 2004); Bettina Stangneth, *Eichmann Before Jerusalem: The Unexamined Life of a Mass Murderer* (New York, 2014); Deborah Lipstadt, *The Eichmann Trial* (New York, 2011).

34. National Archives and Records Administration, College Park, MD, Record Group 238, Official Record, United States Military Tribunals Nürnberg, Case No. 9 Tribunal II A, U.S. v. Otto Ohlendorf et al., v. 2, 659, 662, 664.

35. See, however, the uses of interrogations in Katrin Paehler, *The Third Reich's Intelligence Services: The Career of Walter Schellenberg* (New York, 2017); Steven P. Remy, *The Malmedy Massacre: The War Crimes Controversy* (Cambridge, MA, 2017).

36. See, for example, Zoë Waxman, *Writing the Holocaust: Identity, Testimony, Representation* (New York, 2006); Lawrence Langer, *Holocaust Testimonies: The Ruins of Memory* (New Haven, CT, 1991); Laura Jockusch, *Collect and Record! Jewish Holocaust Documentation in Early Postwar Europe* (New York, 2012); Alexandra Garbarini, *Numbered Days: Diaries and the Holocaust* (New Haven, CT: 2006); Lina N. Insana, *Arduous Tasks: Primo Levi, Translation, and the Transmission of Holocaust Memory* (Toronto, 2009); Camila Loew, *The Memory of Pain: Women's Testimonies of the Holocaust* (New York, 2011); Jürgen Matthäus, ed., *Approaching an Auschwitz Survivor: Holocaust Testimony and its Transformations* (New York, 2009).

37. Annette Wieviorka, *The Era of the Witness* (Ithaca, NY), 43.

38. On this last issue, see also the essays by Arieh J. Kochavi, Boaz Cohen, and Christian Delage in Bankier and Michman, *Holocaust and Justice*, 59–113.

39. *The Trial of Adolf Eichmann,* 7 June 1961, Session No. 68.

SELECT BIBLIOGRAPHY

Albrich, Thomas, Winfried R. Garscha, and Martin F. Polaschek, eds. *Holocaust und Kriegsverbrechen vor Gericht: Der Fall Österreich.* Innsbruck: Studien Ve, 2006.

Arendt, Hannah. *Eichmann in Jerusalem: A Report on the Banality of Evil,* rev. ed. New York: Viking, 1977.

Bankier, David, and Dan Michman, eds. *Holocaust and Justice: Representation & Historiography of the Holocaust in Post-War Trials.* Jerusalem: Yad Vashem, 2010.

Barkan, Elazar. *The Guilt of Nations: Restitution and Negotiating Historical Injustices.* New York: Norton, 2000.

Bass, Gary Jonathan. *Stay the Hand of Vengeance: The Politics of War Crimes Tribunals.* Princeton, NJ: Princeton University Press, 2000.

Baumann, Stefanie Michaela. *Menschenversuche und Wiedergutmachung: Der lange Streit um Entschädigung und Anerkennung der Opfer nationalsozialistischer Humanexperimente.* Munich: Oldenbourg Verlag, 2009.

Bazyler, Michael J. *Holocaust Justice: The Battle for Restitution in America's Courts.* New York: New York University Press, 2005.

———. *Holocaust, Genocide, and the Law: A Quest for Justice in the Post-Holocaust World.* New York: Oxford University Press, 2016.

Bazyler, Michael J., and Frank M. Tuerkheimer. *Forgotten Trials of the Holocaust.* New York: New York University Press, 2014.

Bloxham, Donald. *Genocide on Trial: War Crimes Trials and the Formation of Holocaust History and Memory.* New York: Oxford University Press, 2001.

Breitman, Richard, Norman J. W. Goda, Timothy Naftali, and Robert Wolfe. *US Intelligence and the Nazis.* New York: Cambridge University Press, 2005.

Brochhagen, Ulrich. *Nach Nürnberg: Vergangenheitsbewältigung und Westintegration in der Ära Adenauer.* Hamburg: Junius, 1994.

Buscher, Frank. *The U.S. War Crimes Trial Program in Germany, 1946–1955.* Westport, CT: Praeger, 1989.

Conze, Eckart, Norbert Frei, Peter Hayes, Moshe Zimmermann. *Das Amt und die Vergangenheit: Deutsche Diplomaten im Dritten Reich und in der Bundesrepublik.* Munich: Blessing Verlag, 2010.

de Mildt, Dick. *In the Name of the People: Perpetrators of Genocide in the Reflection of their Post-War Prosecution in West Germany: The "Euthanasia" and "Aktion Reinhard" Cases.* The Hague: Martinus Nijhoff, 1996.

Deák, István, Jan T. Gross, and Tony Judt, eds. *The Politics of Retribution in Europe: World War II and Its Aftermath.* Princeton, NJ: Princeton University Press, 2000.

Dean, Martin, Constantin Goschler, and Philipp Ther, eds. *Robbery and Restitution: The Conflict over Jewish Property in Europe.* New York: Berghahn, 2007.

Diner, Dan, and Gotthart Wunberg, eds. *Restitution and Memory: Material Restoration in Europe.* New York: Berghahn, 2007.

Douglas, Lawrence. *The Memory of Judgment: Making Law and History in the Trials of the Holocaust.* New Haven, CT: Yale University Press, 2001.

———. *The Right Wrong Man: John Demjanjuk and the Last Great Nazi War Crimes Trial.* Princeton, NJ: Princeton University Press, 2016.

Earl, Hilary. *The Nuremberg SS-Einsatzgruppen Trial, 1945–1958: Atrocity, Law and History.* New York: Cambridge University Press, 2009.

Elster, Jon. *Closing the Books: Transitional Justice in Historical Perspective.* New York: Cambridge University Press, 2004.

Felman, Shoshana. *The Juridical Unconscious: Trials and Traumas in the Twentieth Century.* Cambridge, MA: Harvard University Press, 2002.

Felman, Shoshana, and Dori Laub, eds. *Testimony: Crises of Witnessing in Literature, Psychoanalysis, and History.* New York: Routledge, 1991.

Frei, Norbert. *Vergangenheitspolitik: Die Anfänge der Bundesrepublik und die NS-Vergangenheit.* Munich: DTV, 1996.

Frei, Norbert, and José Brunner, eds. *Die Praxis von Wiedergutmachung: Geschichte, Erfahrung und Wirkung in Deutschland und Israel.* Göttingen: Wallstein Verlag, 2009.

Garbarini, Alexandra. "Document Volumes and the Status of Victim Testimony in the Era of the First World War and Its Aftermath." *Études arméniennes contemporaines* 5 (2015): 113–38.

Gellately, Robert, ed. *The Nuremberg Interviews: An American Psychiatrist's Conversations with the Defendants and Witnesses.* New York: Knopf, 2004.

Goda, Norman J. W. *Tales from Spandau: Nazi Criminals and the Cold War.* New York: Cambridge University Press, 2007.

Golsan, Richard, ed. *The Papon Affair: Memory and Justice on Trial.* New York: Routledge, 2000.

Goschler, Constantin. *Wiedergutmachung: Westdeutschland und die Verfolgten des Nationalsozialismus 1945–1964.* Munich: Oldenbourg Verlag, 1992.

———. *Schuld und Schulden: Die Politik der Wiedergutmachung für NS-Verfolgte seit 1945.* Göttingen: Wallstein Verlag, 2005.

Goschler, Constantin, and Jürgen Lillteicher, eds. *Arisierung und Restitution: Die Rückerstattung jüdischen Eigentums in Deutschland und Österreich nach 1945 und 1989.* Göttingen: Wallstein Verlag, 2002.

Greene, Joshua. *Justice at Dachau: The Trials of An American Prosecutor.* New York: Broadway Books, 2003.

Haberer, Erich. "History and Justice: Paradigms of the Prosecution of Nazi Crimes." *Holocaust and Genocide Studies* 19, no. 3 (2005): 487–519.

Hammerschmidt, Peter. *Deckname Adler: Klaus Barbie und die westlichen Geheimdienste.* Frankfurt am Main: Fischer, 2014.

Heberer, Patricia, and Jürgen Mattäus, eds. *Atrocities on Trial: Historical Perspectives on the Politics of Prosecuting War Crimes.* Lincoln, NE: University of Nebraska Press, 2008.

Hébert, Valerie. *Hitler's Generals on Trial: The Last War Crimes Tribunal at Nuremberg.* Lawrence, KS: University Press of Kansas, 2010.

Heller, Kevin Jon. *The Nuremberg Military Tribunals and the Origins of International Criminal Law.* New York: Oxford University Press, 2011.

Heller, Kevin Jon, and Gerry Simpson, eds. *The Hidden Histories of War Crimes Trials.* New York: Oxford University Press, 2013.

Henkys, Reinhard, ed. *Die nationalsozialistischen Gewaltverbrechen: Geschichte und Gericht.* Stuttgart: Kreuz-Verlag, 1965.

Herbst, Ludolf, and Constantin Goschler, eds. *Wiedergutmachung in der Bundesrepublik Deutschland.* Munich: Oldenbourg Verlag, 1989.

Herf, Jeffrey. *Divided Memory: The Nazi Past in the Two Germanys.* Cambridge, MA: Harvard University Press, 1996.

Hilger, Andreas, Ute Schmidt, and Mike Schmeitzner, eds., *Sowjetische Militärtribunale.* 2 vols. Cologne: Bohlau Verlag, 2001–2003.

Himka, John-Paul, and Joanna Beata Michlic, eds. *Bringing the Dark Past to Light: The Reception of the Holocaust in Postcommunist Europe.* Lincoln, NE: University of Nebraska Press, 2013.

Hockerts, Hans Günter, Claudia Moisel, and Tobias Winstel, eds. *Grenzen der Wiedergutmachung: Die Entschädigung für NS-Verfolgte in West- und Osteuropa 1945–2000.* Göttingen: Wallstein Verlag, 2006.

Jockusch, Laura, and Gabriel N. Finder, eds. *Jewish Honor Courts: Revenge, Retribution and Reconciliation in Europe and Israel after the Holocaust.* Detroit, MI: Wayne State University Press, 2015.

Kellenbach, Katharina von. *The Mark of Cain: Guilt and Denial in the Lives of Nazi Perpetrators.* New York: Oxford University Press, 2013.

Langer, Lawrence. *Holocaust Testimonies: The Ruins of Memory.* New Haven, CT: Yale University Press, 1991.

Lebow, Richard Ned, Wulf Kansteiner, and Claudio Fogy, eds. *The Politics of Memory in Postwar Europe.* Durham, NC: Duke University Press, 2006.

Lemkin, Raphael. *Axis Rule in Occupied Europe: Laws of Occupation, Analysis of Government, Proposals for Redress.* Washington, DC: Carnegie Endowment for International Peace, 1944.

Leys, Ruth. *From Guilt to Shame: Auschwitz and After.* Princeton, NJ: Princeton University Press, 2007.

Lillteicher, Jürgen. *Raub, Recht und Restitution: Die Rückerstattung jüdischen Eigentums in der frühen Bundesrepublik.* Göttingen: Wallstein Verlag, 2007.

Ludi, Regula. *Reparations for Nazi Victims in Postwar Europe.* New York: Cambridge University Press, 2012.

Marrus, Michael R. *Some Measure of Justice: The Holocaust Era Restitution Campaign of the 1990s.* Madison, WI: University of Wisconsin Press, 2009.

Olick, Jeffrey K. *In the House of the Hangman: The Agonies of German Defeat, 1943-1949.* Chicago: University of Chicago Press, 2005.

———. *The Politics of Regret: On Collective Memory and Historical Responsibility.* New York: Routledge, 2007.

Osiel, Mark. *Mass Atrocity, Collective Memory, and the Law.* New Brunswick, NJ: Transaction, 1997.

Overy, Richard, ed. *Interrogations: The Nazi Elite in Allied Hands, 1945.* New York: Viking, 2001.

Pendas, Devin O. *The Frankfurt Auschwitz Trial, 1963–1965: Genocide, History, and the Limits of the Law.* New York: Cambridge University Press, 2005.

———. "Seeking Justice, Finding Law: Nazi Trials in Postwar Europe." *Journal of Modern History* 81, no. 2 (2009): 347–68.

Priemel, Kim C., and Alexa Stiller, eds. *Reassessing the Nuremberg Military Tribunals: Transitional Justice, Trial Narratives, and Historiography.* New York: Berghahn, 2012.

Pross, Christian. *Wiedergutmachung: Der Kleinkrieg gegen die Opfer.* Frankfurt am Main: Athenäum Verlag, 1988.

Rückerl, Adalbert. *NS-Verbrechen Vor Gericht: Versuch einer Vergangenheitsbewältigung.* Heidelberg: Juristicher Verlag, 1982.

Schabas, William A. *Genocide in International Law.* New York: Cambridge University Press, 2000.

———. *Unimaginable Atrocities: Justice, Politics, and Rights at the War Crimes Tribunals.* New York: Oxford University Press, 2014.

Smelser, Ronald, ed. *Lessons and Legacies V: The Holocaust and Justice.* Evanston, IL: Northwestern University Press, 2002.

Smith, Bradley F. *Reaching Judgment at Nuremberg.* New York: Basic Books, 1977.

———. *The Road to Nuremberg.* New York: Basic Books, 1981.

———. *The American Road to Nuremberg: The Documentary Record, 1944–1945.* Stanford, CA: Hoover Institute Press, 1982.

Sprecher, Drexel. *Inside the Nuremberg Trial: A Prosecutor's Comprehensive Account,* 2 vols. Lanham, MD: University Press of America, 1999.

Stoltzfus, Nathan, and Henry Friedlander, eds. *Nazi Crimes and the Law.* New York: Cambridge University Press, 2008.

Stonebridge, Lyndsey. *The Judicial Imagination: Writing after Nuremberg.* Edinburgh: Edinburgh University Press, 2011.

Taylor, Telford. *The Anatomy of the Nuremberg Trials: A Personal Memoir.* New York: Norton, 1992.

Tobin, Patrick. "Crossroads at Ulm: Postwar West Germany and the 1958 Ulm *Einsatzkommando* Trial." Ph.D. diss., University of North Carolina at Chapel Hill, 2013.

Torpey, John. *Making Whole What Has Been Smashed: On Reparations Politics.* Cambridge, MA: Harvard University Press, 2006.

Tutorow, Norman E., ed. *War Crimes, War Criminals, and War Crimes Trials: An Annotated Bibliography and Source Book.* New York: Greenwood Press, 1986.

Ueberschär, Gerd R. ed. *Nationalsozialismus vor Gericht: Die alliierten Prozesse gegen Kriegsverbrecher und Soldaten 1943–1952.* Frankfurt am Main: Fischer Verlag, 1999.

Vogel, Rolf, ed. *Ein Weg aus der Vergangenheit: Eine Dokumentation zur Verjährungsfrage und zu den NS-Prozessen.* Frankfurt am Main: Ullstein Verlag, 1969.

Vollnhals, Clemens and Jörg Osterloh, eds. *NS-Prozesse und deutsche Öffentlichkeit: Besatzungszeit, frühe Bundesrepublik und DDR.* Göttingen: Vandenhoeck & Ruprecht, 2012.

Weinke, Annette. *Die Verfolgung von NS-Tätern im geteilten Deutschland: Vergangenheitsbewältigungen 1949–1969.* Paderborn: Ferdinand Schöningh, 2002.

Werle, Gerhard. *Auschwitz Vor Gericht: Völkermord und bundesdeutsche Strafjustiz.* Munich: C. H. Beck, 1995.

Wieviorka, Annette. *The Era of the Witness,* trans. Jared Stark. Ithaca, NY: Cornell University Press, 2006.

Wittmann, Rebecca. *Beyond Justice: The Auschwitz Trial.* Cambridge, MA: Harvard University Press, 2005.

Part I

Literary and Religious Approaches to Holocaust Justice

Chapter 1

Before the Law

The Poetics of Justice in Hannah Arendt's *Eichmann in Jerusalem*

Eric Kligerman

As the Trial of the Major War Criminals at Nuremberg commenced in November 1945, Hannah Arendt wrote to Karl Jaspers:

> The Nazi crimes ... explode the limits of the law; and that is precisely what constitutes their monstrousness (*Ungeheurlichkeit*). For these crimes, no punishment is severe enough. It may well be essential to hang [Hermann] Göring, but it is totally inadequate ... this guilt, in contrast to all criminal guilt, oversteps and shatters any and all legal systems. The viewpoint of our legal institutions and moral standards of judgment cannot deal with this new type of criminal.[1]

Sixteen years later Arendt revisited the problem with the trial of Adolf Eichmann. In her classic *Eichmann in Jerusalem: A Report on the Banality of Evil,* she described how with this "new type of criminal and a new crime ... it was inevitable that the trial would collapse beneath the moral, political and legal problems."[2] Arendt's language suggests that juridical law was incapable of balancing the weight of guilt with a proper mode of punishment.

Critical studies analyzing Arendt's search for the proper language for the Eichmann trial have turned to such representational frameworks as Immanuel Kant's sublime, Walter Benjamin's figure of the storyteller, and Sigmund Freud's psychoanalytic concepts of trauma and mourning.[3] Yet Arendt rejected these metaphysical tenets. She dismissed, for example, the

Israeli judges' position that Kant's moral law could sit in judgment of Eichmann, describing how the court did not arrive at a "clear understanding of the actual horror of Auschwitz."[4] Again, all legal precedents were shattered. Lawrence Douglas eloquently captures what was at stake. Describing how the courts lacked the "proper idiom" to engage the charges against the defendants, Douglas argues that the courtroom failed to grasp the Holocaust in terms of the law.[5] How then did Arendt conceptualize law (political, moral, and judicial) and justice in the aftermath of the Shoah?

One must examine Arendt's literary references for clues. Though Shoshana Felman asserts that Arendt rejected "the contamination between facts and fiction … the confusion and interpenetration between law and literature," the latter indeed informed Arendt's understanding of justice.[6] Far from jettisoning poetic discourse, Arendt employed examples from literature throughout her report. She began with an epigraph from Bertolt Brecht; made references to Shakespeare's Iago, Macbeth, and Richard III; and interspersed dramatic metaphors throughout her study. Jaspers noted that Arendt "had almost taken the path of poetry."[7]

Yet throughout Arendt's political philosophy, she returned repeatedly to Kafka's literature.[8] Her first published essay in the United States was "Franz Kafka: A Revaluation" (1944), and afterwards she worked extensively on Kafka.[9] Later, as I will argue, she placed Eichmann into Kafka's poetic landscape and thus found a new language to investigate justice in relation to genocide. Kafka confronted his readers with a manifold of unresolved legal polemics, and thus provided the proper poetics to form a judgment of Eichmann's guilt. And Arendt's foregrounding of resistance to injustice in Kafka influenced how she comprehended the interplay between judgment and imagination in relation to Eichmann's guilt.

Many scholars have discussed Kafka's influence on Arendt's theory of totalitarianism; Kafka provided the model to the machinery behind the camps.[10] But how did Kafka function as the subtext to Arendt's study of justice in Jerusalem? Bettina Stangneth claims "Hannah Arendt, whose linguistic and conceptual sensibilities had been honed on classical German literature, wrote that Eichmann's language was a roller coaster of thoughtless horror, cynicism, whining self-pity, unintentional comedy and incredible human wretchedness."[11] This blend of horror, comedy, and human wretchedness is more appropriate in describing Kafka's modern literature, not classical German literature. Moreover, with her concept "the banality of evil" Arendt subverted the traditional metaphysical representation of how the individual responsible for evil actions is monstrous and diabolical. Contrary to Richard Wolin's assertion that Arendt desired "to immunize German intellectual and cultural traditions, with which she so profoundly identified, from their share of responsibility for the European catastrophe," it is this very tradition that she critiques throughout her report with the help of Kafka's poetics.[12]

TRANSLATING JUSTICE

Kafka straddled the cultural markers of the German-Jewish tradition in the era of assimilation. Arendt too stood amid the tensions between these German and Jewish traditions, albeit one situated in the ruins of the Shoah, and she searched for a perspective to comprehend both Eichmann and the court's judgment of him. From its opening words, *Eichmann in Jerusalem* searches for the proper language for the legal system to judge the nature of Eichmann's crimes. Her epigraph, from Bertolt Brecht, invokes the house of Germany: "O Germany, pale mother! / Hearing the harangues which echo from your house, / men laugh. / But whoever sees you reaches for a knife." Arendt also underscores the linguistic problems at the trial's core. The opening words of her first chapter, "The House of Justice," are: "*Beth Hamishpath.* The House of Justice."[13] Arriving in a foreign land, Arendt transforms justice into an alien concept with her inclusion of the Hebrew term *Beth Hamishpath,* which shifts between familiar English terms. Arendt moves from Brecht's German house to a Jewish one. Throughout *Eichmann in Jerusalem,* Arendt tried to translate the meaning of justice. She replaced the literal translation of "order in the court" or "all rise" with "the house of justice." She used the word "justice" instead of "judgment" (another term linked to *Hamishpath*).[14] She described the German translation of the trial, specifically geared for the defendant, as "sheer comedy, frequently incomprehensible."[15] Yet Arendt's reflections in her essay on Walter Benjamin on the relation between translation and poetry provides further direction to how we approach this opening scene. In describing Benjamin, Arendt examined how "thinking poetically" involves the interplay between metaphor, translation, and the breakdown of conceptual language. At this moment of linguistic collapse, Arendt quoted Stéphane Mallarmé, "The poem ... philosophically makes good the defects of language."[16] With Mallarmé's words in mind, I would suggest that Arendt approached the breakdown of juridical concepts of law, guilt, and justice in the Shoah's aftermath by turning to Kafka.

Although Arendt may appear to inhabit some uncanny—or *unheimlich*—space between the German and Jewish house through this juxtaposition of citations, she is not some ghostly figure who occupied the Freudian realm of the repressed. Rather, Arendt's in-between perspective is consistent with her concept of the *conscious pariah*: a term she applied to thinkers such as

Heinrich Heine, Bernard Lazere, and Kafka. Marginalized from European society and the Jewish community, the conscious pariah is an emancipated Jew who is aware of the pariah quality of Jewish existence, but who rebels against oppression.[17]

In her *Origins of Totalitarianism* (1951), Arendt had already examined how Kafka anticipated the destruction of "the juridical person in man" through "monstrous" machinery by discussing the fictional Barnabas family from Kafka's *The Castle*. After their daughter Amalia rejects the salacious advances of a castle official, both the village and castle spurn her family. While her father attempts to have his daughter pardoned for her "wrongdoing," he learns that "[b]efore he could be forgiven he had to prove his guilt, and that was denied in all the departments."[18] The machinery of the castle, similar to the one driving Kafka's *The Trial,* ascribes guilt to the system's innocent victims. Arendt cited the following lines from *The Castle*: when K. hears Barnabas's story, the process appears to him as "unjust and monstrous" (*ungerecht und ungeheuerlich*).[19]

Continuing on the interplay between Kafkaesque injustice and the monstrousness of National Socialism, Arendt noted, in describing concentration camps that "[t]he first essential step … is to kill the juridical person in man."[20] The concentration camp world was made up of horrors outside of life and death too "monstrous" for the imagination to grasp.[21] It was a world of malignant fantasies, a phantom world, which had materialized into a world complete with all the sensual data of reality yet lacking the structure of consequence and responsibility without which reality remains for us incomprehensible.[22] The incomprehension stemmed not from representational limits, but from the distortion of ethics. There was no consequence for those who deformed the law via the imagination and who made violence the policy of the state.

One key for Arendt in understanding Eichmann lay in her thoughts concerning history and the individual. In her 1961 preface to *Between Past and Future,* Arendt argued that history had to be approached through its ruptures rather than through assumption of steady progress through the linearity of successive generations. The historian, she said, should explore the biography of a single person and aim for no more than a "*metaphorical approximation* to what actually happened in the minds of men."[23] Arendt emphasized how biography would focus on the juncture between thinking and the act of resistance. Here she examined the French poet and Resistance fighter René Char. Describing how the poet had to turn to a life of action with the advent of political terror, Arendt stressed how the act of resistance necessitates in its aftermath a reflection on its meaning. The historian, Arendt said, must focus on this gap between thought and action: "In history

these intervals have shown more than once that they may contain the moment of truth."[24]

In a revealing analytical shift, Arendt turned to Kafka's parable "HE,"
which illustrates man's antagonistic struggle with temporality. "He" stands
between the forces of the past and future. In her conceptualization of history as a "metaphoric approximation," Arendt described how she found
the "perfect metaphor" for the activity of thought in Kafka's parable, which
illustrates the temporal gap between past tradition and its impact on the
future.[25] In her analysis of "HE," Arendt probed man's search for an epistemological position to engage with history that neither transcends time nor
our earthly realm.

> Seen from the viewpoint of man, who always lives in the interval between past
> and future, time is not a continuum, a flow of uninterrupted succession; it is bro-
> ken in the middle, at the point where "he" stands; and "his" standpoint is not the
> present as we usually understand it but rather a gap in time in which "his" con-
> stant fighting, "his" making a stand against past and future, keeps in existence.[26]

For Arendt, the Eichmann trial represented a temporal rupture that
interferes with our traditional understanding of terms such as justice, law,
and evil. Arendt herself stood in this gap to render her judgment of Eichmann and the courtroom itself, not from some transcendent perspective, but
within the earthly realm of time and space. Several years later in *Life of the
Mind,* Arendt returned to Kafka's "HE." Yet here Arendt avoided reference
to Char. Instead, she described how her preoccupation with the task of thinking stemmed from the Eichmann trial, arguing that her term "banality of
evil" went "counter to our tradition of thought—literary, theological, or philo-
sophic—about the phenomenon of evil" in the aftermath of Auschwitz.[27]

Arendt analyzed not just Eichmann's refusal to think, but also her own
act of philosophical resistance. Describing how she dismantled the concepts
of metaphysics from the Greeks to the present, Arendt challenged traditional
modes of thinking and historical narrative through her reconceptualization
of evil and justice. The concepts that form the cornerstones of metaphysics—
reason, freedom, authority, and justice—become part of this lost tradition.[28]
Within the context of Kafka's parable, the collision between the past and
future signifies a gap in time whereby traditional concepts dissolve.

EICHMANN'S BANALITY

Arendt further understood Kafka's layering of horror and humor throughout his literature as distinct from the genre of surrealism.[29] She famously

struggled with the representations of Eichmann's own monstrousness in Jerusalem. The prosecution referred to Eichmann as a "monster."[30] The judges and prosecution, in her retelling, described the "monstrousness of events" and "monstrous acts."[31] On seeing Eichmann for the first time, however, Arendt labeled him as "*nicht einmal unheimlich*—not even sinister."[32] But later, in her *Life of the Mind,* Arendt noted that while Eichmann's "deeds were monstrous, the doer … was quite ordinary, commonplace, and neither demonic nor monstrous."[33] As she pondered how one could judge this new criminal and his monstrous crimes that had destroyed the frame of juridical understanding, Arendt's reflections guided her to Kafka, who provided her with the proper poetics to form a judgment of Eichmann's guilt.

For Arendt, Eichmann's narrative in his police interviews, prison memoir, and trial testimony also embodied the Kafkaesque elements of horror, comedy, and banality, and she imparted these elements throughout her representation of the trial. What made Eichmann's narrative humorous, according to Arendt, was his tone of a "hard-luck story" to describe how he became part of the extermination process.[34] Like many Kafka characters—Gregor Samsa, K., and Gracchus—Eichmann attributed his trajectory to one of misfortune, or *Unglück.* For instance, instead of remaining with the Freemasons, Eichmann lamented his "accidental" joining of the SS.[35]

Arendt further noted, in representing Eichmann, that "[t]he comedy breaks into horror itself, and results in stories, presumably true enough, whose macabre humor easily surpasses that of any Surrealist invention."[36] Referring to Eichmann's police interrogation by the Israelis, Arendt noted, "The horrible can be not only ludicrous but outright funny. There was something inherently comedic about Eichmann's struggle with the German language."[37] Eichmann emphasized the mundane events surrounding the process of extermination. Despite his supposed memory gaps pertaining to the genocide in Slovakia, for instance, Eichmann recalled bowling with Sano Mach, the Slovak minister of the interior.[38] Arendt highlighted this disconnect in order to evoke the "macabre humor" of his narrative. She framed the court's dilemma as follows: how could one reconcile "the unspeakable horror of the deeds and the undeniable ludicrousness of the man who perpetrated them"?[39]

Arendt's critics deemed her comedic description of Eichmann as a clown, as opposed to a monster, as insensitive to his victims' suffering. Gershom Scholem admonished Arendt for what he described as her lack of love for the Jewish people. Arendt responded that Scholem overlooked the irony of her writing: "I never made Eichmann out to be a 'Zionist.' If you missed the irony of the sentence—which was plainly in *oratio obliqua,* reporting Eichmann's own words—I really can't help it."[40] In discussing the hostile reception of *Eichmann in Jerusalem,* Günter Gauss argued that Arendt's critics rejected not only its content but also its tone. Arendt responded that

> The tone of voice is predominantly ironic ... If people think that one can only write about these things in a solemn tone of voice ... Look, there are people who take it amiss—and I can understand that in a sense—that, for instance, I can still laugh. But I was really of the opinion that Eichmann was a buffoon.[41]

Arendt subverted the traditional metaphysical concepts such as right and wrong, moral and immoral, and evil itself that the court used to understand Eichmann. She employed irony to show the inconsistencies of such concepts when applied to Eichmann. She also employed humor to undermine the monstrousness that the court attributed to Eichmann. Comprised of reversals and paradoxical turns, Arendt's tone corresponds to Richard Grey's description of Kafka's "conscious irony," which discloses how our modern world is a "farcical stage devoid of metaphysical center."[42] Similarly, the paradoxical twists in Arendt's report stem from her preparation to behold a monster in Jerusalem and her ironic confrontation with a clown.

But Arendt's use of laughter and irony points to a second feature of Kafka's literature that she utilized in her encounter with Eichmann. In analyzing Kafka, she remarked that laughter is an act of resistance that "permits man to prove his essential freedom through a kind of serene superiority to his own failures."[43] It embodies the spontaneity that totalitarianism sets out to destroy. In an interview with the French journalist Roger Errera, Arendt remarked:

> When I wrote my *Eichmann in Jerusalem,* one of my main intentions was to destroy the legend of the greatness of evil, of the demonic force, to take away from people the admiration they have for the great evildoers like Richard III or et cetera. I found in Brecht the following remark: "The great political criminals must be exposed and exposed especially to laughter. They are not great political criminals, but people who permitted great political crimes, which is something entirely different. The failure of his enterprises does not indicate that Hitler was an idiot."[44]

Arendt's transformation of Eichmann diminishes the figures responsible for historical violence. Calling the investigation of Eichmann a "comedy of the soul"[45] and stressing his averageness, Arendt dismantled the monster, making him less significant; he was neither a "great man" who moved history in some Hegelian sense nor a tragic Shakespearian villain. Arendt's report functions as a *Purimspiel* designed to disempower, albeit belatedly, any image of "greatness," whether it be deemed monstrous or criminal.

MEANINGS OF JUSTICE

My juxtaposition of Kafka and the Eichmann trial is not fanciful. Legal scholars have cited Kafka in articles on topics such as family, international, employment, and immigration law.[46] Arendt too used Kafka's literature as a template for the meaning of justice and she argued that Kafka provided a "blueprint" to this world of injustice—a world of inscrutable and violent laws—that his characters try to sabotage.[47] Kafka unveiled the hidden structures that had to be resisted. Arendt argued that the main theme of Kafka's novels is the conflict between a world depicted as a seamlessly functioning machine and a protagonist trying to destroy it. But she also described how obedience "is the hidden motor that drives the destructive machinery in which Kafka's protagonists are caught."[48] Contrary to traditional readings of Kafka, with his protagonists trapped in labyrinthine webs of power, Arendt viewed Kafka's characters as emblems of resistance within these authoritarian systems.

Kafka for Arendt thus projects upon history's catastrophic landscape "the image of man as a model of good will [which] exposes the hidden structures of this world almost without knowing it, or wanting to."[49] His protagonists continuously face injustice, as he imagines a "possible world that human beings would construct in which the actions of man depend on nothing but himself and his spontaneity."[50] Arendt continues: "It is always salvation which is the miracle, not ruin; only salvation, and not ruin depends upon the freedom of man and his capacity to change the world and its natural course."[51] If for Arendt, Kafka's writings offered "blueprints" of resistance to totalitarianism, then there was also a connection between justice and resistance in *Eichmann in Jerusalem.*

In a seldom-discussed part of her analysis, Arendt recalled that Kafka himself obtained residence permits for many Eastern European Jews. She imagined that Kafka's actions were outside the law.[52] Kafka knew, she wrote, "that a man caught in the bureaucratic machine is already condemned ... The interpretation of the law became an instrument of lawlessness."[53] In her description of how the "senseless automatism among the lower echelon" was in charge of "the final decision," Kafka, in her view, did not submit to automation; he became his own "man of good will."[54] Arendt praised Kafka's power of imagination, which he used to reach the necessary conclusions to what reality had yet to bring into full focus. We cannot help but hear in her use of terms such as "final decision" and "automation" a description of the Nazis' Final Solution of the Jewish Question. And if Kafka's *The Trial* conveys the warping of justice within the totalitarian system, where the human subject is emptied of the juridical and moral self, *Eich-*

mann in Jerusalem opens up a space to judge those individuals responsible for this system.

In 1915, Kafka wrote "Before the Law" as a freestanding parable, and he eventually included it in the penultimate chapter of *The Trial.*[55] It describes how a man from the country travels to a foreign space to gain entry to the Law. The Law, so believes the man, is something rational and open to all. But when he arrives, a gatekeeper informs him that his entrance has been delayed and that multiple doorkeepers stand in the way to the Law. Contrary to his preconceived understanding that the Law is "open to all," the man dies without ever gaining admission.

Arendt never explicitly references Kafka in *Eichmann in Jerusalem.* Still, how might the architecture of "Before the Law" help us understand Arendt's representation of justice in *Eichmann?*[56] Similarly to *The Trial* Arendt in her report offered a hermeneutics of law, whereby justice is placed in abeyance. With its analysis of the ambiguous relationship between law and justice, Arendt rewrote Kafka's parable:

> These words [*Beth Hamishpath*] … announce the arrival of the three judges, who, bareheaded, in black robes, walk into the courtroom from a side entrance to take their seats on the highest tier of the raised platform. Their long table … is flanked at each end by the court stenographers. Directly below the judges are the translators. … One tier below the translators, we see the glass booth of the accused. Finally, on the bottom tier … are the prosecutor with his staff of four attorneys … and the counsel for the defense, who during the first weeks is accompanied by an assistant.[57]

Arendt's opening description of the courtroom mirrors the topography of Kafka's parable with its multiple tiers. But in her re-formulation it is the audience, including Arendt, who came to behold the man in the glass booth as something concrete and not as a vague abstraction. The audience wishes to "see justice done."[58] Like Kafka, Arendt attempted to look anew at the meaning of law by interrogating our traditional understanding of its relation to justice.

Early in her report Arendt discussed Eichmann's claim that he was not guilty "in the sense of the indictment." His attorney Robert Sevatius remarked that, "Eichmann feels guilty before God, not *before the law.*"[59] We are left to wonder: to which law was Servatius referring? Arendt mentioned a multiplicity of laws throughout the report—judicial, criminal, moral, positive, state, international, natural, the law legislating mass murder, and law of history—and engaged with each of these concepts within her report. Unlike Kafka's man from the country, who fails to reflect on the Law critically, Arendt, using the judges' own words, remarked that the court's judgment needed to be placed under "study and thought."⁶⁰ She contemplated the gatekeepers of the law, including the legal precedents from Nuremberg, the Jerusalem judges, the lawyers, and Eichmann himself, and she examined the juridical, moral, theological, philosophical, and literary narratives surrounding Eichmann's actions.

Placing their faith in traditional concepts of law, justice, and history as embedded within the tenets of the Enlightenment such as reason, free will, and moral law, the methods of the judges and the lawyers in judging Eichmann all relied on the structures of Western metaphysics. While the defense employed a Hegelian model of history and the prosecution inserted the Holocaust within a religious narrative of Jewish persecution, the judges argued with Eichmann about his reflections on Kantian moral thought. Arendt, however, rejected how the judges, lawyers, and Eichmann employed these philosophical concepts to engage questions of guilt, law, and justice. She argued that all modes of judgment, "from the *Zeitgeist* down to the Oedipus complex," were insufficient.⁶¹ Uncovering a *Sonderweg* in Kafka's representation of an indeterminate justice, Arendt found in his poetics a challenge to Western metaphysics' reliance on Hegel and Kant's analysis of reason, historical progress, and moral thought. By turning to Kafka, she subverted the paradigms of jurisprudence and philosophy.

I will narrow my analysis to Arendt's rejection of Kant's moral law within the context of the trial. Despite her affinity for Kant's moral philosophy, in which moral law dwells within each human being, Kant's moral philosophy could not provide an adequate framework to evaluate Eichmann. Arendt illustrated how the Nazis inverted Kant's concepts of duty and obedience to law. Her disagreement with Israel's judges stemmed from their belief that a sense of justice is grounded in every man in the form of conscience. In turn, this conscience could function as a substitute for knowledge of the law. Arendt vehemently rejected this perspective. For a law-abiding citizen in Nazi Germany, Hitler's orders possessed "the force of law." The *Hitler Befehl* became the new categorical imperative.⁶²

Arendt claimed that the judges could not escape considering Eichmann as "not normal."⁶³ Holding to a humanist model concerning the relationship between justice and law and anchored in the Enlightenment's concepts of justice and *mens rea,* while clinging to what Arendt called the "old-fashioned faith in the moral foundations of their profession," the judges failed to see that Eichmann was a "new kind of criminal."⁶⁴ "If a crime unknown before, such as genocide, suddenly makes its appearance," she continued, "justice itself demands a judgment according to a new law."⁶⁵ The judges could argue that they "are not judges outside the realm of law," but Arendt wished that they had "dared" to reach a judgment that circumvented the traditional model.[66] In order to deal with the unprecedented crimes, she argued, "[i]t has become the task of ordinary trial judges to render justice without the help of, or *beyond the limitation* set upon them through, positive, posited laws."[67] Arendt's use of the phrase "beyond the limitation" recalls her letter to Jaspers prior to Nuremberg. Almost two decades later the legal system and juridical concepts applied in Jerusalem remained inadequate to confront state-sanctioned massacres.

Arendt gleaned a single moment when the judges, in determining Eichmann's guilt, liberated themselves from the aforementioned judicial constraints. In considering Eichmann's "monstrous" deeds, she said: "They judged freely ... and did not really lean on the standards and legal precedents with which they more or less convincingly sought to justify their decisions."[68] A few paragraphs later Arendt used the notion of "free judgment" to describe rare acts of resistance against the Third Reich. For those who carried out such actions "[t]here were no rules to be abided by ... They had to decide each instance as it arose, because no rules existed for the unprecedented."[69] Eichmann's judges tried to operate in a similar manner, but ultimately they turned to the "very foundation of their profession," falling back upon the established tools of juridical thought. Thus they missed the trial's greatest moral and even legal challenge. In order for this act of juridical resistance to be complete, they had to circumvent the long-standing metaphysical tradition of moral thought. Since the crimes of the Shoah went beyond the limits of law and experience, Arendt necessitates an act of "free judgment" of the imagination to confront its horrors.

To reach a verdict that did not stem from legal precedent, the judges had to turn to the power of the imagination that Arendt discerned in Kafka and that she linked to Kant's idea of genius. In Kant's *Critique of Judgment,* genius refers to the inborn mental disposition of the artist unbound by existing laws, concepts, experience, or representations. Genius can create out of what is not seen. For Arendt, Kafka was this genius. He created a "thought-landscape" that anticipated "unprecedented and unforeseeable events."[70] Describing how "Kafka invents such aspects freely," Arendt described elsewhere that:

> Blueprints cannot be understood except by those who are willing and able vividly to imagine the intentions of the architect and the future appearances of the building. For the first time in literary history, a writer requires his readers to engage in the very same activity that upholds both him and his work. And this is none other than the imagination ... At every turn, what Kafka demands of his reader is the exertion of the real power of imagination. This is why the purely passive reader, molded and educated as he has been by the tradition of the novel and active only in his identification with one of the characters, does not know what to do with Kafka.[71]

Kafka's power of the imagination goes beyond mere imitation of experience. Creating a literary paradigm, a "new kind of perfection that appears
to be equally removed from all past styles," Kafka's imagination does not
reproduce what is given; instead, his imagination operates outside of literary
tradition and rules of epistemology.[72] In turn, Kafka's readers must forsake
a traditional interpretive approach to his literature and employ the same
power of imagination to enter the architecture behind his texts.

Arendt also associated Kafka's imagination with unprecedented political acts. His imagination provided blueprints to resist the injustice found
in the bureaucracy's violent machinery. Thus for Arendt the judgment of
Eichmann also had to go beyond legal precedents, models and tradition. Accordingly, Arendt created in her epilogue an imaginary judgment, discussing Eichmann's death sentence "beyond the limitation" of positive law. In
their judgment on Eichmann, the judges searched for guilt and innocence
"before the law," that is, by following the structure of the indictment fram-
ing the trial.[73] For Arendt, "Eichmann was brought to justice" because "the
very earth cries out for vengeance."[74] Citing Yosal Rogat, Arendt claimed
that Eichmann must be punished because "evil violates a natural harmony
which only retribution can restore."[75] At first, her imaginary judgment re-
verts to the Greek tragedies of Aeschylus and Sophocles. Her description of
barbaric and long-forgotten principles recalls a primordial justice, unwrit-
ten, before time, and fulfilled by the Furies.

Although Arendt began with a classical depiction of justice as vengeance, her judgment shifts by the end. She concluded:

> The human race cannot be expected to share the earth with someone like Adolf
> Eichmann. For politics is not like the nursery; in politics obedience and support
> are the same. And just as you supported and carried out a policy of not wanting
> to share the earth with the Jewish people and the people of a number of other
> nations ... no member of the human race, can be expected to want to share the
> earth with you. This is the reason, and the only reason, you must hang.[76]

Arendt's goal was to remove the source of injustice from the community. The
emphasis on retribution shifts to a restorative justice that remains incomplete.

Genocide, having now appeared, would always be present. To Arendt,
we must be prepared to imagine the unimaginable.[77] Eichmann's death sentence thus did not stem from barbaric vengeance against his monstrous acts.
Rather it was a sign of the imperative to resist totalitarianism's continuation.
Although Arendt insisted that Eichmann should be judged for his actions,
his death sentence signified that since he embodied the continuation of totalitarianism, as disclosed by his thoughtless, unimaginative, and automated
behavior during the trial, he must be removed from the earth.

Arendt's imaginary judgment also contains her rejection of Eichmann's misuse of Kantian morality to argue that his fulfillment of Hitler's law was analogous to Kant's notion of respect. Her concluding reflections on obedience shift from echoes of vengeance in Greek tragedy to thoughts on both Kant and Kafka. Arendt's judgment of Eichmann alludes again to her Kafka study, wherein she asserts that obedience "is the hidden motor that drives the destructive machinery in which Kafka's protagonists are caught."[78] But Arendt now expanded on her thoughts on obedience. Within the context of National Socialism, Eichmann's obedience was tied to his political support of administrative violence. Arendt countered Eichmann's invocations of the Kantian notion of obedience with the terror of obedience in Kafka.

Arendt's iconic and oft-cited phrase "the banality of evil" does not appear until her description of Eichmann's execution. Thus, her imaginary judgment interpreted the very concept that Arendt contended was the fulcrum of her report. Arendt's use of "banality of evil" to explain Eichmann shifts the focus from both her previous use of the term "radical evil" to describe the camps in *Origins of Totalitarianism* and the judges' verdict that centered on Eichmann's "monstrous acts."[79] For Arendt, Eichmann's cliché-laden final words on the scaffold were a lesson for the trial itself: "The lesson of the fearsome, word-and-thought-defying *banality of evil*."[80] By challenging the perspective that Eichmann was a monster, Arendt altered her former description of "radical evil."[81] Arendt appropriated the term "radical evil" from Kant, but the banality of evil can be traced back to her work on Kafka. Arendt asserted that "Without a doubt Kafka's world is a terrible world," and a few pages later she described how his literature is permeated with "banal events."[82]

In her analysis of Kafka's *The Trial*, Arendt focused on the interplay between truth, lies, and necessity, where the inscrutable laws of the courts adhere to a divine order. Arendt quotes the chaplain, who tells K. that, "'one does not have to accept everything as true, one must only accept it as necessary.'" Arendt continues with K.'s response, "'It fashions the lie into the world order.' ... The power of the machine that grabs and kills K. lies precisely in the appearance of necessity." Those who are caught in this machinery find themselves "in a world of necessity, injustice and lies."[83] In the earlier version of her essay, Arendt writes, "The terror of Kafka adequately represents the true nature of the thing called bureaucracy—the replacing of government by administration and of laws by arbitrary decrees."[84] In the end of *The Trial*, K. submits "like a dog" and becomes one of the "obedient members" of this system. While the murderous system of the courts is still full of terror and horror, evil has become routinized, automated, and thoughtless.

Arendt continued her reading of *The Trial* by describing men's belief that they are part of a society that is representative of God on earth. "The evil of the world," she said, is built out of a "pretense of representing divine necessity."[85] Human laws become like laws of nature, whereby this world order is based on a "mendacious necessity" and "necessary mendacity" that now constitute the "'divinity' of this world order."[86] Arendt returned to "necessary mendacity" in *Eichmann in Jerusalem*: "But the practice of self-deception had become so common, almost a moral prerequisite for survival ... that mendacity had become an integral part of the German national character."[87] But while Kafka emphasized the individuals caught in the machinery, Arendt concentrated on the functionaries who willfully gave themselves over to this system and operated its deadly machinery. Arendt demonstrated how Eichmann, despite his claims of bad luck, shared responsibility. He freely surrendered himself to the necessity of law and relinquished the need for thought, judgment, and imagination.

In her discussion of Kafka, Arendt asserted that "[t]he domination of bureaucracy implied that the interpretation of the law became an instrument of lawlessness, while the chronic inaction of the interpreters was compensated by a senseless automatism among the lower echelons of the bureaucratic hierarchy, who were entrusted with the privilege of final decision."[88] The bureaucratic machinery thus functions like the laws of natural necessity, in which the lowly functionaries become mere instruments in a process that evokes a final solution. In *Eichmann in Jerusalem* the extermination system's bureaucracy is "absurdly complicated."[89] Arendt described the prosecution's difficulties in "finding its way through the labyrinth of parallel institutions" to locate Eichmann's responsibilities within this "incredibly complicated machinery of destruction."[90] Arendt used almost the exact words from her study of Kafka's "evil bureaucratic machine" in her own attempt to pinpoint where Eichmann fit within the obscure hierarchies and the camouflaged language of extermination. Like the officials in *The Castle,* the bureaucrats behind the courts in *The Trial* and the commandant of "In the Penal Colony," Eichmann performed a "specific, limited job" and occupied "the lower echelons" of this system.[91]

ARENDT'S POETICS

Numerous scholars have misread Arendt's representation of Eichmann, as if her study of the trial was shaped exclusively by historiographical methods.[92] Literary scholars have read her differently. The poet Robert Lowell described Arendt's representation of Eichmann as a "masterpiece" and a "terrifying expressionist invention applied with a force no imitator could rival."[93] Capturing the poetic implications behind Arendt's study, Lowell's words invoke Harold Bloom's depiction of a "strong poet." To Bloom, a great poet is also a "strong reader" who swerves from his/her poetic precursors through acts of "misreading." Not only did Arendt read Kafka with an imaginative mind, but she also dared to read Eichmann through such a lens.[94]

Arendt's "banality of evil" intersects with Bloom's notion of "strong readers" of literature. If, as Bloom suggests, strong poets liberate themselves from the literary tradition in a move toward originality, it was Arendt's *misreading* of Kafka that spurred her approach to crimes of genocide. Swerving from her philosophical origins, including the ancient Greeks, Kant, Hegel, and Heidegger, Arendt derived her notion of the banality of evil from her "strong troping" of Kafka. She could then judge Eichmann more freely through her poetic imagination. Bloom writes:

> Yet by "strong misreading" I mean "strong troping," and the strength of trope can be recognized by skilled readers in a way that anticipates the temporal progression of generations. A strong trope renders all merely trivial readings of it irrelevant ... [I]n a strong reader's struggle to master a poet's trope, strong poetry will impose itself, because that imposition, that usurpation of mental space, is the proof of trope, the testing of power by power.[95]

According to Bloom, a "strong trope" creates meaning that could not otherwise exist and "brings about a condition of newness."[96] Just as strong poets misread their predecessors and move toward "something new" in literature as they break from poetic tradition, Arendt's banality of evil constitutes the "something new" in thinking about justice in the aftermath of genocide. Arendt's "strong misreading" of Eichmann has withstood five decades of critical scrutiny, whereby the banality of evil has functioned as the touchstone to juridical thought in relation to crimes of genocide.

Dismissing the notion of hermeneutic precision, Bloom is interested not only in the troping that occurs in poetry but also in the field of criticism.

> To read actively is to make a fiction as well as to receive one, and the kind of active reading we call "criticism" or the attempt to decide meaning, or perhaps to see whether meaning *can* be decided, always has a very large fictive meaning in it. I continue to be surprised that so many literary scholars refuse to see that every stance in regard to texts, however professedly humble or literal or prosaic or "scientific" or "historical" or "linguistic" is always a poetic stance.[97]

Similar to how a strong poem becomes both part of the literary canon and functions as a catalyst for continued debate among critics about the poem's meaning, Arendt's *Eichmann in Jerusalem* is both a canonical text about the Nazi genocide and has served as a flashpoint for deliberations about the significance of Eichmann's guilt. The banality of evil is indicative of Arendt's "poetic stance" toward Eichmann. It functions as a metaphor that resists the attempts to revert to legal precedent and norms as well as traditional philosophical concepts to approach genocide. To use again a phrase from Arendt's analysis of Kafka, the banality of evil provides a "metaphoric approximation to truth" to what unfolded in Jerusalem.[98]

In addition to her claim that the banality of evil contains a lesson for us to learn, Arendt also pondered the extraordinarily rare moments of resistance against National Socialism by individuals who subverted the mechanisms of genocide. Weaving examples of resistance throughout her report, Arendt regarded such acts—like those displayed by Kafka's man of good will—as "miracles," and she wishes to transform these scant instances into lessons for the future. Referring to the rescue of Denmark's Jews in 1943, Arendt writes: "One is tempted to recommend the story for all political science students. What happened there was truly amazing."[99] The preparation for bureaucratic murder faltered, as the Danes protected nearly their entire Jewish population. Even more miraculous for Arendt, the Danes protected non-citizens and refused to surrender stateless refugees to the German occupiers.

Arendt reserved one of the most stirring scenes for Anton Schmid, an Austrian sergeant in the Wehrmacht who assisted Jews during the extermination process in the East. Arendt's poetic thought behind the following passage resonates with elements from Kafka's "HE":

> During the few minutes it took [Abba] Kovner to tell of the help that had come from a German sergeant [Schmid], a hush settled over the courtroom; it was as though the crowd had spontaneously decided to observe the usual two minutes of silence in honor of the man named Anton Schmidt [*sic*]. And in those two minutes, which were like a sudden burst of light in the midst of impenetrable, unfathomable darkness, a single thought stood out clearly, irrefutably, beyond question—how utterly different everything would be today in this courtroom, in Israel, in Germany, in all of Europe, and perhaps in all countries of the world, if only more such stories could have been told.[100]

Waxing poetic, Arendt described how a temporal rupture opened up in the courtroom. There was a moment of thinking ("a single thought stood out clearly") directed toward Schmid's resistance. How did he preserve his juridical self, resist totalitarianism, and not succumb to the banality of evil? Arendt does not answer, but rather describes Schmid's story as "a sudden burst of light in … unfathomable darkness." He signified the mark of wonder within horror that eclipses, for a moment, the flames from "Planet Auschwitz." Arendt concluded, "Politically speaking, most people will comply under conditions of terror, but *some people will not ... it did not happen everywhere.*"[101] Schmid's actions did not gesture to some "higher moral meaning." Rather, "politically speaking ... humanly speaking" such actions are necessary for our planet to be a "place fit for human habitation."[102] Anton Schmid embodied for Arendt the "man of good will" described in her earlier work on Kafka—a just man whose actions counter injustice.

Justice, in short, became Kafkaesque for Arendt, as the act of resistance replaced the axiomatic expression of justice. Arendt appeared to transform Kafka's authoritarian image of justice into an ideal for confronting totalitarianism. In *The Trial,* the painter Titorelli shows Joseph K. his incomplete painting of Dikē, the Greek goddess of Justice, blindfolded and holding scales. But as K. discerns, Dikē is conjoined with two other goddesses: Artemis (the Huntress) and Nikē (Victory). Titorelli further replaces the sword of vengeance with winged feet, thus linking Justice to Hermes, the messenger god. Observing that the figure appears to be running, K. remarks, "[t]hat's a poor combination ... Justice must remain at rest, otherwise the scales sway and no just judgment is possible."[103] For Kafka, Justice is not fixed. It is always on the move. His idea of "protracted" Justice (*Verschleppung*), moreover, shows it to be in a state of perpetual deferment.[104]

Despite its classical Greek components, Kafka's painterly representation of a Justice moving within a violent bureaucratic and autocratic society hearkens to Deuteronomy 16:20, "Justice, justice you should pursue" (*Tzedek, tzedek tirdof*). The passage implies that we too are on the move. But the Hebrew word for "pursue" (*tirdof*) also connotes a sense of hunting down or stalking an animal. In Kafka's adaptation, however, the individual no longer chases justice. Kafka reverses the direction of the pursuit and transforms Deuteronomy's image into a Greek one reminiscent of the Furies; Justice hunts its victim, and ultimately chases down K. to slaughter him "like a dog!"

What can Kafka's incomplete image of Justice tell us about how Arendt approaches Eichmann? For Arendt, the pursuit of justice within the Jerusalem courtroom involved the interplay between judgment and the imagination. In "Truth and Politics" Arendt wrote, "Thinking is truly discursive, running, as it were, from place to place, from one part of the world to another, through all kinds of conflicting views, until it finally ascends from these particularities to some impartial generality."[105] For Arendt, this discursive process was the crux of political thought. In discussing the model of jurisprudence behind the Nuremberg and Eichmann trials—that is, "To weigh the charges brought against the accused, to render judgment and to mete out due punishment"—Arendt described how the judicial process follows a traditional path.[106] The judges could not overstep these limits; they argue that they were not judges outside the realm of law. And yet, as the courts could not locate Nazi crimes in the law books, Arendt wished that they had "dared" to reach a judgment that circumvented the traditional path.One must pursue justice outside the frame of preconceived notions or pre-specified ends.[107]

If the Shoah was an epochal instantiation of injustice in which the scales to measure *Schuld*—a term that means in German both guilt and debt—were ruptured, then the inability to eliminate this *Schuld* suggests the permanence of an injustice. The scales for Arendt, like those in *The Trial*, entailed the image of an unstable calculation of justice.[108] The incalculable suggests neither the failure nor impossibility of justice, nor did Arendt call for the suspension of a legal decision. Arendt agreed with the judges on their sentence. Yet in her search for a justice that lay outside of traditional jurisprudence, Arendt sidestepped judicial law. Reluctant to make a judgment in terms of individual moral responsibility, Arendt turns instead to "political responsibility" in order to calculate Eichmann's *Schuld*.

Like Kafka's inclusion of Hermes in the painting of Dikē, Arendt underscored the hermeneutic element behind justice. At the end of her report she asserted:

> Every act that has once made its appearance and has been recorded in the history of mankind stays with mankind as a potentiality long after its actuality has become a thing of the past ... that the unprecedented, once it has appeared, may become a precedent for the future, that all trials touching upon "crimes against humanity" must be judged according to a standard that is today still an "ideal."[109]

If history involves acts of judgment, then Arendt's report reflected on the history of the Shoah at one particular moment as she searched for an idealized standard of judgment. Arendt's positing of a Holocaust justice remains in a state of abeyance; the sought-for justice entails a protracted resistance to injustice. Thus, the pursuit of justice is perpetually restaged in shifting temporal-historical moments and undergoes a series of dislocations at points of juridical transition. A political community's future depends on an unremitting engagement with the debts left in the wake of a monstrous past: a past that has nonetheless become routinized and all-too common in the present.

Eric Kligerman received his Ph.D. in comparative literature from the University of Michigan. He is an associate professor of German studies at the

University of Florida. In addition to his *Sites of the Uncanny: Paul Celan, Specularity and the Visual Arts* (2007), he has published on such topics as Nazis in American popular culture, representations of the Red Army Faction in New German Cinema, and the paintings of Gerhard Richter. His current research, which focuses on Franz Kafka, examines the intersection between quantum physics and German-Jewish intellectual thought.

NOTES

1. Hannah Arendt and Karl Jaspers, *Correspondence 1926–1969* (New York, 1992), 54.
2. Hannah Arendt, *Eichmann in Jerusalem: A Report on the Banality of Evil,* rev. ed. (New York, 1977), 253.
3. Deborah E. Lipstadt, *The Eichmann Trial* (New York, 2011) and Richard Wolin, "The Banality of Evil: The Demise of a Legend," *Jewish Review of Books,* 14 October 2014, argue that Arendt's reflections on Eichmann's thoughtlessness are related to Heidegger's philosophy. Seyla Benhabib, "Who's on Trial, Eichmann or Arendt?" *New York Times,* 21 September 2014, stresses how Arendt wished to rescue Kantian thought from the horrors of Nazism. Shoshana Felman, *The Juridical Unconscious: Trials and Traumas in the Twentieth Century* (Cambridge, MA, 2002) examines how Arendt used the space of the trial to mourn the loss of her friend Walter Benjamin. Lyndsey Stonebridge, *The Judicial Imagination: Writing after Nuremberg* (Edinburgh, 2012), turns to Arendt as the starting point for a new theory on the relationship between law and trauma.
4. Arendt, *Eichmann in Jerusalem,* 267.
5. Lawrence Douglas, *The Memory of Judgment: Making Law and History in the Trials of the Holocaust* (New Haven, CT, 2000), 173.
6. Felman, *The Juridical Unconscious,* 145.
7. Arendt and Jaspers, *Correspondence 1926–1969,* 62.
8. I will refer to the following essays by Arendt on Kafka: "The Jew as Pariah, A Hidden Tradition" (1944), "Franz Kafka, Appreciated Anew" (1946, originally published in German in *Die Wandlung*) and "Franz Kafka: A Revaluation" (published in 1944 in *The Partisan Review*). The first two essays are located in S.Y. Gottlieb, ed., *Reflections on Literature and Culture* (Palo Alto, CA, 2007). "Franz Kafka: A Revaluation" is reprinted in Arendt's *Essays on Understanding: 1930–1954 Formation, Exile, and Totalitarianism* (New York, 1994).
9. Arendt was an editor on the first volume of Kafka's works published in English at Schocken Books. In addition to the essays mentioned in the previous note, she began the final chapter of *The Human Condition* (1958) with Kafka's aphorism "HE." The prologue to her *Between Past and Future* contains a detailed reading of this very parable. In her last study, *Life of the Mind* (posthumously published in 1978), Arendt again returned to Kafka's "HE" at the end of the

first section on thinking. See Hannah Arendt, *The Human Condition* (Chicago, 1998); *Life of the Mind* (New York, 1978).

10. See Brian Danoff, "Arendt, Kafka, and the Nature of Totalitarianism," *Perspectives on Political Science* 29, no. 4 (2000): 211–18.

11. Bettina Stangneth, *Eichmann before Jerusalem: The Unexamined Life of a Mass Murderer* (New York, 2014), 197.

12. Richard Wolin, "Arendt, Banality, and Benhabib: A Final Rejoinder," *Jewish Review of Books,* 14 October 2014.

13. Arendt, *Eichmann in Jerusalem,* 3.

14. Arendt's translation is "incorrect," if one were to understand translation as a simple act of replacing one word with another. While *Hamishpath* comes closer to the term "judgment" than to "justice," Arendt's word choice also sheds light on her act of exegesis to the trial. Although her report may commence with the term "justice," Arendt ultimately shifts her analysis of the trial to the question of judgment.

15. Arendt, *Eichmann in Jerusalem,* 3.

16. See Arendt's introduction to Walter Benjamin's *Illuminations* (New York, 1968), 50.

17. According to Arendt, the conscious pariah also inhabits Kafka's literature. Through his act of resistance, the conscious pariah becomes an emblem of political rebellion and evolves into what Arendt describes as a "man of good will." See Arendt, "Pariah," 82–90. I will return to this concept later in my analysis.

18. Franz Kafka, *The Castle* (New York, 1998), 214.

19. Arendt, *The Origins of Totalitarianism* (New York, 2004), 246.

20. Ibid., 447.

21. Ibid., 444 and 446.

22. Ibid., 447.

23. Hannah Arendt, *Between Past and Future: Eight Exercises in Political Thought* (New York, 1993), 9, my emphasis.

24. Ibid., 9.

25. Ibid., 12.

26. Ibid., 11.

27. Arendt, *Life of the Mind,* 3.

28. Arendt, *Between Past and Future,* 15.

29. Arendt, "Kafka Appreciated Anew," 104.

30. Arendt, *Eichmann in Jerusalem,* 8.

31. Ibid., 270 and 278.

32. Cited in Elizabeth Young-Bruehl, *Hannah Arendt–For Love of the World* (New Haven, CT, 1982), 329.

33. Arendt, *Life of the Mind,* 4.

34. Arendt, *Eichmann in Jerusalem,* 50.

35. Ibid., 32.

36. Ibid., 50.

37. Ibid., 48.

38. Ibid., 81.

39. Ibid., 54.

40. Letter to Scholem in Hannah Arendt, *The Jewish Writings* (New York, 2007), 468.

41. Arendt, *Essays in Understanding,* 16.

42. Richard T. Grey, et al, eds., *A Franz Kafka Encyclopedia* (Westport, CT, 2005), 139.

43. Arendt, "Kafka Appreciated Anew," 106.

44. Roger Errera, "Interviewing Hannah Arendt," in *Hannah Arendt: The Last Interview and Other Conversations* (New York, 2013), 60.

45. Arendt, *Eichmann in Jerusalem,* 26.

46. Parker Potter, "Ordeal by Trial: Judicial References to the Nightmare World of Franz Kafka," *Pierce Law Review* 3, no. 2 (2005): 195–330.

47. Arendt, "Kafka Appreciated Anew," 104.

48. Ibid.,103.

49. Ibid., 104.

50. Ibid., 108.

51. Ibid., 109.

52. I say "imagined" because I have not found any documentation that Kafka actually performed such actions. In a letter to Felice, Kafka describes his desires of wanting to help Jewish refugee children from Eastern Europe who were living in Berlin. See Franz Kafka, *Letters to Felice,* ed. Erich Heller and Jürgen Born, trans. James Stern and Elisabeth Duckworth (New York, 2013), 500. Despite Arendt's assertion that resistance is a central feature to Kafka's literature, her interpretation is less a misreading of Kafka than an act of imagination that responds to her predicament as a Jewish exile in 1944. It is as if she uses Kafka as a screen to tell her own story of receiving an illegal visa to flee to America. Moreover, it was Arendt who, during her exile in Paris in 1933, worked for Youth Aliyah and helped organize the mass emigration of stateless Jewish children on ships to Palestine in 1935. In actuality, it is Arendt who demonstrates the very traits that she attributes to Kafka.

53. Arendt, "Kafka Appreciated Anew," 97.

54. Ibid.

55. Within *The Trial,* the parable allegorizes how traditional justice is withheld from Joseph K. during his experience within an inscrutable legal system that culminates with his execution.

56. We can hear in her subtitle "A Report on the Banality of Evil" an allusion to Kafka's "Report to the Academy." See S.Y. Gottlieb, "Hannah Arendt: Reflections on Ruin" in *New Formations* 71 (Summer 2011): 110–24.

57. Arendt, *Eichmann in Jerusalem,* 3.

58. Ibid., 277.

59. Ibid., 21, my emphasis.

60. Ibid., 254.

61. Ibid., 297.

62. Arendt noted that "[t]he command of the Führer … is the absolute center of the present legal order." See *Eichmann in Jerusalem,* 24. I do not wish to suggest

that Kafka is Arendt's new categorical imperative. Rather, Kafka's imagination reveals to her the very vulnerability of Kant's law.

63. Arendt, *Eichmann in Jerusalem*, 26–27.
64. Ibid., 146.
65. Ibid., 276.
66. Ibid., 254.
67. Ibid., 274, my emphasis.
68. Ibid., 294.
69. Ibid., 295.
70. Arendt, *Between Past and Future*, 10.
71. Arendt, "Kafka Appreciated Anew," 104.
72. Ibid., 95.
73. Arendt, *Eichmann in Jerusalem*, 278.
74. Ibid., 277.
75. Ibid., 277.
76. Ibid., 279.
77. Ibid., 273.
78. Arendt, "Kafka Appreciated Anew," 103.
79. Arendt, *The Origins of Totalitarianism*, 459.
80. Arendt, *Eichmann in Jerusalem*, 252, emphasis in original.
81. For the connections between radical evil and the banality of evil, see the chapter "From Radical Evil to the Banality of Evil: From Superfluousness to Thoughtlessness," by Richard Bernstein in his *Hannah Arendt and the Jewish Question* (Cambridge, MA, 1996), 137–53.
82. Arendt, "Kafka Appreciated Anew," 100 and 105.
83. Ibid., 96–97.
84. Arendt, *Essays in Understanding*, 74.
85. Arendt, "Kafka Appreciated Anew," 98.
86. Ibid.
87. Arendt, *Eichmann in Jerusalem*, 52.
88. Arendt, "Kafka Appreciated Anew," 97.
89. Arendt, *Eichmann in Jerusalem*, 71.
90. Ibid., 68.
91. Ibid., 84.
92. For an outstanding analysis of how scholars from across disciplines have misread Arendt, see Roger Berkowitz, "Misreading 'Eichmann in Jerusalem'," *The New York Times*, 7 July 2013. In his article, Berkowitz includes how reflections on Arendt by such writers as David Owen, Fred Kaplan, David Cesarani, and Deborah Lipstadt failed to grasp the "unconventional meaning" behind what Arendt meant by "banality of evil." As Berkowitz concludes, there is a need "to free Arendt's book, once again, from the tyranny of the conventional wisdom." Retrieved April 2016 from https://opinionator.blogs.nytimes.com/2013/07/07/misreading-hannah-arendts-eichmann-in-jerusalem/?_r=0.
93. Ibid.

94. Harold Bloom, *Agon: Towards a Theory of Revisionism* (New York, 1983), 286.
95. Ibid., 285.
96. Harold Bloom, *The Best Poems of the English Language: From Chaucer through Frost* (New York, 2004), xv.
97. Harold Bloom, *Agon: Towards a Theory of Revisionism,* 238.
98. Arendt, *Between Past and Future,* 9.
99. Arendt, *Eichmann in Jerusalem,* 129 and 172.
100. Ibid., 231.
101. Ibid., 233, emphasis in original.
102. Ibid.
103. Franz Kafka, *The Trial* (New York, 1998), 145–46.
104. Ibid., 152.
105. Arendt, *Between Past and Future,* 242.
106. Arendt, *Eichmann in Jerusalem,* 253.
107. Ibid., 298.
108. See Jacques Derrida's "Force of Law: The Mystical Foundation of Authority" in *Deconstruction and the Possibility of Justice,* ed. Drucilla Cornell, Michel Rosenfeld, and David Carlson (New York, 1992), 3–67. Derrida argues that an "incalculable justice requires us to calculate" (14). But while Derrida ultimately requires a "sort of obligation towards the law," Arendt's judgment of Eichmann occurs before the law. That is, genocide breaks an altogether "different community" and requires "the emergence of an international penal code" and the "protection of international law." As Arendt contends, the failure in Jerusalem stems from "this yet unfinished nature of international law" (*Eichmann in Jerusalem,* 272–74).
109. Arendt, *Eichmann in Jerusalem,* 273.

SELECT BIBLIOGRAPHY

Arendt, Hannah, ed. Introduction to *Illuminations* by Walter Benjamin, trans. Harry Zohn, 1–55. New York: Schocken, 1968.
——. *Eichmann in Jerusalem: A Report on the Banality of Evil,* rev. ed. New York: Penguin, 1977.
——. *Life of the Mind,* ed. Mary McCarthy, 2 vols. New York: Harcourt Brace Jovanovich, 1978.
——. *Between Past and Future: Eight Exercises in Political Thought.* New York: Penguin, 1993.
——. "Franz Kafka: A Revaluation." In *Essays in Understanding, 1930–1954: Formation, Exile, and Totalitarianism,* ed. Jerome Kohn, 69–80. New York: Harcourt, 1994.
——. *Essays on Understanding. 1930–1954: Formation, Exile, and Totalitarianism,* ed. Jerome Kohn. New York: Harcourt, 1994.
——. *The Origins of Totalitarianism.* New York: Schocken, 2004.
——. "Franz Kafka, Appreciated Anew." In *Reflections on Literature and Culture,* ed. S.Y. Gottlieb, 94–109. Palo Alto, CA: Stanford University Press, 2007.

——. "The Jew as Pariah: A Hidden Tradition" in *Reflections on Literature and Culture,* ed. S.Y. Gottleib, 94–109. Palo Alto, CA: Stanford University Press, 2007.

——. *The Jewish Writings,* ed. Jerome Kohn and Ron H. Feldman. New York: Schocken, 2007.

Arendt, Hannah, and Karl Jaspers. *Correspondence 1926–1969,* ed. Lotte Kohler and Hans Saner, trans. Robert and Rita Kimber. New York: Harcourt Brace Jovanovich, 1992.

Bauman, Zygmunt. *Modernity and the Holocaust.* Ithaca, NY: Cornell University Press, 1989.

Benhabib, Seyla. "Who's on Trial, Eichmann or Arendt?" *New York Times,* 24 September 2014. Retrieved April 2016 from http://opinionator.blogs.nytimes .com/2014/09/21/whos-on-trial-eichmann-or-anrendt/

Berkowitz, Roger. "Misreading 'Eichmann in Jerusalem.'" *New York Times,* 7 July 2013. Retrieved April 2016 from https://opinionator.blogs.nytimes.com/2013/07/07/misreading-hannah-arendts-eichmann-in-jerusalem/?_r=0.

Bernstein, Richard. *Hannah Arendt and the Jewish Question.* Cambridge, MA: MIT Press, 1996.

Bloom, Harold. *Agon: Towards a Theory of Revisionism.* New York: Oxford University Press, 1983.

——. *The Best Poems of the English Language: From Chaucer through Frost.* New York: Harper Collins, 2004.

Danoff, Brian. "Arendt, Kafka, and the Nature of Totalitarianism." *Perspectives on Political Science* 29, no. 4 (2000): 211–18.

Derrida, Jacques. "Force of Law: The Mystical Foundation of Authority." In *Deconstruction and the Possibility of Justice,* ed. Drucilla Cornell, Michel Rosenfeld, and David Carlson, 3–67. New York: Routledge, 1992.

Douglas, Lawrence. *The Memory of Judgment: Making Law and History in the Trials of the Holocaust.* New Haven, CT: Yale University Press, 2000.

Felman, Shoshana. *The Juridical Unconscious: Trials and Traumas in the Twentieth Century.* Cambridge, MA: Harvard University Press, 2002.

Friedlander, Saul, ed. *Probing the Limits of Representation Nazism and the "Final Solution."* Cambridge, MA: Harvard University Press, 1992.

Gottlieb, S.Y. "Hannah Arendt: Reflections on Ruin." *New Formations* 71 (Summer 2011): 110–24.

Grey, Richard T, et al, eds. *A Franz Kafka Encyclopedia.* Westport, CT: Greenwood Press, 2005.

Halberstam, Michael. "Hannah Arendt on the Totalitarian Sublime and Its Promise of Freedom." In *Hannah Arendt in Jerusalem,* ed. Steven Aschheim, 105–23. Berkeley, CA: University of California Press, 2001.

Kafka, Franz. *The Castle,* trans. Mark Harman. New York: Schocken, 1998.

——. *The Trial,* trans. Breon Mitchell. New York: Schocken, 1998.

——. *Letters to Felice,* ed. Erich Heller and Jürgen Born, trans. James Stern and Elisabeth Duckworth. New York: Schocken, 2013.

Lipstadt, Deborah. *The Eichmann Trial.* New York: Schocken, 2011.

Potter, Parker. "Ordeal by Trial: Judicial References to the Nightmare World of Franz Kafka." *Pierce Law Review* 3, no. 2 (2005): 195–330.

Sophocles. *Volume 1: Oedipus the King, Oedipus at Colonus, Antigone,* ed. and trans. David Grene. Chicago: University of Chicago Press, 1991.

Stangneth, Bettina. *Eichmann before Jerusalem: The Unexamined Life of a Mass Murderer,* trans. Ruth Martin. New York: Knopf, 2014.

Stonebridge, Lyndsey. *The Judicial Imagination: Writing after Nuremberg.* Edinburgh: Edinburgh University Press, 2011.

Wolin, Richard. "Arendt, Banality, and Benhabib: A Final Rejoinder." *Jewish Review of Books* (October 14, 2014). Retrieved April 2016 from https://jewishreviewof books.com/articles/1315/arendt-banality-and-benhabib-a-final-rejoinder/

———. "The Banality of Evil: The Demise of a Legend." *Jewish Review of Books* (Fall 2014). Retrieved April 2016 from https://jewishreviewofbooks.com/arti cles/1106/the-banality-of-evil-the-demise-of-a-legend/

Young-Bruehl, Elizabeth. *Hannah Arendt–For Love of the World.* New Haven, CT: Yale University Press, 1982.

Chapter 2

Criminal Trials as Rituals of Purification

Katharina von Kellenbach

In a postcard sent from Jerusalem in 1966, the renowned Jewish scholar Shalom Ben-Chorin quoted Deuteronomy to urge his German Christian colleague Hermann Schlingensiepen to "eradicate evil from their midst and purify the land of the Mulkas and Bradfischs who are still living amongst them."[1] This essay examines the language of defilement and purification that percolated through postwar German legal, political, and religious discourses and explores ecologically informed metaphors of purification to rethink the role of criminal trials in the transformation of guilt and the guilty in post-atrocity societies.

The Protestant theologian and the Jewish scholar began corresponding in 1960 during Israel's preparation for the Eichmann trial in Jerusalem. The retired Professor Schlingensiepen wrote to Eichmann, and later to other Nazi defendants in West Germany, in an effort to provide pastoral counseling and Christian support. By 1966, Shalom Ben-Chorin had become disenchanted with the West German justice system and the German churches' unwillingness to hold Nazi perpetrators accountable. Hundreds of court proceedings before West German courts during the 1960s yielded few convictions and often shockingly lenient sentences. Ben-Chorin quoted Deuteronomy 13:6 in Hebrew, *Ubi 'arta hara' mikirbeha,* and then translated it into German (retranslated here into English). He wrote: "You shall annihilate the evil from your midst. This legal maxim is found in several places in

Deuteronomy (17:7, 12; 19:19; 21:21–22; 24:7) and it is reiterated repeatedly. The Germans as well should listen to this."[2]

Ben-Chorin wrote this shortly after the conclusion of the Frankfurt Auschwitz trial in 1965, at a time when the Ludwigsburg Central Office for the Investigation of National Socialist Crimes had 6,372 open investigations.[3] Robert Mulka and Otto Bradfisch were among the highest-ranking and best-known Nazi convicts. Mulka (1895–1969) was the lead defendant of the Auschwitz trial as the former adjutant of Rudolf Höss, the commandant of Auschwitz. Bradfisch (1903–1994) had commanded Einsatzkommando 8 and overseen the mass executions of Jews in Baranowicze, Bialystok, Bobruisk, Borissow, Gomel, Gorki, Klinzy, Minsk, Mogilew, Nowogrodek, Orscha, Rjetschiza, Rogatschew, and Sluzk as well as the deportation of Jews from Łódź to the Chełmno death camp. Both men received relatively light prison sentences and were subsequently released for health reasons. It was in response to these events that Ben-Chorin expressed his frustration over West Germany's apparent inability to hold individuals accountable for mass murder.

I begin with Ben-Chorin's invocation of Deuteronomy to examine the suggestion that criminal law in general, and retributive justice in particular, serve to purify a community of the contaminating presence of evil and guilt. The language of purification hovers in the background of criminal law and transitional justice.[4] In her analysis of the British and American legal systems, Martha Duncan notes that words like "*pollution, refuse, garbage,* and *scum* were commonly used to refer to the convicts but the dominant metaphor was *stain* or its closely associated term *taint.*"[5] Metaphors of crime as filth, she maintains, and of "criminality as a contagious disease that might spread to noncriminals," convinced the British House of Commons Select Committee in the early nineteenth century to dispatch English convicts into exile to the distant shores of Australia. Exile and quarantine of prisoners to prison systems at the outskirts of civilization continue to inform prison construction, in "places where refuse and garbage are collected."[6] In 1926, the US Supreme Court upheld a zoning ordinance in the city of Euclid, Ohio, which classified "sewage disposal, garbage and refuse incineration, cemeteries, crematories, penal and correctional institutions, insane and feeble-minded institutions, storage of oil and gasoline" as one zone.[7] Refuse, sewage, death, and crime were considered polluting and needed to be contained and restricted outside the borders of the community.

Shalom Ben-Chorin's scriptural reference contains an important ambiguity that moves between "the evil" and "the evildoer" as the source of contamination. This ambiguity has practical consequences as to who or what exactly has to be removed: is it the individual evildoer who must be quarantined, or is it the transpersonal presence of evil that a community must get rid of? The book of Deuteronomy prescribes two rituals for purification: The first demands the physical removal of the evildoer by execution or banishment, while the second symbolically eliminates the community's guilt by association.

The verse following Ben-Chorin's quote demands that everyone in the community participate in the execution of the culprit in order to "purge the evil from your midst ... Show them no pity or compassion and do not shield them. But you shall surely kill them; your own hand shall be the first against them to execute them" (Dt 13:8–9). Only the death of the evildoer as the source of pollution can protect the community against contamination. Failure to punish signals complicity: "At this primitive level," philosopher Bernard J. Verkamp points out, "the purification rite was supposed to remove the contagion in almost a physical sense, or to quarantine the victim from the community at large, lest physical contact in itself pollute others."[8] This notion has found its most prominent modern proponent in Immanuel Kant who feared that the contagion of guilt would spread through a community if it failed to exact punishment. He writes in *The Metaphysical Elements of Justice*:

> Even if a civil society were to dissolve itself by common agreement of all of its members (for example, if the people inhabiting an island decided to separate and disperse themselves around the world), the last murderer remaining in prison must first be executed, so that everyone will duly receive what his actions are worth and so that the bloodguilt thereof will not be fixed on the people because they failed to insist on carrying out the punishment; for if they fail to do so, they may be regarded as accomplices in this public violation of justice.[9]

Retribution must be imposed not only to insure that the culprit receives the punishment they deserve but also to protect the moral health of the community. Punishment serves the community, as much, if not more than the offender whose rehabilitation and deterrence is the stated goal of punitive justice.[10] The duty to punish is incumbent on the community in order to avoid complicity and contamination.

The second ritual described in Deuteronomy focuses on the community. This ritual is obligatory when the evildoer is unknown or cannot be located. In the absence of a culprit, the community is still required to remove the guilt caused by bloodshed. Where culpability cannot be determined beyond reasonable doubt and capital punishment cannot be imposed, the pollution must be removed symbolically. In this case, a young heifer is taken outside the camp and its neck is broken. The elders of the camp wash their hands over the dead animal and declare:

"Our hands did not shed this blood, nor were we witnesses to it. Absolve O LORD, your people Israel, whom you redeemed; do not let the guilt of innocent blood remain in the midst of your people Israel." Then they will be absolved of bloodguilt. So, you shall purge the guilt of innocent blood from your midst (Dt 21:6–9).

The sacrifice of an animal and the ritual washing of hands are universal symbols of purification. All of the world's religions have developed rituals that symbolically cast out moral and spiritual contagion. Different traditions apply different symbolic detergents, most prominently sacrificial blood and (sacred) water, or fire and smoke (e.g., fire sacrifice, smudge sticks, incense, or sweat lodges).[11] The correlation of washing with spiritual or moral purification is well established in the history of religions. Water is used in Christian baptism and Jewish mikveh baths, by Hindu immersions in the holy river Ganges, and by Muslims who wash their hands, feet, and faces before daily prayers. Recent studies by social psychologists have confirmed that people experience a need for physical cleansing when reminded of moral wrongdoing. Social psychologists call this the "Macbeth Effect" based on Shakespeare's gripping portrait of Lady Macbeth's obsessive attempts to wash away the blood of guilt.[12] And Shakespeare invokes the cultural icon of Pontius Pilate who publicly washed his hands while proclaiming his innocence of the conviction of Jesus of Nazareth.

It is therefore not surprising that references to washing circulated through the postwar German rhetoric of coming to terms with the past. *Persilscheine* was the popular term given to letters defending the moral character and personal integrity of Nazi functionaries, which were submitted to denazification panels. The name *Persil* refers to a laundry detergent and signaled the wish that these letters would possess the magic power of whitewashing all traces of culpability. The wave of criminal trials throughout the 1960s generated fierce debates over who or what should be considered dirty. *Nestbeschmutzer* (soiling one's own nest) was the derogatory name applied to those who supported the trials. In their "Memorandum on the Prosecution of National Socialist Crimes in West Germany" published in 1963, the Council of the Protestant Church in Germany scolded: "only ignorance (*Unverstand*) can speak of soiling one's own nest, when in truth one is engaged in cleansing a heavily soiled nest."[13] Judges, politicians and upstanding citizens furiously protected their white vests against mudslinging journalists who exposed past Nazi careers and unleashed international media scandals. Such discourses on dirt, the anthropologist Mary Douglas has pointed out in *Purity and Danger,* are a function of symbolic and political orders:

To conclude, if uncleanness is matter out of place, we must approach it through order. Uncleanness or dirt is that which must not be included if a pattern is to be maintained. To recognize this is the first step towards insight into pollution. It involves us in no clear-cut distinction between sacred and secular ... Defilement is never an isolated event. It cannot occur except in view of a systematic ordering of ideas. Hence any piecemeal interpretation of pollution rules of another culture is bound to fail. For the only way in which pollution ideas make any sense is in reference to a total structure of thought whose keystone, boundaries, margins, and internal lines are held in relation by rituals of separation.[14]

Who or what pollutes a particular social or political order is subject to change. Over the course of the 1960s, the social and moral order of West Germany was redefined and tested by the second wave of criminal Nazi trials. When regimes change and new political orders are instituted, old structures become obsolete and past elites are ousted. The creation and preservation of social order requires radical interventions as well as regular maintenance. When National Socialism came to power, the party used the rhetoric of purification to overcome moral inhibitions against the use of mass violence in order to implement a radical and genocidal vision of purity.[15] The party defined Jews, homosexuals, and communists as out of the social order and depicted them as dirty vermin and depraved parasites. In public rituals, beginning with the burning of books, the removal of "degenerate" art, the demolition of synagogues and businesses, the marginalization, expropriation, deportation, and eventually, mass murder of Jews, the Nazi state dramatically displayed its vision and will to purify the nation. The SS (Schutzstaffel) was charged with cleansing and purifying the German *Volk,* a mission that was considered honorable and heroic.[16]

Genocidal visions of purity are integral to modern political movements that implement ethnic cleansing and ruthlessly eliminate racial sub-humans, biological degenerates, and political subversives from the national body. Racism and antisemitism, argues sociologist Zygmunt Bauman, arise from a distinctly modern need to establish and maintain boundaries. Rooted in metaphors of gardening and hygiene, eliminationist purification, to use Daniel Goldhagen's felicitous term, has become a defining characteristic of the modern world.

Gardening and medicine supplied the archetypes of constructive stance, while normality, health, or sanitation offered the archmetaphors for human tasks and strategies in the management of human affairs. Human existence and cohabitation became objects of planning and administration; like garden vegetation or a living organism they could not be left to their own devices, lest they be infested by weeds or overwhelmed by cancerous tissues. Gardening and medicine are functionally distinct forms of the same activity of separating and setting apart useful elements destined to live and thrive from harmful and morbid ones, which ought to be exterminated.[17]

These modern secular visions of order use necrophilic practices of sterilization and sanitation to create and maintain monocultures. The modern paradigm of purity strives to impose totalitarian systems of monoculture that can be maintained by powerful technologies of destruction that allow the elimination of intrusive weeds, subversive hybrids, and wild admixtures. Anyone who does not fit must be eliminated. We can trace this genocidal impulse into the politics of ethnic cleansing in Romania, Rwanda, and Bosnia to political purges in Cambodia, China, and the Soviet Union,[18] to apartheid systems designed to protect racial purity.[19] More recently, movements such as Islamic State (ISIS) and extremist Christian pro-life groups embrace violence as means to cleanse the world of moral corruption and religious defilement.[20] Internal and external pollution is seen as mortal threat to the health and well-being of a national, ethnic, and religious collective.[21]

SS men who were tasked with racial and political cleansing considered themselves "pure" even as they generated and lived in the extreme filth and depravity of ghettos, extermination camps, and mass execution sites. Famously, Himmler in his Posen Speech of 4 October 1943 lauded his SS soldiers and policemen for remaining *anständig* (decent) while killing thousands. National Socialism pursued a vision of purity that justified mass killings. Their participation in purification did not undermine perpetrators' sense of self-worth. For instance, Robert Mulka explained in a private letter to Professor Hermann Schlingensiepen in June 1965, shortly before his conviction in August:

> I must declare out of deep conviction and after careful consideration of the past events that I will be able to step before HIS chair of justice with a PURE heart and a PURE conscience, possibly very soon, if HE so chooses, and that I trust and hope that HE will keep his word and that HE knows what is right and wrong, as well as what is falsehood and truth.[22]

Mulka's delusional sense of purity was validated by his family and friends, whose support reinforced his loyalty to the National Socialist symbolic universe. He praised the "devoted care of my beloved wife and loyal life companion" and the loving support of "the circle of my dear and faithfully remaining children and grandchildren" and boasted of his network of friends: "The name Mulka has a good reputation in the world, and we have good friends everywhere around the world who stand by me in unbroken loyalty and reassure me that they remain convinced of my innocence."[23] His innocence is rooted not in the denial of his actions but in rejection of culpability. Like other Nazis, Mulka maintained moral indifference to extreme conditions of dehumanization and degradation, which he created and oversaw in Auschwitz. When prodded by Professor Schlingensiepen, Mulka claimed to have suffered from "internal conflicts" over whether "what happened in Auschwitz constituted MURDER for the sake of MURDER, or whether these were [lawful] measures in the context of the former war effort."[24] Mulka refused to recognize culpable wrongdoing because he remained wedded to Nazi ideology, which declared Jews out of the moral universe. In his mind, the killing of Jewish men, women, and children constituted a "lawful measure of war." Jews were dirt that needed to be removed. Like most perpetrators during the trials of the1960s, Mulka emphasized the political responsibility of the German people over his personal culpability and refused to hold himself accountable for actions, such as the construction of gas chambers and supervision of the killing operation. Instead, he implicated the political collective:

> No. My dear Herr Professor, the entire German Volk is guilty, because no one resisted or dared to criticize what was happening. And I count myself among those who often held a different opinion because of my Christian thinking ... I did not become co-guilty (*mitschuldig*) for the later totality of events (*spätere Gesamtgeschehnisse*) like the vast majority of Germans who joined the party for a variety of personal reasons. I had no party affiliation and voted for the *Deutschnationale Volkspartei.*[25]

At the trial, Mulka's claim not to have joined the Nazi party was disproved.[26] But his systematic dispersion and redistribution of culpability undermined the resolve of the judicial system and political culture. Owing to the vagaries of the German penal code and the high standards of proof, the Frankfurt court in August 1965 convicted Mulka as an accomplice to the murder of at least 750 people on four separate occasions. It sentenced him to fourteen years in prison but in January 1966 released him after he suffered what he described as "Herzkollaps." It was this wavering and indecisiveness that unsettled Shalom Ben-Chorin and prompted him to write the letter chiding West Germany for failing to remove evil from its midst.

A growing number of voices within the Evangelical Church in Germany (Evangelische Kirche in Deutschland) agreed with Ben-Chorin. In their 1963 Memorandum, the EKD had called on West German courts "to characterize injustice as reprehensible and to punish it for the sake of the community."[27] The memorandum continues:

> It is not the task of the courts to perform the purification of our entire nation with these trials; they can only hold individual criminals accountable and sentence them. But it is their high office to reestablish in our nation the binding va-

lidity of the law, which had been destroyed in the past, and thereby contribute substantially to the inner recuperation of our people.[28]

The EKD criticized the leniency of punishments for crimes committed "in Nazi times" compared to those committed "in our days," such as sexual assault and ordinary murders. And it assured judges in West Germany that the church would not "leave the courts alone in their grave responsibility." But there were opposing voices in the Protestant Church that insisted that crimes committed "in our days" were fundamentally different. While ordinary criminals break the laws of the state, Nazi perpetrators had followed orders and upheld the laws of state, however reprehensible and perverted. These opposing voices charged judges with hypocrisy if they had been in office "in the past." The complicity of the legal profession with Nazism made judges susceptible to arguments such as the one proposed by a group of sympathetic prison chaplains, who published an open letter in opposition to the EKD memorandum:

> [O]ur people (among them the judges and state attorneys) have supported the [National Socialist] regime and have given those directly involved in Nazi crimes the impression that their actions were legitimate and performed in the name of the people, of the government, and of the legislature. This collaboration in guilt (*Schuldzusammenhang*) between participating perpetrators and our entire people prohibits their condemnation and punishment for something they committed on order and with support of the people.[29]

The moral force of this prohibition against punishment rests on the relationships between the collective and the individual. Unlike the murder for which the book of Deuteronomy demanded purification through the punishment of the murderer, the killings performed during National Socialism were willed and ordered by the leaders of the community. Therefore, sympathizers argued, the community had no right to extricate from the overall guilt by punishing individual culprits. Punishment in this case would not purify the community but indict the collective for inflicting violence on a substitute in order to alleviate its general complicity.

Such critics referred to a different purification ritual: the scapegoat.[30] Unlike the sacrifice of the heifer in Deuteronomy that is killed in order to prevent the spread of guilt incurred by one man, the scapegoat is loaded with the guilt of the entire community. To purge the Hebrews of their sins, God ordered Moses to tell his brother the priest Aaron to

> lay both of his hands on the head of a live goat, and confess over it all the iniquities of the people of Israel, and all of their transgressions, all of their sins, putting them on the head of the goat, and sending it away into the wilderness

> ... The goat shall bear on itself all of their iniquities to a barren region; and the
> goat shall be set free in the wilderness. (Lv 16:22–23)

This ritual expulsion of the scapegoat, performed on the Day of Atonement,
grants reprieve from punishment to the entire community and thereby permits its renewal and reemergence from the violence of the past. The banishment of an expendable substitute saves everyone else.

Perpetrators, their lawyers, and sympathizers used this trope in courtrooms and the media to elicit sympathy and to charge everyone else with
trying to exculpate themselves on the backs of defendants. During his 1963
trial, Otto Bradfisch, senior officer in Einsatzgruppe B in 1941 and 1942,
and later Commander of the Security Police in Łódź, complained that Nazi
convicts

> had to be singled out as lone scapegoats for reasons of state expediency—such
> as restoration of international prestige—in order to load them quite comfortably
> with the guilt and to force them to pay for a mistaken, yes criminal, policy of a
> German government. Don't misunderstand me, please, I recognize that terri-
> ble crimes were committed in the last war, but that confession is linked to the
> question of responsibility for these cruel events ... Did not the highest German
> jurists ... approve and support Hitler's measures of mass murder although they
> had the responsibility to intervene as sworn agents of the law? I have met none
> of these gentlemen, who I consider the intellectual inventors of subsequent
> events, in the many prisons of the Federal Republic, which I was forced to visit
> as a witness ... They enjoy their freedom and "well-deserved" pensions.[31]

Nazi defendants and their lawyers routinely made reference to the
scapegoat to re-invoke the web of collective culpability and to condemn
the community's desire to remove the guilty. The rhetoric of the scapegoat
contained enough kernels of truth to make it politically effective. While all
sides seemed to agree on the need for purification, there was no clarity over
who or what exactly should suffer the consequences and become the subject
of penal suffering. This ambivalence resulted in paralysis and encouraged
clemency. Mulka was released from prison in 1966 after visiting a psychiatric ward. Bradfisch was released into the custody of his friends in 1965
despite separate sentences of ten years in 1961 and thirteen years in 1963.

PENANCE AND PENITENTIARIES

No modern legal theorist claims that the goal of punishment should be the
sacrificial destruction of the offender. But in what way can punishment be

said to be beneficial not only to the community but also to individual convicts? Legal scholar Stephen P. Garvey criticizes major theorists of punishment for failing to distinguish clearly between the benefits of punishment for the perpetrator and those that accrue to the community. Beginning with Kant's retributivist deontology, Jeremy Bentham's utilitarian teleology, and more recent theories of restorative justice, punishment is most often recommended for its cleansing effects on the society. Garvey wants to defend penal suffering as meaningful to perpetrators. He suggests that we consider the sacrifice of (life)time and money, freedom and power, pride and privilege a form of "secular penance."[32] He argues that enduring hardships, both voluntary and involuntary, provides perpetrators with the means to "pay back" moral debts. Garvey reclaims the terminology of atonement to argue that punishment in secular societies ought to be intentional and serve the transformation of perpetrators as well as the restoration of victims:

> Atonement is both a goal and a process. As a goal, atonement seeks the reconciliation of the wrongdoer and the victim, and the reintegration of the wrongdoer back into good standing as a member of the community. As a process, atonement has several steps whose successful completion should ideally lead to atonement-the-goal.[33]

In order to work purposefully toward moral repair and reconciliation, Garvey proposes the concept of "talionic restitution" as a guide for sanctions.[34] His examples are minor but they make the point that punishment should generate restitution to victims and confront perpetrators with the harmful consequences of their actions. He cites a case in which a person convicted of a hit-and-run accident was sentenced to volunteer in a hospital trauma unit, thereby exposing him to the ordeal of crash victims. Another trial convicted someone of tampering with fire alarms and ordered him to clean fire trucks for a year, thereby observing the impact of false fire alarms. Garvey calls these punishments talionic restitution because they fit the crime, actively confront perpetrators with the suffering of victims, and generate opportunities for moral restitution.

The conventional repertoire of punitive codes is already absurd in the face of genocidal crimes. Is the concept of talionic restitution any more incongruous in the context of crimes such as Auschwitz (Mulka) or the Einsatzgruppen (Bradfisch)? Societies mark the gravity of the infringement by the severity of punishment, but in the case of genocide and of the Holocaust there is no appropriate hardship or sacrifice that can be imposed on individuals that would be proportional to the harm.[35] As Hannah Arendt has famously pointed out, "radical evil" exceeds the ability of court systems either to punish or to forgive.

> It is therefore quite significant, a structural element in the realm of human
> affairs, that men are unable to forgive what they cannot punish and that they
> are unable to punish what has turned out to be unforgivable ... All we know
> is that we can neither punish nor forgive such offenses and that they therefore
> transcend the realm of human affairs and the potentialities of human power,
> both of which they radically destroy.[36]

Justice systems struggle to prosecute and convict perpetrators who do
not torture and kill for personal satisfaction or gain, and who do not lose
control over their desires and succumb to envy, lust, greed, or anger.[37] Collective evil is characterized by personal discipline and submission to superior orders, a phenomenon, which Hannah Arendt tried to capture with the
concept of the "banality of evil."[38] Building on these insights, philosopher
Susan Neiman notes:

> Jurisprudence views heinous crimes as those done with malice and forethought.
> Both of these components of intention were often missing in many agents who
> carried out the daily work of extermination ... At every level, the Nazis pro-
> duced more evil, with less malice, than civilization had previously known.[39]

Men like Mulka and Bradfisch remained seemingly incapable of fully grasp-
ing what they had done. The idea of talionic restitution calls for the invention of new penalties that compel ideologically blinded perpetrators as well
as their communities to engage in atoning practices that dismantle moral
indifference and ideological negation of the moral dignity and human
worth of victims. Such penalties strive to generate the conditions in which
individual and collective remorse can emerge. It is contrition over political
wrongdoing that drives personal and political change.

PURIFICATION AS PENANCE

Religious traditions have provided frameworks for repentance that guided
individuals and communities through processes of internal and behavioral
change. These penitential practices consisted of self-imposed hardships and
sacrifices, such as fasting, prayer, abstinence, charity, and service. In the
modern world, these ritual practices have been privatized and often delegit-
imized. The word penance conjures up images of medieval self-flagellation,
hair shirts, and indulgences. It seems quaint to bring up penitential practices
in the context of secular processes of purification and to suggest a reconsid-
eration of such ritual observances in the aftermath of genocide and human
rights abuses. However, what makes these traditional practices an intriguing

option for contemporary, post-genocidal societies is their activist approach to the problem of guilt. Penance transforms guilt into a challenge. It understands guilt as a burden that can and should be carried with dignity. Penitential practices externalize culpability and turn the web of complicity into specific actions that require courage, discipline, and perseverance. Penance transforms guilt from internal shameful secrets into public acts. Penitential practices engage individuals and communities in activities that rebuild self-respect and prescribe specific tasks that break the silence and isolation of wrongdoing. Penance exercises moral agency and confronts self-serving delusions. While penance does not replace punishment imposed on individual perpetrators who must be removed from positions of power and authority, it recruits the community into transformative practice by prescribing reparative and restorative tasks. The political transformations of the 1960s were less the result of purification by punitive removal of the likes of Mulka and Bradfisch than by the growing willingness of German subcultures to engage in penitential practice and substitutionary acts of atonement.[40]

THE ECOLOGY OF PURIFICATION

It is useful to reconsider the metaphors, means, and methods of purification. Instead of imaging purgation as a swift removal of filth, a metaphor that informs the removal of criminals from the community by incarceration, exile, or execution, we should consider more ecological approaches to dirt. In actuality, neither our waste material nor our moral filth simply disappears once it has been moved out of sight. The planet has run out of wild spaces where we can deport and exile people, and we have reached the limits of dumping grounds in which we can bury the waste. Instead, we need visions of purification that take note of global limits, on which nothing disappears and nobody vanishes into exile. Neither our physical garbage nor the moral baggage of personal and collective failures can be expelled into the wilderness. Instead of discarding, we have to learn to recycle and transform existing structures as the only method of disposing unwanted legacies. However, responsible approaches to garbage involve handling toxic materials that require deliberate and intentional remediation strategies. Composting criminal histories of atrocity demands a variety of ritual interventions that include criminal trials, removal of political elites, economic reparations, cultural exchange, and educational programs conceived as a sequence of dynamic remediation steps.

Composting is not usually associated with poisonous and harmful substances. Ordinary gardeners with backyard composts are warned against

adding non-biodegradable contaminants to their compost piles. But industrial superfund sites use composting as a form of bioremediation, as out-
lined by the Environmental Protection Agency:

> Compost bioremediation refers to the use of a biological system of microor-
> ganisms in a mature, cured compost to sequester or break down contaminants
> in water or soil. Microorganisms consume contaminants in soils, ground and
> surface waters, and air. The contaminants are digested, metabolized, and trans-
> formed into humus and inert byproducts, such as carbon dioxide, water, and
> salts. Compost bioremediation has proven effective in degrading or altering
> many types of contaminants, such as chlorinated and nonchlorinated hydro-
> carbons, wood-preserving chemicals, solvents, heavy metals, pesticides, petro-
> leum products, and explosives. Compost used in bioremediation is referred to
> as "tailored" or "designed" compost in that it is specially made to treat specific
> contaminants at specific sites.[41]

Application of the methods of compost bioremediation to the realm of
moral and political transformation highlights the need for systemic interventions and long-term engagement with individual perpetrators as well
as their political ideologies. Purification cannot be enacted by one-time
cathartic experiences, such as high-profile criminal trials or dramatic punishments. Instead, we should envision purification as a process involving
multiple stages and levels that involve individuals and ideologies, social
structures, economic systems, and collective identities. The metaphor of
composting highlights the need for systemic approaches to moral remainders of violent legacies. The idea of "tailored composting" provides new
metaphors for thinking about rituals of purification that move beyond the
punishment of individuals and includes systemic transformation. Ecological approaches to purification of culpability move beyond the "either-or"
of criminal trials versus political processes of reconciliation. Indeed, both
interventions are necessary and need to remain activated for prolonged
periods of time.

The metaphor of composting is not meant to suggest a natural process that eventually allows grass to grow over the mass graves of genocide's
victims. In fact, the goal of the "purification of memory," as suggested by
Pope John Paul II in the Papal Apology of 2000, is not the disappearance of
memory but its decontamination of harmful ideologies (among perpetrator
communities) and of traumatic memories (among victim communities). Purification aims to create a cultural memory that is shared across the chasm
between victim and perpetrator communities.[42] Successful decontamination
prevents the uses of memory to stir up resentment and hatred in the future.
A composted history dissolves narratives of dehumanization and averts

their eruption into the collective unconscious in uncontrollable and irrepressible ways. Instead, it has turned the memory of atrocity into pedagogical and political lessons that honor the moral dignity of victims and creates the ground for peaceful co-existence.

This requires ongoing critical attention to toxic ideologies such as antisemitism, racism, and nationalism, which infect ordinary people and entire communities. National Socialism did not invent antisemitism and Germany was not the only country affected by it. Dehumanizing depictions of Jews are deeply embedded in the Western tradition, as historian David Nirenberg has recently shown.[43] While criminal trials and convictions of the instigators of the Final Solution of the Jewish Question, such as Eichmann, Mulka, and Bradfisch, signaled national and international repudiation of antisemitism, additional cultural work was required to confront the noxious power of this ideology. This included Jewish-Christian dialogue and the theological revision of Christian teachings, such as the 1965 adoption of *Nostra Aetate* at the Second Vatican Council; the assumption of West Germany's diplomatic relations with the state of Israel and the establishment of political, economic and cultural ties between Israel and Germany and the institutionalization of *Politische Bildung*;[44] the criminalization of Holocaust denial and antisemitism as hate crime; and the development of curricula to teach the Holocaust in public schools. Criminal justice is only one force among several others by which communities respond to the obligation to "purify the evil from your midst."

RITUAL VERSUS INSTRUMENTAL MEANS OF PURIFICATION

We should also take more seriously the ritual dimension and symbolic function of criminal trials in the process of purification. If one judges the Frankfurt Auschwitz trial by its instrumental success in purifying the nation of men like Mulka, it failed. These trials did not effectively cleanse the community by removing or quarantining Nazi convicts. But seen as rituals, these trials shifted the boundaries of law, established new codes of public conduct, and forced social and normative changes. Scholars and activists in the field of transitional justice have noted the power of rituals to regenerate order after systematic human rights abuses, mass violence and injustice.[45] In a co-authored provocative essay called "Ritual and Its Consequences: On the Limits of Sincerity," four scholars from Jewish studies, anthropology, psychiatry, and history argue that rituals are necessary particularly in moments of contradictory and fractured transition. In their introduction, they point out that ritual creates and re-creates a world of social convention and authority beyond the inner will of any individual. We argue that the [religious] traditions understand the world as fundamentally fractured and discontinuous, with ritual allowing us to live in it by creating temporary order through the construction of performative, subjunctive world. Each ritual rebuilds the world "as if" it were so, as one of many possible worlds.[46]

Rituals provide formulas and gestures at times when words fail and order collapses in the chaos of transition. Rituals create subjunctive worlds by compelling people to pretend "as if" something were true. For instance, rituals of politeness demand that people act "as if" they were grateful by saying "please" and "thank you," regardless of whether they actually feel appreciation at that particular moment in time. Rituals consist of speech acts and symbolic gestures that generate the appearance of civility, respect, justice, or love, in human lives that are, in truth, complicated, conflicted, and complex. We shake hands with enemies, declare love to people who cause us pain, show respect to judges who disappoint us, and apologize although we do not mean it. Ritual liberates from the obligation to speak genuinely and truthfully. Apologies, understood as ritual speech acts, are effective despite and because of speakers' insincerity. "Faked remorse," Stephen Garvey points out, "is better than nothing. Indeed, doing the right thing, even for the wrong reason, can sometimes lead to doing the right thing for the right reason."[47] By acting "as if" one were apologetic or grateful, ritual speech acts generate consequences and change the external dynamics of human interactions. Eventually, those consequences may include internal feelings that have caught up and then conform to the externally performed actions. Rituals steer people through moments of profound anxiety and ambivalence, by pretending "as if" we lived in a world that is civilized, polite, and orderly.

West Germany's Nazi trials could not achieve the literal purification of the community's moral remainders of Nazi crimes. But as rituals they served to repudiate National Socialism. Each trial ritually turned respected Nazi functionaries into felons and powerbrokers into convicts. Each guilty verdict signaled society's repudiation, despite their failure to expel the culprits. The punitive removal of Mulka and Bradfisch could not have cleansed the German collective of guilt by association. Instead, the recognition of sheltering murderers in its midst forced the (West) German public to reach for alternate means of "coming to terms with the past." To quote Adam Seligman et al., "ritual teaches us to live within and between different boundaries rather than seeking to absolutize them—which is, sadly, often the result of deritualized frames of understanding and action."[48] As West Germany's trials unfolded through the 1960s, Nazi definitions of order and purity were dislodged from the center to the margins of political discourse. The trials reasserted the validity and transgressed the boundaries of law in an effort to arrive at a new social, political, and legal order. This confirms Devin O. Pendas's observations about the Auschwitz trial:

> What these evaluations indicate is that it is more useful to think about the Auschwitz trial in terms of limits and boundaries, rather than relying on the language of success and failure. In other words, rather than first choosing an evaluative criterion—truth or justice—and then applying this to the trial like a yardstick, it makes far more sense to examine what the trial actually *did* in both the juridical and representational domains, where it drew the boundaries between the two and how the internal dynamic of tension and resolution between them unfolded.[49]

Approaching criminal trials as rituals of purification moves beyond literalist cleansing expectations that legitimize retributive violence. Rather than quarantining the guilt and the guilty, the trials opened a public space in which questions of complicity and culpability could be negotiated. Public media coverage of the trials forced families and neighbors, business associates, and political comrades to confront the facts presented in court and to debate their meaning. The trials "aired out West Germany's dirty laundry" and undercut the desire to "sweep the past under the rug." In the language of composting, the trials generated heat and added air to the lingering pile of filth and contributed to the decomposition and transformation of the moral and political remainders of National Socialism, which proved more sustainable than quick purges and punitive expulsions.

Katharina von Kellenbach is a professor of religious studies in the Department of Philosophy and Religious Studies at St. Mary's College of Maryland, the Honors College of the State of Maryland. Her areas of expertise include Holocaust studies, Jewish-Christian relations, feminist theology, and interreligious dialogue. Publications include *Anti-Judaism in Feminist Religious Writings* (1994) and *The Mark of Cain: Guilt and Denial in the Lives of Nazi Perpetrators* (2013).

NOTES

1. Archiv der Evangelischen Kirche im Rheinland (AEKIR), 7 NL 016-67, Shalom Ben-Chorin to Hermann Schlingensiepen, 5 October 1966, Unseren Briefwechsel möchte ich … mit dem Hinweis auf ein Wort im Deuteronomium 13,6 be-

enden: "Ubi 'arta hara' mikirbeha:" "Du sollst das Böse ausrotten aus deiner Mitte." Dieses Rechtsmotiv findet sich im Deut. noch mehrmals: 17,7 + 12, 19, 19; 21,21+22; 24,7. Es wird also wiederholt eingeschärft. Das sollten sich auch die Deutschen gesagt sein lassen; sie müssen das Böse aus ihrer Mitte ausrotten um ihr Land zu reinigen von den Mulkas und Bradfischs, die noch unter ihnen leben.

2. Ibid.
3. Devin O. Pendas, *The Frankfurt Auschwitz Trial: Genocide, History, and the Limits of the Law* (New York, 2006), 21.
4. Martha Grace Duncan, *Romantic Outlaws, Beloved Prisons: The Unconscious Meaning of Crime and Punishment* (New York, 1996), 147–87.
5. Ibid., 153.
6. Ibid., 145.
7. Decision (Village of Euclid, Ohio v. Ambler Realty Co., [1926]) quoted in ibid. See also Walter Weyrauch, "Unconscious Meanings of Crime and Punishment," *Buffalo Criminal Law Review* 2, no. 2 (January 1999), 951.
8. Bernhard J. Verkamp, *The Moral Treatment of Returning Warriors in Early Medieval and Modern Times* (Scranton, PA, 1993), 27; Rita Nakashima Brock and Gabriella Lettini, *Soul Repair: Recovering from Moral Injury after War* (Boston, 2013).
9. Immanuel Kant, *The Metaphysical Elements of Justice: Part I of the Metaphysics of Morals,* (1797), trans. John Ladd, 2nd ed. (Indianapolis, 1999), 140.
10. SpearIt, "Legal Punishment as Civil Ritual: Making Cultural Sense of Harsh Punishment," *Mississippi Law Journal* 82, no. 1 (2013): 3.
11. Mircea Eliade, ed. *Encyclopedia of Religion,* vol. 12 (New York, 1987): 91–100.
12. Chen-Bo Zhong and Katie Liljenquist, "Washing Away Your Sins: Threatened Morality and Physical Cleansing," *Science* 313, no. 5792 (8 September 2006): 1451–52.
13. Rat der EKD, "Wort des Rates der EKD zu den Verbrecherprozessen vom 13. März 1963," in *Die nationalsozialistischen Gewaltverbrechen: Geschichte und Gericht,* ed. Reinhard Henkys (Stuttgart, 1965), 341.
14. Mary Douglas, *Purity and Danger: An Analysis of Concepts of Pollution and Taboo* (London, 1966), 40–41.
15. Götz Aly, Peter Chroust, Christian Pross, eds., *Cleansing the Fatherland: Nazi Medicine and Racial Hygiene* (Baltimore, MD, 1994).
16. Judith Herrin, "Book Burning as Purification," in *Transformations of Late Antiquity: Essays for Peter Brown,* ed. Manolis Papoutsakis and Philip Rousseau (Burlington, VT, 2009), 205–22.
17. Zygmunt Bauman, "Modernity, Racism, Extermination," in *Racism and Anti-Semitism,* ed. Zygmunt Bauman, Les Back, and John Solomos (London, 1999), 216.
18. Alexander Etkind, *Warped Mourning: Stories of the Undead in the Land of the Unburied* (Berkeley, CA, 2013).
19. Robert Meister, *After Evil: A Politics of Human Rights* (New York, 2011).
20. The extremist *Army of God* quotes Numbers 35:33: "So ye shall not pollute the

land wherein ye are: for blood defileth the land: and the land cannot be cleansed of the blood that is shed therein, but by the blood of him that shed it." Retrieved from http://www.armyofgod.com/AOGhistory.html.

21. Jacques Semelin, *Purify and Destroy: The Political Uses of Massacre and Genocide* (New York, 2009).

22. AEKIR, 7 NL 016-67, Robert Mulka to Schlingensiepen, 16 June 1965, p. 1. "Bei aller Anerkennung der Richtigkeit und Wirksamkeit Ihrer lieben Zeilen v.9.ds. muß ich Ihnen, Herr Professor, aber aus voller Überzeugung und nach tiefem Nachdenken über die damaligen Geschehnisse gestehen, daß ich, und wenn es ihm gefällt, vielleicht schon sehr bald, mit REINEM Herzen und REINEM gewissen vor SEINEN Richterstuhl treten kann, und das in der Erkenntnis und Hoffnung, dass ER' uns sein Wort erhält und daß 'ER' weiß was Recht und unrecht, sowie was Lüge und Wahrheit ist. Emphasis in original.

23. Ibid, 2.

24. Ibid, 4. Emphasis in original.

25. Ibid, 2.

26. Pendas, *The Frankfurt Auschwitz Trial,* 132–39.

27. "Wort des Rates der EKD," in Henkys, *Die nationalsozialistischen Gewaltverbrechen,* 340.

28. Ibid., 340.

29. Gerhard Deimling, Friedrich-Wilhelm Eltester, Lothar Hamer, et. al., "Brief der Arbeitsgemeinschaft der Bergischen Gefängnisgemeinde an den Rat der EKD vom 7. September 1963," in Henkys, *Die nationalsozialistischen Gewaltverbrechen,* 343.

30. Rene Girard, *Violence and the Sacred* (Baltimore, MD, 1979); Katharina von Kellenbach, *The Mark of Cain: Guilt and Denial in the Lives of Nazi Perpetrators* (New York, 2013), 112–37.

31. AEKIR, 7 NL 016-17, Bradfisch to Schlingensiepen, 11 July 1965: "scheint mir symbolhaft dafür zu stehen, dass einzelne Sündenböcke aus Gründen der Staatsräson—Wiederherstellung des aussenpolitischen Prestiges—herausgestellt werden mussten, auf die man die Schuld bequem abladen konnte, und die nun den Kopf für eine verfehlte, ja verbrecherische Politik einer deutschen Regierung hinhalten müssen. Verstehen Sie mich bitte nicht falsch, ich bekenne ebenfalls, dass furchtbare Verbrechen in dem vergangenen Kriege geschehen sind … Und jene höchsten deutschen Juristen (Oberlandesgerichtspräsident und Generalstaatsanwälte), haben sie nicht Hitlers Massentötungsmassnahmen gebilligt und gefördert, wo sie als Hüter des ihnen anvertrauten Rechts die Pflicht zum Einschreiten gehabt hätten? Ich bin noch keinem dieser Herren, die ich als Urheber des nachfolgenden Geschehens bezeichnen muss, in den vielen Gefängnissen des Bundesgebietes begegnet, die ich auf meinen Zeugenrundfahrten gemacht habe. Sie genießen alle die Freiheit und die 'wohlverdiente' Pension."

32. Stephen Garvey, "Punishment as Atonement," *UCLA Law Review* 46, no. 6 (August 1999): 1858.

33. Ibid., 1804.
34. Stephen P. Garvey, "Can Shaming Punishments Educate?" *The University of Chicago Law Review* 65, no. 3 (Summer 1998): 788.
35. Joel Feinberg, "The Expressive Function of Punishment," in *Doing and Deserving: Essays in the Theory of Responsibility,* ed. Joel Feinberg (Princeton, NJ, 1970), 96; Linda Radzik and Michael Hand, "Hampton on the Expressive Power of Punishment," *Journal of Social Philosophy* 35, no. 1 (Spring 2004): 79–90.
36. Hannah Arendt, *The Human Condition* (Chicago, 1989), 241.
37. Claudia Card, *The Atrocity Paradigm. A Theory of Evil* (New York, 2002).
38. Hannah Arendt, *Eichmann in Jerusalem: A Report on the Banality of Evil* (New York, 1963).
39. Susan Neiman, *Evil in Modern Thought: An Alternative History of Philosophy* (Princeton, NJ, 2002), 270–71.
40. For example, Aktion Sühnezeichen (Action Sign of Atonement, translated as Action Reconciliation [ARSP]) was founded in 1958 to send volunteers to rebuild countries and communities affected by Nazi violence, retrieved from https://www.asf-ev.de/.
41. U.S. Environmeral Protection Agency Fact Sheet, "Innovative Uses of Compost: Bioremediation and Pollution Prevention," National Service Center for Environmental Publications (NSCEP), 25 January 2016.
42. International Theological Commission, "Memory and Reconciliation: The Church and the Faults of the Past," (Vatican, December 1999). Retrieved from http://www.vatican.va/roman_curia/congregations/cfaith/cti_documents/rc_con_cfaith_doc_20000307_memory-reconc-itc_ge.html.
43. David Nirenberg, *Anti-Judaism: The Western Tradition* (New York, 2013).
44. Retrieved from https://www.bpb.de.
45. Ronald L. Grimes, Ute Hüsken, Udo Simon, and Eric Venbrux, eds., *Ritual, Media and Conflict* (New York, 2011); Catherine M. Cole, *Performing South Africa's Truth Commission: Stages of Transition* (Bloomington, IN, 2010).
46. Adam B. Seligman, Robert P. Weller, Michael J. Puett, and Bennet Simon, *Ritual and Its Consequences: An Essay on the Limits of Sincerity* (New York, 2008), 11.
47. Garvey, "Punishment as Atonement," 1801–58.
48. Seligman et al., *Ritual and Its Consequences,* 7.
49. Pendas, *The Frankfurt Auschwitz Trial,* 291.

SELECT BIBLIOGRAPHY

Aly, Götz, Peter Chroust, Christian Pross, eds. *Cleansing the Fatherland: Nazi Medicine and Racial Hygiene,* trans. Belinda Cooper. Baltimore, MD: Johns Hopkins University Press, 1994.
Arendt, Hannah. *Eichmann in Jerusalem: A Report on the Banality of Evil.* New York: Viking, 1963.

———. *The Human Condition.* Chicago: University of Chicago Press, 1989.

Bauman, Zygmunt. "Modernity, Racism, Extermination." In *Racism and Anti-Semitism,* ed. Zygmunt Bauman, Les Back, and John Solomos, 216–28. London: Routledge, 1999.

Brock, Rita Nakashima, and Gabriella Lettini. *Soul Repair: Recovering from Moral Injury after War.* Boston: Beacon Press, 2013.

Card, Claudia. *The Atrocity Paradigm: A Theory of Evil.* New York: Oxford Universty Press, 2002.

Cole, Catherine M. *Performing South Africa's Truth Commission: Stages of Transition.* Bloomington, IN: Indiana University Press, 2010.

Douglas, Mary. *Purity and Danger: An Analysis of Concepts of Pollution and Taboo.* London: Routledge, 1966.

Duncan, Martha Grace. *Romantic Outlaws, Beloved Prisons: The Unconscious Meaning of Crime and Punishment.* New York: New York University Press, 1996.

Eliade, Mircea, ed. *Encyclopedia of Religion.* New York: Macmillan, 1987.

Etkind, Alexander. *Warped Mourning: Stories of the Undead in the Land of the Unburied.* Berkeley, CA: University of California Press, 2013.

Feinberg, Joel. *Doing and Deserving: Essays in the Theory of Responsibility.* Princeton, NJ: Princeton University Press, 1970.

Garvey, Stephen P. "Can Shaming Punishments Educate?" *The University of Chicago Law Review* 65, no. 3 (1998): 733–794.

———. "Punishment as Atonement." *UCLA Law Review* 46, no. 6 (1999): 1801–58.

Girard, René. *Violence and the Sacred,* trans. Patrick Gregory. Baltimore, MD: Johns Hopkins University Press, 1979.

Grimes, Ronald L., Ute Hüsken, Udo Simon, and Eric Venbrux, eds. *Ritual, Media and Conflict.* New York: Oxford University Press, 2010.

Henkys, Reinhard, ed. *Die nationalsozialistischen Gewaltverbrechen: Geschichte und Gericht.* Stuttgart: Kreutz-Verlag, 1965.

Herrin, Judith. "Book Burning as Purification." In *Transformations of Late Antiquity: Essays for Peter Brown,* ed. Manolis Papoutsakis and Philip Rousseau, 205–22. London: Routledge, 2016.

International Theological Commission. "Memory and Reconciliation: The Church and The Faults of the Past." Vatican, 1999. Retrieved 9 February 2017 from http://www.vatican.va/roman_curia/congregations/cfaith/cti_documents/rc_con_cfaith_doc_20000307_memory-reconc-itc_ge.html.

Kellenbach, Katharina von. *The Mark of Cain: Guilt and Denial in the Lives of Nazi Perpetrators.* New York: Oxford University Press, 2013.

Kant, Immanuel. *The Metaphysical Elements of Justice: Part I of the Metaphysics of Morals* (1797), trans. John Ladd, 2nd ed., Indianapolis, IN: Hackett, 1999.

Meister, Robert. *After Evil: A Politics of Human Rights.* New York: Columbia University Press, 2011.

Neiman, Susan. *Evil in Modern Thought: An Alternative History of Philosophy.* Princeton, NJ: Princeton University Press, 2002.

Nirenberg, David. *Anti-Judaism: The Western Tradition.* New York: Norton, 2013.

Pendas, Devin O. *The Frankfurt Auschwitz Trial, 1963–1965: Genocide, History, and the Limits of the Law.* New York: Cambridge University Press, 2005.

Radzik, Linda, and Michael Hand. "Hampton on the Expressive Power of Punishment," *Journal of Social Philosophy* 35, no. 1 (2004): 79–90.

Seligman, Adam B., Robert P. Weller, Michael J. Puett, and Bennet Simon. *Ritual and Its Consequences: An Essay on the Limits of Sincerity.* New York: Oxford University Press, 2008.

Semelin, Jacques. *Purify and Destroy: The Political Uses of Massacre and Genocide.* New York: Columbia University Press, 2009.

SpearIt. "Legal Punishment as Civil Ritual: Making Cultural Sense of Harsh Punishment." *Mississippi Law Journal* 82, no. 1 (2013): 1–43.

Weyrauch, Walter. "Unconscious Meanings of Crime and Punishment." *Buffalo Criminal Law Review* 2, no. 2 (1999): 947–61.

Verkamp, Bernhard J. *The Moral Treatment of Returning Warriors in Early Medieval and Modern Times.* Scranton, PA: University of Scranton Press, 1993.

Zhong, Chen-Bo, and Katie Liljenquist. "Washing Away Your Sins: Threatened Morality and Physical Cleansing." *Science* 313, no. 5792 (8 September 2006): 1451–52.

Part II

Testimony and Narrative

Chapter 3

What Kind of Narrative is Legal Testimony?

Terezín Witnesses before Czechoslovak, Austrian, and German Courts

Anna Hájková

What kind of narrative is the legal testimony of a Holocaust survivor? This question connects two fields of historical inquiry, those of Holocaust justice and of narrative analysis. Scholars have generally addressed one or the other. However, only a few historians have looked at survivors' witness statements within the legal context as texts that are also within the narrative genre. Holocaust historians have often used victim depositions to write history as it happened; some have used them to write Holocaust history focused on the perpetrators.[1] Rather than unearthing the history of an atrocity, however, this essay examines testimony as a part of narrative studies.[2]

Historians who have discussed the narrative character of legal testimony include Annette Wieviorka, Aleida Assmann, Karel Berkhoff, and Alexandra Garbarini. In examining Avraham Suzkever's testimony at the Trial of the Major War Criminals at Nuremberg, Wieviorka shows the critical importance of having one's voice heard, standing face to face with the perpetrators, and having the final word as the witness to the catastrophe.[3] Assmann demonstrates the constraints placed on the testifying witnesses: a trial is far more interested in establishing the "truth" rather than exploring the wartime biography of the individual.[4] Garbarini shows that authenticity and truth were in the forefront for the defense team of Sholem Schwarzbard, who in Paris in 1926 assassinated Simon Petliura, the Ukrainian leader under whom pogroms erupted following the Russian Revolution. Schwarzbard's defenders compiled eyewitness testimonies to be used at the trial.[5] Finally, Berkhoff's careful tracing of the multiple testimonies of Dina Pronicheva, one of the very few survivors of Babi Yar, shows a strikingly consistent narrative of the only person to testify to this atrocity.[6]

As important as this scholarship is, these authors only make comments in passing rather than undertake a systematic inquiry concerning trial testimony and narrative. This essay examines the nexus of survivor legal testimony and narrative study. I examine the differences as well as commonalities between legal testimonies and other types of self-testimony. I also look at how the content and style of the testimonies change over time and how intended audiences shape the testimony. What makes a legal testimony appear true and reliable? And what makes it moving? Gender, I show, is a crucial factor here. I build on Benjamin Frommer's remark that trials are truthful, but that they do not necessarily produce true history.[7] Devin Pendas points out that what while trials are particularly successful at establishing facts, the facts cannot speak for themselves. How the facts are arranged into a meaningful narrative depends on interpretative frameworks.[8]

I examine the depositions of Terezín survivors in the proceedings that focused on the ghetto there. These witness statements from trials concerning Terezín represent a large collection of early Holocaust testimonies, one that to date has not been examined in this light.[9] Witnesses who testified at trials related to Terezín were generally born between 1900 and 1910. Most of them died before the launch of the large oral history projects in the 1990s. Their legal testimonies are often the only self-testimony they left behind.

This essay has four parts. First, I sketch a history of the Terezín ghetto, the crimes committed there, and the laws with which perpetrators were prosecuted. Second, I discuss the testimony of Terezín survivors at the early legal proceedings, offering a map of the testimonies and their context. The third section follows the development in the narratives over time and examines the types of witnesses and main narrative patterns. I also examine the testimonies of those who bore witness more than once and in different contexts. The fourth part examines the gendered perceptions of "hard facts" and use of emotions against the backdrop of the liberalization of Czechoslovakia during the 1960s.[10]

HISTORICAL BACKGROUND

The SS (Schutzstaffel) created Terezín (Theresienstadt in German) as a transit ghetto in November 1941. It was the only ghetto still in existence when the war ended in May 1945.[11] Altogether, 143,000 prisoners were deported there: the largest group were Czech Jews, followed by Jewish deportees from Germany, Austria, the Netherlands, Denmark, Slovakia, and Hungary. A Jewish Council of Elders administered the ghetto under the direction of the SS. The majority of Terezín's prisoners, 87,000, were sent east and murdered; another 34,000, particularly the elderly, died in Terezín itself from starvation-related diseases.

Compared to concentration camps, ghettos have received less attention from historians as sites of atrocity.[12] Concentration camps became the topoi of Nazi cruelty and have come to signify genuine suffering. But in all, ghettos had higher mortality rates, and thanks to their double function as transit and labor sites they were arguably a locus of comparable suffering. Even though there were numerous postwar prosecutions against ghetto-related crimes, ghettos remain relatively understudied in the context of Holocaust trials.[13] The Terezín-related trials fit this pattern, and also make for particularly significant case studies. Terezín generated a large number of trials, which were transnational with regard to people, places, and later developments concerning witness depositions. In addition, core witnesses bore testimony several times, inside and outside the legal context. Moreover, prosecutors had to construct cases for direct violence since the act of running a transit ghetto was theoretically not prosecutable in the countries in which trials were held.

There were altogether thirty-five legal proceedings with a main focus on crimes in Terezín. Twenty-three took place in Czechoslovakia, nine in Austria, and three in West Germany. East Germany had several legal proceedings that touched on the topic of Terezín, but these trials never had the ghetto as their focus.[14] Twenty-eight of the proceedings were actual trials and seven were investigations or pre-trial investigations. Twenty-one of the proceedings were directed against German or Austrian perpetrators. Another ten were directed against Jews who were blamed for "collaboration."[15] Finally, four proceedings charged Czech gendarmes who guarded the ghetto. Several defendants were prosecuted in two trials and/or extradited: Rudolf Haindl, who had served as deputy to the camp inspector Karl Bergel from 1942 to 1945, was extradited from his trial in Vienna to Litoměřice. The first commandant Siegfried Seidl (1941–1943) was convicted in Vienna and had a trial in Litoměřice in absentia. Both were sentenced to death and executed; Seidl in Vienna in 1947, and Haindl in Czechoslovakia in 1948.

Despite the miserable conditions in Terezín, the SS was usually absent from the everyday life in the ghetto. Emanuel Herrmann, a prewar attorney who in Terezín worked as a baker, recalled: "Often three weeks passed without meeting a German."[16] The SS did not administer Terezín but rather exercised control through "constructive violence."[17] Thus, after the war, rel-

atively few specific crimes from Terezín were adjudicated. In January and
February 1942, the SS ordered first nine, and later another seven men, sixteen in all, executed for contact with the outside. These hangings, at the
Außig Barracks, were staged for a select audience: the Council of Elders, the
Jewish ghetto police, and house elders were forced to be present. Later, the
SS closely observed the smuggling of items forbidden in the ghetto. Smug-
glers who were caught were interrogated, brutally tortured, and, if still alive,
transferred to the nearby Gestapo prison in Terezín's nearby Small Fortress.[18] Most did not survive. In August 1943, Heinrich Himmler arranged
for 1,200 Jewish children to be transferred from the Białystok Ghetto to
Terezín; he was negotiating with Jewish aid organizations to exchange the
children for payment. Some forty of the children who were ill were separated
upon arrival and the SS driver Johann Vostrel shot them in the Small Fortress.[19] The negotiations failed, and the remaining children were deported
to Auschwitz-Birkenau and murdered. In addition to these crimes, some SS,
in particular the more brutal such as Vostrel, beat inmates when they passed
through the ghetto's streets.[20] During the ghetto's existence and in the early
postwar years, the Außig Barracks executions of winter 1942 formed a central part of the master narrative of how the inmates and early survivor community understood the ghetto.[21]

After the war, the Czechoslovak and Austrian governments pursued
transitional justice based on the Moscow Declaration.[22] They employed special people's courts—*lidové soudy* and *Volksgerichte* respectively—which tried all
of the Czechoslovak and Austrian Terezín-related proceedings.[23] They operated under extraordinary laws—in Czechoslovakia special retribution decrees and in Austria the *Kriegsverbrechergesetz* and *Verbotsgesetz*. The trials were
swift and the sentences severe. For their own part, neither West nor East
Germany had such statutes for transitional justice. The basis of criminal law
in both Germanys remained the 1871 Penal Code, though its application
varied between the two states in the prosecution of Nazi criminals.[24]

No state made Terezín the center of judicial proceedings, despite its
deportations and annihilation. Still, the ghetto came up in various trials
and investigations. The Czechoslovak people's courts could apply §5 of
the retribution decree against enslavement, human trafficking, kidnap-
ping, and "unlawful restriction of personal freedom," which were capital
offences. Austria's *Kriegsverbrechergesetz* included §5a, eviction from home,
which was punishable by death for main organizers. The West German
Central Office of the Judicial Authorities for the Investigation of National
Socialist Crimes in Ludwigsburg, founded in 1958, prepared in the early
1960s investigations against Terezín perpetrators living in West Germany.
The key figures were Karl Bergel, the former "camp inspector," and Anton

Burger, the second commandant. West German investigators cooperated with Czechoslovak authorities in assembling evidence, though neither case actually went to trial.

Witnesses in the early people's court trials in Czechoslovakia and Austria often came forward of their own volition after the state advertised a call for witnesses. In Czechoslovakia, for example, witnesses learned of investigations from the major newspapers or from the Bulletin of the Council of Jewish Religious Communities, the periodical of the Council of Jewish Religious Communities in Bohemia and Moravia. Before the Czechoslovak trial of Karl Rahm, Terezín's last commandant from February 1944 to May 1945, the state authorities also advertised the call for witnesses in survivors' organizations and Jewish communities abroad. In addition, the state attorney approached the Council of Jewish Religious Communities for witnesses' addresses and for further recommendations. The Council, for its own part, set up a department for prosecution of war criminals, headed by the lawyer Kurt Wehle.[25] In addition to collecting information and contacting witnesses, Wehle's department collected sworn affidavits and sent them to courts outside of Prague and also to the people's courts in Vienna. Some of the survivors who testified later became historians of Terezín. These included Zdeněk Lederer, Miroslav Kárný, and Josef Lagus.[26]

Terezín witnesses testified either at the trials of SS and police perpetrators or at trials against the Jewish "collaborators."[27] The latter trials started immediately after the liberation. On 18 May 1945, a committee of Terezín survivors who were members of the Czechoslovak Communist Party drafted a list of suspects and passed it to party headquarters and the people's committees.[28] The overwhelming majority of witnesses volunteered, seemingly with no requests by the state attorney for witnesses or recommendations from the Jewish community. The Jewish community closely monitored the investigations of Benjamin Murmelstein, the last and only surviving Jewish elder of Terezín, not wishing for these investigations to become too public.[29] Volunteer witnesses in this and other "collaboration" proceedings gave statements that were passionate, personal, and defamatory, with reproaches often based on hearsay. The victim community perceived cooperation with the enemy—whether real, alleged, voluntary, or forced—as repulsive, and survivors felt the need to pose an example of what they perceived as wrong behavior, thus enabling a return to normality.[30] At the trials of German and Austrian perpetrators, which occurred a bit later, some witnesses volunteered but witnesses were often summoned by the state's attorney after recommendation by the Jewish community. In a few cases, defendants also requested witness statements. These testimonies tended to be more "factual" in nature.

In the meantime, all early pretrial depositions were acts of reintegration into the Czech society, aimed at fitting into the dominant narrative of what was perceived as the authentic suffering of those who were deported. In Czechoslovakia, as elsewhere, this narrative focused on resistance, political prisoners, and their torment in concentration camps. Terezín survivors who published memoirs in the immediate postwar period fashioned their stories accordingly. They referred to Terezín as a concentration camp, Czech survivors staged their Czech-related activities in the ghetto as a resistance, and they presented their persecution in a way that included them in the Czech community of suffering.[31] We can see this narrative in the openings of various witness testimonies. Some start with a variation of the phrase: "I was arrested because of my affiliation with the Jewish religion and sent to the concentration camp Terezín." In the 1952 Vienna trial of Johann Vostrel, the brutal driver of the SS headquarters, the thirty-year old Prague merchant Pavel Lužický (formerly Langweil) testified: "As an affiliate of the Jewish religion I was seized on 1 December 1941 by the German authorities, then transferred to the concentration camp-ghetto Theresienstadt, where I remained until liberation."[32] Similarly, the forty-year old Olomouc attorney Edmund Repper, who worked in the ghetto crematorium, opened his statement to the police with: "Since 8 April 1942, I was, as an affiliate of the Jewish religion, [a] prisoner in the ghetto in Theresienstadt."[33] Even the forty-one-year old Adolf Beneš, the former functionary in the Jewish community and the director of the American Jewish Joint Distribution Committee in Czechoslovakia at the time of his affidavit, formulated the circumstances of his deportation thus: "In July 1943, I was detained as an affiliate of the Jewish religion and transferred to the concentration camp-ghetto Theresienstadt, where I remained until October 1944."[34]

The use of the passive voice in these statements makes a stilted impression, and indeed, is grammatically incorrect on occasion. A proper formulation might be: "As a Jew/Being a Jew I came to Terezín" (which would be in German, "Ich kam als Jude nach Theresienstadt," or in Czech, "Jako žid jsem přišel do Terezína/jako žida mě deportovali do Terezína"). However, the reason for deportation is instead given as an attribute, a modifier. The narrator does not call himself directly a Jew, nor is the reason for his deportation that he is a Jew. This indirect expression describes someone affiliated with Judaism as a religion, not something that one simply is, religiously, culturally, or ethnically. Moreover, the phrasing echoes the language used in the context of deportations of political prisoners: one is *transferred* or *seized,* by the *German authorities.*

Beneš and others moreover denoted Terezín as a "concentration camp" with the name "Ghetto-Terezín."[35] This contradictory phrasing is also striking: Terezín was a ghetto, and the inmates and the SS referred to it as such. Indeed within the ghetto itself, "Terezín" and "ghetto" became synonymous terms. The survivors framed Terezín as a concentration camp only *after* the war because they now lived in a society that coded camps as the only sites of the legitimate, authentic suffering. A ghetto was nothing familiar; it was something potentially lesser, and it did not fit the preferred narrative. The re-labeling of Terezín from a ghetto to a camp helped in having one's story accepted. The long-standing postwar debate as to whether Terezín was a ghetto or a concentration camp began, I believe, with these early designations.[36]

One could possibly counter-argue that these phrases might have originated from the typist as a part of the court terminology. However, these statements were collected in heterogeneous conditions: some were sworn pretrial testimonies (affidavits, protocols) in front of local police, collected to be sent to Kurt Wehle's department within the Jewish community; others were voluntary submissions, sent also to Wehle's department or directly to the state prosecutor. Indeed, the same phrasing is found in other trials across time and space. Twenty years later in the mid-1960s, Emil Jockel, then a fifty-six-year old director of a hotel in Znojmo, the sixty-three-year old emigré to West Germany Vilém Hostovský (who now wrote his name Wilhelm Hostovsky), and the fifty-six-year old lawyer Jan Franĕk (former Friedmann), opened their statements with variations of the same phrase:

> For reasons of racial discrimination I was sent to the ghetto of Terezín.[37]

> On 24 November 1941, I was registered in Prague for a transport to concentration camp (KL) Theresienstadt. The transfer to the KL occurred for racial reasons.[38]

> I was incarcerated for racial reasons in the concentration camp Terezín-ghetto, Auschwitz, and Friedland.[39]

The language here has changed in one detail. Persecution on the basis of Jewish religion has turned into one based on race. The reason may lie in the changing meaning of the 1946 Czechoslovak law on reparations for soldiers and resistance fighters, clause 255/1946, which defined beneficiaries as individuals persecuted for political, national, racial, or religious reasons.[40] In terms of reparations, the relative weight of types of persecution differed when the law was issued, political persecution ranking most highly. But by the 1960s, racial persecution was politically more opportune than religious.

The trials, complex affairs with actual defendants or taking place in absentia, became all the more complex—and for later historians, difficult to disentangle—because of the differing ways in which testimonies were col-

Figure 3.1. Portrait of Emil Jockel (ca. 1951). With permission from the Pavel Jockel Family Archive

lected and how they emerged outside Czechoslovakia. Wehle's department and the state's attorney summoned dozens of people and had them give testimony for the Vienna people's trials. The witnesses accordingly gave statements concerning all perpetrators prosecuted in Austria. These included trials against Johann Vostrel (1948–1952) and Ernst Girzick (1946–1948), the latter an employee of the Prague Central Office for Jewish Emigration and one of Adolf Eichmann's subordinates, with some affidavits addressing Franz Stuschka, the brutal commandant of Terezín's Wulkow labor commando.[41] Apparently, the Jewish community created a list of Terezín survivors who were there during the aforementioned January and February 1942 Außig Barracks executions. Witnesses from these lists were passed to Austrian state's attorneys when they asked for assistance. They became the "go-to" witnesses, considered able to testify regarding the few prosecutable crimes in Terezín, and they did so repeatedly. They gave pretrial testimonies, speaking with the police and the state's attorneys, and at a latter point, they traveled to the trials, all while busy building new lives.[42]

These standard witnesses were also at the forefront in the early 1960s when West German state's attorneys in the Central Office in Ludwigsburg took up investigations against Karl Bergel and Anton Burger.[43] Copies of earlier witness statements were easily obtained from the Austrian authorities. In 1964, the Central Office also approached the Czechoslovak Governmental Commission for Prosecution of National Socialist Criminals for cooperation.[44] The Commission, founded in 1959 initially as a branch of the Ministry of Justice, also turned to the postwar witness testimonies from earlier people's courts.[45] Indeed in researching Terezín, one can repeatedly find in German files copies of affidavits, charges, and judgments from the people's courts, often translated, sometimes without dates and without information about the legal proceeding the statements originated from.

Trials concerning Terezín gained an additional transnational character owing to postwar emigration. Many survivors left Czechoslovakia to escape postwar Czech antisemitism and the communist regime, as well as to build new lives elsewhere. German and Austrian Jewish survivors also emigrated. Thus, as the Austrian trial against SS driver Johann Vostrel began in 1952, witnesses' addresses changed. For example, Vilém Hostovský lived initially in Prague, then in Jablonec, and, by the time of his final affidavit in 1952, in an Israeli moshav.[46] In 1959, he moved to Frankfurt am Main.[47] In Theresienstadt, he met Ruth Weitz from Berlin, and they married in June 1945. Ruth's German background was possibly the reason why when the Hostovskýs left Israel and moved to West Germany. Here, Vilém testified against Karl Bergel in 1963.

A final transnational aspect stemmed simply from the character of the transit ghetto itself. In the Czechoslovak trials, for example, dozens of witnesses from Austria, Germany, and the Netherlands submitted affidavits. Interestingly, some non-Czech witnesses, unlike their Czech counterparts, wrote detailed testimonies or later published memoirs.[48] Many of the Terezín perpetrators were Austrian.[49] The people's trials in Vienna, meanwhile, were largely built on the statements of younger Czech survivors, as very few Austrian Jews survived Terezín—fewer than 2,000—and the Außig Barracks execution in January and February 1942 had taken place before the first deportation from Vienna to Terezín in June.

LEGAL AND OTHER TESTIMONIES COMPARED

We can categorize survivors who testified at the early trials into two groups based on their motivations. The larger group comprised witnesses whose family members died in Terezín or who believed themselves to have been otherwise harmed there expressly due to actions by the accused. Their testimonies tended to be more emotional and less detail-oriented. Both men and women were in the first group. The second, smaller group comprised former Jewish functionaries, prisoner physicians, and those who were harmed themselves in concrete crimes. These witnesses were recommended by Kurt Wehle's department or summoned by the accused. Their depositions tended to be more factual, detailed, and technical. The second group was predominantly male.

Among the dozens and perhaps hundreds of Terezín survivors who gave testimony, six men did so repeatedly: Rudolf Freiberger (1906–1978), Jiří Vogel (1904–1994), Emil Jockel (1907–1993), Emanuel Herrmann (1910–1991), Vilém Hostovský (1900–1987), and Otakar Růžička (1911–?). These men were deported to Terezín in three early and exclusively male transports,[50] and therefore were in the ghetto during the early 1942 Außig Barracks executions. However, only Freiberger and Vogel, who had to be present at the executions as members of the Council of Elders, were direct eyewitnesses. Freiberger, meanwhile, did not testify in perpetrator trials. In Terezín, he was the head of production in the Economic Department, which oversaw forced labor for the Germans in a mica splitting workshop. The work here was tedious but workers were protected from transport. As the overseer, Freiberger was perceived as the Germans' henchman. After the war, together with Benjamin Murmelstein, he was arrested for "collaboration," and spent eighteen months in detention in the Pankrác prison before the state's attorney dropped the charges in 1947.[51] In his interrogations and voluntary statements, Freiberger was careful, saying nothing, for example, about witnessing the executions. The danger of a harsh sentence was real.[52] Possibly, Freiberger's past as a Jewish "collaborator" was the reason why the Czechoslovak authorities sent his testimony to Ludwigsburg only after a delay of two years.[53]

The testimonies of these standard witnesses tend to fall into the more "factual" rather than the more emotional category. It is useful to follow the similarities and further developments in their statements, comparing the earlier legal depositions with later oral history

Figure 3.2. Portrait of Rudolf Freiberger (1941). With permission from the Jewish Museum in Prague

testimonies that are more biographical self-testimonies.[54] In the late 1960s and early 1970s, Jockel, Herrmann, and Růžička gave oral history interviews to the Terezín memorial.[55] In 1992, Vogel, who was then old and ill, was interviewed for the Prague Jewish Museum.[56]

Venue influenced narrative.[57] For instance, Vilém Hostovský's statement to the Frankfurt police in 1963 for the trial of Karl Bergel differs from his earlier statements. The content is similar, but the style less detailed. In 1946, speaking in Vienna at the trial of Siegfried Seidl, Hostovský described his first weeks in Terezín, after his arrest for a similar offense that led to the execution of sixteen other men:

> They told us in Prague that we go to work and come back on Saturday. When we arrived in Terezín, we were brought into a barrack, the door closed behind us, and we were inside … I was in a coal mine, and when I came back to the camp I found out that I was blamed of sabotage because I carelessly loaded a piece of wood, which had the consequence that now the coal mine could not operate, and I was to be deported. I then made up a story that I was of mixed background, and so I escaped the transport. That was my second detention. The first one occurred because I brought in a parcel with bacon and bread. Because of bringing in this parcel I came into detention between 3 and 24 January 1942.[58]

In 1963, his depiction of the same event is less meandering:

> On 3 January 1942, I was brought into the camp prison because of alleged illegal trading, that is, bringing in food and tobacco into the camp. During

my body search by the Czech gendarmerie, who also guarded the camp, small amounts of food and tobacco were found.[59]

The West German prosecutor might have already made clear to Hostovský that he was interested only in statements relating to the executions, not prison biography.

Otakar Růžička had a similar experience in Czechoslovakia in 1972. He came forward to give testimony at the Ministry of the Interior, having heard that the police were interviewing witnesses about the murder of the Białystok children. The protocol is written in a standard secret police style:

> I was imprisoned as prisoner in ghetto Theresienstadt from November 1941 until the end of the war. I had the transport number AK 147. This transport was for reason[s] unknown to me protected by the Gestapo from transports to other concentration camps. After the evacuation of the Sudeten barracks I was moved with the brothers ARNŠTAIN who came from Unhošť near Kladno into a little store that I can point out.[60]

One policeman grew suspicious of why Růžička had volunteered to testify and ordered an inquiry into why Růžička had come forward and who had informed him about the investigations. The openness of the Prague Spring of 1968 was by now over, and the "normalization" had started. Public appearances of Holocaust survivors were eyed with suspicion.[61]

Scholars like Sigrid Weigel and Aleida Assmann have argued that in the legal context, survivor statements are necessarily reduced to their function as evidence only, thus implying that witnesses have no leeway to shape their narratives.[62] But my reading of Terezín testimonies suggest differently. Witness narratives are indeed shaped by respective legal contexts, which can flatten the narrative, but the experience and social capital of the witness equally influence the testimony.[63] Czechoslovak and Austrian people's trials, for instance, gave the witnesses more space for expression. West German trials are the most often analyzed case studies, but it would be wrong to generalize their structure to all witness statements. There are several examples of this trend.

In the 1960s, the Terezín witnesses had a number of additional and strong motivations to speak. Several desired to see just punishment for the Nazi criminals, Karl Bergel and Anton Burger, who had lived safely in West Germany for two decades. Witness depositions thus became more causal. Jiří Vogel, who in the Terezín ghetto was a leading functionary of the Technical Department and who became the last Elder of the Jews in the ghetto's final days, stressed how paltry the SS justifications were for the Außig Barracks executions in early 1942. One victim had talked with his wife, who had come to visit from Prague. Another had left the barracks to buy gingerbread. Vogel added that for the entire period of the ghetto's existence, there were no normal court sessions against the Jews.[64] Vogel's insistence on the break from normality and injustice was absent in the early trials, and the fervor to testify helps to explain it. Several witnesses made statements similar to that of Emanuel Herrmann, who concluded his own affidavit: "I am happy to come to any court anywhere, even abroad, and give testimony in front of judges."[65]

For some, testifying was motivated by a search for more personal justice. While Vilém Hostovský and Emanuel Herrmann, like many others, lost close friends owing to Nazi atrocities, Ota Růžička's narrative of imprisonment was a history of wrongs. He listed everyone who made his life difficult. Růžička came forward at four people's court trials including those of Karl Rahm, Rudolf Haindl, and Karl Bergel.[66] But he also testified in the trial of Paul Raphaelson, who served as a Jewish kapo at Wulkow. Růžička's depositions are akin to general Holocaust testimonies, which often reinstate the author's sense of self. In describing wrongs he had suffered, Růžička put himself into the center of his own persecution story. In this retelling, he had a monopoly over interpretation. This emotionality hints at another signifi-

Figure 3.3. Portrait of Emanuel Herrmann. Alena Štěpánková's Family Collection

cant feature of witnessing, namely testimony as its own form of agency—as coming to terms with traumatic past characterized by powerlessness. Historian Saul Friedländer points out that powerlessness was a key experience for Holocaust victims.[67] Ability to tell the story of one's persecution is a powerful means to regain control, which was even more the case when the personal account contributes to rendering justice to the perpetrator.[68]

Emanuel Herrmann's 1960s testimony aimed to avenge and commemorate a lost friend.[69] It also shows how knowledge acquired subsequently influences witnesses' memories. Herrmann's friend Vilém Heller had worked in the *Expositur,* the connecting office between the Jewish community and the Central Office for Jewish Emigration, which expelled and later deported Jews. Both Karl Bergel and Karl Rahm worked in the Central Office; Bergel until November 1941, Rahm until February 1944. During the large deportations to Auschwitz-Birkenau in fall 1944, Rahm met Heller in the ghetto bakery and put him, his wife, and his young daughter on transport. Bergel, who accompanied the transports to Auschwitz, noticed that Heller had survived the selection, and arranged that Heller be sent to the gas chambers. Herrmann witnessed the scene and survived. In 1947, he testified against Rahm, only briefly describing the selection at Auschwitz.[70] But in the later deposition for Ludwigsburg in 1965, he gave a more dramatic and elaborate scene of Bergel's intervention.[71] Probably, his memory came to include the iconic moment of the Auschwitz ramp.

Over the postwar decades, the legal testimonies remained remarkably consistent in terms of style and substance. Vogel had an excellent memory and concentrated on details, technicalities, and character features. Herrmann liked to describe networks, and how the ghetto was a class society. Růžička liked to speak about himself, and was judgmental and spiteful toward others. But there are several shifts between depositions and general oral-history testimonies. Former Jewish functionaries, such as Vogel and Herrmann, who worked for the Prague Jewish community, explicitly stated their former jobs in their earlier legal depositions. In the later oral history interviews, however, they were more vague concerning their functions. This vagueness was a consequence of the charged postwar perception of Jewish functionaries, who could be marked as "collaborators." And oral history interviews offered more leeway than a legal affidavit in representing oneself; in particular, the narrator knows that his testimony will stand in direct comparison to that of former colleagues or acquaintances.

Finally, a striking difference between the legal depositions and later general testimonies is that the Nazi crimes themselves, the very focal point of the depositions, are rarely mentioned in the interviews. Emil Jockel was the only one in this group who addressed in his oral history interview the

Außig Barracks executions of January and February 1942.[72] Vogel, Růžička, and Herrmann did not mention the executions, nor did they discuss other specific German crimes. Though interviewers did not explicitly ask about crimes, the interviewees could have mentioned anything they considered important. In his interview for the Terezín memorial in 1971, Herrmann mentioned his testimony at the Rahm trial, but no longer spoke of his murdered friend Vilém Heller.[73]

THE GENDER OF WITNESSING

All the standard witnesses in the initial judicial proceedings concerning Terezín were men. The reasons were partly structural. Members of the Council of Elders were all male, and ghetto guards and house elders included women only in the latter stages of the war. Hence the direct eyewitnesses of the critical Außig Barracks executions, for example, were all male. Even so, just two of the six were actually present at the executions. There were thousands of women inmates in Terezín in early 1942 who were related to or knew the executed victims, and many of these women lived in Czechoslovakia in the 1960s. But these women were never asked to testify about the executions, or, by extension, to speak of the official crimes.

However, another major trial, the in absentia East German trial of Hans Globke in 1963, indicates key gendered functions of women witnesses. Globke, as is well-known, co-authored the legal commentary of the 1935 Nuremberg Laws as well as a number of other anti-Jewish statutes. After the war, he served in West Germany as the state secretary to Federal Chancellor Konrad Adenauer. In the wake of the 1961 Eichmann trial in Jerusalem, the East German authorities staged a show trial of Globke in order to demonstrate that the West German state was dominated by revanchist ex-Nazis.[74] All five witnesses representing Czechoslovakia were women. The East Germans wanted testimony that would, as in Jerusalem, create an emotional effect.

One of the Czech witnesses was the politician Gertruda Sekaninová-Čakrtová. She was a lawyer whose first husband, Ivan Sekanina, contributed to the defense of Georgi Dimitrov in the 1933 Reichstag Fire Trial in Leipzig.[75] After the occupation of Czechoslovakia, Sekanina was arrested and eventually murdered in Sachsenhausen in 1940. Sekaninová herself was placed in Terezín. There she worked as a caretaker in a youth home for teenaged *Geltungsjuden,* girls of mixed parentage deported without their parents and alone in Terezín. After the war, Sekaninová became Czechoslovakia's deputy minister of foreign affairs. She was the only Jew to survive the

Figure 3.4. Czechoslovak witnesses at the 1963 Globke trial. With permission from the Bundesarchiv Lichterfelde

Slánský trials in function. In the 1960s, she became a Member of Parliament. Sekaninová-Čakrtová was an experienced politician and lawyer and in the 1963 Globke trial, she described the everyday of Theresienstadt. But when Friedrich Wolff, the defense attorney in the Globke trial, asked her as a jurist about the legal basis for the deportations from Czechoslovakia, Sekaninová-Čakrtová responded not as a lawyer, nor a "normal human being," but as a "prisoner who underwent all this."[76] She gave a moving testimony about children in the ghetto and about her work in a children's home. She showed the book *I Never Saw Another Butterfly* and read aloud two poems, including Pavel Friedmann's "I have never seen another butterfly."[77] She also spoke about the last moment she saw her mother at the selection in Auschwitz:

> Immediately after arrival ... we came to an SS officer ... He asked me if I was able to work. I said yes and he simply showed a direction with one hand. That meant that I had to separate from my mother. I asked him if I may not reside with my mother—today I am almost ashamed that I used the word "reside"

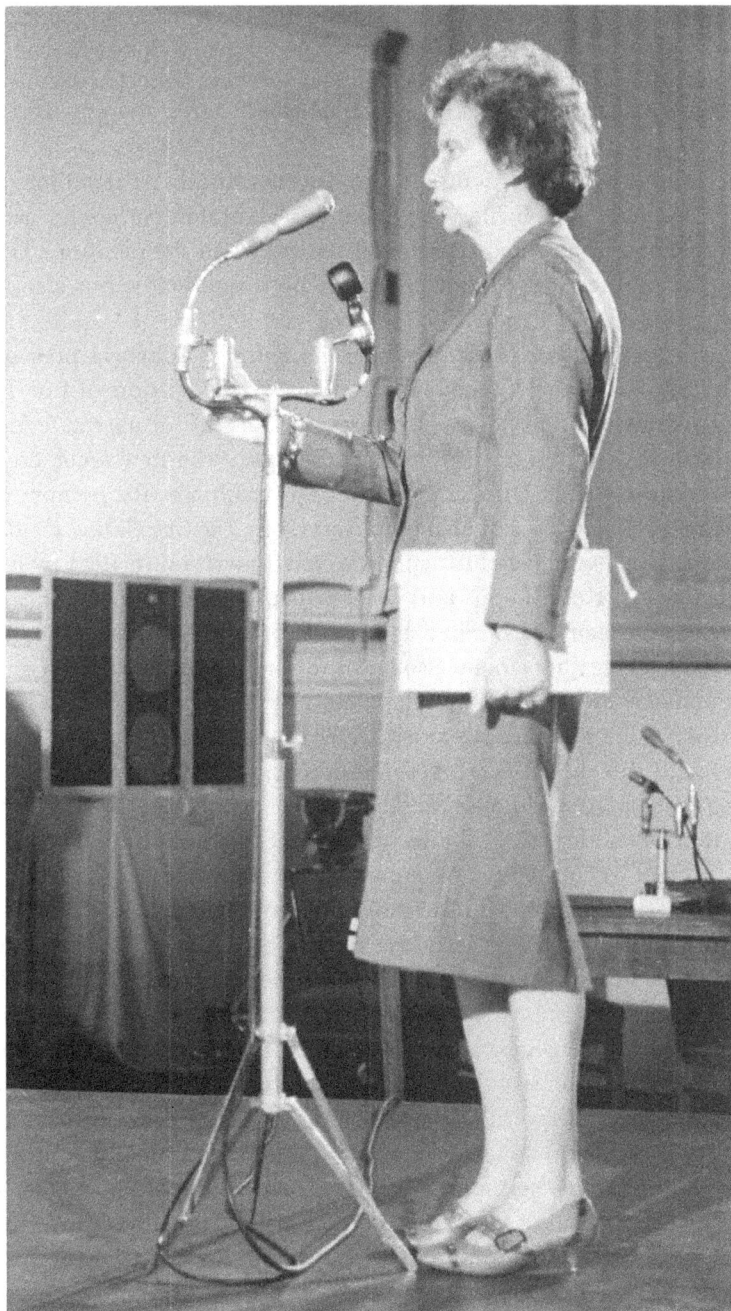

Figure 3.5. Gertruda Sekaninová-Čakrtová at the Globke trial holding *I Never Saw Another Butterfly*. With permission from the Bundesarchiv Lichterfelde

[*wohnen*] because there is such incredible naiveté in it—namely I thought that a
working person may reside in one barrack with a non-working prisoner. He just
shook his head. It would be difficult and it also does not belong here to try to
describe the look of my mother in that moment.[78]

In describing the last moment with her mother and her shame for not understanding what Auschwitz was, Sekaninová's statement comes across as
remarkably emotional. The effect is reinforced when she mentioned the last
look of her mother while describing it as both impossible but also for the
court irrelevant.

I Never Saw Another Butterfly, which Sekaninová-Čakrtová presented in
East Berlin, was Hana Volavková's and Jiří Weil's edition of the Terezín
children's drawings and poems. It represented a shift of narrative focus toward children and cultural activities in Terezín. The new focus created a
sentimentalized portrayal of the ghetto that dominates its memory to this
day.[79] This reimagining can also be observed in *The City Behind the Bars,* an
important Czech-language history of the ghetto written in 1964 by two survivor historians, Karel Lagus and Josef Polák. The book includes a child's
drawing of an execution, implied as a depiction of the famous executions of
winter 1942, suggesting violence so omnipresent that even children drew it.[80]
Yet the actual drawing of a hanging by the 12-year-old Josef Novák, however,
is a cartoon telling a detective story, in which a criminal is pursued, justice
prevails, and the culprit is hanged ["Popraven!"]. It is this fragment of the
hanging that Lagus and Polák used.[81]

In the 1960s, the political atmosphere in Czechoslovakia became more
liberal.[82] The Czechoslovak government cautiously cooperated when Western German authorities in Ludwigsburg asked for help in the investigation
of Nazi perpetrators. Because of the nature of the West German law, the
guilt could be proven only with the establishment of "hard," "reliable" facts.
To secure such testimony, the experts of the Governmental Commission
selected almost exclusively male testimonies from earlier trials. The male
testimonies were ostensibly fashioned to tell history with hard facts: this is
why their testimonies were oriented around concrete events of the official,
prosecutable crimes. The purpose of the 1963 Globke trial, in contrast, had
been to demonstrate the monstrosity of racism in the Holocaust, to which
Globke's work in writing the Nuremberg laws had contributed. Women witnesses gave testimony of children deported alone, separated from their families by racial madness, and often murdered. This focus on topics marked as
particularly upsetting supplied the emotions to manifest how heartrending
the genocide was. Women's testimonies were perceived and presented as
emotional while men's would seem as factual.

Figure 3.6. Josef Novák's cartoon from Terezín. With permission from the Jewish Museum in Prague.

Yet in 1964, a year after her testimony in the Globke trial, Sekaninová-Čakrtová spoke in the Czechoslovak Parliament against the statute of limitations for Nazi crimes. She raised her previous year's testimony, which, she stressed, took place in East rather than West Germany, where debates concerning the statute of limitations for Nazi crimes were underway. Her speech in Parliament conformed to the formal structure, but with an almost conscious switching between official, dry, and formal statements, and emotional ones.[83] It was the legal setting together with gender that dictated the form of Sekaninová's testimony.

CONCLUSION

These proceedings had little impact on the memory of Terezín. The only legacy of the people's trials that remains is the stigma of the "collaborator." The investigations of the Czechoslovak Governmental Commission for Prosecution of National Socialist Criminals are largely forgotten. The same applies for the dozens, if not hundreds, of witness depositions: today, none of the children of the witnesses know about their fathers' court testimonies.[84]

The executions and other crimes, although not forgotten, are not at the fore-front of the Terezín master narrative today.

The main difference between a trial witness and general oral testimony was that of genre context. In the legal proceedings, independent of the re-spective legal framework, state attorneys concentrated on concrete crimes and questioned the witnesses accordingly; the content of the depositions did not change much. In their later oral testimonies, survivors concentrated on the autobiographical rather than the structural or organizational. The genre and the setting thus influenced the content. However, it did not shape the style. The survivors kept their tone, interpretations, and figures of speech, whether they spoke to a state's attorney or to a historian.

Witness testimony is a part of the category of testimony, and, like any other testimony, it is a social narrative. What we expect and recognize as truth or fact is subject to the surrounding culture and is also deeply gen-dered. Each narrative genre—in this case, legal testimony concerning Nazi crimes—shapes what can be narrated and how the speaker tells the story. Gender, a powerful societal category, leaves its own mark on how the nar-ratives are told, and even more importantly, how they are perceived. We should see these genre constraints alongside the historical and societal ones. Statements change over time and are influenced by dominant narratives. They also changed so that the story told helped make sense within the nar-rator's biography. In this sense, the perpetrators' narratives analyzed by Ker-stin von Lingen (chapter 4) were shaped in ways similar to those of survivors. Such a statement may come across as unexpected; but both groups of nar-ratives were similar in one crucial way: both groups are made up of people and all people tell their life stories in similar ways.

What differentiates the depositions of the victims and perpetrators is, however, not the nature of the genre, but that of ethics. As Alexandra Gar-barini has pointed out, the survivors were consumed by stressing that theirs were truthful accounts.[85] Their motivation to testify is thus different than that of the murderers. The survivors are the only ones who can speak for the dead. And so, after the profound powerlessness of the persecution, bearing testimony of the crime was a critical moment of agency.

Anna Hájková received her Ph.D. in history from the University of Toronto. She is an assistant professor of modern continental European history at the University of Warwick. Her book manuscript *The Last Ghetto: An Everyday His-tory of Theresienstadt, 1941–1945,* was awarded the Irma Rosenberg as well as the Herbert Steiner Prizes. She has served as coeditor of *Theresienstädter Stu-dien und Dokumente,* and also co-edited with Doris Bergen and Andrea Löw, *Alltag im Holocaust: Jüdisches Leben im Großdeutschen Reich, 1941–1945* (2013).

NOTES

I would like to thank Maria von der Heydt and Hilary Earl for advice on legal matters, to Katrin Stoll on what legal testimony is, and to Maria and Norman Goda for their comments on various drafts of this article.

 1. There is a wealth of literature. See among others Andrej Angrick and Peter Klein, *The "Final Solution" in Riga: Exploitation and Annihilation, 1941–1944*, trans. Ray Brandon (New York, 2009). Angrick and Klein's doctoral advisor was Wolfgang Scheffler, a historian of the Holocaust who served as expert witness at several German legal proceedings, and who worked closely with the sources they produced. The "Scheffler School" stands for a prominent use of legal proceedings in establishing historical truth.

 2. Shoshana Felman and Dori Laub, eds., *Testimony: Crises of Witnessing in Literature, Psychoanalysis, and History* (New York, 1991); Annette Wieviorka, *The Era of Witness,* trans. Jared Stark (Ithaca, NY, 2006); Alexandra Garbarini, *Numbered Days: Diaries and the Holocaust* (New Haven, CT, 2006); Veronika Zangl, *Poetik nach dem Holocaust: Erinnerungen-Tatsachen-Geschichten* (Munich, 2009).

 3. Wieviorka, *The Era of Witness,* 31–32; see also her discussion of Ada Lichtman's testimony at the Eichmann trial, 74–78.

 4. Aleida Assmann, "History, Memory, and the Genre of Testimony," *Poetics Today* 27, no. 2 (2006): 261–73. See also Sigrid Weigel, "Klage und Anklage: Die Geste des Bezeugens in der Differenz von 'identity politics,' juristischem und historiographischem Diskurs," *Zeugnis und Zeugenschaft: Jahrbuch des Einstein-Forums* (2000): 111–35.

 5. Alexandra Garbarini, "Document Volumes and the Status of Victim Testimony in the Era of the First World War and Its Aftermath," *Études arméniennes contemporaines* 5 (2015): 113–38.

 6. Karel Berkhoff, "Dina Pronicheva's Story of Surviving the Babi Yar Massacre: German, Jewish, Soviet, Russian, and Ukrainian Records," in *The Shoah in Ukraine: History, Testimony, Memorialization,* ed. Ray Brandon and Wendy Lower (Bloomington, IN, 2010), 291–310.

 7. Benjamin Frommer, "The Jewish Department of the Prague Police: What its Czech Directors Did During the War, and How They Escaped Justice Afterwards," presentation at the Association for Slavic, East European, and Eurasian Studies, New Orleans, 15–18 November 2012. Frommer paraphrases Charlotte Delbo: "I am not sure that what I wrote is true. I am certain that it is truthful." Charlotte Delbo, *None of Us Will Return,* trans. John Githens (New York, 1968), 1.

 8. Devin Pendas, "Truth and Its Consequences: Reflections on Political, Historical and Legal Truth in West German Holocaust Trials," *Traverse: Zeitschrift für Geschichte/Revue d'histoire* 11, no. 1 (2004): 25–38. Ida Fink's play "The Table" speaks powerfully to this point. See Ida Fink, "The Table," in *A Scrap of Time and Other Stories,* ed. Ida Fink (Evanston, IL, 1995), 139–65.

 9. In addition to these legal testimonies, there was a Czechoslovak Jewish historical commission, the Documentation Action, on which see Magda Veselská,

Early Documentation of the Shoah in the Czech Lands: The Documentation Project and the Prague Jewish Museum (1945-1947), *Judaica Bohemiae* 52, no.1 (2017): 47–85.

10. A note on terminology: The instances in which the witnesses participated in Czechoslovak, Austrian, and West German trials included witness hearings, sworn testimonies (affidavits/protocols), written submissions, and also witness statements at actual trials. I attempted to translate the original description of every statement truthfully, and denote them as such below.

11. For a history of Terezín, see Anna Hájková, "The Prisoner Society in Terezín Ghetto, 1941–1945," Ph.D. diss., University of Toronto, 2013.

12. Martin Dean, ed. "Editor's Introduction," in *The United States Holocaust Memorial Museum Encyclopedia of Camps and Ghettos 1933–1945*, vol. 2: *Ghettos in German-Occupied Eastern Europe*, gen. ed. Geoffrey Megargee (Bloomington, IN, 2012), xlvi.

13. Wolfgang Scheffler and Helge Grabitz, *Der Ghetto-Aufstand Warschau 1943 aus der Sicht der Täter und Opfer in Aussagen vor deutschen Gerichten* (Munich, 1993); Katrin Stoll, *Die Herstellung der Wahrheit. Strafverfahren gegen ehemalige Angehörige der Sicherheitspolizei für den Bezirk Białystok* (Berlin, 2012).

14. In the East German Waldheim trials, Richard Hesse, the former chairman of the Halle branch of the Reich Association of German Jewry who was subsequently deported to Terezín, was sentenced to eighteen years in prison. Uta Franke, Heidi Bohley, Falco Werkentin, *Verhängnisvoll verstrickt: Richard Hesse und Leo Hirsch–zwei jüdische Funktionäre in zwei Diktaturen* (Halle, 2014). Terezín also played a role in the Globke trial, described below. See Erika Schwarz, *Juden im Zeugenstand: Die Spur des Hans Globke im Gedächtnis von Überlebenden der Schoa* (Berlin, 2009).

15. I use here "collaboration," as this term carries a problematic moralizing undertone. See also Anna Hájková, "Der Judenälteste und seine SS–Männer: Benjamin Murmelstein, der letzte Judenälteste in Theresienstadt und seine Beziehung zu Adolf Eichmann und Karl Rahm," in *"Der Letzte der Ungerechten:" Der Judenälteste Benjamin Murmelstein in Filmen 1942–1975*, ed. Ronny Loewy and Katharina Rauschenberger (Frankfurt am Main, 2011), 75–100.

16. Testimony of Emanuel Herrmann, 5 December 1971, Archiv Památníku Terezín [Archive of the Terezín Memorial] [hereafter APT], A, 564.

17. On violence as means of a new order, see Walter Benjamin, "Zur Kritik der Gewalt," *Archiv für Sozialwissenschaft und Sozialpolitik* 47, no. 3 (1920/1921): 809–32.

18. Testimony of Julius Taußig, APT, A, 51.

19. Testimony of Artur Holzer, 17 November 1947, trial of Anton Burger, copied Archiv bezpečnostních složek [Security Services Archive], Prague [hereafter ABS], 325-15-5 (Czech contribution to Ludwigsburg preliminary proceedings against Burger and Erwin Weinmann).

20. See, for example, Wolf Glücksmann, "Das Leben des Baron von Hirsch, und wie er unter den Nazis gelitten hat," interview, 23 January 1946, Yad Vashem Archives [hereafter YVA], M1E, 18.

21. Report of Otto Schütz, 28 March 1945, Moreshet Archive, A, 553; Testimony

of Jacob Plaut, YVA, M1E, 1942; Menasche Mautner Munisch, YVA, O1, 163; Edith Ornstein, YVA, O7, 291, Mirko Tůma, *Ghetto našich dnů* (Prague 1946); Benjamin Murmelstein, *Geschichtlicher Überblick*, Wiener Library, 1073, 3.

22. The Moscow Declaration on atrocities was one of the four declarations at the 1943 Allied conference. It pledged that German mass crimes would be prosecuted, and most perpetrators extradited to the country where they committed their crimes.

23. Mečislav Borák, *Spravedlnost podle dekretu : retribuční soudnictví v ČSR a Mimořádný lidový soud v Ostravě, 1945–1948* (Šenov u Ostravy, 1998); Benjamin Frommer, *National Cleansing: Retribution against Nazi Collaborators in Postwar Czechoslovakia* (New York, 2005); Brigitte Rigele, *Verhaftet: Verurteilt. Davongekommen: Volksgericht Wien 1945–1955* (Vienna, 2010). See also the website of the Austrian Forschungsstelle Nachkriegsjustiz, www.nachkriegsjustiz.at.

24. For an overview, see Devin O. Pendas, *The Frankfurt Auschwitz Trial, 1963–1965: Genocide, History, and the Limits of the Law* (New York, 2006), ch. 2; Devin O. Pendas, "Retroactive Law and Proactive Justice: Debating Crimes against Humanity in Germany, 1945–1950," *Central European History* 43, no. 3 (2010): 428–63.

25. Interview Kurt Wehle, 25 May 1995, University of Southern California Shoah Foundation, Visual History Archive, Los Angeles, CA, interview code 2859.

26. They spoke at different trials, with varying motivations. Lederer and Lagus testified at Rahm's trial, whereas Kárný stepped forward to give an accusing testimony against Benjamin Murmelstein. See Kárný to inspector Mužík, no date (1946), 305-633-1, ABS. Other survivors who became historians such as Ruth Bondy and H.G. Adler did not testify.

27. Only one person, Ota Růžička, spoke at both types of proceedings.

28. Memorandum, 18 May 1945 (Prague survivors to Terezín with a list whom to arrest), Ghetto Fighters' House, Lohamei HaGeta'ot, 3338; Memorandum, May 28, 1945 (Terezín survivors with a similar, yet longer list), ABS, 305-639-5.

29. Karel Stein to Kurt Wehle (on investigation of Benjamin Murmelstein), 4 March 1960, Archiv Židovského Muzea [Archive of the Jewish Museum], Prague [hereafter ŽMP], Kurt Wehle Papers, box 1. Thanks to Magda Veselská for drawing my attention to it.

30. Hájková, "Der Judenälteste und seine SS–Männer," 75–100; Beate Meyer, *A Fatal Balancing Act: The Dilemma of the Reich Association of Jews in Germany, 1939–1945,* trans. Bill Templer (New York, 2013), ch. 5; Laura Jockusch and Gabriel N. Finder, eds., *Jewish Honor Courts: Revenge, Retribution, and Reconciliation in Europe and Israel after the Holocaust* (Detroit, 2015).

31. Lisa Peschel, "The Prosthetic Life: Theatrical Performance, Survivor Testimony and the Terezín Ghetto, 1941–1963," Ph.D. diss., University of Minnesota, 2009; Anna Hájková, "To Terezín and Back: Czech Jews and their Bonds of Belonging between Theresienstadt and Postwar Czechoslovakia," *Dapim: Studies on the Holocaust* 28, no. 2 (March 2014): 52–53.

32. Affidavit Pavel Lužický, 18 November 1947, Wiener Stadt- und Landesarchiv [hereafter WStLA], People's Trial Vienna, Vr 314/50 gg. Johann Vostrel. The Czech originals are not in this file.

33. Affidavit Edmund Repper, 17 November 1947, WStLA, People's Trial Vienna, Vr 314/50.
34. Affidavit Adolf Beneš, 18 November 1947, WStLA, People's Trial Vienna, Vr 314/50.
35. Affidavit Rudolf Gerstmann, 28 May 1947, WStLA, People's Trial Vienna, Vr 314/50.
36. See Miroslav Kárný, "Zur Typologie des Theresienstädter Konzentrationslagers," *Judaica Bohemiae* 1, no. 17 (1981): 3–14; Peter Klein, "Theresienstadt: Ghetto oder Konzentrationslager?" *Theresienstädter Studien und Dokumente* 12 (2005): 111–23.
37. Deposition Emil Jockel, 3 November 1964, ABS, 325-82-2. Copies and German translations of most of the Czech statements are in the Bundesarchiv Ludwigsburg [hereafter BA Ludwigsburg], B 162, 1885, fol. 1.
38. Hearing of Wilhelm Hostovsky (Polizeipräsidium Kriminalpolizei Frankfurt am Main), 26 September 1963, BA Ludwigsburg, B 162, 1885, fol. 1.
39. Deposition of Jan Franěk, (investigations of Karl Bergel), 11 May 1965; ABS, 325-82-2.
40. The full name is the Law on Members of the Czechoslovak Army Abroad and Some Other Participants of the National Struggle for Liberation, issued 19 December 1946.
41. WStLA, People's Trial Vienna, Vr 314/50 gg. Johann Vostrel, and Vr 8881/46 gg. Ernst Girzick.
42. For instance, Doris Schimmerlingová had to postpone her high school final examinations to come to Prague and bear testimony against Theodor Janeček, the head of the gendarmes. Státní okresní archiv Praha [State Regional Archive Prague] [hereafter SOAP], People's Court, LS 428/46; interview Doris G. (née Schimmerlingová), 17 and 27 May 1996, Vzpomínky, ŽMP. Schimmerlingová, however, was not a standard witness.
43. Karla Müller Tupath, *Verschollen in Deutschland: Das heimliche Leben des Anton Burger, Lagerkommandant von Theresienstadt* (Hamburg, 1994).
44. Jan Volejník to *Hlas Revoluce* (asking to publish a search for witnesses), 23 April 1964, ABS, 325-82-2. Founded in 1959, this commission was first a branch of the Ministry of Justice that sought to procure the extradition of Nazi criminals. It later became independent. Lenka Šindelářová, "50 Jahre Zentrale Stelle in Ludwigsburg: Strafverfolgung von NS-Verbrechen am Beispiel des 'Lagerinspekteurs' von Theresienstädter Ghetto," *Theresienstädter Studien und Dokumente* 15 (2008): 95–97.
45. Bergel: ABS, 325-82-2; Burger: ABS, 325-15-5.
46. Affidavit Vilém Hostovský, 25 January 1952, WStLA, People's Trial Vienna, Vr 314/50 gg. Johann Vostrel.
47. Ruth Hostovský to Richard Host, 15 July 1997. Thanks to Richard Host for sending me a copy.
48. See Albert Hess, 21 December 1947, Státní okresní archiv Litoměřice [State Regional Archive Litoměřice] [hereafter SOAL], People's Trial, 147/48, box 154;

Albert Hess, letters and a report, Netherlands Institute for War Documentation, Amsterdam, 250d, box 28. Alice Randt, *Die Schleuse: Die Erlebnisse der Jüdin Alice Randt im Ghetto Theresienstadt* (Hannoversch Münden, 1974).

49. Gabriele Anderl, "Die Lagerkommandanten des jüdischen Ghetto Theresienstadt," in *Theresienstadt in der "Endlösung der Judenfrage,"* ed. Miroslav Kárný, Vojtech Blodig, and Margita Kárná (Prague, 1992), 213–22; see also Hans Safrian, *Eichmann und seine Gehilfen* (Frankfurt am Main, 1995).

50. AK and J, the two construction commandos, and Stab, transport of Jewish functionaries. Emanuel Herrmann was deported to Theresienstadt in summer 1943.

51. Archiv ministerstva vnitra [Archive of the Ministry of the Interior], Prague [hereafter AMV], 305-633-1.

52. One Jewish "collaborator," Paul Raphaelson, who had been a kapo in Wulkow, had been sentenced to death. Paul Raphaelson, SOAP, People's Court Prague, LS 414/47. See also Pavla Plachá and Jiří Plachý, "Der Wulkower Kollaborateur vor dem Außerordentlichen Volksgericht in Prag," *Theresienstädter Studien und Dokumente* 15 (2008): 48–63; Holger Hintzen, *Paul Raphaelson und Hans Jonas: Ein jüdischer Kapo und ein bewaffneter Philosoph im Holocaust* (Cologne, 2011).

53. Freiberger gave his affidavit on 12 October 1965, but Ludwigsburg received it from the Czechoslovak authorities only in March 1967. See Šindelářová, "50 Jahre," 94.

54. None of these six men were interviewed by the Documentation Action.

55. Růžička, APT, A, 834; Jockel, APT, A, 148; and Herrmann, APT, A, 564.

56. Interview Jiří V. (no date, ca. 1991), ŽMP, Vzpomínky, 5.

57. Stoll, *Herstellung der Wahrheit,* ch. 6.

58. Witness statement of Vilém Hostovský during the trial of Siegfried Seidl, copy, 28 September 1946, WStLA, People's Court Vienna, Vr 314/50 gg. Johann Wostrel, 205.

59. Affidavit Hostovsky, (Polizeipräsidium Kriminalpolizei Frankfurt am Main) 26 September 1963, Bundesarchiv Ludwigsburg, B 162, 1885 fol. 1.

60. Affidavit Růžička, 18 August 1972, ABS, 325-15-5.

61. For the change of tone in the interpretation of the Holocaust, see Peter Hallama, *Nationale Helden und jüdische Opfer: Tschechische Repräsentationen des Holocaust* (Göttingen, 2015), 135–41, 271–75.

62. Weigel, "Zeugnis und Zeugenschaft;" and Assmann, "Genre of Testimony," 266.

63. See Katrin Stoll's analysis of Artur Bejlin in "Narratives in the Audio Testimony of the Witness Dr. Aron Bejlin in the Bielefeld Białystok Trial," unpublished paper presented at conference "The Future of Holocaust Testimonies," Western Galilee College, Akko, 26–28 January 2010.

64. Affidavit Vogel, 5 January 1965, BA Ludwigsburg, B 162, 1885 fol. 1.

65. Affidavit Herrmann, 14 May 1965, BA Ludwigsburg, B 162, 1885 fol. 1. Similarly, another witness František Suchařípa, stated not only that he was pleased to bear witness in front of a West German court, but that he could do so in

German, as he was a professional court interpreter. Affidavit Suchařípa, 11 May 1963, ABS, 325-82-2.

66. Testimony in the trial against Karl Rahm, 23 April 1947, SOAL, LSP 441/4, box 135; affidavit in the trial against Rudolf Haindl, 17 June 1948, SOAL, People's Court, 147/48, box 154; affidavit against Bergel, 21 June 1948, SOAL, People's Court, Lsp 159/48, box 156.

67. Saul Friedländer, *Nazi Germany and the Jews,* 2 vols. (New York, 1998–2006), v. 2: 8–9, 438–43; also Amos Goldberg, "The Victim's Voice in History and Melodramatic Esthetics," *History and Theory* 48, no. 3 (2009): 220–37.

68. Here I am building on Wieviorka, *The Era of Witness,* 31–32.

69. On testifying as revenge, see Laura Jockusch, *Collect and Record! Jewish Holocaust Documentation in Early Postwar Europe* (New York, 2012).

70. Herrmann's testimony in trial against Rahm, 23 April 1947, SOAL, LSP 441/47, box 135.

71. Affidavit Herrmann, 14 May 1965, BA Ludwigsburg, B 162, 1885 fol. 1.

72. Testimony Emil Jockel, APT, A, 148.

73. Testimony Emanuel Herrmann, APT, A, 564.

74. See Annette Weinke, *Die Verfolgung von NS-Tätern im geteilten Deutschland: Vergangenheitsbewältigungen 1949–1969* (Paderborn, 2002), 151–57; Schwarz, *Juden im Zeugenstand,* 9–22.

75. In addition to Marinus van der Lubbe, the four communists on trial, Ernst Torgler, Georgi Dimitrov, Blagoi Popov, and Vasil Tanev, were accused of taking part in a broader conspiracy. For Sekanina's participation, see Petr Sekanina, *Ivan Sekanina, 1900–1940* (Prague, 2005), 130–36.

76. Deposition of Gertruda Sekaninová-Čakrtová, July 1963, BA Ludwigsburg, DP 2/763, 609-699, 628. Thanks to Susanne Heim for help in obtaining the deposition.

77. Deposition of Gertruda Sekaninová-Čakrtová, BA Ludwigsburg, DP 2/763, 622. See also interview of Gertruda Sekaninová-Čakrtová, 24 July 1985, family archive. Thanks to Martin Čakrt.

78. Deposition of Gertruda Sekaninová-Čakrtová, BA Ludwigsburg, DP 2/763, 625.

79. Hana Volavková, ed., *Children's Drawings and Poems Terezín 1942–1944,* with introduction by Jiří Weil; trans. Jeanne Němcová (Prague, 1959).

80. Lagus and Polák, *Město za mřížemi* (Prague, 1964), 286, #19.

81. Josef Novák, ŽMP, photo archive, drawings, no. 129.190.

82. Hugh Agnew, *The Czechs and the Lands of Bohemian Crown* (Stanford, CA, 2004), ch. 13; Andrew Evans, "The Last Gasp of Socialism: Economics and Culture in 1960s East Germany," *German Life and Letters* 63, no. 3 (July 2010): 331–44.

83. Statement by Gertruda Sekaninová-Čakrtová, Minutes of the Czechoslovak Parliament, 24 September 1964. Retrieved February 2017 from http://www.psp.cz/eknih/1964ns/stenprot/002schuz/s002010.htm.

84. Erika Schwarz comes to the same conclusion. Indeed, even the witnesses questioned in the preparation of the trial did not remember testifying, whereas the

Terezín witnesses remembered their appearance in court well. Schwarz, *Juden im Zeugenstand,* 15.
85. Garbarini, "Document Volumes and the Status of Victim Testimony," 113.

SELECT BIBLIOGRAPHY

Agnew, Hugh. *The Czechs and the Lands of Bohemian Crown.* Stanford, CA: Stanford University Press, 2004.

Angrick, Andrej, and Peter Klein. *The "Final Solution" in Riga: Exploitation and Annihilation, 1941–1944,* trans. Ray Brandon. New York: Berghahn, 2009.

Assmann, Aleida. "History, Memory, and the Genre of Testimony." *Poetics Today* 27, no. 2 (2006): 261–73.

Benjamin, Walter. "Zur Kritik der Gewalt," *Archiv für Sozialwissenschaft und Sozialpolitik* 47, no. 3 (1920/1921): 809–32.

Berkhoff, Karel. "Dina Pronicheva's Story of Surviving the Babi Yar Massacre: German, Jewish, Soviet, Russian, and Ukrainian Records." In *The Shoah in Ukraine: History, Testimony, Memorialization,* ed. Ray Brandon and Wendy Lower, 291–310. Bloomington, IN: Indiana University Press, 2010.

Borák, Mečislav. *Spravedlnost podle dekretu: retribuční soudnictví v ČSR a Mimořádný lidový soud v Ostravě, 1945–1948.* Šenov u Ostravy: Tilia, 1998.

Dean, Martin. "Editor's Introduction." In *The United States Holocaust Memorial Museum Encyclopedia of Camps and Ghettos 1933–1945,* vol. 2: *Ghettos in German-Occupied Eastern Europe,* gen. ed. Geoffrey Megargee. Bloomington, IN: Indiana University Press, 2012.

Delbo, Charlotte. *None of Us Will Return,* trans. John Githens. New York: Beacon Press, 1968.

Evans, Andrew. "The Last Gasp of Socialism: Economics and Culture in 1960s East Germany." *German Life and Letters* 63, no. 3 (2010): 331–44.

Felman, Shoshana, and Dori Laub, eds. *Testimony: Crises of Witnessing in Literature, Psychoanalysis, and History.* London: Routledge, 1991.

Fink, Ida. "The Table." In *A Scrap of Time and Other Stories,* ed. Ida Fink, 139–65. Evanston, IL: Northwestern University Press, 1995.

Franke, Uta, Heidi Bohley, Falco Werkentin. *Verhängnisvoll verstrickt: Richard Hesse und Leo Hirsch–zwei jüdische Funktionäre in zwei Diktaturen.* Halle: Hasenverlag, 2014.

Friedländer, Saul. *Nazi Germany and the Jews,* 2 vols. New York: HarperCollins, 1998–2006.

Frommer, Benjamin. *National Cleansing: Retribution against Nazi Collaborators in Postwar Czechoslovakia.* New York: Cambridge University Press, 2005.

———. "The Jewish Department of the Prague Police: What its Czech Directors Did During the War, and How They Escaped Justice Afterwards." Association for Slavic, East European, and Eurasian Studies, New Orleans, 15–18 November 2012.

Garbarini, Alexandra. *Numbered Days: Diaries and the Holocaust.* New Haven, CT: Yale University Press, 2006.

——. "Document Volumes and the Status of Victim Testimony in the Era of the First World War and Its Aftermath." *Études arméniennes contemporaines* 5 (2015): 113–38.

Goldberg, Amos. "The Victim's Voice in History and Melodramatic Esthetics." *History and Theory* 48, no. 3 (2009): 220–37.

Hájková, Anna. "Der Judenälteste und seine SS–Männer: Benjamin Murmelstein, der letzte Judenälteste in Theresienstadt und seine Beziehung zu Adolf Eichmann und Karl Rahm." In *"Der Letzte der Ungerechten:" Der Judenälteste Benjamin Murmelstein in Filmen 1942–1975,* ed. Ronny Loewy and Katharina Rauschenberger, 75–100. Frankfurt am Main: Campus Verlag, 2011.

——. "The Prisoner Society in Terezín Ghetto, 1941–1945." Ph.D. diss., University of Toronto, 2013.

——. "To Terezín and Back: Czech Jews and their Bonds of Belonging between Theresienstadt and Postwar Czechoslovakia." *Dapim: Studies on the Holocaust* 28, no. 2 (2014): 38–55.

Hallama, Peter. *Nationale Helden und jüdische Opfer: Tschechische Repräsentationen des Holocaust.* Göttingen: Wallstein Verlag, 2015.

Hintzen, Holger. *Paul Raphaelson und Hans Jonas: Ein jüdischer Kapo und ein bewaffneter Philosoph im Holocaust.* Cologne: Greven Verlag, 2012.

Jockusch, Laura. *Collect and Record! Jewish Holocaust Documentation in Early Postwar Europe.* New York: Oxford University Press, 2012.

Jockusch, Laura, and Gabriel N. Finder, eds. *Jewish Honor Courts: Revenge, Retribution, and Reconciliation in Europe and Israel after the Holocaust.* Detroit, MI: Wayne State University Press, 2015.

Kárný, Miroslav. "Zur Typologie des Theresienstädter Konzentrationslagers." *Judaica Bohemiae* 17, no. 1 (1981): 3–14.

Klein, Peter. "Theresienstadt: Ghetto oder Konzentrationslager?" *Theresienstädter Studien und Dokumente* (2005): 111–23.

Lagus, K., and J. Polák. *Město za mřížemi.* Prague: Naše vojsko, 1964.

Meyer, Beate. *A Fatal Balancing Act: The Dilemma of the Reich Association of Jews in Germany, 1939–1945,* trans. Bill Templer. New York: Berghahn, 2013.

Müller Tupath, Karla. *Verschollen in Deutschland: Das heimliche Leben des Anton Burger, Lagerkommandant von Theresienstadt.* Hamburg: Konkret, 1994.

Pendas, Devin O. 2004. "Truth and Its Consequences: Reflections on Political, Historical and Legal Truth in West German Holocaust Trials." *Traverse: Zeitschrift für Geschichte/Revue d'histoire* 11, no. 1 (2004): 25–38.

——. *The Frankfurt Auschwitz Trial, 1963–1965: Genocide, History, and the Limits of the Law.* New York: Cambridge University Press, 2006.

——. "Retroactive Law and Proactive Justice: Debating Crimes against Humanity in Germany, 1945–1950." *Central European History* 43, no. 3 (2010): 428–63.

Peschel, Lisa. "The Prosthetic Life: Theatrical Performance, Survivor Testimony and the Terezín Ghetto, 1941–1963," Ph.D. diss., University of Minnesota, 2009.

Plachá, Pavla, and Jiří Plachý. "Der Wulkower Kollaborateur vor dem Außerordentlichen Volksgericht in Prag," *Theresienstädter Studien und Dokumente* (2008): 48–63.

Randt, Alice. *Die Schleuse: Die Erlebnisse der Jüdin Alice Randt im Ghetto Theresienstadt.* Hannoversch Münden: Gauke, 1974.

Rigele, Brigitte. 2010. *Verhaftet: Verurteilt. Davongekommen: Volksgericht Wien 1945–1955.* Vienna: Wiener Stadt- und Landesarchiv, 2010.

Scheffler, Wolfgang and Helge Grabitz, *Der Ghetto-Aufstand Warschau 1943 aus der Sicht der Täter und Opfer in Aussagen vor deutschen Gerichten.* Munich: Siedler Verlag, 1993.

Schwarz, Erika. *Juden im Zeugenstand: Die Spur des Hans Globke im Gedächtnis von Überlebenden der Schoa.* Berlin: Hentrich & Hentrich, 2009.

Sekanina, Petr. *Ivan Sekanina, 1900–1940.* Prague: Orego, 2005.

Stoll, Katrin. "Narratives in the Audio Testimony of the Witness Dr. Aron Bejlin in the Bielefeld Białystok Trial." "The Future of Holocaust Testimonies." Akko, Western Galilee College, 26–28 January 2010.

———. *Die Herstellung der Wahrheit: Strafverfahren gegen ehemalige Angehörige der Sicherheitspolizei für den Bezirk Białystok.* Berlin: de Gruyter, 2012.

Šindelářová, Lenka. "50 Jahre Zentrale Stelle in Ludwigsburg: Strafverfolgung von NS-Verbrechen am Beispiel des 'Lagerinspekteurs' von Theresienstädter Ghetto." *Theresienstädter Studien und Dokumente* (2008): 95–97.

Tůma, Mirko. *Ghetto našich dnů.* Prague: Salvar, 1946.

Veselská, Magda. "Early Documentation of the Shoah in the Czech Lands: The Documentation Project and the Prague Jewish Museum (1945–1947)." *Judaica Bohemiae* 52, no.1 (2017): 47–85

Volavková, Hana, ed. *Children's Drawings and Poems Terezín 1942–1944,* with introduction by Jiří Weil, trans. Jeanne Němcová. Prague: Jewish Museum, 1959.

Weigel, Sigrid. "Klage und Anklage: Die Geste des Bezeugens in der Differenz von 'identity politics,' juristischem und historiographischem Diskurs." *Zeugnis und Zeugenschaft: Jahrbuch des Einstein-Forums* (2000): 111–35.

Weinke, Annette. *Die Verfolgung von NS-Tätern im geteilten Deutschland: Vergangenheitsbewältigungen 1949–1969.* Paderborn: Ferdinand Schöningh, 2002.

Wieviorka, Annette. *The Era of the Witness,* trans. Jared Stark. Ithaca, NY: Cornell University Press, 2006.

Zangl, Veronika. *Poetik nach dem Holocaust: Erinnerungen-Tatsachen-Geschichten.* Munich: Fink Verlag, 2009.

Chapter 4

A Morality of Evil

Nazi Ethics and the Defense Strategies of German Perpetrators

Kerstin von Lingen

When former Waffen-SS General Karl Wolff was touring South America with the journalist Gerd Heidemann in June 1979, they had a remarkable conversation at Santiago de Chile. After just having met Walter Rauff, the inventor of the infamous gas vans, Wolff's memory—which had in the past been somehow obfuscated in the several legal proceedings against him—became remarkably clear. He revealed to Heidemann his feelings about watching the killings of 120 Jews by an Einsatzgruppen squad near Minsk on the occasion of an official visit there with Heinrich Himmler some thirty-eight years earlier, in August 1941: "I was really sick, not because [the Jews] were brought to death, but because it was so unworthy; they had not even received a verdict that they [were] now to be shot, as I had expected. Nothing. They were just transported there to be killed in a pit."[1] Although the total absence of pity for the dead is disturbing, this phrase also reveals a certain, albeit distorted, moral framework transported in the term "unworthy" that shows the persistence of what we might call "Nazi ethics." It is not the killings themselves that are questionable. Rather Wolff rejects the way in which they were carried out incongruent with German rules or customs, or even "decency."

How did senior Nazi perpetrators testify about their crimes? How did they discuss them in private? The answers can tell us something about how senior figures from the Third Reich represented their crimes in court and to one another, and they can perhaps even tell us about the mentality of killers as they committed their acts. There have been many studies about Holocaust testimony as such. But most of the literature relates to victim testimony and the degree to which trauma affects truth. Though perpetrator testimony has been used in studies about the motivations of killers, it has not been deconstructed in quite the same way. This essay focuses on a few senior perpetrators in two different settings. Karl Wolff was Heinrich Himmler's personal secretary and later the highest SS (Schutzstaffel) and police commander for Italy. Walter Rauff was the architect of the gas vans and was employed later with the task of liquidating the Jews of Tunisia, but he was never brought before a court, as extradition from Chile failed.[2] Klaus Barbie was the Gestapo chief in Lyon from 1942 to 1944, and was brought to trial in 1987 after extradition from Bolivia to France.[3]

In this chapter, transcripts from informal talks between three former high ranking Nazi officials are scrutinized for the first time. Wolff was a witness at Nuremberg in 1947, underwent denazification in 1949, and faced a criminal trial for murder in 1964. The transcripts of his testimonies in court have been available for years. But in 1979, Wolff, Rauff, and Barbie met in South America, where the latter two former SS officers lived as fugitives. This material has surfaced only recently as part of the private archive of Gerd Heidemann, a journalist for *Der Stern,* most famous for the Hitler diary hoax of 1983. Heidemann granted the author access to his transcripts.

In the 1950s *Der Stern* had campaigned for the release of convicted German army officials from Allied custody.[4] In the 1960s and 1970s it turned more toward scandals and journalistic scoops including Nazi hunting. In the 1970s, Heidemann was interested in Karl Wolff's "secret surrender" to the Americans in Italy, known as Operation Sunrise. Wolff met Heidemann in Hamburg and in 1979 Heidemann offered Wolff a trip to South America at the magazine's expenses. The recent West German broadcast of the American television miniseries *Holocaust* had spurred German interest in the Final Solution. *Der Stern's* editors tasked Heidemann to locate Doctor Joseph Mengele and to write a story about the opaque Nazi pathway to South America. By taking Wolff, a high-ranking officer, Heidemann expected to gain access to the other high-ranking former Nazis.

In private settings or quiet restaurants, the former Nazi officials sat down to talk about their past. Heidemann recorded them and later produced written transcripts that today form a unique source of evidence. The material contains dialogues in a banal, everyday tone and colloquial, blood-chilling language (the original German is in the footnotes). The content is important for at least two reasons. First, it reveals a certain "banality of evil," as described by Hannah Arendt. It was the daily work of perpetrators who gave no thought to the human lives they were extinguishing. At the same time, talk about actual deeds shows that the perpetrators in question did not see themselves as guilty of the killings that they describe in detail. Even among themselves, they represented their crimes as ideological duty. This perpetrator testimony reveals a certain Nazi "morality"—a "morality of evil" as Arendt put it, whereby the killers justify their crimes while simultaneously distancing themselves from their own criminality. Such a morality was based on what we might call a loose system of "Nazi ethics" concerning mass killings, which manifests itself in the perpetrators' public defense strategies or in the ways old comrades spoke privately about details while trying to avoiding mention of the killings themselves.

NAZI MORALITY

Nazi ethics, though a seeming oxymoron, is a growing research field.[5] Claudia Koonz argues that the "popularizers of anti-Semitism and the planners of genocide followed a coherent set of severe ethical maxims derived from broad philosophical concepts."[6] Raphael Gross develops this idea further in his book *Staying Decent,* which examines conscious participation in crimes, the positive feelings many Germans had toward National Socialism, and their support for its measures and policies.[7] Psychological research, meanwhile, shows the intersection between ideological regimes and new moral codes. Albert Bandura notes:

> The conversion of socialized people into dedicated fighters is achieved not by altering their personality structures, aggressive drives, or moral standards. Rather, it is accomplished by cognitively redefining the morality of killing so that it can be done free from self-censure. Through moral justification of violent means, people see themselves as fighting ruthless oppressors, protecting their cherished values, preserving world peace, saving humanity from subjugation, or honoring their country's commitments. Just war tenets were devised to specify when the use of violent force is morally justified.[8]

Wolfgang Bialas usefully defines Nazi ethics as a new morality that replaced the "universal ethics based on unconditional empathy and charity [toward] all human beings ... with the selective ethics of racial superiority and inferiority."[9] The new ethical system was free of moral constraints imposed previously by religious beliefs. Human rights were no longer universal, but applied only to the *Volksgemeinschaft.*[10] Nazi ethics unleashed an "unprecedented wave of barbarism, intellectually justified in the name of the highest ideals."[11] The Nazis thus turned the ethics of humanism upside down and replaced them with "particularistic selective racial ethics and the pragmatics of eugenics and racial extermination politics."[12] In this worldview, the "moral conditioning of Nazi perpetrators aimed at developing a kind of 'ethnic conscience,' which restricted moral obligations to members of their own race community."[13] Perpetrators, from desk murderers to on-site killers, insisted that their actions were not only necessary, but also correct—"appropriate in the given situation."[14] Thus Nazi morality "combined absolute virtues that demanded unconditional obedience with the attitude of social engineering, and replaced common sense intuitions with an ideological catalogue of virtues and commands."[15] The most prevalent concepts used in Nazi ideology were "decency," "honor," "loyalty" and "duty," and in view of a soldierly ethic, these virtues were flanked by "struggle," "strength of character" and "willingness to sacrifice."[16] Bialas emphasizes that SS members "were trained to ignore, deny, and overcome their personal feelings if [these feelings] contradicted the attitudes they were expected to develop to fulfill their duties as political soldiers or racial warriors."[17] This system, Bialas argues, worked better when perpetrators had the chance to suppress any doubts by expressing their feelings of humanity toward people who they felt deserved it: their wives, their children, and their friends.[18]

Yet as Didier Pollefeyt points out, it is too simple to see Nazi perpetrators as free from moral restraints: "The Germans were not suddenly deprived of their capacity to distinguish good from evil. They did not act out of purely immoral desires or out of moral insensitivity, but precisely because they were ethically sensitive. Nazism was sustained by a very strict, almost puritanical, ethical code."[19] Pollefeyt underlines that "[t]he executioners of the Nazi genocide failed to suffer bad conscience not because they were perverted completely (immorality) nor because they were thoughtless machines (amorality), but because they devoted themselves consciously, creatively and with passion to the meaning that the Nazi ethic gave their (camp) behavior."[20]

And exceptions within the system for weakness in the face of killing were possible. To Heinrich Himmler, this "temporary tolerance" constituted an "intermediate stage of racial maturity."[21] Thus members of killing squads who abstained from shooting operations were excused for their "temporary weakness," so long as they did not question the politics of the extermination as a whole.[22] Himmler also called on SS members to act without "unnecessary cruelty."[23] In his infamous Posen speech before high-ranking SS officers and Gauleiter in October 1943, Himmler claimed that SS men must be honest, decent, and loyal, showing camaraderie only to members of their own race. When discussing mass killing, Himmler insisted: "To have gone through this and yet—apart from a few exceptions, examples of human weakness—to have remained decent fellows, this is what has made us hard. This is a glorious page in our history that has never been written and shall never be written."[24] Konrad Kwiet underlines that this use of the word "decent" encapsulates the perversion of ethics; the entanglement between old values and distorted new meanings.[25]

The assumption that Nazi perpetrators acted within a moral framework shifts the research focus, as Bialas puts it, "from discerning why they committed such atrocities to how they managed to manipulate their conscience to the point that they became indifferent to the suffering of their victims."[26] He suggests examination of the distinction between the terms "immoral" and "amoral." Examination of immoral behavior implies an ability to understand why perpetrators acted the way they did, but examining motivations for amoral behavior would mean to scrutinize why the perpetrators failed to grasp that their actions were wrong.[27] Public pressure, political repression, and moral indoctrination may alter the cultural meaning of good and evil, and all these seemingly eradicate an independent faculty of moral judgment.[28]

THE COURTROOM DEFENSES OF KARL WOLFF

Karl Wolff's career is well documented. He served as chief of Himmler's personal staff from the mid-1930s. In mid-September 1943, he became highest SS and police commander in northern Italy. He was implicated in numerous war crimes including the Final Solution. In August 1941, Wolff witnessed mass killings of Jews at Minsk when on an inspection tour there with Himmler. An execution of a hundred "partisans," among them Jewish women, took place to "honor" the high-ranking Nazi visitors.[29] Wolff was personally involved in the deportation of Jews to Treblinka in 1942 by organizing railroad transportation, and he expressed satisfaction when the transport was accomplished, stating that "with utmost pleasure, I have received your report that for a fortnight already, 5,000 members of the 'chosen people' leave every day for Treblinka."[30] In January and February 1943, Order Police Chief Kurt Daluege reported directly to Wolff on the statistical composition, internal organization, and regional distribution of Order Police units deployed for mass killing.[31]

Yet after the war, there was a feather in Wolff's cap. Following secret negotiations with US envoy and Office of Strategic Services (OSS) representative Allen Dulles in Switzerland in 1945, Wolff had managed to bring about an early surrender for northern Italy, codenamed Operation Sunrise. This "secret surrender" opened the way through the feared Alpine Redoubt into southern Germany in early May, and helped to bring about the overall European surrender on 8 May 1945.[32] Dulles afterward argued that Sunrise had spared countless US soldiers' lives, although the effect is hard to prove numerically. Wolff, meanwhile, insisted privately on several occasions later that during the Sunrise negotiations he had received promises that he would not be prosecuted. Wolff's well-documented and researched case shows a certain ambiguity. On one side stood a man in high office, who was able at a certain moment to act against his regime. On the other, was a man complicit in the Final Solution who organized rail transport of Jews to Treblinka.[33] Wolff was a typical "desk murderer," who could also use his role in Operation Sunrise to erase his guilt.

Regardless, Wolff spent a lot of time in courtrooms after the war. After the four-power Trial of the Major War Criminals before the International Military Tribunal in Nuremberg (IMT) from 1945 to 1946, the US staged twelve subsequent trials before the US Military Tribunal, also in Nuremberg, which involved different layers of Nazi elites as defendants, ranging from doctors to judges to industrialists.[34] Wolff testified as a witness in Case 4, the trial of the SS Economic and Administrative Main Office, the lead defendant of which was Oswald Pohl, who was eventually hanged. Chief prosecutor Jack Robbins suggested that, given Wolff's seniority and the documentation at hand, Wolff must have approved of the extermination campaign.[35] Wolff indeed testified on 4 June 1947 that he had been made aware of the transport from the Warsaw ghetto by way of a report from the German National Railroad, but he retracted this testimony the following day with the explanation that he had only signed—not personally dictated— an answer to Reichsbahn Commissioner Albert Ganzenmüller.[36]

Wolff was protected owing to his role in Operation Sunrise. Telford Taylor, the US chief of counsel, remembered that a meeting with Wolff in early August 1947 had given him the impression that an immunity agreement existed. Wolff actually met with Judge Michael Musmanno, the presiding judge in Case 4, asking him to halt any prosecution proceedings against him.[37] Despite Wolff's contradictory testimony concerning deportations during that case, any further explanation of his involvement in the persecution of Jews in Poland under Operation Reinhard—the murder of the Jews there—was indeed deemed unnecessary. This hints at possible intervention of high-ranking US officials.[38] Judge F. Donald Philips later remembered that American judges had received orders to keep in mind that, when considering Wolff as a potential defendant, the surrender of German forces to the US in northern Italy was in part Wolff's achievement.[39]

Nazi party members after 1946 had to undergo individual proceedings in so-called denazification courts (*Spruchkammer* trials). These courts, which were presided over by German citizens, sorted German society into five categories: major offenders, offenders, lesser offenders, followers, and persons exonerated. Once cleared by the *Spruchkammer,* the citizen could start afresh. Most defendants were grouped under Category IV ("followers" of Nazi politics), and the whole process of denazification was soon given the nickname "follower-factory" by critics, indicating that apparently no high-ranking Nazi had ever existed and that all simply followed orders. It became apparent that the courts selected a few scapegoats in order to prove the non-liability of the majority.[40] Denazification thus became, contrary to the Allies' intent, a vehicle for reintegrating a large portion of the old party warriors into postwar German society.

Wolff's denazification proceeding occurred in February 1948 in Hamburg. When the verdict was read on 6 November, Wolff was declared guilty and sentenced to four years of imprisonment. But in pondering his deeds during his service, the court classified him as a "lesser incriminated Nazi" (Category III) for mere "nominal membership" in the SS. Wolff also received credit for his pre-trial custody by the Americans. Affidavits and intervention by his US interlocutors from the Sunrise negotiations helped to create this outcome. The conflicted verdict thus read: "The defendant, as one of the highest-ranking SS leaders was indeed aware of this link [between deportation and annihilation] and is therefore incriminated by the knowledge of those criminal measures involving Jewish persecution in which the SS did not directly participate."[41] It continued that "by virtue of his offices" Wolff had had "information but no specific knowledge of the crimes committed by the SS." Presiding Judge Dr. Roscher reduced the already lenient sentence by suspending Wolff's remaining weeks in prison and then announced that "the defendant leaves the courtroom with a spotless white vest."[42] Seldom has a trial been more ambiguous.

Thanks to the intervention of Jewish victim groups and following preliminary investigations by the Central Office for the Investigation of Nazi Crimes in Ludwigsburg, Wolff was finally arrested in 1962. He came before a Munich court in 1964, charged with having been an accessory to the murder of 300,000 Jews by organizing their rail transport to Treblinka. His trial occurred within the context of the 1961 trial of Adolf Eichmann in Jerusalem and the 1963–1965 Frankfurt Auschwitz trial. Both sets of proceedings sensitized public opinion to the extent of Nazi atrocities. In addition, witnesses and experts in both trials mentioned Wolff's name, linking him directly to Nazi crimes.[43] In light of the overwhelming evidence, Wolff's defense was limited to reacting to the many accusations.[44] And unlike at Nuremberg where the Americans were in charge, there was little opportunity to use the Sunrise narrative as a mitigating influence.

In minute detail, the Munich Regional Court reconstructed all of Wolff's statements concerning deportation transports in the trials before the US Military Tribunal at Nuremberg—the Pohl trial,[45] but also at the US trials of Friedrich Flick and of the Supreme Command of the Armed Forces.[46] Wolff's counter claims were stunning.[47] Wolff posed as a "good SS officer"—an "alien element in the SS." When discussing the shootings at Minsk by Einsatzgruppe B, which Wolff had witnessed with Himmler, Wolff insisted that he had no clue what was happening, and that he was nonetheless "disgusted" by the way killings were carried out.[48] Although the judgment later conveyed the court's view that Wolff's visit had a "motivating effect on soldiers and officers employed with the killings to carry on with the lawless murders," this particular charge was dropped [*vorläufig eingestellt*] on 21 September 1964 without explanation.[49] For the rest, Wolff posed almost as a subaltern. He explained the deportation order concerning Treblinka as follows: "I just had to play mailman between Himmler and [Foreign Minister Joachim von] Ribbentrop, who could not stand each other personally. The thing played out between the Foreign Ministry and the Reich Security Main Office. Since the matter did not affect my official duties, I did not read the report or at most [I] scanned it."[50] When the judge asked Wolff rhetorically whether he thought that Himmler forwarded these reports to him "so that you would know what was going on," Wolff dismissed the point by saying "I cannot tell you why he did that. Himmler was often very unorthodox in the way he worked."[51]

In fact, Wolff's guilt could not be covered up. Ulrike Meinhof, later a Red Army Faction terrorist, but in 1964 a journalist observing the Wolff trial, remarked that Wolff's was "the first trial that proved the nature of National Socialism and Nazi deeds based on testimony from its supporters, not from its victims."[52] And the truth could not be hidden. Witness Erich von dem Bach-Zelewski, a former SS general who served Himmler on the Eastern Front and elsewhere, conceded during cross-examination that it was "impossible" for a higher SS officer not to have known about the extermination of the Jews.[53] Historian Dr. Hanns von Krannhals, called as an expert witness in court, confirmed that "the circle of people who knew about the mass killings in the General Government was large," and Wolff was undoubtedly "an aide designated to implement Himmler's orders."[54]

In the meantime, the aforementioned Nazi ethics raised their head at the Wolff trial. Specifically, temporary tolerance and even mercy by SS members came up. Defense witnesses described Wolff as someone willing to help rescue an individual in need. Gerhard Engel, army liaison officer in the Führer Headquarters between 1941 and 1943 testified that "Wolff helped Jews in dozens of cases. He liberated Jews, if I may say so."[55] Specifically,

Engel testified as to Wolff's attempts to rescue "Jewish friends of members of the Wehrmacht."[56] The reaction was open sarcasm. The prosecution asked Engel what Wolff was saving these Jews from if he knew nothing about the threats to their lives, a connection lost on both Engel and Wolff.[57] The *Abend-zeitung* argued that one could hardly agree to "mitigating circumstances for a bank robber ... just because he did not shoot all the bank employees in his line of fire, but spared the lives of a few."[58] Former resister Hans von Winterfeld doubted in court that Wolff was motivated to help people because he opposed National Socialism; instead, Winterfeld argued that Wolff did it as a personal favor.[59] He continued that Wolff "was a believing, naïve supporter of the regime, a romantic dreamer who could not bring himself to realize that the National Socialist dictatorship was linked to dreadful terror."[60]

State Attorney Benedict Huber went a step further, actually attempting to use the ethical argument against Wolff.[61] Why, Huber asked, did Wolff expend energy on "quasi-private amusement" for SS officers [namely exterminations] instead of the Eastern front, specifically concerning rolling stock which might have aided surrounded German soldiers in Stalingrad? "The Jews penned up in the ghettos could have waited still a while," Huber said, while "the wounded German soldiers could not."[62] In fact the troops in the Stalingrad area were not surrounded in July 1942 when Wolff was corresponding with Ganzenmüller about deportation transports. Huber's point was to appeal to the German public, which viewed Stalingrad as the singular catastrophe that turned the tide of the war. Aside from obviating Wolff's heroic Sunrise tale, the reference to Stalingrad would turn any argument of SS ethics on its head. In fact, Huber flirted with a new stab-in-the-back legend, this time implicating the SS itself against a supposedly "clean" military. Regardless, Wolff's letter to Ganzenmüller concerning Treblinka was at the center of the prosecution's strategy, and it led to Wolff's conviction on 30 September 1964. Wolff was found guilty of being an "accessory to a crime that has no precedent"—an accessory rather than a murderer owing to the eccentricities of the German murder statute.[63]

The judgment's narrative was conflicted in part owing to the quandary over Nazi ethics. It indicated that Wolff was an ethical man, albeit within the upside-down Nazi ethical system. Wolff "was trapped in the delusion of Nazism and was fixed on the idea, despite all scruples, that he was to fulfill a historic mission."[64] Yet his subservience to Himmler and his acceptance of SS racial theory and the Final Solution meant that his ethical compass was "not reconcilable with the character of an upright man."[65] Meanwhile, the sentence was conflicted as well. A life sentence was certainly possible when the trial began. But the court fell back on the legal definition of murder, which demanded that initiative and bloodlust be proved. Wolff, the judgment read, acted neither out of conviction nor in pursuit of office, and he lacked authority in the extermination of the Jews.[66] He received a sentence of fifteen years and a ten-year loss of civil rights. *Der Spiegel* noted: "[Wolff] will never understand that one can be guilty without dirtying one's own hands."[67] Ulrike Meinhof observed critically that the verdict had not punished the defendant as placeholder of a murderous regime; but the lenient sentence had indeed "unburdened [and] marginalized the regime altogether."[68]

IN CONVERSATION BETWEEN COMRADES

In 1979, Gerd Heidemann offered Wolff a trip to South America at *Der Stern*'s expense. Heidemann and Wolff flew first to Argentina, then to Chile, and finally to Peru and Bolivia. Over the course of the trip, Heidemann and Wolff met with Walter Rauff, who lived in a German colony in Chile, and in Bolivia Klaus Barbie, who had a colorful postwar career working for US, Bolivian, and West German intelligence. Heidemann recorded and transcribed the conversations. He still holds these collections, parts of which are presented here for the first time, in his Hamburg home.[69] The transcripts contain banalities, but they are also an invaluable source concerning patterns of reflection by senior Nazi perpetrators. The old comrades in conversation here carried different ranks. Wolff was an SS general who gave orders; Rauff and Barbie, meanwhile, were actually involved in killing missions. Wolff had been Rauff's superior in Italy in 1944. Wolff had never met Barbie before travelling to South America.

Hans Gross has argued that as a precondition to murder, shared morality and absolute loyalty among perpetrators is necessary. Nazi ethics are themselves part of the crime.[70] When analyzing ways in which perpetrators discuss killing, Bialas suggests that the perpetrators often complain that their values of hard work and discipline had been abused and that they themselves had thus fallen victim to circumstances.[71] These arguments are especially visible among old comrades after the fact, particularly in a relaxed and free atmosphere. They rarely admit that they acted on their own initiative. Rather they acted as members of military units.[72] A familiar defense strategy is the claim that "ideologically induced moral brutalization entitled them to reduced criminal responsibility," while at the same time Nazi perpetrators remain responsible for their deeds, even when "historical constellations beyond their control made them perpetrators."[73]

In Heidemann's recorded conversations, the speakers do not avoid discussing crimes; on the contrary, they discuss their deeds in detail. But they stay on the purely technical plane. Moreover, they never mention the Final Solution as such. Instead they discuss individual instances of mass killings by giving the names of villages or commanders in charge, or even by the amount of ammunition used in a given operation. There is thus an obsession with seemingly incidental detail. But there is also the argument that mass killing was a hated job. "Decency," "honor," "loyalty," and "duty" are recurrent terms deployed in new formulations to justify one's actions. In the meantime there is no remorse.[74]

Heidemann recorded two kinds of conversations: direct conversations and reflections afterward between Wolff and Heidemann after they met Rauff and Barbie. For example, on the evening of 26 June 1979, Wolff and Heidemann discussed their earlier meeting with Rauff in Chile. Wolff discussed how he witnessed with Himmler the shootings of Jews near Minsk. At his Munich trial, Wolff had not denied being there, but had pointed out that it was just by chance and not part of his actual duties.[75] Yet with Heidemann Wolff describes in detail what he witnessed at the visit of Einsatzgruppe B on 15 August 1941, when 120 Jews were shot.[76] Wolff reveals the organizational aspect of mass murder, namely how the SS men assembled in the yard, mounted on vans, drove to the outskirts of Minsk, and took their positions near the pits. Afterwards he describes how the victims had to lie down and were shot from behind, their brains splattering.

When discussing Himmler and his insistence on watching the killings, Wolff became agitated. Three times he mentions that he and SS Obersturmbannführer Otto Bradfisch, who commanded Einsatzkommando 8 at Minsk, were about twenty meters behind Himmler, "as we did not want to witness this." Wolff described how Himmler became sick when brains splattered on his coat. He then admitted to having seen the shootings from nearby, but he qualified this admission: "This was the moment when I came nearer, as I feared [Himmler] would stumble and fall, and then he would be laying amongst the Jews. Well, that would have suited him right [laughter]!"[77] Wolff claims to have commented along with Bradfisch, "That suits him right, he shall see the burden he is inflicting on his own men!"[78] The conversation is interesting in two regards. First, Heidemann makes reference to the representation of the shooting at Babi Yar in the miniseries *Holocaust*, asking Wolff, "Was it like in the film?" Wolff states that it was "a bit different," thus confirming that Wolff had in fact watched the television series. Second, Wolff, unusually for him, critiques Himmler, not for his involvement in mass murder, but for the burden inflicted upon the SS.

The conversation afterward seeks redemption. Wolff tells Heidemann of a lengthy dialogue he had with Himmler in which Wolff, in this retelling, tried to spare two women accused of sabotage. It was ignoble, he said, to kill women, and he then described them to Heidemann as "decent women," "not prostitutes," and "quite good looking." The women were not spared, for another officer pointed to the duty to protect German soldiers from sabotage. But Wolff evidently hoped to maintain a chivalrous image, which would shine all the more beside the character of other Nazis.

Heidemann asked Wolff how he felt about the killings—a question never raised in Wolff's court proceedings. Wolff discussed his astonishment that no one tried to escape. Jewish men prayed loudly or cried, he said, but they did not curse the killers. He claims to have found the entire business disgusting: "I was really sick, not because [the Jews] were brought to death, but because it was so unworthy; they had not even received a verdict that they are now to be shot, as I had expected. Nothing. They were just transported there to be killed in a pit."[79] Wolff thereby emphasizes his own contemporaneous decency of a type emphasized by Himmler himself, absent of any actual pity for the dead. Indeed, he emphasized that he was not in his soul even an SS man. He had joined the ranks, he said, for honorable reasons—he believed in its exclusiveness as a separate "order."[80]

The shooting of the two women was the last straw, Wolff continued. He sounded agitated insofar as his wording stopped referring to himself in the first person in lieu of the expression "oneself." Himmler should have spared everyone the terrible spectacle.[81] Wolff even accuses Himmler of perverting the chivalrous ideals of the SS. "Was there no other way of deterrence? Did one have to be so inhumane and unchivalrous? What is it that two strong men drag two women into a pit, and four others blow their heads away, and that's it? This was so disgusting, and one needed a schnapps afterwards, as it was really so disgusting." Heidemann and Wolff wonder afterward whether this episode triggered Himmler's subsequent order to Rauff to invent more "humane" ways of killing, such as gas vans (the topic had not been raised between Rauff and Wolff directly). Wolff spoke much more freely with Heidemann here than he did in court or with his former comrades, and also reveals his feelings. But this remarkable discussion also indicates a last remaining moral framework to which Wolff tried to cling.

Heidemann's other surviving interviews are direct conversations. The most interesting are between Wolff and Klaus Barbie, then living under the alias Klaus Altmann in Bolivia. In 1971 Barbie's identity and location had been discovered by the Nazi hunter Beate Klarsfeld, but he thought himself safe in these discussions, and in fact was not extradited to France until 1983. Interestingly, Wolff and Barbie seem to have been talking to themselves rather than to each other. Rarely does a real conversation evolve between them, and usually only with regard to small details or extraneous information. In addition, the defense strategies deployed at Nuremberg emerge as a

kind of child's game—one man starts a sentence, and the other ends it with
well-worn arguments.

The following conversation provides details about the killings and at the
same time argues that non-prosecution by the Allies implied innocence.[82]

> Wolff: I did nothing more than follow a telephone request to solve a railroad
> standstill in Poland, by writing a letter to the secretary in the Ministry of Trans-
> portation, Dr. Ganzenmüller. None of these foreign courts have ever brought
> me to trial for this. I have survived the denazification court, although the [de-
> nazification] court at Hamburg-Bergedorf was communist [*sic*]. But afterwards,
> they claimed I must have been aware what was going on, as I was a close aide of
> Hitler, Himmler, and Mussolini.
>
> Barbie: I have also been convicted for war crimes but in France.[83] The trials
> have been lock, stock, and barrel, following the Lex Oradour. Have you ever
> heard of what happened at Oradour?[84]
>
> Wolff: Yes, I know, our battalion commander had been murdered, and then the
> soldiers had ...
>
> Barbie: Yes, and then the soldiers returned. Shit happens. I mean, it is true.
>
> Wolff: Yes, sadly, it's true.
>
> Barbie: I remember a similar incident, in France, not in Russia. They had mur-
> dered a whole company of our Landsturm, honest 40-year-old men ...
>
> Wolff: Who were just on guard.
>
> Barbie: Yes, they were guarding prisoners and so on. They were in the car, to
> get spare parts for the plane, when they were caught by the Maquis. They were
> murdered so cruelly. They were blinded, then their legs broken, and then they
> were laid down in rank order.
>
> Wolff: Understandable that [after that] one cannot guarantee the soldiers stay
> calm.
>
> Barbie: I reported to the headquarters, and the Luftwaffe came immediately.
> The commanding officer was unsure what to do. Then they decided to put up
> two machine guns and surround the whole village, so nobody could escape, and
> the whole hick town was leveled.
>
> Wolff: Where did that happen?
>
> Barbie: Near Mâcon. It was in the area of Wilhelm Brückner's Feldkomman-
> dantur. Remember, he was the adjutant of Adolf [Hitler].

The conversation in fact has two parts. In the first, the Oradour massacre of June 1944 is admitted as being cruel. But both Wolff and Barbie
distance themselves from the crime. In discussing the deaths of German
comrades near Mâcon, both men show empathy, and here, Barbie even
admits he ordered the reprisal that followed. Still, when they might have

expressed some empathy toward the innocent villagers, Barbie justifies the massacre by pointing to German soldiers murdered by French resistance fighters, and the French reprisal victims are not mentioned even in passing. This tu quoque argument was a common strategy going back to the Trial of the Major War Criminals at Nuremberg. One's own guilt is diminished by pointing to the crimes of the enemy.

Another conversation between Wolff and Barbie shows a similar pattern: Barbie, when discussing attempts to bring him back to Europe for trial, noted:

> All pigs, the Jews. I have never been an ardent antisemite, I guess none of us really were. But after the war I became one! First, the bad treatment in Oberursel camp—the interrogating US officers were all Jewish! Mine had the name Mr. Kuddelwasher, I think the name is telling. And then, they found me again with help of this Jewish woman—as you know, Beate Klarsfeld is not Jewish, she is just married to a Jew—and she came with this Jewish witness who claimed I had personally shot her four children, with seventeen shots. Which was pure nonsense, no gun has seventeen shots.[85]

Barbie does not deny having shot Jewish children. He simply points to the "nonsense" of the charge on its more technical grounds. It was not possible to connect this episode to a concrete date of any Gestapo action in the Lyon area. But the incident might have happened in spring of 1943, after Barbie had taken over the *Judenreferat* of the Gestapo office in Lyon and he is reported at that time to have been hunting down Jews personally in their homes, displaying special cruelty in murdering children before the eyes of their terrified parents.[86]

Barbie also portrayed his crimes as accidental bureaucratic snafus. Barbie discussed with Wolff his April 1944 arrest and deportation of the forty-four children hidden in the farming village of Izieu south of Lyon. All of the children were murdered on arrival in Auschwitz-Birkenau.[87] Izieu was one of the crimes for which Barbie was convicted on the charge of crimes against humanity in 1987. There is little doubt concerning his involvement. Yet with Wolff Barbie obscures the matter by quibbling over numbers. Only the Jews, he said, would prosecute him over a mere forty-four lives. He told Wolff:

> They have accused me on the basis of one single telegram. It could be true, but I simply do not remember. It had to do with a Jewish orphanage. I was accused for having signed the [order], because the man in charge from Eichmann's staff[88] wasn't available, and someone else had brought to my attention that a decision was needed. I think it's plausible. But I can't remember, I can't say for sure. But of course, in the end, the victims are not 40 but 40,000 [*sic*],

and Mengele even gets 4 million on his plate. They don't care about a million, a zero more or less is nothing for them.[89]

Another recurrent pattern in the discussions concerns the duty to obey a superior's order, and the strength necessary for the cruel everyday work of a racial warrior. In 1940 and 1941, Barbie was stationed in the Netherlands under Willy Lages, the SD commander in The Hague. In 1941 the killing of a Dutch Nazi prompted the Germans to seal off the Jewish quarter of Amsterdam. Raids led by Barbie ensued. Some 425 Jews were arrested, mostly young men, and most were sent to Mauthausen and murdered. Barbie also headed the firing squad that killed a German Jewish leader who booby-trapped his business, injuring German policemen. In discussing the reprisal arrests and subsequent killings, Barbie viewed his acts as legitimate counter-insurgency and fell back on the well-worn theme of decency. Yet his comments also insist that he held himself to an ethical standard.

Barbie: And then they were sentenced to death and were to be shot [outside of] Amsterdam. I led the command. This was when I felt really sick, when I saw all the brains splattering. Oh, that was really cruel, to shoot like that … [Heidemann, sympathetic, agrees that executions are different from fighting at the front, and Barbie nods]. You are right, but shooting like this "Ready! Fire!" and then all the splattering, this was awful, not decent [*richtig*]. But we had to do it. It took three weeks, all the combat and the executions.[90]

The concept of loyalty also appears in Barbie's recollections. It was shameful, the former SS men argued, that the Reichsführer himself had escaped judgment by committing suicide. Himmler, they argued, violated the most eternal SS principle, "Our honor is loyalty." Barbie bitterly resented:[91] "They [the superiors] always expected us to be perfect with everything: Espionage, counter-espionage, soldier, civilian—and always retain the highest moral standards! We little folks! Fiercely fighting, until the end if necessary. And we knew how to die!" Worse, SS veterans learned after the war that Himmler had launched secret peace negotiations with the Allies, an unthinkable betrayal in their eyes.[92]

"I can see the point," Barbie told Wolff when considering Himmler's suicide: that one reacts in a distorted way when everything breaks down. But I would have expected him to stand up for us and say, I am the Reichsführer SS, and I will take the responsibility! On the other hand, I guess that would not have served the cause, would it?

Wolff: No, probably not.

Barbie: But his record would have been much different.

Wolff: And our young boys would not have been so disappointed. Of course, the Führer was unable to take the responsibility ... the attempt to murder [him] in 1944 had broken his strength. But Himmler! After doing this all behind our backs, how could he dare to sneak out (and leave us behind)?[93]

Interestingly the former SS officers' outrage is directed against Himmler for burdening them with the tasks of mass killing on the one hand, and then in escaping the responsibility, leaving them to take it. It was, according to this conversation, a dereliction of duty.

CONCLUSION

Wolfgang Bialas argues that "Nazi ethics provided a framework through which Nazi leaders could legitimize mass murder as moral and induce ordinary Germans to actively participate in, or at least acquiesce to, the violence."[94] Racial politics were seen as "a necessary means to avert danger for the *Volksgemeinschaft*." Nazi ethics thus also spared perpetrators the burden of human empathy towards their victims and relieved any doubts.[95]

Two things become apparent in the perpetrator testimonies and private discussions above. The upper echelons of the SS imbued Nazi ethics to the point where they leaned on them years after the war. Apart from the aim of avoiding legal guilt, such perpetrators also avoided pangs of conscience. Bialas has pointed out that, "the good conscience demonstrated by Nazi perpetrators is disturbing." Most of the actual perpetrators and desk murderers insisted that what they had done was correct and necessary—"appropriate in the given situation."[96] Loyalty among comrades transcends the crime and its memory. As Gabriele Taylor writes, "Guilt, unlike shame, is a legal concept."[97] Shame is not linked to the violation of legal norms, and can thus be avoided under the right conditions.

Redefining the morality of killing was perhaps the Nazis' most successful project. Old comrades remained completely free from self-censure. By morally justifying violent mass crimes, they represented themselves as fighting ruthless military men, protecting their cherished values, saving Germany from a perceived Jewish subjugation, or honoring their country's commitments. Moments of critique show the margins of Nazi morality by pointing to the persistence of older values: for example, protecting women, or soldiers. This is especially visible within the concept of "decency" when killing people. The absence of remorse about death or the actual process of killing together with the focus on tangential details reveals a surprising moral dilemma of perpetrators and their decision to leave things unsaid.

In his famous essay on German guilt, Karl Jaspers emphasized that moral guilt consisted of "blindness for the misfortune of others, lack of imagination of the heart, inner indifference toward the witnessed evil."[98] Most Nazi perpetrators did not acknowledge their blindness; they maintained the moral ground on which they stood when they committed their deeds. They dismissed the unbearable facts and avoided sober analysis of their motives. According to Bialas, even those who act immorally must have a clear understanding of what is good and what is evil.[99] This is certainly true when reviewing the material presented here: the men knew they were committing murder, but they insisted that within the Nazi frame of morality it was carried out mostly in a "decent" way. For perpetrators, avoiding a bad conscience in the postwar period was thus crucial, as analysis of their argumentation shows. Their main concern remained whether one of their peers—especially Himmler—had violated this rule by betraying his followers and not taking on the responsibility these crimes required, leaving the blame to the actual perpetrators, in other words, to them.

Kerstin von Lingen is a historian and researcher/lecturer at Heidelberg University where she leads the research project "Transcultural Justice: Legal Flows and the Emergence of International Justice within the East Asian War Crimes Trials, 1946–1954." Her books include *Kesselring's Last Battle: War Crimes Trials and Cold War Politics, 1945–1960* (2009) and *Allen Dulles, the OSS and Nazi War Criminals: The Dynamics of Selective Prosecution* (2013). She has also edited or coedited three volumes on war crimes and memory including *Kriegserfahrung und Nationale Identität in Europa nach 1945. Erinnerung, Säuberungsprozesse und nationales Gedächtnis* (2009).

NOTES

1. Gespräch mit Walther Rauff und Karl Wolff in Santiago, 26./27.6.1979. Evening conversation Heidemann and Wolff, on shootings at Minsk, page 48, Private Archive, Gerd Heidemann, Hamburg. "Also, es war mir speiübel zumute, nicht weil es den Tod betraf, sondern weil diese ganze Handlung so ablief. Es ist nicht vorher, was ich erwartet hätte, ein Todesurteil verlesen worden. 'Sie sind wegen völkerrechtswidrigen Widerstandes zum Tode verurteilt worden, das Urteil wird jetzt vollstreckt.' Nein, nichts. Sie wurden hingebracht und in die Grube geschickt."

2. Martin Cüppers, *Walther Rauff – In Deutschen Diensten: Vom Naziverbrecher zum BND Spion* (Darmstadt, 2013).

3. Background in Tom Bower, *Klaus Barbie: The Butcher of Lyons* (New York, 1984); Peter Hammerschmidt, *Deckname Adler: Klaus Barbie und die westlichen Geheimdienste* (Frankfurt am Main, 2014).

4. Ulrich Kröger, "Die Ahndung von NS-Verbrechen vor westdeutschen Gerichten und ihre Rezeption in der deutschen Öffentlichkeit 1958–1965, unter besonderer Berücksichtigung von *Spiegel, Stern, Zeit, SZ, FAZ, Welt, Bild, Hamburger Abendblatt, NZ* und *Neuem Deutschland*," (Ph.D. diss. Hamburg 1973).

5. In general, Eve Garrand and Geoffrey Scarre, eds., *Moral Philosophy and the Holocaust* (Burlington, VT, 2003).

6. Claudia Koonz, *The Nazi Conscience* (Cambridge, MA, 2003), 1.

7. Raphael Gross, *Anständig geblieben: Nationalsozialistische Moral* (Frankfurt am Main, 2010), 17. Others have addressed the problem in more detail. See Rolf Zimmermann, *Philosophie nach Auschwitz: Eine Neubestimmung* (Hamburg, 2005); Rolf Zimmermann, *Moral als Macht: Eine Philosophie der historischen Erfahrung* (Hamburg, 2008); Herline Pauer-Studer and J. David Vellemann, "Distortions of Normativity," *Ethical Theory and Moral Practice,* 14, no. 3 (2011): 329–56; Werner Konitzer, "Moral oder Moral? Einige Überlegungen zum Thema Moral und Nationalsozialismus," in *Moralität des Bösen: Ethik und nationalsozialistische Verbrechen,* ed. W. Konitzer and R. Gross (Frankfurt am Main, 2009), 97–115.

8. Albert Bandura, "Moral Disengagement in the Perpetration of Inhumanities," *Personality and Social Psychology Review* 3, no. 3 (1999): 194–95.

9. Wolfgang Bialas, "Nazi Ethics: Perpetrators with a Clear Conscience," *Dapim: Studies on the Holocaust* 27, no. 1 (2013): 4.

10. Bialas, "Nazi Ethics," 5.

11. Peter J. Haas, *Morality after Auschwitz: The Radical Challenge of the Nazi Ethic* (Philadelphia, PA, 1987), 124.

12. Bialas, "Nazi Ethics," abstract.

13. Ibid.

14. Ibid., 3.

15. Ibid., 6.

16. Ibid., 7.

17. Ibid., 5.

18. Ibid., 6.

19. Didier Pollefeyt, "The Kafkaesque World of the Holocaust: Paradigmatic Shifts in the Ethical Interpretation of the Nazi Genocide," in *Ethics after the Holocaust: Perspectives, Shifts and Responses,* ed. J. Roth (St. Paul, MN, 1999), 229.

20. Pollefeyt, "Kafkaesque World," 228.

21. Bialas, "Nazi Ethics," 18.

22. Ibid., 18.

23. Ibid., 18.

24. The German text of Himmler's Posen speech is printed in *Vierteljahreshefte für Zeitgeschichte* 1, no. 4 (1953): 357–94, and online at http://www.ifz-muenchen .de/heftarchiv/1953_4_6_eschenburg.pdf. The translation here is from Bialas, "Nazi Ethics," 24.

25. Konrad Kwiet, "Rassenpolitik und Völkermord," in *Enzyklopädie des Nationalsozialismus,* 2nd ed. (Munich, 1998), 64.

26. Bialas, "Nazi Ethics," 9.

27. Ibid., 9.
28. Ibid., 10.
29. Raul Hilberg, *The Destruction of the European Jews* (Chicago, 1961), 343, 555. For Erich von dem Bach Zalewski's account of Himmler and Wolff's visit to Minsk, see an article in *Aufbau*, 23 August 1946, 1–2. Other witness accounts are contained in Case Wolff, 10a Js 39/60, particularly Z-Prot II/vol.2; cited in Magnus Linklater, Isabel Hilton, and Neal Ascherson, *The Fourth Reich* (London, 1984), 331; Martin Gilbert, *The Holocaust: The Jewish Tragedy,* (London, 1987), 190–91.
30. Adelheid L. Rüter-Ehlermann and C. F. Rüter, eds., *Justiz und NS-Verbrechen: Sammlung deutscher Strafurteile wegen nationalsozialistischer Tötungsverbrechen 1945–1999,* (Amsterdam, 1971), v. 20 (12.4.1964–20.3.1965), Case No. 580, Karl Wolff, 380–504, here, 458: letter from Wolff to Ing. Dr. Ganzenmüller, 13 August 1942.
31. Daluege to Wolff, 28 February 1943, cited in Hilberg, *Destruction,* 203.
32. Kerstin von Lingen, *Allen Dulles, the OSS and Nazi War Criminals: The Dynamics of Selective Prosecution* (New York, 2013); Kerstin von Lingen, "Conspiracy of Silence: How the 'Old Boys' of American Intelligence shielded SS-General Karl Wolff from Prosecution," *Holocaust and Genocide Studies* 22, no. 1 (2008): 74–109; Kerstin von Lingen and Michael Salter, "Contrasting Strategies within the War Crimes Trials of Kesselring and Wolff," *Liverpool Law Review,* 26, no. 3 (2005): 225–66.
33. This ambivalence is also underlined by the first biography on Wolff written by Heidemann's colleague, *Der Stern* journalist Jochen von Lang, *Karl Wolff: Der Adjutant* (Hamburg, 1982). While telling his life story, Wolff even lived in von Lang's home for several months.
34. For an overview see Kevin Jon Heller, *The Nuremberg Military Tribunals and the Origins of International Criminal Law* (New York, 2011); Kim C. Priemel and Alexa Stiller, eds., *Reassessing the Nuremberg Military Trials: Transitional Justice, Trial Narratives and Historiography* (New York, 2012).
35. *Trials of War Criminals before the Nuremberg Military Tribunals under Control Council Law No. 10* (hereafter *TWC*), 14 vols. (Washington, DC, 1950–1952), 5: 774–76.
36. *TWC,* vol. 5, 5 June 1947, 2216–18.
37. See Wolff to Musmanno, 10 August 1947, on being deleted from the CROWCASS list, in Norbert Barr Papers, Columbia University, Rare Books and Manuscripts Library, NYCR89-A47, box 7.
38. Richard Breitman and Robert Wolfe, "Case Studies of Genocide," in *US Intelligence and the Nazis,* Richard Breitman, Norman J.W. Goda, Timothy Naftali, and Robert Wolfe (New York, 2005), 73–92, here 86.
39. Breitman and Wolfe, "Case Studies," 86n65. The reference is to a letter from the Allen Dulles Collection, Princeton University, Seely G. Mudd Manuscript Library, Affidavit F. Donald Philips, 11 December 1962.
40. For example, Lutz Niethammer, *Die Mitläuferfabrik: Die Entnazifizierung am Beispiel Bayerns* (Bonn, 1982).
41. Prozessakten Karl Wolff (Hamburg 1948), verdict of 8 November 1949, Bundesarchiv [hereafter BA] Koblenz, Z 42/III 2670. The English version of the text is located in Telford Taylor Papers, Columbia University, Diamond Law School, Signature 5-4-3-38, Judgment re Karl Wolff, 3 June 1949.

42. "Vier Jahre Gefängnis für Wolff. Haftbefehl aufgehoben. Die Anklage konnte keine Belastungszeugen vorführen," *Hamburger Allgemeine,* 7 June 1949; "'Sie gehen mit fleckenlosem Kleide.' SS General Wolff erhielt 4 Jahre Gefängnis," *Die Welt,* 4 June 1949; "Vier Jahre Gefängnis für General Wolff: 'Der Angeklagte verläßt mit fleckenlosem Kleide den Gerichtssaal,'" *Hamburger Freie Presse,* 4 June 1949.

43. Two witnesses claimed at first to have once seen Wolff accompanying Himmler in Auschwitz, but they later revoked this testimony. It was also reported that Robert Mulka, the main defendant in the Auschwitz trial, transferred from Frankfurt to Munich, had testified that Wolff had definitely not accompanied Himmler. See "Wolff begleitete Himmler durchs Vernichtungslager," *Münchner Abendzeitung,* 5 August 1964; "Widersprüchliche Zeugenaussagen im Wolff-Prozess," *Neue Zürcher Zeitung,* 3 September 1964.

44. Unfortunately scholars have not yet analyzed the still-closed papers of Wolff's attorney Rudolf Aschenauer, at the Bundesarchiv/Militärarchiv in Freiburg im Breisgau (BA-MA).

45. Testimony Wolff for Oswald Pohl, 1948, BA Ludwigsburg, B 162/5020.

46. BA Ludwigsburg, B 162/5037: Case 7, 5038: Case 5, testimony Wolff.

47. "Ex-Nazi Aide Denies He Knew Jews' Fate," *New York Times,* 16 July 1964.

48. Markus Riverein, "Das einwandfreie" Leben des Waffen-SS Generals Karl Wolff: Der Münchner Prozess gegen Himmlers Adjutanten 1964," in *NS-Prozesse und deutsche Öffentlichkeit. Besatzungszeit, frühe Bundesrepublik und DDR,* ed. Clemens Vollnhals and Jörg Osterloh (Göttingen, 2012), 334, cites an article in *Süddeutsche Zeitung,* titled "Wolff: Mir wurde speiübel."

49. Riverein, "Das einwandfreie Leben," 329.

50. "Es wird immer deutlicher: Wolff war über Himmlers wichtige Pläne informiert," *Münchner Abendzeitung,* 12 August 1964. See also the newspaper clippings in the Simon Wiesenthal Archiv, Vienna, Akt Karl Wolff (no signature).

51. "Himmler—ein Meister der Tarnung. Wolff durch weitere Dokumente belastet. Kinderraub in Polen geplant," *Süddeutsche Zeitung,* 14 August 1964.

52. Cited in Riverein, "Das einwandfreie Leben," 324.

53. "Schwarzer Tag für SS-Wolff," *Münchner Abendzeitung,* 31 July 1964.

54. "Großer Kreis wußte von Massentötungen," *Münchner Abendzeitung,* 3 September 1964. Krannhals deposited his collection of private papers, which include his preparations for various expert testimonies, in the Bundesarchiv Koblenz, where they are accessible under BA Koblenz, ZFg 122; the Wolff trial is found in the number sequel 9, 13, 14, 46, 64–68.

55. "Zeuge entlastet Karl Wolff," *Die Welt,* 21 July 1964.

56. "Der Prozess gegen SS-General Wolff: Ein Entlastungszeuge," *Neue Zürcher Zeitung,* 23 July 1964.

57. "Wolff stand zwischen Pflicht und Neigung," *Münchner Merkur,* 21 July 1964; "Witness Says Few Knew of Jews' Fate," *New York Times,* 21 July 1964.

58. "Mildernde Umstände?" *Münchner Abendzeitung,* 24 July 1964.

59. The topic was also raised here about the alleged attempt by Wolff's second wife Ingeborg to blackmail her brother-in-law Albrecht von Bernsdorff, who later

died in a concentration camp. Wolff was said to have helped with the blackmail, but this was neither proved nor disproved in court.

60. "Wolff Prozess geht zu Ende. Zeuge: er war ein gläubig-naiver Anhänger," *Münchner Abendzeitung*, 9 September 1964.

61. "Die Ausrottung der Warschauer Juden: Zeugenaussage Reich-Ranizkis im Wolff-Prozess," *Neue Zürcher Zeitung*, 28 August 1964.

62. US Holocaust Memorial Museum, DD 247, W 64, no. 5, 1990, report by Tuvia Friedmann, "Himmler's deputy SS-General Karl Wolff arrested!" p. 10.

63. See the chapter by Lawrence Douglas in this volume.

64. "Urteil im Wolff-Prozess," *Neue Zürcher Zeitung*, 2 October 1964.

65. "Verurteilt wegen Beihilfe zu einer Tat, die ohne Beispiel ist," *Münchner Abendzeitung*, 1 October 1964.

66. Ibid.

67. "Himmler nannte ihn 'Mein Wölffchen,'" *Der Spiegel*, 22 July 1964. Although this quote is taken from an article that was published at the trial's beginning, this aspect of Wolff's character became more obvious during the course of the trial, which justifies that the quote be used here.

68. Ulrike Marie Meinhof, "Das 'einwandfreie Leben' des Waffen-SS-Generals Karl Wolff," in *Blätter für deutsche und internationale Politik* 9 (1964): 909. "Das Urteil im Karl-Wolff-Prozess … ist der Kompromiss, den ein bundesdeutsches Gericht zwischen seinen eigenen Rechtsnormen und dem Nationalsozialismus geschlossen hat. … Es muss nunmehr festgestellt werden, … dass der Angeklagte entlastet wurde, indem man das Regime bagatellisiert hat."

69. Martin Cüppers and Peter Hammerschmidt also drew on these transcripts for their work on Rauff and Barbie. I am indebted to Peter Hammerschmidt for making the Barbie transcripts available to me, which proved to be an interesting addition to the Wolff and Rauff transcripts that I had already seen. Within the Stasi Archives Berlin [Bundesbeauftragte für die Unterlagen des Staatssicherheitsdienstes der ehemaligen Deutschen Demokratischen Republik, hereafter BStU] there is a second copy available.

70. Gross, *Anständig geblieben*, 91.

71. Bialas, "Nazi Ethics," 10.

72. Ibid., 11.

73. Ibid., 11.

74. The following translations are mine, and they are not always literal, especially as the old men used colloquial language, and by translating, sometimes words were inserted to make the earlier context clearer. If special expressions are used, the German original is reported in the footnote.

75. Gespräch mit Walther Rauff und Karl Wolff in Santiago, 26./27.6.1979. Evening conversation Heidemann and Wolff, on shootings at Minsk. Pagination 43–53, Private Archive, Gerd Heidemann.

76. Martin Cüppers, *Wegbereiter der Shoah: Die Waffen-SS, der Kommandostab Reichsführer-SS und die Judenvernichtung 1939–1945* (Darmstadt, 2005), 183. In his report on the shootings Cüppers analyzes the radicalization effect Himmler's visit had on the troops.

77. Wolff: "Da nun niemand da war, bin ich vorgegangen die paar Schritte, weil ich ja nicht wusste, übergibt er sich, wird ihm schlecht, und dann fällt er in die Grube und liegt oben auf den Juden drauf! Gegönnt hätte ich es ihm, haha." Pag. 46, Private Archive, Gerd Heidemann.

78. Wolff: "Ich weiß nicht ob ich es gesagt habe oder der Bradfisch zu mir. Jedenfalls ist das Wort gefallen ,Es geschieht ihm ganz recht, er soll ruhig sehen, was er seinen Leuten zumutet!' ich glaube, dass ich das gesagt habe." Pag. 46, Private Archive, Gerd Heidemann.

79. Wolff: "Also, es war mir speiübel zumute, nicht weil es den Tod betraf, sondern weil diese ganze Handlung so ablief. Es ist nicht vorher, was ich erwartet hätte, ein Todesurteil verlesen worden, 'Sie sind wegen völkerrechtswidrigen Widerstandes zum Tode verurteilt, das Urteil wird jetzt vollstreckt.' Nein nichts, sie wurden hingebracht und in die Grube geschickt." Pag. 48, Private Archive, Gerd Heidemann.

80. See for Wolff's ethics Lingen, *Allen Dulles,* 82; also Riverein, "Einwandfreies Leben," 332, cites a statement Wolff made in this regard during his Munich trial in 1964.

81. Wolff: "Wir waren alle so aufgewühlt und innerlich so erschüttert und verbiestert und haben gesagt: Musste das denn sein? Das konnte uns dieser Unmensch doch ersparen, nachdem wir ihm gesagt hatten, dass wir den Tod in allen Lebensarten kennengelernt hatten. Das konnte er uns doch ersparen. Wir hatten ihn gebeten, anständig, korrekt, nicht unflätig oder fordernd oder maulend oder meuternd. Musste das sein? Verkrampft und verbittert ging man zum Wagen und fragte sich: ist das jetzt Aufgabe des Ritterordens?" Pag. 52–53, Privae Archive, Gerd Heidemann.

82. Gespräch mit Klaus Altmann/Barbie (und Heidemann), La Paz, Bolivien, 15.8.1979, Pag. 20, BStU Sig 000262 and Private Archive Gerd Heidemann. Wolff: Ich habe auch nichts weiter gemacht, als eine telefonische Bitte um Behebung einer Transportstockung in Polen an den Staatssekretär im Verkehrsministerium in Berlin, Dr. Ganzenmüller, durchzugeben. Kein Ausländer hat mich angeklagt. Ich habe die Entnazifizierung mit einer persönlichen Ehrenerklärung im roten Hamburg-Bergedorf durchgestanden. Aber hinterher haben sie behauptet, ich müsste davon (Judenvernichtung) gewusst haben, da ich ja das Vertrauen von Hitler, Himmler und Mussolini gehabt hätte.
Altmann: Ich bin in Frankreich ja auch zum Tode verurteilt worden. Die Prozesse sind in Bausch und Bogen durchgeführt worden, nach der lex Oradour. Sie kennen die Geschichte mit Oradour?
Wolff: Ja, wo dieser Battaillons Kommandeur von uns ermordet worden war und dann die Soldaten …
Altmann: Ja, dann kamen die Soldaten! Das passiert. Ich meine, das ist wahr.
Wolff: Ja, das ist leider Gottes wahr.
Altmann: Ich hatte ungefähr die gleiche Schweinerei. Das war in Frankreich, nicht im Osten. Da haben sie eine Kompanie von unserem Landsturm ermordet, das waren vierzigjährige brave Leute
Wolff: Die nur Wachdienst geschoben haben.

Altmann: Ja, Gefangene bewachen, usw. Die waren mit einem Wagen unter-
wegs, um Flugzeugersatzteile abzuholen und sind der Maquis in die Hände
gefallen. Sie sind grausam ermordet worden. Man hat ihnen die Augen ausge-
stochen, die Arme gebrochen und hat sie nach Dienstgrad hingelegt.
Wolff: Da kann man die Truppe nicht mehr ruhig halten.
Altmann: Das habe ich gemeldet, und dann kam die Luftwaffe da an. Der Offi-
zier wusste gar nicht mehr, was er da machen sollte. Dann haben sie zwei Ma-
schinen geholt, und wir haben das ganze Nest umstellt, damit keiner rauskam,
und das ganze Kaff ist da restlos von oben bis unten zerstört worden.
Wolff: In welcher Gegend war das?
Altmann: Das war in der Gegend von Macon. Da war der Wilhelm Brückner
Feldkommandant, der Adjutant von Adolf.

83. Barbie was tried in absentia in France in 1952 and 1954, both times sentenced
to death.
84. Concerning the German reprisal destruction of the town Oradour-sur-Glane
on 10 June 1944. The French *Lex Oradour* in 1948 allowed convictions of individuals for war crimes if they had belonged to units involved in specific crimes,
whether or not personal responsibility could be proved. See Claudia Moisel,
*Frankreich und die deutschen Kriegsverbrecher: Politik und Praxis der Strafverfolgung nach
1945* (Göttingen, 2004), 148–58.
85. Gespräch mit Klaus Altmann (und Heidemann), La Paz, Bolivien, 15.8.1979, S.
25, BStU Sig. 000295. Altmann (über die Juden, die seine Auslieferungen bean-
tragt hätten): Schweine sind das. Ich war nie ein fanatischer Antisemit in dem
Sinne, wir alle nicht, aber nach dem Kriege bin ich es geworden. Nach dem
Kriege! Erst mal die Behandlung in Oberursel—das waren ja nur Juden. Mein
Vernehmer hiess Mr. Kuddelwasher, mehr brauche ich Ihnen nicht zu sagen.
Und dann kamen sie das zweite Mal wieder mit einer Jüdin, die Klarsfeld ist ja
keine Jüdin, die ist nur mit einem Juden verheiratet. Die behauptete dann, ich
hätte ihre vier Kinder mit 17 Schuss getötet. So ein Quatsch, das wurde ihr vor
Gericht auch nachgewiesen, keine Pistole hat 17 Schuss."
86. Bower, *Barbie,* gives several examples.
87. Serge Klarsfeld, *The Children of Izieu: A Human Tragedy* (London, 1985).
88. Probably Aloïs Brunner.
89. Gespräch mit Klaus Barbie/Altmann (und Heidemann), La Paz, Bolivia,
15.8.1979, Pag. 94, BStU Sig. 000364. Altmann: "Was man mir vorwirft, in
Nürnberg, ist ein Fernschreiben. Das kann absolut möglich sein, ich weiß es
nicht. Es betrifft die Auflösung eines jüdischen Kinderheims. Ich soll es unter-
schrieben haben, weil der zuständige Mann von Eichmann nicht da war und
der andere hat mir eine Meldung gegeben, und ich habe das weitergegeben.
Das ist möglich. Ich weiß es aber nicht, kann es nicht sagen. Aber natürlich
macht man da aus vierzig 40.000, und bei Mengele sind es vier Millionen. Es
kommt ja auf eine Million nicht an, eine Null ist ja nichts."
90. Gespräch mit Klaus Barbie/Altmann (und Heidemann), La Paz, Bolivia,
15.8.1979, Pag. 73–74, BStU Sig. 000343 and 344. Altmann (über Erschießun-

gen von Aufständischen in Amsterdam 1941): "Und dann wurden die offiziell zum Tode verurteilt und wurden in der Nähe von Amsterdam erschossen. Ich hatte das Kommando. Und da ist mir schlecht geworden, als ich die ganzen Gehirne wegspritzen sah. … Ja, das war schlecht, so schießen, ja." [Heidemann: Im Kampf ist es etwas anderes, da ist man aufgeregt oder in Euphorie.] Altmann: Ja, aber so: 'Legt an—Feuer!' Und dann spritzt der ganze Laden da weg, das ist nicht das Richtige. Aber wir mussten das machen. Drei Wochen hat dieses Unternehmen gedauert."

91. Gespräch mit Klaus Altmann (und Heidemann), La Paz, Bolivien, 17.8.1979, S. 228 (BStU 000498).
    Altmann: "Aber von uns wurde ja wirklich alles verlangt: Spionage, Gegenspionage, Soldat, Zivilist—mit allerhöchster Moral! Von uns kleinen Leuten! Und eisern kämpfen und bis zum letzten Mann. Und wir sind gestorben!"

92. Richard Breitman, "A Deal with the Nazi Dictatorship? Himmler's Alleged Peace Emissaries in Autumn 1943," *Journal of Contemporary History* 30, no. 3 (1995): 411–30.

93. Gespräch mit Klaus Barbie/Altmann (und Heidemann), La Paz, Bolivia, 15.8.1979, Pag. 18, BStU Sig. 000260. Altmann: über Himmler: Ich verstehe, dass man falsch reagiert, wenn einem nun alles kaputt geht. Ich hätte von ihm erwartet, er stellt sich hin und sagt 'Ich bin der Reichsführer-SS und nehme alle Verantwortung auf mich!' Obwohl das auch nichts genützt hätte, nicht?
    Wolff: Nein, aber…
    Altmann: Er wäre in die Geschichte anders eingegangen
    Wolff: Und unsere Jugend hätte nicht diese Bitternis gehabt. Denn dass der Führer nach dem Attentat nicht mehr konnte, weil ihn das seelisch gebrochen hat, ist eine andere Sache. Aber er [Himmler]—wenn er das hinter unserem Rücken macht—kann sich nicht einfach davon stehlen!

94. Bialas, "Nazi Ethics," 9.

95. Bialas, "Nazi Ethics," 3.

96. Bialas, "Nazi Ethics," 3.

97. Gabriele Taylor, *Pride, Shame and Guilt: Emotions of Self-Assessment* (New York, 1985), esp. chapter "Guilt and Remorse," 85–107, here 85.

98. Karl Jaspers, *Die Schuldfrage* (Munich, 1996), 47; English edition: *The Question of German Guilt* (New York, 2000).

99. Bialas, "Nazi Ethics," 8.

SELECT BIBLIOGRAPHY

Bandura, Albert. "Moral Disengagement in the Perpetration of Inhumanities." *Personality and Social Psychology Review,* 3, no. 3 (1999): 194–95.

Bialas, Wolfgang. "Nazi Ethics: Perpetrators with a Clear Conscience." *Dapim: Studies on the Holocaust* 27, no.1 (2013): 3–25.

Bower, Tom. *Klaus Barbie: The Butcher of Lyons.* New York: Pantheon, 1984.

Breitman, Richard, Norman J.W. Goda, Timothy Naftali, and Robert Wolfe. *US Intelligence and the Nazis.* New York: Cambridge University Press, 2005.

Browning, Christopher. *Ordinary Men: Reserve Police Battalion 101 and the Final Solution in Poland.* New York: Harper Collins, 1992.

Cüppers, Martin. *Wegbereiter der Shoah: Die Waffen-SS, der Kommandostab Reichsführer-SS und die Judenvernichtung 1939–1945.* Darmstadt: WBG, 2005.

———. *Walther Rauff – In Deutschen Diensten: Vom Naziverbrecher zum BND Spion.* Darmstadt: WBG, 2013.

Garrand, Eve, and Geoffrey Scarre, eds. *Moral Philosophy and the Holocaust.* Burlington, VT: Ashgate, 2003.

Gilbert, Martin. *The Holocaust: The Jewish Tragedy.* London: Fontana, 1987.

Gross, Raphael. *Anständig geblieben: Nationalsozialistische Moral.* Frankfurt am Main: Fischer Verlag, 2010.

Haas, Peter J. *Morality after Auschwitz: The Radical Challenge of the Nazi Ethic.* Philadelphia, PA: Fortress, 1987.

Hammerschmidt, Peter. *Deckname Adler: Klaus Barbie und die westlichen Geheimdienste.* Frankfurt am Main: Fischer Verlag, 2014.

Heller, Kevin Jon. *The Nuremberg Military Tribunals and the Origins of International Criminal Law.* New York: Oxford University Press, 2011.

Hilberg, Raul. *The Destruction of the European Jews.* Chicago: Aubrey Durkin, 1961.

Jaspers, Karl. *Die Schuldfrage.* Munich: Piper Verlag, 1996.

Klarsfeld, Serge. *The Children of Izieu: A Human Tragedy.* London: Harry N. Abrams, 1985.

Konitzer, Werner, and Raphael Gross, eds. *Die Moralität des Bösen: Ethik und nationalsozialistische Verbrechen.* Frankfurt am Main: Campus Verlag, 2009.

Konitzer, Werner. "Moral oder 'Moral'? Einige Überlegungen zum Thema Moral und Nationalsozialismus," in *Moralität des Bösen,* ed. W. Konitzer and R. Gross, 97–115. Frankfurt am Main: Campus Verlag, 2009.

Koonz, Claudia. *The Nazi Conscience.* Cambridge, MA: Harvard University Press, 2003.

Kröger, Ulrich. "Die Ahndung von NS-Verbrechen vor westdeutschen Gerichten und ihre Rezeption in der deutschen Öffentlichkeit 1958-1965, unter besonderer Berücksichtigung von *Spiegel, Stern, Zeit, SZ, FAZ, Welt, Bild, Hamburger Abendblatt, NZ* und *Neuem Deutschland,*" Ph.D. diss. Hamburg 1973.

Kwiet, Konrad. "Rassenpolitik und Völkermord," in *Enzyklopädie des Nationalsozialismus,* 2nd ed. Munich: DTV, 1998.

Lang, Jochen von. *Karl Wolff: Der Adjutant.* Hamburg: Ullstein Verlag, 1982.

Lingen, Kerstin von. "Conspiracy of Silence: How the 'Old Boys' of American Intelligence Shielded SS-General Karl Wolff from Prosecution." *Holocaust and Genocide Studies* 22, no. 1 (2008): 74–109.

———. *Allen Dulles, the OSS and Nazi War Criminals: The Dynamics of Selective Prosecution.* New York: Cambridge University Press, 2013.

Lingen, Kerstin von, and Michael Salter. "Contrasting Strategies within the War Crimes Trials of Kesselring and Wolff." *Liverpool Law Review,* 26, no. 3 (2005): 225–66.

Linklater, Magnus, Isabel Hilton, and Neal Ascherson, eds. *The Fourth Reich.* London: Hodder and Stoughton, 1984.

Meinhof, Ulrike Marie. "Das 'einwandfreie Leben' des Waffen-SS-Generals Karl Wolff." *Blätter für deutsche und internationale Politik* 9 (1964): 906–10.

Niethammer, Lutz. *Die Mitläuferfabrik: Die Entnazifizierung am Beispiel Bayerns.* Bonn: Dietz, 1982.

Pauer-Studer, Herlinde, and J. David Vellemann. "Distortions of Normativity." *Ethical Theory and Moral Practice* 14, no. 3 (2011): 329–56.

Pollefeyt, Didier. "The Kafkaesque World of the Holocaust: Paradigmatic Shifts in the Ethical Interpretation of the Nazi Genocide." In *Ethics after the Holocaust: Perspectives, Shifts and Responses,* edited by J. Roth, 210–42. St. Paul, MN: Paragon House, 1999.

Priemel, Kim C., and Alexa Stiller, eds. *Reassessing the Nuremberg Military Trials: Transitional Justice, Trial Narratives and Historiography.* New York: Berghahn, 2012.

Riverein, Markus. "'Das einwandfreie' Leben des Waffen-SS Generals Karl Wolff: Der Münchner Prozess gegen Himmlers Adjutanten 1964." In *NS-Prozesse und deutsche Öffentlichkeit. Besatzungszeit, frühe Bundesrepublik und DDR,* ed. Clemens Vollnhals and Jörg Osterloh, 323–48. Göttingen: Vandenhoeck & Ruprecht, 2012.

Rüter-Ehlermann, Adelheid L., and C. F. Rüter, eds. *Justiz und NS-Verbrechen: Sammlung deutscher Strafurteile wegen nationalsozialistischer Tötungsverbrechen 1945–1999,* Amsterdam: Amsterdam University Press, 1971.

Waller, James E. *Becoming Evil: How Ordinary People Commit Genocide and Mass Killing.* New York: Oxford University Press, 2007.

Zimmermann, Rolf *Philosophie nach Auschwitz: Eine Neubestimmung.* Hamburg: Rowohlt, 2005.

——. *Moral als Macht: Eine Philosophie der historischen Erfahrung.* Hamburg: Rowohlt, 2008.

Part III

*Approaches to Justice
in the Killing Fields*

Chapter 5

The "Second Wave" of Soviet Justice
The 1960s War Crimes Trials

Alexander V. Prusin

The 1964 Soviet film *Gosudarstvennyi prestupnik* (State Criminal) opens with a scene from a war crimes trial. The dock is empty and witness Nina Semenova tells the court that the defendant, a German named Berg, "is hiding somewhere in the West." Semenova lost her sight during the war. Choked with emotions, she recalls how Berg and his native accomplices indiscriminately murdered old men, women, and children. The court is packed with people of different ages. They are visibly shaken by Semenova's testimony. In the name of the victims, Semenova pledges that the Soviet people will "never forgive nor forget" Nazi crimes. She urges Soviet authorities to search for Berg's most vicious native accomplice still at large, one Zolotitskii. After a long search the KGB (Komitet gosudarstvennoy bezopasnosti or Committee for State Security) arrests Zolotitskii, who for two decades had lived under assumed name.[1]

Released in November 1964, the film echoed the "second wave" of war crimes trials that took place in several Soviet cities in the 1960s and constituted a particular chapter in the history of Soviet prosecution of war crimes. The first stage of Soviet postwar justice began during the war itself and lasted until the early 1950s. Soviet courts convicted approximately 31,000 German military personnel and as many as 400,000 Soviet citizens.[2] Then the drive to punish war criminals and collaborators lost momentum, as it did elsewhere in Europe. Soviet courts thereafter treated all German culprits, including the notorious chief organizer of the Einsatzgruppen Bruno Streckenbach, as prisoners of war. In 1953, the "Extraordinary Commission for the Investigation of German-Fascist Crimes," which had been created during the war to investigate Nazi atrocities, was dissolved.[3] On 17 September 1955, the Soviet government declared general amnesty, and the majority of foreign nationals and Soviet citizens who had served in the German army, police, and special units were released. The amnesty did not apply to "perpetrators" (*karateli*), who directly took part in punitive expeditions, murder, and torture of Soviet citizens.[4] A few days later, the Presidium of the Supreme Council paroled all German prisoners; 749 individuals sentenced for war crimes were repatriated to East and West Germany.[5]

In the late 1950s, however, the Soviet government initiated a series of war crime trials that lasted almost a decade. With a few exceptions, all defendants were Soviet citizens of different nationalities who had collaborated with the Axis powers.[6] Some had already been tried in the 1940s and 1950s as "accomplices" (*posobniki*), but after a more thorough investigation revealed new facts about their criminal activities, they were put on trial again, this time as "perpetrators."[7] All in all, approximately 130 defendants were sentenced to death or long prison terms; some were tried in groups in accordance with their membership in the German-sponsored collaborationist units. Several trials became media events (see the incomplete list below)— they were conducted openly, reported by the local and all Union press, and broadcast on the radio. A few trials were filmed and some of these films were shown in public cinemas.[8]

If looked at through the prism of the Stalinist "show" trials, where law was subordinated to political expediency and the question of individual guilt was irrelevant, such publicity casts grave doubts on the methods of Soviet justice. Perhaps for this reason, in contrast to several excellent studies on the wartime and immediate postwar trials,[9] the "second wave" has barely received the attention of Western scholarship.[10]

It is my contention, however, that although Soviet justice was governed by political expediency, the 1960s trials exposed new legal practices. Owing to Nikita Khrushchev's partial de-Stalinization campaign, the KGB investigations were more comprehensive and the Soviet courts used more conventional legal standards, comparable to those in Western courts. In this context, I seek to answer three related questions. First, what was the ideological and political framework of the "second wave"? To put it differently, since all political trials (including those in democratic societies) are rooted in both legal and political agendas, how did the 1960s trials relate to Soviet internal and external policies? Second, how reliable was evidence, especially in comparison to the wartime and immediate postwar trials? Finally, given

Table 5.1 Soviet War Crimes Trials of the 1960s

Year	Site of the Trial	Defendants
March 1959	Krasnodar	7 members of the German Secret Field Police (GFP)
July 1959	Rostov	5 members of the auxiliary police
February 1960	Lugansk	Policeman (Vasilii Podtynnyi) in Krasnodon[a]
January 1961	Tartu	3 (two were tried in absentia) concentration camp functionaries
March 1961	Riga	3 (?) concentration camp guards
October 1961	Minsk	13 members of the Dirlewanger battalion[b]
March 1962	Kyiv	12 Trawniki guards[c]
July 1962	Krasnodar	9 auxiliaries of the German Security Police in Radom (Poland)
October 1963	Krasnodar	9 members of the Sonderkommando 10a
June 1965	Krasnodar	6 Trawniki guards
October 1965	Riga	6 members of the Latvian police and collaborationist administration (3 were tried in absentia)
December 1965	Lugansk	Policeman (Ivan Mel'nikov) in Krasnodon
April 1966	Vitebsk	5 members of the GFP
February 1966	Mineral'nye Vody	6 members of the Sonderkommando 10a
February–March 1966	Luga	Auxiliary (Vasilii Dolin) of the German Security Police
December 1966	Lviv	6 Trawniki guards
November 1967	Gomel'	10 members of the GFP
December 1967	Krasnodar	13 members of the "Caucasian company" (an auxiliary unit of the Einsatzgruppe D)
January–February 1968	Elista	4 members of the Kalmyk Cavalry Corps[d]
December (?) 1970	Leningrad	Five members of the GFP

a. Vasilii Podtynnyi and Ivan Mel'nikov (tried in Lugansk) participated in tortures and executions of the members of the "Young Guard" — the Krasnodon youth organization, which became one of the most celebrated symbols of Soviet heroism and suffering during the war.

b. Made up of German poachers, convicted criminals, concentration camp inmates, and native collaborators, the unit gained a particular notoriety for atrocities in Belorussia and Poland.

c. Soviet POWs recruited by the Germans and trained in the Trawniki camp in Poland. All in all, about 5,000 Trawniki guards took active part in the genocide of Jews. The investigators and the courts used the term vakhmans—the Russified form of the German *Wachmann* or *Wachmänner*.

d. A mobile collaborationist unit formed by the Germans in Kalmykia in 1942.

the background of ambivalent Soviet attitudes toward the "Jewish question," how was the Holocaust treated in the courtroom?

IDEOLOGICAL AND LEGAL CONTEXT

A major factor that seems to have spurred the "second wave" was the atmosphere of augmented international tension that permeated East-West
relations since the mid-1950s. The rise of West Germany as a major European power caused grave concern in the Kremlin. Whether by coincidence
or design, exactly ten years after the capitulation of the Third Reich—on 9
May 1955—West Germany formally joined NATO, and in November of the
same year the West German armed forces, the Bundeswehr, were called into
being. A few days later, the Soviet government responded by announcing the
creation of the Warsaw Pact, a defensive alliance among the East European
states minus Yugoslavia, and Moscow issued several declarations to Bonn
regarding the militarization of West Germany. Although in September 1955
the USSR and West Germany established diplomatic relations, affairs between the two states remained strained, especially since the creation of the
Bundeswehr entailed the integration of some former Wehrmacht officers
into its command structure and NATO forces.[11] For example, in 1957 Adolf
Hitler's one-time army chief of staff, Adolf Heusinger, became the inspector-
general of the Bundeswehr, and in 1961 he was appointed the chairman of
the NATO Military Committee.

Nor were former Wehrmacht officers the only problem. From 1958 to
1965 the East German judiciary published lists of hundreds of former Nazi
functionaries who had taken positions in the West German civil service.[12]
Similarly, the Polish press reported that about six hundred former Nazi
judges were employed in the West German judicial system, while many
other former Nazi functionaries occupied prominent posts in the state apparatus, economy, and industry. Thus Hans Globke, who had participated
in the formulation of Nazi anti-Jewish legislation and served as an expert
on the "Jewish question" in the Ministry of Interior during the Nazi period,
joined the Federal Chancellor's Office under Konrad Adenauer in 1953 as
a state secretary and became one of Adenauer's closest advisers.[13] In April
1960, a press conference in Moscow accused Adenauer's minister for refugee affairs, Theodor Oberländer, of war crimes. In his book titled *Unmask-
ing,* a prominent Soviet essayist Vladimir Beliayev alleged that in July 1941,
under Oberländer's supervision, a Ukrainian nationalist battalion took part
in the murder of the Polish intelligentsia in Lviv.[14]

The mounting crisis over the four-power status of Berlin after 1958 generated an increasingly belligerent wave of Soviet propaganda. It accentuated how West German courts, based on the restrictive German homicide statute, meted out comparatively mild sentences or acquitted Nazi war criminals entirely, and how entire categories of war criminals such as judges and industrialists were spared prosecution completely. It stands to reason that the Soviet government also felt it necessary to react to the renewed prosecution of Nazi criminals in West Germany. In July–August 1958, the trial of ten Einsatzkommando members in Ulm became a landmark event that centered on the mass murder of Jews in the USSR. The trial was a media affair, especially as it revealed that many perpetrators smoothly integrated themselves into West German society and lived normal lives. Consequently, later in the year, the West German Ministry of Justice established the Central Office for Investigations of Nazi crimes in Ludwigsburg.

These events, in turn, facilitated the debate over the statute of limitations for wartime murders and the reluctance of the West German government to extend the twenty-year statute of limitations on murder for Nazi crimes engendered particularly withering criticism from Moscow.[15] On 14 December 1964, the Soviet government issued a declaration condemning West Germany for violating broader international principles regarding war crimes established by the St. James Declaration (1942) and the Moscow Declaration (1943), which recognized no time limits for punishment.[16] Soviet jurists, including the attorney-general of the USSR Roman Rudenko, the chief Soviet prosecutor at the Trial of the Major War Criminals at Nuremberg in 1945, insisted that international legal norms trumped national laws.[17] On 17 January 1965 the Soviet government issued a note to Bonn, stressing that the USSR was committed to prosecuting Nazi criminals in accordance with international principles, and in April, the Soviets reminded the governments of the United States, Great Britain, and France that they "were also responsible for the eradication of German militarism and Nazism and the punishment of Nazi criminals, residing on the territory of the Federal Republic of Germany."[18]

On 4 March 1965, the Presidium of the Supreme Council of the USSR signed a decree "[o]f the punishment of individuals, guilty of crimes against humanity and war crimes, regardless of the time of the commission of crimes." It stated that the Soviet Union suffered the heaviest losses during the war and could not tolerate "fascist barbarians" living unpunished. In accordance with the principles of international law, the Soviet Union, therefore, would prosecute Nazi criminals guilty of war crimes and the gravest atrocities against peace and humanity, regardless of the time elapsed since their commission.[19] On 11 March 1969, the Presidium of the Supreme Council ratified the United Nations' "Convention of the Non-Applicability of Statutory Limitations to War Crimes and Crimes against Humanity."[20]

Accordingly, Soviet propaganda stressed the Soviet Union's determination to prosecute war criminals in contrast to the apparent immunity enjoyed by former Nazis in the West. With the launching of the "second wave" of trials, press reports consistently named German perpetrators living in West Germany and who were employed there as civil servants. For example, in June 1965, during the trial of six Trawniki camp guards in Krasnodar, *Pravda* reported that alongside the "traitors in the dock invisibly sit their masters—Gustav Wilhaus, Franz Wartzok, Fritz Gebauer, Richard Rokita, Gustav Wirt, Johann Schwartz, Franz Göring, Gustav Wagner, and other war criminals who [have] built nests under the patronage of Bonn. Inevitably, these [German] criminals would face retribution."[21] Before the trial of six Latvian collaborators in Riga in October 1965, the Soviet authorities requested the extradition of Boļeslavs Maikovskis, Albert Eichelis, and Harald Puntulis (they were tried in absentia), who lived in the United States, West Germany, and Canada respectively. In its verdict, the court stressed that the former chief of the German Security Police in Daugavpils Günther Tabbert, who supervised the activities of the defendants, was living undisturbed in Düsseldorf.[22] Similarly, a press release on the trial in Mineral'nye Vody in February 1966 named several members of Einsatzgruppe D such as the former SS-Sturmbannführer Friedrich Nägele, now a senior official in the West German police in Stuttgart.[23] The indictment in Gomel' included the name of the commander of the 221st Security Division, Lieutenant General Hubert Lendle, under whose command collaborationist police operated.[24]

In October 1963, Leon Mazrukho filmed the trial in Krasnodar of nine former members of the Sonderkommando 10a of Einsatzgruppe D, which operated on the eastern coast of the Black Sea and west of the Caucasus. Entitled *Vo imia zhyvykh* (In the Name of the Living), the film praised the Soviet Union's adherence to its international declarations twenty years after the first Krasnodar trial in July 1943 and emphasized that Nazi criminals in the West remained immune from prosecution.[25] Similarly, a chapter in the documentary film *Obyknovennyi fashizm* (Ordinary Fascism) by prominent Soviet director Mikhail Romm portrayed West Germany as a safe haven for former Nazis and the cradle of neo-Nazism.[26] In December 1967, the Soviet government accused Bonn of tolerating the rise of neo-fascism, headed by Nazi criminals. Responding to rumors that Martin Bormann was alive in Brazil, an article in *Izvestiia* insinuated that the West German government demanded his extradition only because it wanted to protect him.[27]

For external consumption, the Soviet propaganda campaign related to the "second wave" of trials aimed at two interconnected objectives: to portray the Soviet Union as the only true adherent to the principles of international law established during and after World War II and to prove that Soviet courts dispensed justice in the name of all humanity. At the same time, after Khrushchev's exposure of Stalin's crimes in the 20th Congress of the Communist Party in February 1956, the "second wave" served an important function in the cult of the Great Patriotic War, which was the name of World War II in the USSR and was hailed as the second founding myth, after the October Revolution, of the first socialist society. In this context, the patriotic education of the masses was considered of paramount importance. War memories acquired a sacral form and museums of military glory, meetings of youngsters with war veterans, and public manifestations were all to remind the world that humankind was saved by the heroism and untold suffering of the Soviet people. On 9 May 1965, Victory Day again became an official day off of work (it had been a day off from 1945 to 1948), and numerous books, articles, and war films aimed at promoting Soviet patriotism.[28]

On the legal side, matters were more complicated. Although criminal activities described in Soviet courts in the 1960s essentially constituted the Nuremberg definitions of war crimes and crimes against humanity, the Soviet criminal codes themselves did not have specific articles related to these categories of crimes. Instead, all defendants in war crimes trials were charged with high treason (*izmena Rodinie*) under Article 58 of the 1926 Criminal Code. Amended several times, the article defined high treason as the most grievous political crime, encompassing a wide range of offenses from anti-state propaganda to collaboration with the enemy and flight abroad. It was punishable by the death penalty or lengthy prison terms.[29] Still, the Soviet leadership considered the existing laws inadequate in wartime and on 19 April 1943 the Presidium of Supreme Soviet signed a special decree № 39, "Of the Punishment Measures against the German-Fascist Villains, Spies, the Traitors of the Motherland, and Their Accomplices Guilty of Murder and Mistreatment of the Soviet Civilian Population and POWs." It stipulated death by hanging for perpetrators and long prison terms for accomplices, providing a lynch-format for the adjudication of war crimes trials.[30]

With Khrushchev's drive to re-introduce "socialist legality" after Stalin, the application of the April 1943 decree was discontinued. But political crimes were still adjudicated under Article 58 (since 1960 under Article 64) of the RSFSR Criminal Code and its equivalent of the Union's individual republics. For example in Ukraine, high treason was adjudicated under Article 56, Part 1 of the Criminal Code.[31] In December 1958 the Supreme

Soviet of the USSR introduced the Fundamental Principles of Criminal Legislation, which abolished some of the worst Stalinist legal practices. Particularly, Article 6 of the Fundamental Principles stipulated that *corpus delicti* and "punishment were to be determined by the law in force at the time the act was committed." Thus, the non-retroactivity of law, which under Stalin had been rejected as a "bourgeois notion," ostensibly became a key concept of the Soviet justice system.[32]

The liberalization of Soviet legal practices, however, had its limits and, when considered necessary, the Soviet government could pass a decree or a resolution that had priority over the law.[33] In February 1962, in contravention to Article 6 of the Fundamental Principles, the Presidium of the Supreme Soviet passed a resolution allowing the court in Kyiv to apply the death penalty retroactively toward the twelve Trawniki guards (tried in March 1962).[34] On 3 September 1965, the Presidium of the Supreme Council passed a directive that expanded the application of the 4 March 1965 decree, including the death penalty for "those Soviet citizens, who during the Great Patriotic War 1941–1945 took active part in punitive actions (*karatel'naia deiatel'nost'*) and personally participated in the murder and torture of the Soviet people."[35]

Such gross violation of the law of retroactivity in the post-Stalinist context was to demonstrate the determination of the Soviet Union to prosecute war crimes regardless of time limitations. It is also possible that such measures were generated by a new campaign of vigilance against internal and external enemies. This campaign began in the late 1950s with the dissolution of the Gulag system. Thousands of Lithuanians, Estonians, Latvians, and Ukrainians, who had been deported in the late 1940s with their family members as nationalist guerrillas, came home. Alarmed by the release of so many potential troublemakers, regional party and state authorities urged Moscow to mitigate the process.[36] More stringent nationality policies followed, whereby native communist cadres in the Baltic Republics, western Ukraine, and Moldavia were increasingly sidelined by ethnic Russians or Russified natives. The drive against "bourgeois" nationalism entailed trials of the members of nationalist organizations although some of the defendants had served in the German-sponsored collaborationist police and as guards in Nazi concentration camps.[37]

EVIDENCE AND IDEOLOGY

Undoubtedly, all Soviet war crimes trials were "political" and were conducted within prescribed ideological confines. In wartime, the expedited format of the trials often entailed physical and psychological pressure on the defendants, who consequently admitted and even exaggerated their guilt. For example, although the evidence in the Krasnodar trial in July 1943 was mostly circumstantial (only two defendants were directly linked to German crimes) all eleven defendants readily admitted their guilt and the military tribunal sentenced eight to death and three to long prison terms merely on the basis of their collaboration with the Germans.[38]

Under Khrushchev, the Soviet leadership attempted to rehabilitate the judicial system and the security services. Accordingly, the KGB was placed under stricter party control and increasingly employed more conventional methods of investigation—surveillance, forensic evidence, and witness testimonies. Although the KGB retained physical and psychological pressure in its arsenal, especially when dealing with political dissidents, "Zionists," or "bourgeois" nationalists, such methods were often unnecessary in war crimes cases for several reasons.

Since the war, the security services maintained special registries that contained information on all individuals suspected in anti-state activities and this data was constantly expanded. Accordingly, by the 1960s pretrial investigation provided an extensive body of evidence in the form of documents and witness testimonies, which allowed KGB interrogators to forego physical pressure and to confront the suspect instead with testimonies from other culprits, who would in turn reveal gaps in the suspect's answers. Conversely, individuals charged with collaboration were rarely paragons of high moral standards. In the hope of saving their necks, they readily revealed the names and activities of other suspects who served with them during the war.

Upon discovering the name of a suspect, the KGB launched an investigation, which involved surveillance of the suspect's family, perusal of his and his family's correspondence, and the questioning of survivors, eyewitnesses, or the suspect's former colleagues. Some suspects were arrested after being recognized by their victims or neighbors. Sometimes the search for culprits lasted for years.[39] In addition to forensic evidence and depositions of witnesses (copies of many of these are deposited at United States Holocaust Memorial Museum), the KGB had in its possession numerous Soviet and German documents. In the trials of the so-called Trawniki guards, investigators could consult the captured German registration cards (*Fragebogen*) containing the biographical information of the guards, their photos, their thumb impressions, their time and places of service, their orders of assignment, and oaths signed at the time of enlistment. For example, during the trial in Lviv in December 1966 the *Fragebogen* of some defendants were shown in the courtroom on a large screen.[40] Investigators, therefore, could verify the suspects' and witnesses' testimonies against the *Fragebogen* or other existing records and establish the extent to which the suspect participated in atrocities and whether he acted voluntarily or under duress.[41]

Since most defendants in the "second wave" were members of the Red Army when they committed high treason, their cases fell under the jurisdiction of military tribunals. In accordance with the Fundamental Principles, all political cases in which the law stipulated the death penalty in peacetime were also tried by military tribunals. Moreover, if a court case involved a group of defendants and one defendant's activities fell under the jurisdiction of a military tribunal, the entire group was tried by a military tribunal.[42] In accordance with the continental European tradition, the Soviet criminal procedure placed special emphasis on pretrial investigation and the court decided upon the sentence largely based upon the conclusions of investigators.

Thus, the investigation and the subsequent trial of six Trawniki guards in June 1965 in Krasnodar revealed that they had taken part in mass executions of Jews at the Janowska camp in Lviv and in the deportation and murder of about 100,000 Jews in the Sobibór and Bełżec death camps. For two years prior to the trial, investigators questioned witnesses, collected forensic evidence, and searched for the culprits, some living in the remote areas of Siberia and Central Asia.[43] The defendants I. Matviyenko, V. Beliakov, I. Nikoforov, I. Zaitsev, V. Podienok, and F. Tikhonovskii conceded to the charges, but tried to minimize their personal involvement in camp operations. Beliakov told his interrogators that he and other guards in Janowska only "periodically" shot Jews, but since there were so many executions, he did not remember all of them. Matviyenko recalled that he and other guards pushed Jews into a ditch, where they were shot by the Germans, while Podienok admitted that many guards in Bełżec enriched themselves by robbing victims of valuables. The defendants also revealed the personal data, physical description, specific criminal activities, and possible residence of other Trawniki guards, who were still at large.[44]

The KGB also located several Jewish survivors, who recognized some defendants and offered gripping descriptions of their cruelties. Edmund Zeidel saw Matviyenko, Beliakov, and Nikiforov tormenting and killing prisoners in the Janowska camp.[45] Leopold Tsimmerman told the court about an execution of 12,000 Lviv ghetto residents, in which the guards took an active part. Other witnesses recalled that many prisoners died each day from malnutrition and epidemics, while the Germans and the defendants amused themselves by forcing emaciated inmates to carry out hard and useless work. They mockingly called those who moved heavy beams from place to place "vitamin B recipients" and those who carried bricks as "vitamin C recipients." The Germans and the guards shot those who could no longer "receive vitamins."[46]

Similarly, in December 1966 another Trawniki trial in Lviv involved a thorough pre-trial investigation. Noticeably, all the defendants had been arrested in the 1940s, but they concealed their service in the camps and were sentenced to prison terms only for collaboration. They were subsequently granted amnesty in the 1950s, but after their names were mentioned in other cases, they were arrested again, this time for participation in mass murder. Indeed, the KGB-collected evidence and witness testimonies provided gruesome details on the activities of the defendants. After training at the SS (Schutzstaffel) camp at Trawniki, they were transferred to the Jewish ghettos and camps in East Galicia and other localities in the General Government, where they soon became notorious as the most vicious German hirelings.[47]

Defendant A. Zhukov admitted that he and other guards took part in several "actions"—the German euphemism for mass executions—and once he almost fell into a ditch, filled with victims' blood. Defendant Pankratov's testimony stirred the courtroom when, in a monotonous tone, he described how he shot three prisoners in cold blood.[48] Witness Stanisława Gogołowska told the court that commandant Gustav Wilhaus celebrated Hitler's fifty-fourth birthday (20 April 1943) by selecting and personally shooting fifty-four prisoners.[49] The defendants and witnesses recalled the Janowska camp orchestra made up of prominent performers. Formed on the orders of Wilhaus, the orchestra played music when prisoners were escorted for work or to execution sites.[50] Summoned as a witness, the former guard Litvinenko testified that the Germans allowed the guards to take belongings and clothes of the victims. The guards then sold these to local residents. Anticipating that sooner or later they would have to answer for their crimes, he said, the guards drowned fear with alcohol.[51] Witness Dmitriev, also a former guard, told the court that when the camp was liquidated in November 1943, a special detail of prisoners burned corpses in the open and the "smoke and stench enveloped the camp, so that it was difficult to breathe."[52]

In some cases, the KGB investigation was corroborated by the West German authorities. For example, in December 1967 the military tribunal of the North Caucasian Military District tried thirteen former members of the so-called Caucasian Company—a collaborationist unit created in Simferopol in early 1942 from Soviet POWs and attached to Einsatzgruppe D. The company participated in shooting and gas van operations in Simferopol. One of the defendants was German Walter Kehrer, who had formed the Caucasian Company, and who was tried in absentia.[53] In 1965, the West German judiciary began an investigation against Kehrer and established that under his supervision the "Caucasian Company" indeed left a bloody trail in the Caucasus and the General Government.[54]

While retribution was a key element of war crimes trials, they also served as a public forum to shape popular memory.[55] In fact, since the days of the Bolshevik revolution, the Soviet leadership stressed the role of trials in educating citizens in the spirit of devotion to socialism. In 1947, the Chief Justice of the Supreme Court I.T. Goliakov stated that the first task of the Soviet court was combating criminal elements, and its second task was to transform the "trial into an instrument of propaganda for Soviet law and the just foundations of our life ... and [to mobilize] the attention of the masses."[56]

In this regard, the "second wave" certainly achieved its didactic purpose. Set up in facilities capable of accommodating large audiences, the courtrooms were packed with members of the party and state apparatus, journalists, students, and representatives of professional associations. Love of the Motherland was the dominant ideological theme of the trials and conversely, the courts attempted to explain what compelled the defendants to commit treason and so many violent crimes. In one of the most emotive episodes of Mazrukho's film *In the Name of the Living,* the camera closes in on the dock while a voiceover inquires, "Who are these people? What internal spring broke down in them, paralyzing their conscience and reason?" For obvious reasons, Soviet propaganda maintained that collaborators were but a "handful" of individuals, who sided with the enemy, driven by specific sociological factors such as the membership in anti-Soviet organizations or previous criminal records. For example, the key defendant in the Mineral'nye Vody trial, E. Zavadskii, had a criminal record before the war. Thus it was "natural" that he deserted from the Red Army and offered his services to the Germans, who appointed him the city chief of police.[57]

Since many defendants lacked such an "asocial" background, Soviet propaganda emphasized that high treason alone automatically entailed the erosion of human qualities. Thus, a press release on the Trawniki trial in Lviv informed readers that the culprits were a "pitiful few who had lost human dignity and betrayed the Motherland."[58] An article titled "The Wolfish Snarl of the Traitors" similarly emphasized that once the defendants betrayed the "Motherland, they left behind any trace of dignity and humanity and turned into a gang of vicious killers."[59]

The conduct of the defendants only reinforced these messages. Defendants tried to minimize their guilt by citing the inhuman conditions in German POW camps or their fear of German reprisals if they refused orders. In the June 1965 trial in Krasnodar, defendant Beliakov admitted that he "betrayed the Motherland out of fear for his life." Once he put on a Trawniki-guard uniform, he burned all bridges to the past and carried out superior orders.[60] Hoping that the death penalty could not be applied to them retroactively (after the issuance of the Fundamental Principles in December

1958), some defendants in the Trawniki trial in March 1962 in Kyiv freely admitted that they killed scores of prisoners in Sobibór. Defendant Vasilenko revealed that he shot between ten and fifteen people, Karpliuk ten, and Shul'tz "only" three.[61]

Defendants also blamed each other, revealing gruesome details of their colleagues' crimes. When the court chairman in the Lviv trial questioned defendant Minochkin whether his colleague Prikhod'ko took part in the one-day execution of four thousand prisoners in Janowska in May 1943, Minochkin replied: "Surely he did. We were standing side by side and shooting. Prikhod'ko also participated in the suppression of [the] prisoners' uprising in November 1943." Defendant Lagutin described the execution of laborers in a lime factory near Lviv. "[S]ome victims were wounded and still moving. We got orders to finish them off and I shot two-three times." Upon the question of the chairman as to whether Lagutin really fired only "two-three times," Lagutin responded: "yes, two-three times and not because I did not want to shoot more, but because all of them were dead."[62] Such testimonies frequently caused an emotional reaction from the public.[63] For example, when defendant Pankratov in Lviv insisted that in one *Aktion* he killed "only three prisoners," the courtroom was visibly shaken.[64]

Hence, when the prosecution asked for the death penalty, it was met by public approval. In Lviv, the public prosecutor V. Zvarich called upon the court to sentence all the defendants to death: "there are no circumstances that could justify murder; mothers, whose children were taken away by the defendants won't forgive it, thousands of prisoners won't forgive. In the name of the dead, I ask the court to sentence these henchmen, on whose hands is the blood of thousands of victims, to death."[65] The court obliged. The press reports that the sentences were "greeted with satisfaction by all present" were surely not far-fetched.[66]

The themes of high treason and the depravity of traitors were integrated into Soviet feature films, which emphasized that those who once betrayed the Motherland, in a suitable situation would once again become agents of the imperialist West or commit other criminal acts. For example, in a highly popular Soviet spy film *Oshibka rezidenta* (A Secret Agent's Blunder), a foreign agent reactivates several former members of Sonderkommando 10a. A part of Mazrukho's documentary on the trial in Krasnodar is also skillfully integrated into the film's narrative. In the TV series *Soviest'* (Conscience), aired in 1974, a former camp guard, after a chance meeting with a former prisoner, goes on a killing spree, attempting to eliminate all potential witnesses against him.[67]

Another visible function of the "second wave" of trials in the 1960s was the rehabilitation of the security services, the reputation of which was severely damaged by its role in Stalinist terror. The press now hailed the professionalism of the KGB officers, whose vigilance helped expose the culprits, "robbers and murderers," who long hid from justice.[68] A report on the trial in Mineral'nye Vody indicated that the key defendant Matias Gab changed his name from Dmitrii Gabov and lived in South Sakhalin, an island in the Pacific Ocean, but that the KGB nonetheless found him.[69] A press release on the trial in Vitebsk of five former auxiliaries of the Secret Field Police (GFP) informed readers that the culprits hid from justice for twenty years, but eventually were uncovered by the KGB.[70] Contrary to the traditional practice of keeping the names of KGB functionaries secret, a report on the trial of ten GFP auxiliaries in Gomel' revealed that "although time has erased many traces, the perseverance and skill of Lieutenant Colonel Konstantin Yashin, Captains Dmitrii Plotnikov, Vasilii Astashenok, and Evgenii Tsybul'skii, and [the] support of the Soviet people helped [to] unravel a complex tangle of the defendants' crimes."[71]

THE HOLOCAUST IN THE COURTROOM

After the outbreak of the Soviet-German war, Soviet propaganda tended to subsume Holocaust victims into a much broader category of "Soviet citizens." When presenting gruesome descriptions of Nazi atrocities at Babi Yar and elsewhere, media statements omitted the particular anti-Jewish character of the atrocities while downplaying the exceptional nature of Jewish suffering. Even the prominent Soviet Jewish journalist Ilya Ehrenburg referred to thousands of victims in Kharkov as "Russians, Jews, Ukrainians, teachers, workers, doctors, women, babies, and the aged."[72]

The reasons for obscuring Jewish victimization were manifold. The Stalinist leadership was concerned that too much emphasis on Jews as the Germans' primary targets would make the war against Hitler a "Jewish war," thus undermining the official propaganda effort to accentuate the alleged unity of all nationalities in the struggle against Germany. In this regard, Soviet media was not unlike its Western counterparts, which also tended to universalize the Nazis' victims. Still, recent research has demonstrated that official Soviet attitudes toward Jewish victims were neither consistent nor systematic and fluctuated in accordance with the political situation. Although wartime Soviet publications avoided references to the Jewish nature of Hitler's Final Solution, they frequently implied—albeit in disguised form—that it was Jews who were systematically murdered.[73]

In public trials of German military personnel in 1945 and 1946, at least half of the eighty-nine defendants were specifically charged with organizing and perpetrating the mass murder of Jews. For example, Friedrich Jeckeln, the former supreme SS and police commander in the Baltic region, told the court that in Latvia his forces alone murdered 87,000 Jews. In Kyiv, Jewish survivor Dina Pronicheva described the massacre in Babi Yar in detail. In the courtroom and in press reports, the victims were either interchangeably referred to as "Jews" or "citizens of Jewish nationality," or as "Soviet citizens." Sometimes, the press mentioned Jews along with other ethnic groups.[74] With the ascendance of the "anti-cosmopolitan" campaign in the late 1940s, even veiled references to Jewish victimization once again disappeared from the Soviet official discourse. When the Soviet press reported on war crimes trials, it did so without ever mentioning Jews.[75]

But in the trials of the 1960s the genocide of Jews again became a key feature. Without proper documentation, it is hard to ascertain what ideological instructions the courts received in regard to emphasis on Soviet Jews. However, judging by the trial records and press reports it appears that even if the courts were advised to downplay Jewish victimization, they were also not ordered to ignore it entirely.

It is noteworthy that the war crimes trials in the 1960s occurred during a mounting anti-Zionist campaign initiated by the Soviet government. After the Suez Canal crisis of 1956, hostility toward Israel reached new heights and the Soviet ideological establishment churned out hundreds of anti-Zionist articles and pamphlets. On 23 May 1961, during the trial of Adolf Eichmann in Jerusalem, the newspaper *Krasnaia Zvezda* (Red Star), the organ of the Soviet Defense Ministry, insinuated that Bonn and Tel Aviv had struck a secret agreement whereby in exchange for profitable trade agreements, the Israelis would not reveal the names of the former Nazis (ostensibly revealed by Eichmann during his interrogation) in the West German administration.[76]

The anti-Zionist campaign had clear antisemitic overtones. The press highlighted a series of the so-called economic trials in several cities, wherein many of the defendants were Jews. In December 1962 Khrushchev attacked the poet Yevhenii Yevtushenko for emphasizing Jewish suffering in his poem *Babi Yar*. Jewish religious leaders in Kyiv, Minsk, and Vilnius were harassed and removed from their positions, with some arrested and sentenced on charges of espionage. The campaign culminated in the publication of the pamphlet entitled *Judaism without Embellishment* (1964), a Soviet emulation of the notorious *Protocols of the Elders of Zion*. The pamphlet caused great embarrassment to European communist parties owing to its content. The antisemitic campaign gained momentum especially after the severance of diplomatic relations between the Soviet Union and Israel in the wake of the Six-Day War in June 1967. Some publications even accused the Zionists of collaborating with the Nazis.[77]

In this context, the Soviet government faced a dilemma. On the one hand, the anti-Zionist campaign indicated that antisemitism remained a key element in Soviet nationality policy. On the other hand, the Soviet government consistently denied the existence of antisemitism in the "brotherly family of the Soviet people."[78] One can speculate, therefore, that since the Holocaust often constituted the only basis for indictment of collaborationist defendants, for example, in the trials of the Trawniki guards, its treatment as a Jewish event in the courtroom and in the press was left to the discretion of the judges or the local party apparatus. Consequently, the "second wave" discussion of the Jewish catastrophe varied from its integration into the general framework of the suffering of the "Soviet people" to explicit descriptions of Jewish suffering. For example, some publications mentioned Jews, but alongside the communists and the partisans. The media reports on Eichmann's trial made only limited references to Eichmann's crimes against Europe's Jews, but still exposed Soviet citizens to previously unknown information.[79]

Even though the KGB officers and the judges referred to victims as "individuals of Jewish nationality," "Soviet citizens," or simply "prisoners of the concentration camps," many defendants explicitly named their victims as "Jews" or "citizens of Jewish nationality" and described the extermination process in chilling detail.[80] For example, the defendants in Lviv told their interrogators that the Trawniki training camp was created for the single purpose of "preparing specialists in the extermination of the Jewish population."[81] Defendant Beliakov described how during the mass *Aktion* in May 1943 in the Janowska camp, the Germans and the guards shot several thousands of "Jewish men, women, and children in a conveyor fashion."[82] Defendants and witnesses sometimes related stories of the heroism of Jewish prisoners who resisted and attacked the guards. For example, during the liquidation of the Janowska camp in November 1943, prisoners broke through the barbed wire and tried to escape. Most died in the attempt.[83] On 25 December 1966, the court verdict in Lviv specified that the defendants committed high treason, whereby their "practical" activities entailed helping the Germans murder between 15,000 and 20,000 people of "Jewish nationality regardless of gender and age."[84] In accordance with the Decree of 4 March 1965, all defendants were sentenced to death (one sentence was later commuted).[85]

Press reports on the trials varied from naming the ethnicity of victims to referring to victims in only general terms. The *Krasnaia Zvezda* report on the trial of the Sonderkommando 10a members in Krasnodar mentioned only that the defendants were charged with high treason.[86] A press release on the trial of the Trawniki guards in Krasnodar in June 1965 described that the "fascist hirelings" took part in mass annihilation of the "peaceful population in the USSR and Poland—200,000 in the Janowska camp and more than one million in the death camps of Bełżec and Sobibór." It did not mention that these camps were set specifically for the confinement and murder of Jews.[87] *Vil'na Ukrayina* (Free Ukraine) referred to the Janowska camp as a Nazi extermination camp for "all prisoners," with only oblique references to the Jews.[88]

In contrast, a series of press releases on the Trawniki trial in Lviv consistently named Jews or the "Soviet people of Jewish nationality" as the primary victims, and one press release referred to the mass murder of Jews as "genocide."[89] A *Pravda* report on the same trial used more ambiguous terms, confirming that the defendants were "willful executioners of Nazi orders for the systematic destruction of the Jewish population and the Soviet party and state activists."[90] A newspaper article on the trial in Mineral'nye Vody in February 1966 stated that on 2–9 September 1942, the Germans and their native helpers murdered the "entire Jewish population[s] of Mineral'nye Vody, Piatigorsk, Essentuki, and Kislovodsk." The executions claimed several prominent members of Soviet Jewish intelligentsia—"Professor P.I. Efrussi, Doctor of Medicine L.M. Chatskii, and scientist M.S. Shvartsman."[91]

At the same time, publications and films intended for general audiences tended to omit the Holocaust or mention it only in passing. A chapter on the October 1963 trial in Krasnodar in a book on the history of the KGB briefly referred to the murder of thousands of "peaceful citizens of Jewish nationality" by gas or by shooting.[92] Mazrukho's film did not mention Jews at all, while Lev Ginzburg's documentary novel on the same trial referred to Jews as Nazi victims along other Soviet citizens and POWs.[93] A book chapter in a major publication on trials of foreign spies and traitors described in detail the June 1965 Krasnodar trial, but referred to the Janowska camp as the site of suffering of "thousands of people of many nationalities."[94]

CONCLUSION

Prosecution of war crimes was an important, but secondary issue for the Soviet political establishment and served as a propaganda tool for external and internal policies, whereby ideological guidelines reflected the official representation of the past. To this end, the trials aimed at several objectives: they were to shape the memories of the Great Patriotic War and to present the Soviet Union as a monolithic polity, whereas trials of a "handful of traitors" underscored the mass heroism of the Soviet people. In the international context, the "second wave" was to demonstrate that, in contrast to the West, where war criminals received light sentences, were acquitted, or were not tried at all, the USSR punished the culprits in accordance with its official declarations. Accordingly, some trials were made into media events, generating articles, pamphlets, and films.

Such publicity certainly put in doubt the veracity of trial materials, especially given the background of the Stalinist purges, when Soviet interrogators used threats, blackmail, and torture to obtain confessions or simply fabricated investigation materials. The priority of government decrees over laws and the retroactive application of the death penalty also point to critical flaws in the Soviet justice system. War crimes trials in Estonia, Latvia, Lithuania, and western Ukraine against local nationalists indicated that the trials might also have been a part and parcel of the struggle against "bourgeois nationalism."[95]

Nevertheless, a distinction should be made between the Stalinist show trials and later war crimes trials. The former proceedings were fully within the realm of political power, but outside the rule of law. The latter pursued political aims, but also a legal agenda, and were largely within the rule of Soviet law.[96] A number of scholars have convincingly demonstrated that when matched against other available materials, interrogation and trial records become credible sources of information on the functioning of the German and native administration, the mechanisms of the Holocaust, and the dynamics of local collaboration with the occupiers.[97] For ideological purposes some trials in the Baltic republics and western Ukraine were integrated into the suppression of "bourgeois nationalism," but undoubtedly anti-Soviet sentiments, combined with Nazi ideology, resonated among the local right-wing elements who volunteered to serve with the Germans and participated in the Holocaust.[98]

Comprehensive KGB investigation entailed collecting large amounts of data on the defendants' criminal activities, whereas their own confessions revealed many details of atrocities as well as the names of their accomplices. A number of survivors and witnesses recognized the culprits and could testify about specific crimes—in contrast to the 1940s, when witnesses often provided a general description of German terror. Hence, the high conviction rate in Soviet trials—often interpreted as the proof of indiscriminate retribution campaign—resulted from substantial evidence.[99]

The 1960s trials became a part of the broad patriotic-educative effort rather than merely a retaliatory campaign motivated by a desire for retribution. The main charge against all defendants was the penultimate crime—high treason—with actual war crimes as its consequence. Accordingly, propaganda on the trials highlighted two themes, the heroism and sacrifice of the Soviet people and the depravity and exceptionality of those who sided with the enemy and betrayed the Motherland. And even though about a million

Soviet citizens served with the Axis powers in different capacities during the war, the courts made efforts to portray collaborators as a handful of political or social outcasts. To this effect, they largely ignored that some individuals indeed may have committed treason under the threat of death. In truth, most Trawniki guards volunteered to serve due to the atrocious character of the German POW camps, and about 10 percent of them deserted (most, however, at the end of the war). At the same time, the majority served to the end, often matching the SS in zeal and brutality.[100]

Since all defendants were charged with high treason, the Holocaust in the Soviet Union became a tributary aspect of the war crimes trials. Still, witness testimonies and documentary evidence resisted official attempts to merge Jewish victims, undifferentiated, with the death toll of the non-Jewish victims. Conversely, the Soviet leadership used the Final Solution as a tool of socialist education to highlight the immense suffering of the Soviet people in World War II and to exhibit the determination of the USSR to prosecute war criminals regardless of time limitations.[101]

The "second wave" offers a compelling study of Soviet ideology, law, and the politics of memory. Although the prosecution drive subsided in the early 1970s, the Soviet courts into the 1980s punished individuals whose behavior was compromised by collaboration with the Axis powers, reminding the population of the regime's long memory and reach.[102]

Alexander V. Prusin holds a Ph.D. in history from the University of Toronto. He is a professor of history at New Mexico Institute of Mining and Technology. His publications include *Nationalizing a Borderland: War, Ethnicity, and Anti-Jewish Violence in East Galicia, 1914–1920* (2005); *The "Lands Between": Conflict in the East European Borderlands, 1870–1992* (2010); and *Serbia under the Swastika: A World War II Occupation, 1941–1944* (2017).

NOTES

I would like to thank Norman Goda for his invaluable comments and advice. I am also indebted to Vadim Altskan for his help in my research.
   1. *Gosudarstvennyi prestupnik* (1964), director Nikolai Rozantsev.
   2. Andreas Hilger, Ute Schmidt, and Günther Wagenlehner, eds., *Sowjetische Militärtribunale*, vol. 1: *Die Verurteilung deutscher Kriegsgefangener 1941–1953* (Cologne, 2001), 13; Viacheslav Zviagintsev, *Voina na vesakh Femidy: voina 1941–1945 gg. v materialakh sudebno-sledstvennykh del* (Moscow, 2006), 15–16.
   3. Michael Parrish, *The Lesser Terror: Soviet State Security, 1939–1953* (Westport, CT, 1996), 127; Lukasz Hirszowicz, "The Holocaust in the Soviet Mirror," in *The Holocaust in the Soviet Union: Studies and Sources on the Destruction of Jews in the Nazi-*

Occupied Territories of the USSR, 1941–1945, ed. Lucjan Dobroszycki and Jeffrey S. Gurock (Armonk, NY, 1993), 39–40.

4. "Ob amnistii sovietskikh grazhdan, sotrudnichavshikh s okkupantami v period Velikoi Otechestvennoi Voiny 1941–1945 gg.," 17 September 1955, in *Sbornik zakonov SSSR i ukazov Presidiuma Verkhovnogo Sovieta SSSR, 1938–1975,* 4 vols., ed. V.I. Vasil'yev, P.P. Gureev, and M.I. Iumashev (Moscow, 1975), 3: 411–14.

5. "O dosrochnom osvobozhdenii germanskikh grazhdan, osuzhdennykh sudieb-nymi organami SSSR za sovershennye imi prestupleniia protiv narodov Sovi-etskogo Soiuza v period voiny," 28 September 1955, in Vasil'yev et al., *Sbornik zakonov SSSR,* 3: 414–15.

6. At least in one case, a defendant was a former Soviet citizen (A. Stroganov) who returned to the USSR from abroad. Possibly in 1959 the KGB in East Berlin kidnapped a former German officer Aksel Ganzen (Yensen), who at the time was a Swedish resident, and brought him to trial in Minsk.

7. In accordance with the September 1955 amnesty, individuals who were not di-rectly involved in executions and tortures of civilians and POWs were classified as "accomplices."

8. Some cities witnessed more than one trial. For example, there were at least five trials in Krasnodar—in March 1959, July 1962, October 1963, June 1965, and December 1967. A.M. Belyaev et al., *Kuban' v gody Velikoĭ Otechestvennoĭ Voĭny, 1941–1945: khronika sobytiĭ* (Krasnodar, 2000–2003), 2: 419n2.

9. For example, Ilya Bourtman, "Blood for Blood, Death for Death": The Soviet Military Tribunal in Krasnodar, 1943," *Holocaust and Genocide Studies* 22, no. 2 (2008): 246–65; Tanja Penter, "Local Collaborators on Trial: Soviet War Crimes Trials under Stalin (1943–1953)," *Cahiers du monde russe et sovie'tique* 49, no. 2–3 (2008): 782–90; Diana Dumitru, "An Analysis of Soviet Postwar Investigation and Trial Documents and Their Relevance for Holocaust Studies," in *The Ho-locaust in the East: Local Perpetrators and Soviet Responses,* ed. Michael David-Fox, Peter Holquist, and Alexander M. Martin (Pittsburgh, 2014), 142–57.

10. I am aware of four studies related to the subject: Sergei Kudryashov, "Ordi-nary Collaborators: The Case of the Travniki Guards," in *Russia: War, Peace and Diplomacy: Essays in Honour of John Erickson,* ed. Ljubica Erickson and Mark Erickson (London, 2005), 226–39; Vanessa Voisin, "'Au nom des vivants,' de Léon Mazroukho: rencontre entre dénonciation officielle et hommage person-nel," *Kinojudaica: Les représentations des Juifs dans le cinéma russe et soviétique* (Paris, 2012), 365–407; Lev Simkin, "Death Sentence Despite the Law: A Secret 1962 Crimes-against-Humanity Trial in Kiev," *Holocaust and Genocide Studies* 27, no. 2 (2013): 299–312; Richards Plavnieks, "Nazi Collaborators on Trial during the Cold War: The Cases against Viktors Arâjs and the Latvian Auxiliary Secu-rity Police," Ph.D. diss., University of North Carolina at Chapel Hill, 2013, 94–129.

11. "Predstavlenie Sovetskogo pravitel'stva pravitel'stvu FRG po voprosu o proiz-vodstve v Zapadnoi Germanii rakietnogo oruzhiia," 4 February 1964, in *Vnesh-niaia politika Sovetskogo Soiuza i mezhdunarodnye otnosheniia: sbornik dokumentov,*

1964–1965 gody, ed. I.A. Kirilin, V.A. Kaliakina, and N.F. Potapova (Moscow, 1966), 4–6.

12. I.A. Lediakh and F.M. Reshetnikov, "Kazhdyi natsistkii prestupnik dolzhen poniesti nakazanie," *Sovietskoe gosudarstvo i pravo* 2 (1965), 25–27.

13. *Trybuna Ludu,* n. 295 (3512), 22 October 1958, p. 2; n. 16 (3596), 16 January 1959, p. 2; n. 17 (3597), 17 January 1959, p. 2; n. 49 (3629), 18 February 1959, p. 1.

14. *Krovavye zlodeianiia Oberlendera: Otchet o press-konferentsii dlia sovietskikh i inostran-nykh zhurnalistov, sostoiavsheysia v Moskve 5 aprelia 1960 goda* (Moscow, 1960); Vladimir Beliayev, *Razoblachenie: Dokumental'nye ocherki i povesti* (Lviv, 1960), 5–33.

15. In March 1965, after heated debate in the Bundestag, the twenty-year statute of limitation on murder in West Germany was extended so that the start of the limitations period would be 1949, not 1945, for homicides committed during the Nazi period. In 1969, it was extended to thirty years, and in July 1979 it was suspended altogether.

16. "Zayavlenie Sovietskogo pravitel'stva po povodu namereniia pravitel'stva FRG prekratit' privlechenie k otvetsvennosti voyennykh prestupnikov," 24 December 1964, in Kirilin et al., *Vneshniaia politika,* 95–98.

17. R. Rudenko, "Hitlerovskie palachi nie dolzhny uiti ot vozmezdiia," *Sotsialis-ticheskaia zakonnost'* 3 (1965), 4; G.N. Aleksandrov, "Prestupleniia natsistov nie mogut byt' predany zabveniiu," *Sovietskoe gosudarstvo i pravo* 2 (1968), 117–18. In contrast, the Soviet media highlighted "socialist" justice in Poland and East Germany, where war criminals were sentenced to death or lengthy prison terms. Since the creation of East Germany in 1949, its courts convicted 12,807 culprits, or double the number convicted in West Germany. Slavomir Orlovskii and Radoslav Ostrovich, *Erich Koch pered polskim sudom* (Moscow, 1961), 15–16; Lediakh, "Kazhdyi natsistkii prestupnik," 26–27.

18. "Nota Sovietskogo pravitel'stva pravitel'stvu FRG po voprosu o nakazanii nat-sistkikh voyennykh prestupnikov," 17 January 1965, in Kirilin et al., *Vneshniaia politika,* 104–5; "Zayavlenie Sovietskogo pravitel'stva po voprosu o nakazanii natsistkikh voyennykh prestupnikov," 27 April 1965, Kirlin et al., *Vneshniaia politika,* 190–92.

19. "O nakazanii lits, vinovnykh v prestupleniiakh protiv mira i chelovechnosti i voyennykh prestupleniiakh, niezavisimo ot vremeni soversheniia prestuplenii," 4 March 1965, in Vasil'yev, et al., *Sbornik zakonov SSSR,* 3: 343–44.

20. "O ratifikatsii konventsii o nieprimenimosti sroka davnosti k voyennym prestu-pleniiam i prestupleniiam protiv chelovechestva," 11 March 1969, in Vasil'yev et al., *Sbornik zakonov SSSR,* 2: 253.

21. *Pravda,* n. 153 (17105), 2 June 1965, p. 4. During the war, some of these individu-als were superiors of the defendants. Gustav Wilhaus, Franz Wartzok, Fritz Geb-auer, and Richard Rokita served at the Janowska camp in Lviv; Gustav Wagner served in Sobibór. The article did not indicate what connected Gustav Wirt, Johann Schwartz, Gustav Wagner, and Franz Göring to the defendants. The So-viets may have not known or omitted on purpose that some of these individuals were already dead (Wilhaus was presumed killed at the end of the war).

22. A. Anan'yev and F. Tulinov, "Tragediia na Anchupanskikh kholmakh," in *Neo-tvratimoe vozmezdie: po materialam sudebnykh protsessov nad izmennikami Rodiny, fash-istskimi palachami i agentami imperialisticheskikh razvedok,* ed. N.F. Chistiakov and M.E. Karyshev (Moscow, 1973), 287–88.

23. *Pravda,* n. 32 (17349), 1 February 1966, p. 4; n. 45 (17362), 14 February 1966, p. 6.

24. *Pravda,* n. 320 (18002), 16 November 1967, p. 6.

25. Voisin, "'Au nom des vivants,'" 375–76. Frequently referred to as the "first" war crimes trial of the war, the July 1943 trial in Krasnodar was in fact preceded by several less publicized trials.

26. *Obyknovennyi fashizm* (1965), director Mikhail Romm.

27. Aleksandrov, "Prestupleniia natsistov," 118; *Izvestiia,* n. 159 (15553), 8 July 1967, p. 2. Several sightings of Bormann were reported after the war. The Soviets may have not known that he was killed during the last phase of the war, but used such rumors for anti-Western propaganda.

28. Nati Cantorovich, "Soviet Reactions to the Eichmann Trial: A Preliminary Investigation 1960–1965," *Yad Vashem Studies* 35, no. 2 (2007): 105.

29. Postanovlenie TsIK SSSR ot 8 iunia 1934 g. "O dopolnenii Polozheniia o prestupleniiakh gosudarstvennykh (kontrrevolutsionnykh i osobo dlia Soiuza SSR opasnykh prestupleniiakh protiv poriadka upravleniia) stat'yami ob izmenie Rodinie," in *Istoriia gosudarstva i prava Rossii v dokumentakh i materialakh 1930–1990-e gg.,* ed. I.N. Kuznetsov (Minsk, 2003), 73–74.

30. The text of the decree in V.A. Zolotarev and A.S. Emelin, eds., *Velikaia Otechest-vennaia* (Moscow, 1993–1999), 2/3: 130–31. The motives behind the issuance of the April decree are unclear. It is possible that the Soviets reacted to the initiative of the Polish government-in-exile, which on 30 March 1943 signed a decree about the punishment of Nazi crimes. The Polish decree became the first Allied legislation that specifically dealt with the prosecution of war criminals (soon Moscow severed diplomatic relations with the London Poles over the discovery of the mass graves of Polish officers in Katyn'). I also believe that after spring 1943, when the Red Army began liberating large swaths of German-occupied territories, the decree served as a message of deterrence to real and potential collaborators.

31. "Ugolovnaia otvetstvennost' za gosudarstvennye i za voinskie prestupleniia," in Vasil'yev et al., *Sbornik zakonov SSSR,* 25 December 1958, 3: 351.

32. "Osnovy ugolovnogo zakonodatel'stva Soiuza SSR i soiuznykh respublik," in Vasil'yev et al., *Sbornik zakonov SSSR,* 25 December 1958, 3: 311.

33. Concerned with widespread black market and corruption in the Soviet economy, in 1961 Khrushchev forced a Moscow court to replace earlier prison sentences with the death penalty to three defendants who had been convicted for "illegal currency transactions."

34. Simkin, "Death Sentence Despite the Law," 299–312.

35. "O primenenii Ukaza Presidiuma Verkhovnogo Sovieta SSSR ot 4 marta 1965 goda 'O nakazanii lits, vinovnykh v prestupleniiakh protiv mira i chelovech-

nosti i voyennykh prestupleniiakh, nezavisimo ot vremeni sоversheniia prestuplenii,'" 3 September 1965, Vasil'yev et al., *Sbornik zakonov SSSR,* 3: 344.

36. Gerhard Simon, *Nationalism and Policy Toward the Nationalities in the Soviet Union: From Totalitarian Dictatorship to Post-Stalinist Society* (Boulder, CO, 1991), 246–55; Amir Weiner, "War Crimes Trials and Public Justice Soviet Style: Western Ukraine, 1940s–1980s," paper presented on June 2005 at workshop "Prosecuting the Perpetrators of the Holocaust: War Crimes Trials in the Soviet Union and Eastern Europe," United States Holocaust Memorial Museum, Washington, DC, 16–18; also, Amir Weiner, "The Empires Pay a Visit: Gulag Returnees, East European Rebellions, and Soviet Frontier Politics," *Journal of Modern History* 78, no. 2 (2006): 333–76.

37. Rain Liivoja, "Competing Histories: Soviet War Crimes in the Baltic States," in *The Hidden Histories of War Crimes Trials,* ed. Kevin Jon Heller and Gerry Simpson (New York, 2013), 252.

38. Bourtman, "Blood for Blood," 252–54.

39. V.M. Chebrikov, G.F. Grigorenko, N.A. Dushin, and F.D. Bobkov, *Istoriia sovietskikh organov gosbezopasnosti* (Moscow, 1977), 356, 477–78; Igor' Panchishin, "V rozyske oborotni," in *Kontrrazvedka,* ed. V.K. Kirilov and V.P. Krasnopevtsev (Pskov, 1995), 254–76.

40. *L'vovskaia Pravda,* n. 247, 18 December 1966, p. 4.

41. Kudryashov, "Ordinary Collaborators," 227–29; David Allan Rich, "Reinhard's Footsoldiers: Soviet Trophy Documents and Investigative Records as Sources," in *Remembering for the Future: The Holocaust in the Age of Genocide,* vol. 1: *History,* ed. John K. Roth and Elisabeth Maxwell (New York, 2011), 689–90, 696–97; Peter Black, "Foot Soldiers of the Final Solution: The Trawniki Training Camp and Operation Reinhard," *Holocaust and Genocide Studies* 25, no. 1 (2011): 1–99.

42. "Ob utverzhdenii polozheniia o voyennykh tribunalakh," 25 December 1958, Vasil'yev et al., *Sbornik zakonov SSSR,* 4: 25–26.

43. United States Holocaust Memorial Museum (USHMM), RG-31.018M.073, "Postwar Crimes Trials Related to the Holocaust, 1937–1943," reel 15, frame 1546.

44. USHMM, RG-31.018M.073, reel 15 frame 1534–46, 1554–57, 1571–72.

45. M. Tokarev, "V zamknutom krugie," in Chistiakov and Karyshev, *Neotvratimoe vozmezdie,* 188–89. The camp was established in August 1941 as an industrial enterprise of the SS Economic and Administrative Main Office (WVHA), but was directly subordinated to the office of the SS and police commander in East Galicia and integrated into the annihilation process. Thomas Sandkühler, "Das Zwangsarbeitslager Lemberg-Janowska 1941–1944," in *Die nationalsozialistischen Konzentrationslager,* vol. II: *Entwicklung und Struktur,* ed. Ulrich Herbert, Karin Orth, and Christoph Dieckmann (Göttingen, 1998), 606–35.

46. USHMM, RG-31.018M.073, reel 15, frame 1594–96.

47. Ibid., frame 1469. The General Government was an administrative region, which included the bulk of German-occupied Poland. After the invasion of the USSR, East Galicia, which in 1939–1941 was annexed by the Soviet Union, was integrated into the General Government.

48. Ibid., frame 1495–98.
49. Tokarev, "V zamknutom krugie," 189. The April execution became one of the defining scenes in film *Ivanna,* directed by Victor Ivchenko in 1959. The film accused the Greek-Catholic Church in western Ukraine of collaboration with the Nazis.
50. *L'vovskaia Pravda,* n. 248, 20 December 1966, p. 4. Made by an employee at the camp kitchen, the photograph of the orchestra would later become damning evidence of the Nazi genocide.
51. USHMM, RG-31.018M.073, reel 15, frame 1501–3, 1508.
52. Ibid., frame 1483.
53. *Pravda,* n. 356 (18038), 22 December 1967, p. 6. In his recent article, Martin Dean corroborates the role of Walther Kehrer as the supervisor of the "Caucasian company." Martin Dean, "Soviet Ethnic Germans and the Holocaust in the Reich Commissariat Ukraine, 1941–1944," in *The Shoah in Ukraine: History, Testimony, Memorialization,* ed. Ray Brandon and Wendy Lower (Bloomington, IN, 2008), 261–62.
54. Bundesarchiv Ludwigsburg, B 162/2860, "Ermittlungsverfahren gegen Walter Kehrer," pp. 1177–80. In 1980 the case was closed due to Kehrer's "inability to stand trial." I am grateful to Tomasz Frydel for providing me with this source.
55. Lawrence Douglas, "The Didactic Trial: Filtering History and Memory in the Courtroom," in *Holocaust and Justice: Representation and Historiography of the Holocaust in Post-War Trials,* ed. David Bankier and Dan Michman (Jerusalem, 2010), 11, 18.
56. I.T. Golyakov, *The Role of the Soviet Court* (Washington, 1948), 15–18.
57. *Pravda,* n. 32 (17349), 1 February 1966, p. 4.
58. *L'vovskaia Pravda,* n. 245, 15 December 1966, p. 4.
59. *L'vovskaia Pravda,* n. 249, 21 December 1966, p. 4.
60. USHMM, RG-31.018M.073, reel 15, frame 1573.
61. Simkin, "Death Sentence Despite the Law," 301.
62. *L'vovskaia Pravda,* n. 247, 18 December 1966, p. 4.
63. *L'vovskaia Pravda,* n. 249, 21 December 1966, p. 4; USHMM, RG-31.018M.073, reel 15, frame 1495–98, 1504–05, 1510.
64. USHMM, RG-31.018M.073, reel 15, frame 15.
65. *L'vovskaia Pravda,* n. 252, 25 December 1966, p. 6. The public prosecutor was an official appointed to represent the general public in court.
66. *Pravda,* n. 45 (17362), 14 February 1966, p. 6; n. 60 (17377), 1 March 1966, p. 6; n. 356 (18038), 22 December 1967, p. 6.
67. *Oshibka rezidenta* (1968), director Veniamin Dorman; *Soviest',* (1974), director Iurii Kavtaradze. In the 1980s in the TV series *Protivostoianie* (Confrontation) a former collaborator murders three individuals and tries to escape abroad. *Protivostoianie* (1985), director Semen Aranovich.
68. *Pravda,* n. 153 (17105), 2 June 1965, p. 4.
69. *Pravda,* n. 32 (17349), 1 February 1966, p. 4.
70. *Pravda,* n. 144 (17431), 24 April 1966, p. 1.

71. *Pravda*, n. 320 (18002), 16 November 1967, p. 6.

72. *The Trial in the Case of the Atrocities Committed by the German Fascist Invaders and Their Accomplices in Krasnodar and Krasnodar Territory, Heard July 14–17, 1943* (Moscow, 1943); Jeffrey Brooks, *Thank You, Comrade Stalin! Soviet Public Culture from Revolution to Cold War* (Princeton, NJ, 2000), 173.

73. Karel C. Berkhoff, "'Total Annihilation of the Jewish Population': The Holocaust in the Soviet Media, 1941–45," in David-Fox et al., *Holocaust in the East*, 111–13; Mordechai Altshuler, "The Holocaust and Soviet Mass Media during the War and in the First Postwar Years Re-examined," *Yad Vashem Studies* 39, no. 2 (2011): 121–67.

74. Alexander V. Prusin, "'Fascist Criminals to the Gallows!' The Holocaust and Soviet War Crimes Trials, December 1945–January 1946," *Holocaust and Genocide Studies* 17, no. 1 (2003), 9–14.

75. Hirszowicz, "Holocaust in the Soviet Mirror," 39–40.

76. Cantorovich, "Soviet Reactions," 114, 120.

77. Gregor Aronson, Jakob Frumkin, Alexis Goldenweiser, and Joseph Lewitan, ed., *Russian Jewry 1917–1967* (New York, 1969), 2: 451–52, 476; Cantorovich, "Soviet Reactions," 107.

78. Benjamin Pinkus and Jonathan Frankel, eds., *The Soviet Government and the Jews, 1948–1967: A Documented Study* (New York, 1984), 426–27.

79. Cantorovich, "Soviet Reactions," 114–16, 151.

80. USHMM, RG-31.018M.073, reel 15, frame 1470–72, 1518–9, 1522–23.

81. Ibid., frame 984–85, 1017–19, 1023–26, 1086, 1119, 1157.

82. Ibid., frame 1522–23, 1534–35, 1544–45, 1571–72.

83. Ibid., frame 1509, 1524.

84. Ibid., frame 1518–19, 1522–23.

85. Ibid., frame 1528–29, 1532–33.

86. *Krasnaia Zvezda*, n 253/12163, 25 October 1963, p. 4.

87. *Pravda*, n. 153 (17105), 2 June 1965, p. 4.

88. Tarik Cyril Amar, "A Disturbed Silence: Discourse on the Holocaust in the Soviet West as an Anti-Site Memory," in David-Fox et al., *Holocaust in the East*, 179–80.

89. *L'vovskaia pravda*, n. 245, 15 December 1966, p. 4; n. 248, 20 December 1966, p. 4.

90. *Pravda*, n. 45 (17362), 14 February 1966, p. 6.

91. *Pravda*, n. 32 (17349), 1 February 1966, p. 4.

92. L. Kuleshov, ed., *Chekisty* (Moscow, 1972), 345–51.

93. Voisin, "'Au nom des vivants,'" 366–67; Lev Ginzburg, *Bezdna: povestvovanie, osnovannoe na dokumentakh* (Moscow, 1967), 18–19, 54–55, 64–65.

94. Tokarev, "V zamknutom krugie," 187.

95. Andrew Ezergailis, "The Holocaust's Soviet Legacies in Latvia," in *Lessons and Legacies V: The Holocaust and Justice,* ed. Ronald Smelser (Evanston, IL, 2002), 272–74.

96. Ronald Christenson, "A Political Theory of Political Trials," *The Journal of Criminal Law and Criminology* 74, no. 2 (1983), 551.

97. Tanja Penter, "Collaboration on Trial: New Source Material on Soviet Postwar Trials against Collaborators," *Slavic Review* 64, no. 4 (2005): 782–90; Dumitru, "Analysis of Soviet Postwar Investigation," 142–57.

98. See, for example, USHMM, RG-31.018M, reel 2, case 43111; reel 3, case 46872; RG-26.004M, "War Crimes Investigation and Trial Records from the Former Lithuanian KGB Archives, 1944–1992," case 24618.

99. Chebrikov et al., *Istoriia organov,* 455; Dumitru, "Analysis of Soviet Postwar Investigation," 151.

100. Kudryashov, "Ordinary Collaborators," 233.

101. USHMM, RG-31.018M.073, reel 15, frame 1501–05, 1508; *Krasnaia Zvezda,* n. 253/12163, April 13, 1963, p. 4; *L'vovskaia Pravda,* 20 December 1966, p. 4.

102. According to one source, in 1981–1986 the Soviet courts tried sixty collaborators. M.I. Semiriaga, *Kollaboratsionism: Priroda, tipologiia i proiavleniia v gody vtoroi mirovoi voiny* (Moscow, 2000), 781.

SELECT BIBLIOGRAPHY

Archival Sources

Bundesarchiv Ludwigsburg, B 162/2860 "Ermittlungsverfahren gegen Walter Kehrer."
United States Holocaust Memorial Museum (USHMM), RG-31.018M.073 "Post-war Crimes Trials Related to the Holocaust, 1937–1943."
United States Holocaust Memorial Museum, RG-26.004M "War Crimes Investigation and Trial Records from the Former Lithuanian KGB Archives, 1944–1992."

Published Documents

Kirilin, I.A., V.A. Kaliakina, and N.F. Potapova, ed. *Vneshniaia politika Sovietskogo Soiuza i mezhdunarodnye otnosheniia: sbornik dokumentov, 1964–1965 gody.* Moscow: Izdatel'stvo Instituta Miezhdunarodnych Otnoshenii, 1966.
Vasil'yev, V.I., P.P. Gureev, and M.I. Iumashev, ed. *Sbornik zakonov SSSR i ukazov Presidiuma Verkhovnogo Sovieta SSSR, 1938–1975.* 4 vols. Moscow: Izdatel'stvo "Izvestiia Sovietov deputatov trudiashchikhsia SSSR," 1975–1976.
Zolotarev, V.A., and A.S. Emelin, ed. *Velikaia Otechestvennaia.* 9 vols. Moscow: Terra, 1993–1999.

Newspapers

Izvestiia, Moscow
Krasnaia Zvezda, Moscow
L'vovskaia Pravda, Lviv
Pravda, Moscow
Trybuna Ludu, Warsaw

Secondary Sources

Aleksandrov, G.N. "Prestupleniia natsistov nie mogut byt' predany zabveniiu." *Sovietskoe gosudarstvo i pravo* 2 (1968): 117–18.

Altshuler, Mordechai. "The Holocaust and Soviet Mass Media during the War and the First Postwar Years Re-examined." *Yad Vashem Studies* 39, no. 2 (2011): 121–67.

Aronson, Gregor, Jakob Frumkin, Alexis Goldenweiser, and Joseph Lewitan, eds. *Russian Jewry 1917–1967.* 2 vols. New York: Thomas Yoseloff, 1969.

Belyaev, A.M., I.Iu. Bondar', and T.K. Orlova. *Kuban' v gody Velikoĭ Otechestvennoĭ Voĭny, 1941–1945: khronika sobytiĭ.* 2 vols. Krasnodar: Sovietskaia Kuban', 2000–2003.

Belyaev, Vladimir. *Razoblachenie: Dokumental'nye ocherki i povesti.* Lviv: Knizhno-zhurnal'noe izdatel'stvo, 1960.

Bankier, David, and Dan Michman, eds. *Holocaust and Justice: Representation and Historiography of the Holocaust in Post-War Trials.* Jerusalem: Yad Vashem, 2010.

Black, Peter. "Foot Soldiers of the Final Solution: The Trawniki Training Camp and Operation Reinhard." *Holocaust and Genocide Studies* 25, no. 1 (2011): 1–99.

Brandon, Ray, and Wendy Lower, eds. *The Shoah in Ukraine: History, Testimony, Memorialization.* Bloomington, IN: Indiana University Press, 2010.

Brooks, Jeffrey. *Thank You, Comrade Stalin! Soviet Public Culture from Revolution to Cold War.* Princeton, NJ: Princeton University Press, 2000.

Bourtman, Ilya. "Blood for Blood, Death for Death": The Soviet Military Tribunal in Krasnodar, 1943." *Holocaust and Genocide Studies* 22, no. 2 (2008): 246–65.

Cantorovich, Nati. "Soviet Reactions to the Eichmann Trial: A Preliminary Investigation 1960–1965." *Yad Vashem Studies* 35, no. 2 (2007): 103–41.

Chebrikov, V.M., G.F. Grigorenko, N.A. Dushin, and F.D. Bobkov. *Istoriia sovetskikh organov gosbezopasnosti.* Moscow: Vysshaia Krasnoznamennaia Shkola Komiteta Gosudarstvennoi Bezopasnosti pri Soviete Ministrov SSSR imeni F.E. Dzerzhinskogo, 1977.

Chistiakov, N.F., and M.E. Karyshev, eds. *Neotvratimoe vozmezdie: po materialam sudebnykh protsessov nad izmennikami Rodiny, fashistskimi palachami i agentami imperialisticheskikh razvedok.* Moscow: Voyenizdat, 1973.

Christenson, Ronald. "A Political Theory of Political Trials." *The Journal of Criminal Law and Criminology* 74, no. 2 (1983): 547–77.

David-Fox, Michael, Peter Holquist, and Alexander M. Martin, eds. *The Holocaust in the East: Local Perpetrators and Soviet Responses.* Pittsburgh, PA: University of Pittsburgh Press, 2014.

Dobroszycki, Lucjan, and Jeffrey S. Gurock, eds. *The Holocaust in the Soviet Union: Studies and Sources on the Destruction of Jews in the Nazi-Occupied Territories of the USSR, 1941–1945.* Armonk, NY: M.C. Sharpe, 1993.

Erickson, Ljubica, and Mark Erickson, eds. *Russia: War, Peace and Diplomacy: Essays in Honour of John Erickson.* London: Weidenfeld & Nicolson, 2007.

Ginzburg, Lev. *Bezdna: povestvovanie, osnovannoe na dokumentakh.* Moscow: Sovietskii pisatel', 1967.

Golyakov, I.T. *The Role of the Soviet Court.* Washington, DC: Public Affairs Press, 1948.

Heller, Kevin Jon, and Gerry Simpson, eds. *The Hidden Histories of War Crimes Trials.* New York: Oxford University Press, 2013.

Herbert, Ulrich, Karin Orth, and Christoph Dieckmann, eds. *Die nationalsozialistischen Konzentrationslager.* 2 vols. Göttingen: Wallstein Verlag, 1998.

Hilger, Andreas, Ute Schmidt, and Günther Wagenlehner, eds. *Sowjetische Militärtribunale.* 2 vols. Cologne: Bohlau Verlag, 2001–2003.

Kirilov, V.K., and V.P. Krasnopevtsev, eds. *Kontrrazvedka.* Pskov: Izdatel'stvo Organizatsionno-metodicheskogo tsentra, 1995.

Krovavye zlodeianiia Oberlendera: Otchet o press-konferentsii dlia sovietskikh i inostrannykh zhurnalistov, sostoiavsheysia v Moskve 5 aprelia 1960 goda. Moscow: Izdatel'stvo literatury na inostrannykh iazykakh, 1960.

Kuleshov, L., ed. *Chekisty.* Moscow: Molodaia gvardiia, 1972.

Kuznetsov, I.N., ed. *Istoriia gosudarstva i prava Rossii v dokumentakh i materialakh 1930–1990-e gg.* Minsk: Amalfeia, 2003.

Lediakh, I.A., and F.M. Reshetnikov. "Kazhdyi natsistkii prestupnik dolzhen ponesti nakazanie." *Sovietskoe gosudarstvo i pravo* 2 (1965): 24–33.

Orlovskii, Slavomir, and Radoslav Ostrovich. *Erich Koch pered polskim sudom.* Moscow: Izdatel'stvo Instituta Miezhdunarodnykh Otnoshenii, 1961.

Parrish, Michael. *The Lesser Terror: Soviet State Security, 1939–1953.* Westport, CT: Praeger, 1996.

Penter, Tanja. "Collaboration on Trial: New Source Material on Soviet Postwar Trials against Collaborators." *Slavic Review* 64, no. 4 (2005): 782–90.

———. "Local Collaborators on Trial: Soviet War Crimes Trials under Stalin (1943–1953)." *Cahiers du monde russe et soviétique* 49, no. 2–3 (2008): 341–64.

Pinkus, Benjamin, and Jonathan Frankel, eds. *The Soviet Government and the Jews, 1948–1967: A Documented Study.* New York: Cambridge University Press, 1984.

Plavnieks, Richards. "Nazi Collaborators on Trial during the Cold War: The Cases against Viktors Arâjs and the Latvian Auxiliary Security Police." Ph.D. diss., University of North Carolina at Chapel Hill, 2013.

Prusin, Alexander V. "'Fascist Criminals to the Gallows!' The Holocaust and Soviet War Crimes Trials, December 1945–January 1946." *Holocaust and Genocide Studies* 17, no. 1 (2003): 1–30.

Roth, John K. and Elisabeth Maxwell, eds. *Remembering for the Future: The Holocaust in the Age of Genocide.* 3 vols. New York: Palgrave Macmillan, 2001.

Rudenko, R. "Hitlerovskie palachi nie dolzhny uiti ot vozmezdiia." *Sotsialisticheskaia zakonnost'* 3 (1965): 2–7.

Semiriaga, M.I. *Kollaboratsionism: Priroda, tipologiia i proiavleniia v gody vtoroi mirovoi voiny.* Moscow: Rossiiskaia politicheskaia entsiklopediia, 2000.

Simkin, Lev. "Death Sentence Despite the Law: A Secret 1962 Crimes-against-Humanity Trial in Kiev." *Holocaust and Genocide Studies* 27, no. 2 (2013): 299–312.

Simon, Gerhard. *Nationalism and Policy toward the Nationalities in the Soviet Union: From Totalitarian Dictatorship to Post-Stalinist Society.* Boulder, CO: Westview Press, 1991.

Smelser, Ronald, ed. *Lessons and Legacies V: The Holocaust and Justice.* Evanston, IL: Northwestern University Press, 2002.

The Trial in the Case of the Atrocities Committed by the German Fascist Invaders and Their Accomplices in Krasnodar and Krasnodar Territory, Heard July 14–17, 1943. Moscow: Foreign Languages Publishing House, 1943.

Voisin, Vanessa. "'Au nom des vivants,' de Léon Mazroukho: rencontre entre dénonciation officielle et hommage personnel." In *Kinojudaica: Les représentations des Juifs dans le cinéma russe et soviétique,* ed. V. Pozner and N. Laurent, 365–407. Paris: Nouveau Monde Editions, 2012.

Weiner, Amir. 2005. "War Crimes Trials and Public Justice Soviet Style: Western Ukraine, 1940s–1980s." Paper Presented at Workshop, "Prosecuting the Perpetrators of the Holocaust: War Crimes Trials in the Soviet Union and Eastern Europe," United States Holocaust Memorial Museum, Washington, DC, 5 June 2005.

———. "The Empires Pay a Visit: Gulag Returnees, East European Rebellions, and Soviet Frontier Politics." *Journal of Modern History* 78, no. 2 (2006): 333–76.

Zviagintsev, Viacheslav. *Voina na vesakh Femidy: voina 1941–1945 gg. v materialakh sudiebno-sledstvennykh del.* Moscow: Terra, 2006.

Chapter 6

"Not Quite Klaus Barbie, but in That Category"

Mykola Lebed, the CIA, and the Airbrushing of the Past

Per Anders Rudling

One morning in January 1986, three journalists from the left-liberal New York newspaper *The Village Voice* appeared on the doorstep of 76-year-old Mykola Lebed in Yonkers. The journalists asked specific and pointed questions regarding the old man's background as an alumnus of a German Security Police School in Zakopane, in Nazi-occupied Poland, in 1940 as Germany was preparing for war against the Soviet Union.[1] Having briefly answered the questions in the negative, Lebed slammed the door on the journalists. As he did so, they managed to snap his picture. The photo accompanied a large article with the sensational headline, "To Catch a Nazi," which appeared a couple of weeks later.[2]

The article in *The Village Voice,* with its detailed description of war crimes, collaboration in the Holocaust, and allegations that the CIA was sheltering a terrorist and convicted assassin, triggered an historiographical firestorm with a massive Ukrainian nationalist response—coordinated partially by the CIA. Only now, following the opening of the Soviet archives and the release of documents in accordance with the Nazi War Crimes Disclosure Act in 2005 and 2007 can the remarkable story of Mykola Lebed and the CIA be told.[3] As the case of SS Hauptsturmführer and Gestapo officer Klaus Barbie illustrates, Nazi war criminals in the service of Western intelligence

services during the Cold War can be a politically sensitive issue.[4] By study-
ing one—particularly prominent—case, this article aims at expanding our
understanding the CIA's use of former Nazis and collaborators in the spy
games of the Cold War, with a particular focus upon how the community of
interest impacted the representation of a difficult past.

WHO WAS MYKOLA LEBED?

The old man living on the upper floor of a two-story building, above that
of the building's owner, his former driver and bodyguard "from the days
of World War II clandestine operations in Western Ukraine,"[5] was not just
any New York suburbanite. A former leader of the far-right Organization
of Ukrainian Nationalists (OUN) and the organizer of its dreaded security
service, the Sluzhba Bezpeky (SB OUN), Mykola Lebed (1909/10–1998) was
a convicted murderer with a long resume of political violence, including a
stint as a collaborator with Nazi Germany. In 1934, Lebed attended a training camp near Rome, run by the Croatian Ustaša.[6] He was instrumental in
the assassination of Bronisław Pieracki, the Polish minister of the interior,
in June of that year. In January 1936, Lebed was sentenced to death for having organized the murder, a sentence commuted to life in prison.[7] Released
after the German attack on Poland in 1939, Lebed became one of the leading figures in the more radical wing of the OUN following the 1940 split of
the organization.[8]

This organization, known as the OUN-Bandera, or OUN(b) after
its leader, Stepan Bandera (1909–1959), sought to establish a totalitarian
Ukrainian state under its control.[9] In an unsuccessful attempt on 30 June
1941 to establish Ukrainian statehood, the OUN(b) "Prime Minister" Iaroslav Stets'ko (1912–1986) declared that his new state was to "cooperate
closely with National Socialist Greater Germany … under the Führer Adolf
Hitler."[10] Stets'ko assured Adolf Hitler, Benito Mussolini, Francisco Franco,
and Ante Pavelić that the new state was a new, committed member of Hitler's New Order in Europe.[11] The state proclamation was accompanied by a
wave of pogroms in over 140 localities across western Ukraine, organized by
the OUN(b) in the summer of 1941, in which thousands of Jews were murdered.[12] Lebed, the number three person in the OUN(b) hierarchy, arrived
in Lviv on 3 July 1941.[13]

Declarations of loyalty notwithstanding, Hitler had no interest in an
OUN(b) state. His plan was to colonize Ukraine. OUN(b) activities were soon
sharply curtailed. Bandera and Stets'ko were brought to Berlin where they
were interrogated, but otherwise free to move around the city and to con-

tinue to pester the German authorities with pleas to cooperate with their group.[14] Following the assassination of two high-profile Ukrainian national-ists from the rival Melnyk wing of the OUN, which stood in open coopera-tion with the Gestapo and refused to acknowledge the 30 June declaration, Bandera and Stets'ko were detained. They spent much of the war held as *Ehrenhäftlinge* in the Zellenbau, a special annex to the Sachsenhausen camp used for particularly important political figures.[15] The Gestapo issued an ar-rest warrant for Lebed, and, in connection with this, issued a wanted poster for Lebed on 4 October 1941. Lebed went underground and, between Sep-tember 1941 and May 1943 he served as acting leader of the OUN(b).

During this period, the OUN(b) actively infiltrated various German auxiliary police units in the occupied Soviet Union, gaining weapons train-ing and combat experience, but also getting intimately involved in the ex-ecution of the Holocaust in Ukraine and Belorussia.[16] In February 1943, the OUN(b) and its paramilitary branch, the Ukrainian Insurgent Army (Ukrains'ka Povstans'ka Armiia, UPA), launched a coordinated campaign of ethnic cleansing and mass murder against the civilian Polish population in western Ukraine, claiming between 60,000 and 100,000 lives.[17] The precise date of the OUN(b) decision to remove the Poles is unclear, as is the exact role of Lebed. Archival sources, including a postwar Polish interrogation with a local OUN(b) commander make explicit references to an SB OUN(b) "Order No. 1," for a "massive liquidation of the Polish population, start-ing in Polissia and then in Volhynia," issued in early 1943, at a time when Roman Shukhevych (1907–1950) was eclipsing Lebed as the dominant fig-ure of the OUN(b).[18]

Upon Bandera's release in August 1944, the OUN(b) again resumed its strategic collaboration with the German authorities.[19] The contact was es-tablished by Lebed, through his intermediary Ivan Hryn'okh (1907–1994).[20] At the same time, the OUN(b) sought to establish contact with the Western allies. Lebed was tasked with establishing relations with US intelligence. The unreconstructed totalitarians Bandera and Stets'ko remained commit-ted to one-party dictatorship, authoritarianism, and political terror, whereas Lebed's group, after the German defeat at Stalingrad, paid lip service to a certain degree of political pluralism. The fallout between Lebed and Bandera was personal, political, and violent, culminating in Lebed firing a pistol at Bandera during a dispute in mid-March 1947, upon which Ban-dera, in turn, ordered Lebed's assassination.[21] Bandera's group, the Foreign Section of the OUN (Zakordonne Chastyny OUN, ZCh OUN) parted ways with Lebed's Foreign Representation of the Ukrainian Supreme Liberation Council (Zakordonne Predstavnytstvo Ukrains'koi Holovnoi Vyzvol'noi Rady, zpUHVR) in 1948. In western Ukraine, the UPA continued armed resistance against the Soviets until 1949–1950. The insurgency was crushed with utmost brutality, claiming the lives of an estimated 153,000 people.[22]

Centered in Munich, Bandera's group, the largest and most militant émigré political organization, soon lost the support of the United States due in equal measure to its reliance on political assassinations, organized crime, drug and alcohol black marketeering, and the counterfeiting of US banknotes.[23] The OUN(b) continued, however, to work with British, Italian, and West German intelligence until the end of the 1950s, at which time it came to rely increasingly on Franco's Spain and Chiang Kai-Shek's Taiwan for funding.[24] Bandera was himself assassinated by a Soviet Ukrainian agent in 1959, but his organization continued its clandestine and largely unsuccessful attempts to infiltrate the USSR throughout the Cold War.[25] In Canada, where many of its followers settled, the OUN(b) benefited from government funding under the aegis of official multiculturalism after 1971.[26] In 1992, the OUN(b) repatriated much of its organization to Ukraine.

Lebed's group was tiny by comparison. It consisted of two overlapping CIA-funded organizations, the above-mentioned zpUHVR, and the OUN abroad (*zakordonnyi*), or OUN(z), established in 1954. In 1949, the CIA secretly brought Lebed to the United States, where he came to run one of the most successful and long-lasting covert programs aimed against the Soviet Union. In the immediate postwar years Lebed appears to have been involved in the program OHIO (later BINGO, 1949–1950), a US government program that used Ukrainian nationalist agents in the Displaced Person (DP) camps to track down and liquidate suspected Soviet moles in the US zones of occupation in Germany and Austria.[27] From 1948 to 1952, Lebed and his associate Evhen Stakhiv (1918–2014) played key roles in CIA covert operations in which OUN members loyal to his faction were airdropped into the Ukrainian Soviet Socialist Republic (SSR) in conjunction with anti-Soviet guerilla operations.[28] From 1952 until 1977, Lebed led the CIA's covert action program AERODYNAMIC (later QRDYNAMIC and QRPLUMB), which operated until President George H.W. Bush discontinued its funding in September 1990. Its objective was "to exploit and increase nationalist and other dissident tendencies in the Soviet Ukraine."[29] A primary task was the smuggling of anti-Soviet materials, published in New York by a front organization titled Prolog Research Corporation, Inc., into the Ukrainian SSR. From 1961, Prolog published the journal *Suchasnist'* [Modern Times]. Different in tone and content from the militant, ideologically inflexible journals of Bandera's OUN(b), *Suchasnist'* became one of the most important journals of the Ukrainian emigration. By not admitting any new members into his inner circle of confidents until the 1970s, Lebed's zpUHVR—unlike other émigré nationalist organizations—avoided KGB penetration. The CIA described the AERODYNAMIC program as the "principal vehicle through which the Agency conducts its operations against the Ukrainian Soviet Socialist Republic. The main purpose of the project is to exploit contacts with Soviet Ukrainian citizens in order to encourage national and intellectual unrest in the Ukrainian SSR."[30]

Lebed's clandestine circle, which the CIA characterized as "more 'moderate' than most, i.e., it is not fanatically anti-Bolshevik, monarchist or neo-Fascist,"[31] was an unlikely vehicle for its aim "to encourage liberal sentiment in the USSR as a whole."[32] In this marriage of convenience, the CIA supported, in the name of liberal democracy, an ethnonationalist group run by a convicted assassin whereas the zpUHVR/OUN(z), in turn, worked for a government that did not support their cause of Ukrainian independence.[33]

Over the course of the 1950s and 1960s, the Holocaust spurred limited attention in North America. Whereas dissenting liberal and socialist émigré voices occasionally raised concerns about Lebed's wartime past, much of the criticism of Lebed originated from the OUN(b), which resented the CIA funding for Lebed's group. This changed in the late 1970s, as the Holocaust entered Western historical memory, through, among other things, the broadcast in 1978 of the miniseries *Holocaust*.[34] To many postwar Ukrainian émigrés and their offspring this development was often a painful process. As a disproportionate number of the roughly 250,000 Ukrainian Displaced Persons that remained in Western Europe by 1947 had served the German occupation authorities in various capacities during the war, the émigré community was sensitive to allegations of war criminality or complicity in the Holocaust.[35] Many émigrés were stung by accounts of Ukrainian collaboration, perceiving it as besmirching their national honor.[36] The relative ignorance of the general public further complicated matters: the average American often knew little about these Eastern Europeans, other than their reputation as antisemites and as collaborators in the Holocaust.[37]

The creation of the Office of Special Investigations (OSI) within the Department of Justice in 1979 increased the unease within the Ukrainian émigré community. The OSI was charged with investigating the past of immigrants who had entered the United States after World War II who were suspected of having collaborated with the Nazi regime. Following investigations, the OSI undertook denaturalization proceedings in civil courts on the grounds that its targets had lied on their visa forms when entering the United States. Ideally, guilty subjects would be stripped of their US citizenship and then deported. Allegations of war criminality and collaboration with the Nazis served as a rallying cry for much of the Ukrainian diaspora.[38] The case of John Demjanjuk (1920–2012), a former Sobibór death camp guard who had immigrated to the United States in 1952 and settled in Ohio, became a cause célèbre for much of the Ukrainian community, which raised over $1 million for his legal defense alone.[39] And Demjanjuk was but one of several alleged war criminals facing denaturalization and deportation in the 1980s. Former Treblinka death camp guard Fedor Fedorenko (1907–1987) was denaturalized in 1981 and sent back to the Ukrainian SSR in December 1984 where he was found guilty of war crimes, sentenced to death, and executed by firing squad in 1986 or 1987. Estonian concentration camp guard Karl Linnas (1919–1987) was denaturalized and deported to the USSR in 1987, where he died in a prison hospital awaiting trial.[40] Other prominent cases included Andrija Artuković (1899–1988), former minister of the interior in the fascist Croatian Ustaša government, who was arrested in November 1984 and extradited to Yugoslavia in November 1986.[41] These cases stirred strong emotions with the Ukrainian community in North America.[42]

Lebed was one of twelve individuals investigated by the US General Accounting Office (GAO) in its 1985 report.[43] Concerned about a possible exposure of Lebed and his connection to the Agency, on 16 August 1985, the CIA approached the OSI chief Neil Sher directly concerning its involvement with the old nationalist. Sher, according to the CIA's records, "agreed to protect the secrecy of QRPLUMB if and when the investigation of P/2 [Lebed] resumed and promised that OSI would inform CIA of any new developments in P/2's case. This agreement was re-confirmed in December 1985 when OSI informed CIA that it planned to approach the Polish government on the case."[44]

The CIA followed the Lebed case with increasing concern after October 1985 when the OSI began looking into Lebed's background "on allegations that he may have collaborated with the Germans and as a leader of the OUN during World War II [and that] he may have been responsible for the OUN's alleged war crimes" and conducted an interview with the former OUN(b) leader.[45] Roman Kupchinsky (1944–2010),[46] Lebed's successor as Prolog president, was convinced the Soviets were behind the allegations and demanded that both the CIA and GAO apologize to Lebed.[47] The transcript of that communication remains inaccessible to researchers, but the materials available indicate that some form of agreement was reached:

> Agency representatives from the Office of the General Counsel and this office met with the Head of the Office of Special Investigation (OSI) [Neil Sher] at the Department of Justice and advised him of the case and our concern for the security of QRPLUMB operations. Chief, OSI stated that his office does not have a file on Mr. Lebed and at the moment has no basis for initiating an investigation of him; and if such investigation is warranted in the future, he will inform the Agency of his action. He advised against taking any action intended to correct the public GAO statement on Mr. Lebed lest it attract unfavorable

media investigative reporting. Additionally, he recommended that we inform
our Congressional oversight committees and Congressman [Peter W.] Rodino
[D-NJ] of the case and our security concerns, especially since he had indications
that Congressman Rodino was under pressure from certain quarters to hold a
hearing on the GAO report.[48]

The CIA's concerns were justified. Soon thereafter, Lebed's case caught
the attention of investigative journalists. The first serious journalistic inquiry into Lebed's wartime past was not initiated by one of the large New
York papers, but by a relatively small, left-liberal community newspaper, *The
Village Voice*. A research team of investigative journalists, led by the young
journalist Joe Conason (b. 1954) spent months researching Lebed's wartime
past before approaching the OUN veteran and CIA operative in his Yonkers home in January 1986.[49] Conason went through a wealth of sources,
including partially redacted records from the US Army Counterintelligence
Corps (CIC) obtained under the Freedom of Information Act, immigration
records, interviews with Ukrainian émigrés, and eyewitness accounts, obtained via a research fellow at Yad Vashem in Jerusalem.[50] Even more alarm-
ing for the CIA was that Conason's article contained a specific, detailed
timeline of Lebed's whereabouts in 1939–1941. These details posed a direct
challenge to the Ukrainian diaspora's—and the CIA's—official versions of
Lebed's past.[51] A key focus was on his background as a Nazi collaborator:
"Only hints of what Lebed was actually doing in 1940 and 1941 appear in
the CIC file ... a card in the CIC file identifies Lebed as 'a graduate of the
Zakopane, Poland criminal police school,'" Conason wrote.

Conason further cited the memoirs of Mykyta Kosakivs'kyi,[52] a fellow
alumnus and one of the older OUN members trained at the Zakopane
school, on how a "Ukrainian Training Unit" was established in November
1939: "According to [Lebed's] declaration, the Ukrainian unit was organized
by the OUN leadership and by permission of the German Security Service.
It included 120 specially selected trainees ... 'The Ukrainian commandant
... was Mykola Lebid [*sic*].' The curriculum ... emphasized 'exercises in the
hardening of hearts.'" Conason cited Kosakivs'kyi's recollection how,

> At sundown, ... Krüger, Rosenbaum, Lebid [*sic*] and a few students would go
> to Zakopane, enter some Jewish home on the way, grab a Jew, and bring him
> to the Unit. One evening, late in November or early in December 1939, they
> returned with a young Jew. In the presence of Ukrainian seniors, including my-
> self, Krüger and Rosenbaum, fortified with alcohol, [they] proceeded with their
> demonstration of the proper methods of interrogation.

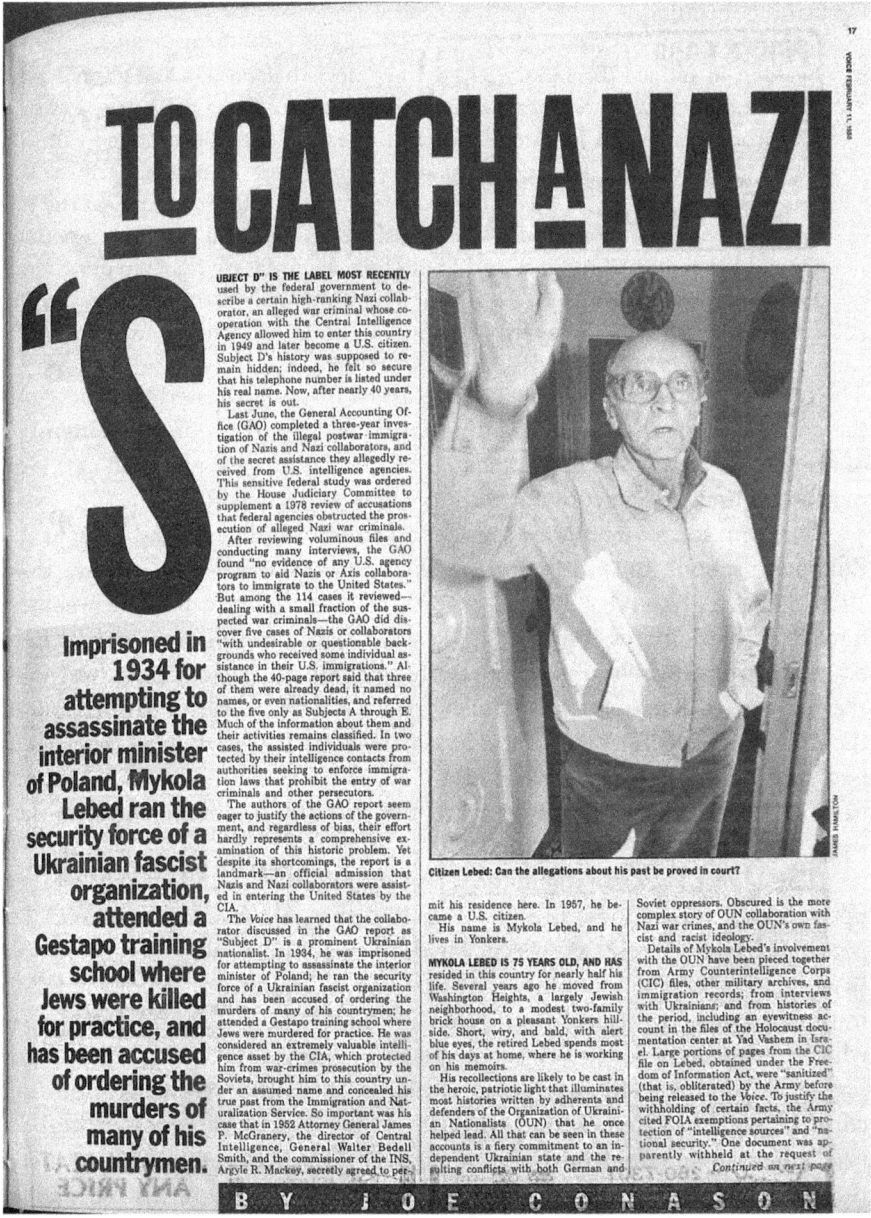

TO CATCH A NAZI

"SUBJECT D" IS THE LABEL MOST RECENTLY used by the federal government to describe a certain high-ranking Nazi collaborator, an alleged war criminal whose cooperation with the Central Intelligence Agency allowed him to enter this country in 1949 and later become a U.S. citizen. Subject D's history was supposed to remain hidden; indeed, he felt so secure that his telephone number is listed under his real name. Now, after nearly 40 years, his secret is out.

Last June, the General Accounting Office (GAO) completed a three-year investigation of the illegal postwar immigration of Nazis and Nazi collaborators, and of the secret assistance they allegedly received from U.S. intelligence agencies. This sensitive federal study was ordered by the House Judiciary Committee to supplement a 1978 review of accusations that federal agencies obstructed the prosecution of alleged Nazi war criminals.

After reviewing voluminous files and conducting many interviews, the GAO found "no evidence of any U.S. agency program to aid Nazis or Axis collaborators to immigrate to the United States." But among the 114 cases it reviewed—dealing with a small fraction of the suspected war criminals—the GAO did discover five cases of Nazis or collaborators "with undesirable or questionable backgrounds who received some individual assistance in their U.S. immigrations." Although the 40-page report said that three of them were already dead, it named no names, or even nationalities, and referred to the five only as Subjects A through E. Much of the information about them and their activities remains classified. In two cases, the assisted individuals were protected by their intelligence contacts from authorities seeking to enforce immigration laws that prohibit the entry of war criminals and other persecutors.

The authors of the GAO report seem eager to justify the actions of the government, and regardless of bias, their effort hardly represents a comprehensive examination of this historic problem. Yet despite its shortcomings, the report is a landmark—an official admission that Nazis and Nazi collaborators were assisted in entering the United States by the CIA.

The *Voice* has learned that the collaborator discussed in the GAO report as "Subject D" is a prominent Ukrainian nationalist. In 1934, he was imprisoned for attempting to assassinate the interior minister of Poland; he ran the security force of a Ukrainian fascist organization and has been accused of ordering the murders of many of his countrymen; he attended a Gestapo training school where Jews were murdered for practice. He was considered an extremely valuable intelligence asset by the CIA, which protected him from war-crimes prosecution by the Soviets, brought him to this country under an assumed name and concealed his true past from the Immigration and Naturalization Service. So important was his case that in 1952 Attorney General James P. McGranery, the director of Central Intelligence, General Walter Bedell Smith, and the commissioner of the INS, Argyle R. Mackey, secretly agreed to permit his residence here. In 1957, he became a U.S. citizen.

His name is Mykola Lebed, and he lives in Yonkers.

MYKOLA LEBED IS 75 YEARS OLD, AND HAS resided in this country for nearly half his life. Several years ago he moved from Washington Heights, a largely Jewish neighborhood, to a modest two-family brick house on a pleasant Yonkers hillside. Short, wiry, and bald, with alert blue eyes, the retired Lebed spends most of his days at home, where he is working on his memoirs.

His recollections are likely to be cast in the heroic, patriotic light that illuminates most histories written by adherents and defenders of the Organization of Ukrainian Nationalists (OUN) that he once helped lead. All that can be seen in these accounts is a fiery commitment to an independent Ukrainian state and the resulting conflicts with both German and Soviet oppressors. Obscured is the more complex story of OUN collaboration with Nazi war crimes, and the OUN's own fascist and racist ideology.

Details of Mykola Lebed's involvement with the OUN have been pieced together from Army Counterintelligence Corps (CIC) files, other military archives, and immigration records; from interviews with Ukrainians; and from histories of the period, including an eyewitness account in the files of the Holocaust documentation center at Yad Vashem in Israel. Large portions of pages from the CIC file on Lebed, obtained under the Freedom of Information Act, were "sanitized" (that is, obliterated) by the Army before being released to the *Voice*. To justify the withholding of certain facts, the Army cited FOIA exemptions pertaining to protection of "intelligence sources" and "national security." One document was apparently withheld at the request of

Continued on next page

Imprisoned in 1934 for attempting to assassinate the interior minister of Poland, Mykola Lebed ran the security force of a Ukrainian fascist organization, attended a Gestapo training school where Jews were killed for practice, and has been accused of ordering the murders of many of his countrymen.

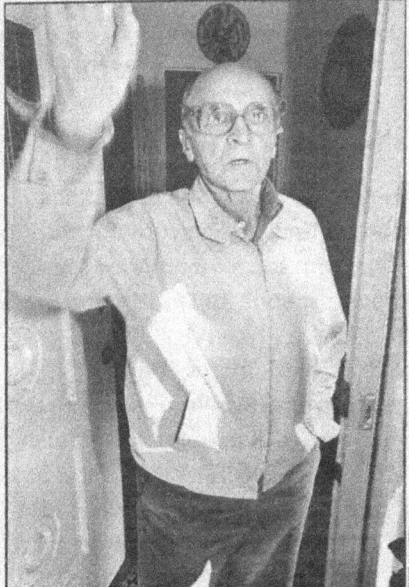

Citizen Lebed: Can the allegations about his past be proved in court?

BY JOE CONASON

Figure 6.1. First page of Joe Conason's "To Catch a Nazi," *The Village Voice*, 11 February 1986

Conason continued:

> Seeking to induce the innocent Jew to confess that he had raped an Aryan
> woman, the German officers beat and tortured him, using their fists, a sword,
> and iron bars. When he was bloody from head to toe, they applied salt and
> flame to his wounds. The broken man then confessed his fictional crimes. But
> that was not the end ... [According to Kosakivs'kyi,] "Rosenbaum beat the Jew
> again with an iron pipe and Lebed too assisted manually in that 'heroic action.'
> One of the senior Ukrainians and I withdrew from the spectacle to our rooms.
> We learned afterwards that the tortured man was stripped naked, stood-up in
> front of the school as 'a sentry' and doused with water in heavy frost."

The next day, Kosakivs'kyi recalled, he and a friend protested to Lebed, but
the commandant told them bluntly that "it was the duty of every member
of the OUN to show the Germans that his nerves are just as tough as a German's and that the heart of any nationalist is as hard as steel."

On Conason's direct question, Lebed conceded that he had been at the
Zakopane school, but said it was in the winter of 1940–1941, rather than
1939–1940, as Kosakivs'kyi had stated, adding "I left after five weeks. I
have exactly the dates. I quit."[53] Conason's team not only researched Lebed's background in the Zakopane training camp, but also his postwar CIA
service, for which they presented very strong indications. Even though
the CIA had declined to comment on the matter, *The Village Voice* felt it
had secured enough evidence to state, unambiguously, "The CIA brought
Mykola Lebed to the US under an assumed name and concealed his past
from the INS."[54]

The *Village Voice* story generated significant interest and was soon taken
up by larger outlets including the *New York Post, The Herald Statesman,*[55] *The
New York Times*[56] as well as several Jewish community newspapers.[57] The article quickly became a liability that threatened to unravel one of the CIA's
most extensive covert action programs. Unlike Demjanjuk and Fedorenko,
who had not been politically active after the war, Lebed had been a senior
operative who headed a propaganda outfit and who retained important
connections and support from the CIA. With decades of experience of covert action and clandestine operations, Lebed was not one to accept quietly
the exposure of his and his organizations' pasts. Utilizing his old Prolog
contacts, he fought back. Roman Kupchinsky, Lebed's successor, launched
a coordinated counteroffensive in the Ukrainian press in North America.
Whereas the CIA was well aware of Lebed's past—and by 1986 of his training in Zakopane—in *The Ukrainian Weekly,* Kupchinsky denied everything,
responding with a litany of direct and deliberate falsehoods. Kupchinsky
charged *The Village Voice* with sloppy journalism and ignorance, dismissed

the article as part of a Soviet conspiracy, and questioned Conason's mental health. "[Lebed's] friends spent [World War II] in jail," Kupchinsky said. "His wife spent the war held by Germans, his daughter was born in a concentration camp. Anyone who says [Lebed] is a Nazi war criminal is downright loony," Kupchinsky told *The Herald Statesman.*[58]

The Ukrainian Weekly launched its own attack on Conason. *The Village Voice*, it asserted, had "a well-honed reputation for engaging in a type of reporting known as muckracking journalism." It also quoted a source close to Lebed, who asked not to be identified, who noted that "the story was obviously orchestrated by Moscow."[59] The following week *The Ukrainian Weekly* published an interview with Kupchinsky, who claimed *The Village Voice* article contained "nothing to show that he [Mr. Lebed] was a collaborator," and denied Lebed had ever commanded the SB.[60] Curiously, while denying Lebed's collaboration with the Nazis, Kupchinsky admitted Lebed's Zakopane training, but presented it as a rather unproblematic episode of the past, for which Lebed had accounted fully.[61] "Lebed never hid the fact that he was at Zakopane ... He was there for only five weeks and he left after he discovered it was a Gestapo police school." Kupchinsky attached a copy of the Gestapo wanted poster of 4 October 1941. The poster, which *The Ukrainian Weekly* published, Kupchinsky explained, "raises further doubt about Mr. Lebed's alleged close association with the Nazis." Conason had pointed out that Prolog, in addition to its New York office, maintained mysterious offices in Munich, London, and Cairo, and that its publication of eight to ten volumes annually, plus two or three small-circulation magazines would hardly provide a sufficient source of revenue to maintain activity on this scale.[62] Kupchinsky went on to deny both Lebed's and Prolog's connection to the CIA, insisting that Prolog's book publishing program and donations from the Ukrainian community provided the organization's funding. "Lebed," he said,

> has nothing to hide ... He came to this country perfectly legally and he was never a CIA agent. The bottom line is that this article is an attack on anybody who supports Ukrainian independence ... The Soviets have consistently tried to discredit the Ukrainian liberation movement, and the *Voice* article appears at a time when the Soviets are continuing to smear the Ukrainian underground.

Kupchinsky claimed that Prolog "for years has been trying to improve Ukrainian-Jewish relations" and he called on the Ukrainian community "not to perceive this latest attack on Ukrainian nationalists as a 'Jewish conspiracy.'"[63] Kupchinski cast Lebed's legacy as one of reconciliation while, at the same time seeking to preempt expressions of open antisemitism from his community.

On its end, *The Ukrainian Weekly* urged the Ukrainian community to rally their wagons and unite around Lebed, whom they equated with Ukraine itself and to "unmask" what it described as a Muscovite conspiracy:

> The Ukrainian community should unite to unmask and fight the smear campaign which originates in Moscow. Likewise, the Ukrainian community should oppose the disinformation disseminated by Western elements, regardless of whether they are the result of ignorance or deliberate malice. It is the duty of the entire Ukrainian community to enlighten those who defame its noble struggle for freedom and denounce its inalienable right to seek justice for Ukrainians to determine their own fate in their homeland. The most recent attacks are not directed against a single person, or one political group, this is an offensive against our entire community, against the honor of Ukrainians and their good name. We can defend the truth successfully only as a single community and a united front.[64]

Lebed summoned the aid of historian and OUN veteran Taras Hunchak,[65] who Lebed's successor Kupchinsky had recruited to serve as editor of *Suchasnist'* in 1984.[66] Hunchak admired Lebed and shared his commitment to the pro-nationalist historical narrative.[67] In his memoirs Hunchak describes how "attacks" on alleged war criminals from Ukraine, constituted "an affront to my feelings of national dignity and therefore I reacted to them, writing replies to papers and journals."[68] Hunchak wrote to *The New York Times* as an academic and scholar. Signing as "Taras Hunczak, Professor of History," he lamented their 6 February 1986 article, titled, "C.I.A. Said to Have Let Nazi into U.S.," which he claimed to have read "with considerable dismay":

> I find it difficult to understand how Mr. Lebed can be referred to as a "Nazi collaborator" when from July 1941, he was a de facto leader of the Ukrainian Anti-Nazi underground movement known as the Organization of Ukrainian Nationalists. As all modern nationalist movements, that Ukrainian movement aimed at the establishment of an independent Ukrainian state—an objective that conflicted with the Nazi objectives in Eastern Europe. The struggle of the OUN against the Nazis is a matter of record for which there is indisputable evidence.

Hunchak thereafter repeated the diaspora's canonical narration: the OUN's victimization at the hands of the Nazis, with particular emphasis on Bandera's and Stet'sko's imprisonment in Sachsenhausen. Hunchak, who did not forget to submit a copy of Lebed's 1941 wanted poster, emphasized that Lebed's wife and daughter spent time in the Ravensbrück concentration camp. Hunchak concluded, "In view of the above facts it should be obvious that a

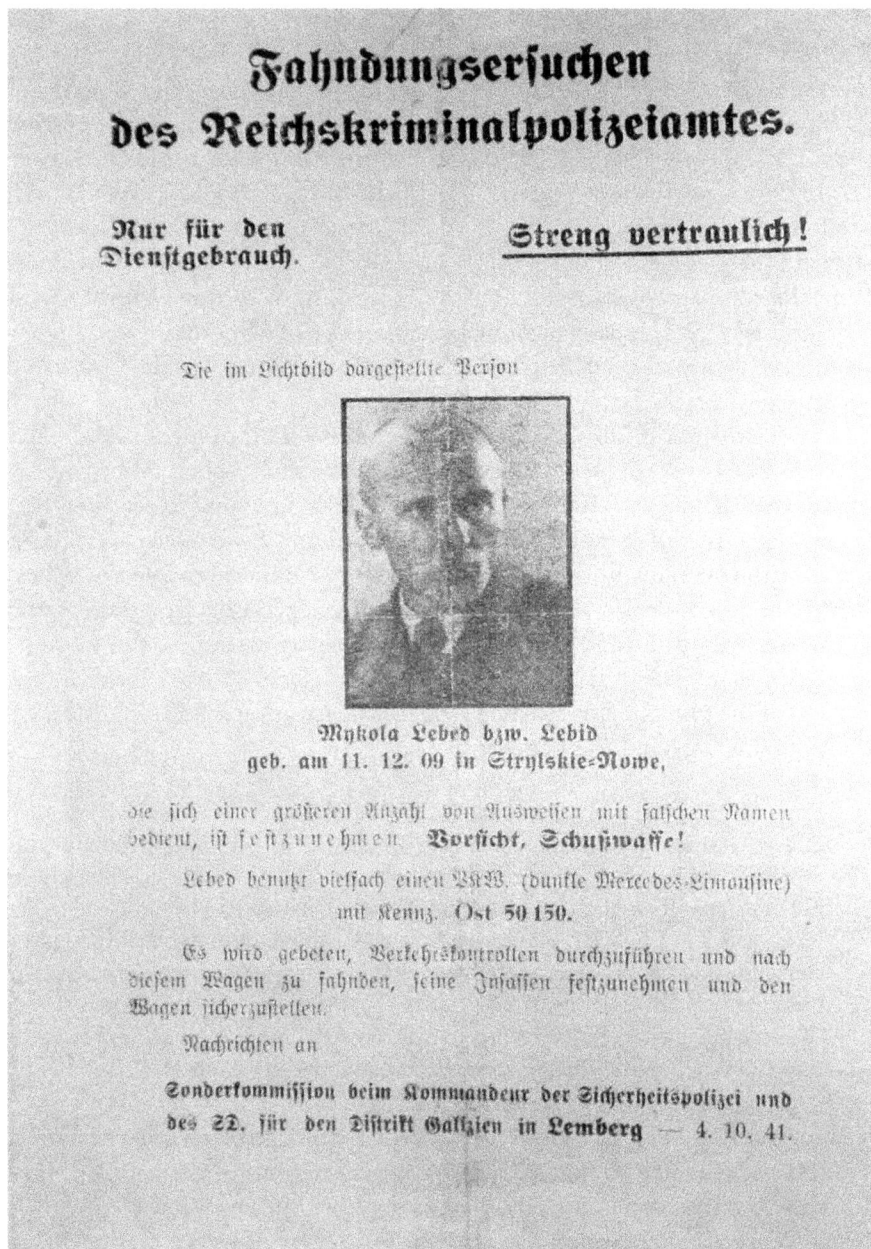

Figure 6.2. German Wanted Poster of Mykola Lebed (October, 1941). Of all the documents in the Mykola Lebed Archive at the Harvard Ukrainian Research Institute, this one appears most frequently. As he seeded his archive in the 1970s and 1980s, Lebed and Prolog made dozens of copies of the poster, distributing them across multiple folders in his archive.

charge of collaboration with the Nazis on the part of Mr. Lebed is absurd."[69] *The New York Times* did not publish his letter. It appeared, the following month, in *The Ukrainian Weekly,* the leading Ukrainian diaspora newspaper.[70]

Evidently troubled by the renewed, massive interest in Lebed's person, the CIA responded by placing a new coat of whitewash on Lebed's past. On 18 February, the CIA's acting chief of Political and Psychological Staff spelled out the Agency's strategy: "[We] see no reason at this time not to stick by the established cover story for QRPLUMB."[71] "We are," a report from the following week said, "currently working with our Central Cover Staff and legal people to determine possible areas of vulnerability in Agency relationship with the QRPLUMB organization and ensure the cover and security of this relationship."[72]

To the dismay of the CIA, on 14 March, Lebed himself entered the discussion. In a letter to the editor of *The Jewish Chronicle,* Lebed described the *Village Voice* article as "attempts at character assassination." He argued that "contrary to the allegations made by Mr. Conason, I was never in collaboration with Germany nor with any other power. Neither was I ever involved in any anti-[S]emitic activities, directly or indirectly."[73] Like Kupchinsky and Hunchak, Lebed illustrated his story by attaching a copy of the Gestapo wanted poster. Lebed also wrote *The New York Times* to offer an alternate version of the past. He approached *New York Times* journalist Ralph Blumenthal, who had covered the Lebed story.

> I was never a Nazi nor did I collaborate with the Germans. I was never trained in any German police school nor was I engaged in persecuting Jews or any other nationals. After the head of the Organization of Ukrainian Nationalists (OUN) Stepan Bandera and his deputy Yaroslav Stetsko had been placed under house arrest in July 1941, subsequently to be incarcerated at the Sachsenhausen concentration camp from September 1941 to September 1944, I headed the underground anti-Nazi resistance of the OUN (mid-July 1941 to May 1943) ... Our struggle has never been directed against any other people; we opposed only those foreign powers which enslaved and aided the enslavement of Ukraine.[74]

Through his lawyer Nestor L. Olesnycky, Lebed drafted an answer for *The Village Voice,* in which he questioned all the major points in Conason's article. Lebed's response systematically denied the OUN(b)'s anti-Jewish violence, instead depicting Ukrainian nationalists as rescuers of Jews while reversing the roles of victims and perpetrators by linking Jews to Stalinist terror:

> Mr. Conason does not give any concrete proof that Lebed was a Nazi collaborator, ... Mr. Lebed never ran the security force of the OUN, ... As to the alleged fascism of the OUN, Mr. Conason throws this phrase out without any proof.

How was the OUN fascistic? Did it, in its program call itself "Fascist"? No. Did it propagate the killing of Jews? No. The OUN might not have been particularly pro-Jewish, for understandable reasons … It is abundantly clear that the Ukrainians suffered terribly at the hands of the GPU, OGPU and NKVD. Thus it is understandable to some degree why they were not particularly pro-Jewish. It must also be kept in mind that Jews in Ukraine did not always share the concerns of their countrymen, the Ukrainians, on the vital question of Ukrainian independence … It was only in 1943 when the UPA was formed, that some Jews joined the UPA as doctors, printers and arms specialists.[75]

In regard to the more specific claims, Lebed, through his attorney, denied them completely:

Mykola Lebed never attended a Gestapo training school or any other police school. He never took part in any anti-Jewish activities. From the later part of December 1939 to January 1940 Lebed was in a camp in Zakopane, Poland. During his stay there, there were two members of the German SD, an officer Kruger, and an NCO "Mutti," whose name was never given. The Germans did not interfere in the daily life of the camp. On January 22, 1940, Kruger told Lebed that the aim of Hitler's policy is to expand the German Reich on the territory of the Soviet Union and that in the near future all participants in the camp will have to fill out personnel questionnaires and be photographed. Lebed then left the camp.[76]

Having Lebed dragged into a public discussion about his terrorist past, his relations with Nazi Germany, the role of the OUN during the Holocaust, and not least, his long-term affiliation with the CIA was a growing liability for the Agency. Officers at CIA headquarters instead suggested the following response: "Write a serious, well-documented letter to prominent newspapers with the goal of clearing Lebed" and "Have a prominent Ukrainian scholar prepare a scholarly study explaining Lebed's role in the OUN organization during World War II for … an appropriate publication."[77] At the same time the Agency sought to dissuade the Ukrainian community from filing a libel action: "[T]here is pressure from within the Ukrainian community," noted a CIA report, "to pursue a libel suit against the 'Village Voice' as a means of clearing [Lebed's] name and the reputation of the Ukrainian community." Having been advised that Lebed was considering taking legal action, Political and Psychological Staff representatives requested a meeting to discuss options and consequences: "Our main objective has been to avoid any legal action which could jeopardize the current Agency relationship with the organization, QRPLUMB."[78] The CIA secured Lebed's cooperation. He agreed "not to initiate a libel suit against the 'Village Voice' at this time since he understands that such action on his part could destroy the QRPLUMB organization."[79] The CIA also feared incidents of vigilante justice. Even though Lebed already had a bodyguard, the agency considered whether they should relocate Lebed "to some other place outside the New York metropolitan area ... The FBI will be in contact if and when they believe Lebed was in danger. The local police force was also contacted and made aware of the situation."[80]

If Kupchinsky coordinated the media response, Professor Hunchak provided academic legitimacy to the denial and, the third leg of the effort to clear Lebed was political. *The Ukrainian Weekly* published a statement of blanket denial by the zpUVHR in English; *Suchasnist'* carried it in Ukrainian.[81] The argument was not new, but one that the émigré nationalists had mechanically repeated since the mid-1940s. Lebed, it read, "was never in collaboration with Nazi Germany or any other power;" the OUN fought Hitler from 1941, and OUN members "were incarcerated in Auschwitz, Dachau, Sachsenhausen, Bergen-Belsen and other death camps. Many perished, including the two brothers of Stepan Bandera who were murdered by the Nazis in Auschwitz." The OUN "was never fascist in any way ... although it had elements of authoritarianism in its founding program, it never espoused racism, xenophobia or anti-Semitism." Rather, in August 1943, "it adopted a democratic program with guaranteed equal rights to all citizens of Ukraine regardless of their nationality, race or religion." The OUN "was a revolutionary organization of freedom-fighters—not a terrorist organization. Only the oppressors of the Ukrainian nation refer to OUN members as terrorists." Contrary to Conason's claims, the OUN "was not counting on Nazi Germany as the liberator or ally of Ukraine. In the first weeks of the Nazi occupation of Ukraine, the OUN began an underground resistance against the occupation which continued for three years."

In September 1986, *Suchasnist'* returned to the topic, publishing a statement by the Political Council of the Organization of Ukrainian Nationalists Abroad, OUN(z).[82] The OUN(z) statement presented Conason and *The Village Voice* as tools of Moscow, dedicated to destroying the Ukrainian nation: "The groundlessness of the entire complex of 'Nazi collaborator' accusations were revealed immediately following the German occupation of the Ukrainian territory. The OUN, under the leadership of Stepan Bandera—and, in his absence from the country—Lebed, fought the National Socialist occupation authorities actively and violently."[83] In connection with the denunciation of the "dishonoring of the Ukrainian name" an open letter, signed by 110 well-known community leaders and émigré politicians was published. The signatories expressed "alarm" about how "Communist Moscow" "exterminates all expression of cultural particularities of the Ukrainian people." They lamented how "the Muscovite communists and their representatives in Ukraine falsify our history, blacken our traditions, spread lies against our fighters for the freedom of the Ukrainian people as supposed servants of foreign powers." To the OUN(z), Conason's article was part of a broader campaign by Moscow and "Mykola Lebed ... one of the most outstanding organizers of the anti-German struggle during the time of the Nazi occupation of Ukraine."[84]

This damage control was coordinated and professionally managed by the QRPLUMB organization. Documentary evidence, recording all the rebuttals were forwarded to Lebed, who, although retired, remained a regular visitor and grey cardinal of sorts at the Prolog office on 875 West End Avenue. The zpUHVR statement was published no less than thirteen times in Ukrainian and English in Ukrainian diaspora papers in the United States, Great Britain, Australia, and Canada.[85] By 10 June 1986, the Prolog circle could report to Lebed that no less than fifty-nine articles in rebuttal to Conason had appeared in the Ukrainian émigré press.[86] The strategy was to maintain a fixed narrative of World War II in Ukraine, with the OUN both as the Nazis' primary victim and leader of the anti-Nazi resistance in Ukraine. Lebed himself was placed at the heart of this narrative, using the October 1941 Gestapo wanted poster akin to a "get out of jail free" card, while dismissing *The Village Voice* as a tool of the KGB.

Despite the significant resources mobilized in order to clear Lebed's record, the results were mixed. The interest in Lebed would not dissipate. In 1987 and 1988, the CIA noted with concern the continued OSI inquiries into Lebed's past, commenting that "if OSI were to bring formal charges, this could subject our relationship with the QRPLUMB organization to closer scrutiny, possible exposure."[87] The categorical denial of CIA operatives stand in contrast to the concerned tone of the CIA's internal correspondence. Well aware of the OUN's collaboration with Nazi Germany, the CIA internally acknowledged this much. It was concerned less with maintaining a sanitized and heroic account of the OUN than about the political liabilities of the Agency's long-term collaboration with Lebed should his past become publicly known.

> Although we do not believe P/2 [Lebed] ever engaged in a war crime himself, he was, during WW II, leader of the Organization of Ukrainian Nationalists (OUN) during the absence of Stepan Bandera, who spent the war in a Nazi concentration camp for having proclaimed an independent Ukrainian republic after the Nazi invasion in July 1941. For a few weeks after the German invasion, the OUN did collaborate with the Nazis. The collaboration ended quickly, however, and Bandera was incarcerated, as were P/2's wife and daughter who also spent WW II in a Nazi concentration camp. (We have given the OSI a copy of a Gestapo "wanted" poster issued in 1941 for the capture of P/2.) ... There is

a strong likelihood that the Poles and possibly the Soviets will publicize such a request and thus try to link P/2–an old nemesis–to war crimes, knowing, as they would, the significance that the request had come from OSI. This not only would damage our Ukrainian program, but would personally tarnish P/2, who is 78 and has served us for nearly 40 years. Also, if we fail to protect P/2 from inquiries [by] the Poles, there would be a strong reaction from the Ukrainian (indeed, probably the entire East European) émigré community, with whom we work closely, particularly if the Poles publicize the case. We do believe that there is some risk that our attempt to block an inquiry [by] the Poles could become public through a leak in the Justice Department. This could bring about a difficult issue for us–not quite Klaus Barbie, but in that category–but we still recommend that we request Justice refrain from contacting any bloc country with regard to its investigation of P/2.[88]

As the Cold War came to an end, the administration of George H. W. Bush ended the funding of the QRPLUMB project, which was terminated on 30 September 1990. *Suchasnist'* was transferred to Kyiv in January 1992 and lost its institutional affiliation with the zpUHVR circle.[89] The OSI continued to take an interest in Lebed until the end of his life. On 4 October 1991, the OSI informed the CIA that they intended "to initiate inquiries with the governments of Germany, Poland and the USSR re P/2's [Lebed's] activities during World War II."[90] Yet, following the termination of the QRPLUMB program, the CIA's internal documentation suggests that the Agency treated the allegations rather dismissively. As one report noted, "Other than a few allegations, possibly politically motivated by hostile Ukrainian émigré informants, OSI has not pursued the case since 1985 ... [Lebed] is now 78 years old and in poor health. Aside from potential security considerations (possible exposure of CIA support of the QRPLUMB project for 43 years) there is also the human factor to be considered."[91] When Congresswoman Elizabeth Holtzman (D-NY) in 1992 requested access to the CIA's files on Lebed, the CIA replied that "no records have been found on Lebed."[92] This point-blank denial continued until Lebed's death.[93]

Lebed's final years were darkened by illness. He suffered from Alzheimer's disease and died peacefully in his bed in Pittsburgh, on 18 July 1998 at the age of 89.[94] He faced no legal consequences for his wartime activities. During a tense period of the Cold War, when alleged war criminals without Lebed's connections were fully investigated and sometimes denaturalized, Lebed's case stands out. To a Ukrainian émigré community heavily vested in an airbrushed and highly ideological version of the recent past, the stakes were high; if Lebed fell, so would their entire wartime narrative. To the CIA, it would have risked exposure of one of their most long-running covert action programs, which Lebed—a terrorist and convicted murderer—ran for more than a quarter century. While significant CIA materials on Lebed remain inaccessible, materials available from Polish, German, Ukrainian, American, and Russian archives support historian Jeffrey Burds's characterization of Lebed as "a major war criminal, perhaps the highest ranking Nazi murderer ever to arrive in America."[95] Conason's investigative journalism in 1986 was no minor feat at a time when historians were only beginning to understand the complex and violent past of the OUN and UPA. If one objection was to be raised, it is that Conason's heavy focus on Lebed's collaboration with Nazi Germany distracted attention from the atrocities carried by the OUN(b) during Lebed's tenure as acting leader of that organization. The OUN(b) and UPA massacres of tens of thousands of Poles, and thousands of Jews, and the SB OUN(b)'s political violence against political rivals inside Ukraine and in the American and British occupation zones in the immediate postwar years greatly eclipse the atrocities committed in the Zakopane school.

CIA loyalty to a long-term employee and valuable asset resulted in Lebed receiving preferential treatment that other, less prominent alleged war criminals, did not enjoy. Lebed's central role as a CIA operative provided him a platform from which his circle launched a counter-initiative, rallying the politically active segments of his community to his defense. Having taken little, if any, interest in Lebed's past in the Zakopane training camp when he first arrived in the United States, the CIA, in 1986, accepted, at face value, Lebed's own claims of having attended the Zakopane training school for several weeks without knowledge of its sponsors.[96] Available documentation strongly suggests the CIA intervened for their long-term operative, partly as a reward for his long and faithful service to the Agency, but also because a community of interest formed over the decades: an inquiry into Lebed's criminal and terrorist past would also incriminate the CIA. Émigré nationalist politics, clandestinely funded by the CIA, not only delayed inquiry into Mykola Lebed's past until after his death; it hampered our understanding of the role of Ukrainian nationalists during World War II generally.

Per Anders Rudling received his Ph.D. in history from the University of Alberta. He is an associate professor of history at Lund University, Sweden, and a senior visiting fellow at the Department of History, National University of Singapore. His publications include *The OUN, the UPA, and the Holocaust: A Study in the Manufacturing of Historical Myths* (Pittsburgh, 2011) and *The Rise and Fall of Belarusian Nationalism, 1906–1931* (Pittsburgh, 2015).

NOTES

1. Whereas the Zakopane school was located in the building used by the local Gestapo headquarters, it was a school run by the *Abwehr*, and the units trained by Lebed and Shukhevych were so-called *peredovye hrupy*, diversionary soldiers from among nationalist volunteers who would go on to serve in the Nachtigal and Roland Battalions and other units in June 1941. Later, the Zakopane school moved to Rabka where Ukrainian militia were trained. According to testimonies by Jewish survivors, as many as three hundred Jews were murdered at the center, many of whom were women and children. Robin O'Neill, *The Rabka Four: A Warning From History* (London, 2011), 27; Karel C. Berkhoff, *Harvest of Despair: Life and Death in Ukraine Under Nazi Rule* (Cambridge, MA, 2004), 289; "Protokol doprosa osuzhdennogo BIZANTSA Al'freda Ioganovicha ot 23 noiabria 1949," Haluzevyi derzhavnyi arkhiv Sluzhby bezpeky Ukrainy, Kyiv [hereafter HDA SBU], f. 65, spr. S-7448, ark. 15–22, published in Volodymyr Serhiichuk, ed., *Roman Shukhevych u dokumentakh radians'kykh organiv derzhavnoi bezpeky (1940–1950), Tom II* (Kyiv, 2007) 381–92.

2. Joe Conason, "To Catch a Nazi," *The Village Voice*, 11 February 1986, 17–21. The issue was actually published a week earlier.

3. Notable recent studies include Richard Breitman, Norman J.W. Goda, Timothy Naftali, and Robert Wolfe, *U.S. Intelligence and the Nazis* (New York, 2005); Richard Breitman and Norman J.W. Goda, *Hitler's Shadow: Nazi War Criminals, U.S. Intelligence, and the Cold War* (Washington, DC, 2010); Peter Hammerschmidt, *Deckname Adler: Klaus Barbie und die westlichen Geheimdienste* (Frankfurt am Main, 2014), and Kerstin von Lingen, *Allen Dulles, the OSS, and Nazi War Criminals: The Dynamics of Selective Prosecution* (New York, 2013). Important studies on this topic are currently being undertaken by Jared McBride and Jeffrey Burds. Since 2009, some of the former operatives themselves have written about their experiences within AERODYNAMIC/QRPLUMB. Anatol Kamins'kyi, *Proloh u kholodnii viiny proty Moskvy: Prodovzhennia vyzvol'noi borot'bi iz-za kordonu* (Hadiach, 2009); Taras Kuzio, "U.S. Support for Ukraine's liberation during the Cold War: A Study of Prolog Research and Publishing Corporation," *Communist and Post-Communist Studies* 45, nos. 1–2 (March-June, 2012): 51–64.

4. Klaus Barbie was a former SS-Hauptsturmführer who commanded the Security Police in Lyon from 1942 to 1944. In 1947, he was recruited as an agent for the US Army Counter Intelligence Corps (CIC) as part of their efforts to further anti-communist efforts in Europe. The CIC helped him flee French extradition requests to Bolivia through the "rat line." In 1965 he was recruited by West German intelligence, for which he worked until 1971. In 1987, he was convicted to life imprisonment in Lyon for war crimes, dying in prison in 1991. On Barbie, see Alan A. Ryan, Jr. *Klaus Barbie and the United States Government: A Report to the Attorney General of the United States* (Washington, DC, 1983), retrieved March 2016 from https://www.justice.gov/sites/default/files/criminal-hrsp/legacy/2011/02/04/08-02-83barbie-rpt.pdf.

5. "Memorandum for the Record. Subject: Meeting with QRPLUMB/2," 8 May 1990, Mykola Lebed Name File, National Archives Records Administration [hereafter NARA], College Park, MD, Record Group [RG] 263, Records of the Central Intelligence Agency, entry ZZ-18, box 16, folder 2 of 2.
6. "Mykola Lebed," biographical sketch, (1st draft) p. 2," undated, (February 1986), "Lebed Archives, Biographical materials about Mykola Lebed (1935–1992)," Ukrainian Research Institute Archives, Harvard Ukrainian Research Institute, UI0019, [hereafter URIA-HURI], Mykola Lebed Papers, box 1, Biographical material: Mykola Lebed.
7. Grzegorz Rossoliński-Liebe, *Stepan Bandera: The Life and Afterlife of a Ukrainian Nationalist. Fascism, Genocide, and Cult* (Stuttgart, 2014), 117–66.
8. Oleksandr Panchenko, *Mykola Lebed': zhyttia, diial'nist, derzhavno-pravivi poliady* (Hadiach, 2001). A lawyer by training, Panchenko is a local political activist for the far-right party VO Svoboda. Highly ideological in nature, his Lebed biography needs to be treated with caution.
9. The most detailed study on the OUN is Franziska Bruder, *"Den ukrainischen Staat erkämpfen oder sterben!": Die Organisation Ukrainischer Nationalisten (OUN) 1929–1948* (Berlin, 2007).
10. Volodymyr Serhiichuk, ed., *OUN-UPA v roky viiny: novi dokumenty i materialy* (Kyiv, 1996), 239.
11. Grzegorz Rossoliński-Liebe, "The 'Ukrainian National Revolution' of 1941: Discourse and Practice of a Fascist Movement," *Kritika* 12, no. 1 (2011): 99.
12. Kai Struve, *Deutsche Herrschaft, ukrainischer Nationalismus, antijüdische Gewalt: Der Sommer 1941 in der Westukraine* (Oldenburg, 2015), 671.
13. Ibid., 262n64.
14. Rossoliński-Liebe, *Stepan Bandera*, 247–49; Marco Carynnyk, "'A Knife in the Back of Our Revolution,' A Reply to Alexander J. Motyl's 'The Ukrainian Nationalist Movement and the Jews: Theoretical Reflections on Nationalism, Fascism, Rationality, Primordialism, and History,'" Website for The American Association for Polish-Jewish Studies, retrieved January 2017 from http://aapjstudies.org/manager/external/ckfinder/userfiles/files/Carynnyk%20Reply%20to%20Motyl%202%20.pdf.
15. The two assassinated members of the more conservative OUN wing under Andrii Melnyk (1890–1964), known as OUN(m), were Omelian Senyk (1891–1941) and Mykola Sts'ibors'kyi (1898–1941), killed in Zhytomyr on 30 August 1941. Kai Struve, *Deutsche Herrschaft*, 202; Rossoliński-Liebe, *Stepan Bandera*, 249.
16. Gabriel N. Finder and Alexander V. Prusin, "Collaboration in Eastern Galicia: The Ukrainian Police and the Holocaust," *East European Jewish Affairs* 34, no. 2 (2004): 105–6; Timothy Snyder, "The Causes of Ukrainian-Polish Ethnic Cleansing 1943," *Past and Present* 179 (2003): 210; Martin Dean, *Collaboration in the Holocaust: Crimes of the Local Police in Belorussia and Ukraine, 1941–44* (New York, 2000), 106.
17. Jared McBride, "Peasants into Perpetrators: The OUN-UPA and the Ethnic Cleansing of Volynia, 1943–1944," *Slavic Review* 75, no. 3 (Fall 2016): 630–54.

A recent work by the author of the most detailed study of the OUN-UPA anti-Polish violence estimates the number of Polish victims at 91,200, 43,987 of which are known by name. Ewa Siemaszko, "Stan badań nad ludobójstwem dokonanym na ludności polskiej przez Organizację Nacjonalistów Ukraińskich i Ukraińską Powstańczą Armię" in *Prawda historyczna a pradwa polityczna: Ludobójstwo na Kresach południowo-wschodnich Polski w latach 1939–1946,* ed. Bogusław Paź (Wrocław, 2011), 311–36.

18. See Instytut Pamięci Narodowej, Warsaw [hereafter IPN] 0192/354, t. 1, k. 100-109 and IPN 0192/354, t. 1, k. 309-312, published in Serhii Bohunov et al., eds., *Pol'shcha ta Ukraina u trydtsiatykh-sorokovykh rokakh XX stolittia: Nevidomy dokumenty z arkhiviv spetsial'nykh sluzhb, Tom 4, Poliaky i ukraintsi mizh dvoma totalitarnymy systemamy 1942–1945: Chastyna persha* (Warsaw, 2005), 186 and 194. For the background and discussion of this order, see Jared McBride, "A Sea of Blood and Tears': Ethnic Diversity and Mass Violence in Nazi-Occupied Volhynia, Ukraine, 1941–1944," Ph.D. diss., UCLA, 2014, 324–25 and Jared McBride, "Peasants into Perpetrators," 637.

19. Rossoliński-Liebe, *Stepan Bandera,* 285.

20. "O sovmestnoi deial'nosti OUN-UPA s okhrannoi politsiiei i nemetskoi 'SD'," 7 October 1944, Derzhavnyi arkhiv l'vivs'koi oblasti (DALO) f. 3, op. 1, d. 67, ll. 78-104, published in Dzheffri [Jeffrey] Burds, *Shpionazh i natsionalizm: Pervyi gody 'kholodnoi voiny' na Zapadnoi Ukraine (1944–1948)* (Moscow, 2010), 146–72. Ivan Hryn'okh (1907–1994), a former chaplain on the Ukrainian Nachtigal Battalion and OUN(b) liaison with the Germans in 1944 would later become vice president of the zpUVHR. A witting CIA operative, Hryn'okh was also Lebed's man in Munich.

21. Jeffrey Burds, *The Early Cold War in Soviet West Ukraine, 1944–1948 = The Carl Beck Papers in Russian and East European Studies,* no. 1505 (Pittsburgh, 2001), 16; "Dokladnaia zapiska o sostoianii OUN za kordonom i meropriiatiiakh MVD USSR protiv zarubezhnykh natsionalisticheskikh tsentrov," 1953, HDA SBU, f. 16, op. 1, spr. 9, ark. 151.

22. In addition, 134,000 were arrested, and 203,000 people deported from Western Ukraine. Grzegorz Motyka, *Ukraińska partyzantka 1942–1960: Działalność Organizacji Ukraińskich Nacjonalistów i Ukraińskiej Powstańczej Armii* (Warsaw, 2006), 649.

23. Breitman and Goda, *Hitler's Shadow,* 83.

24. "Zvernennia chleniv provodu ZCh OUN do vsikh chleniv OUN," p. 4. March 1960, Libraries and Archives Canada, Ottawa, ON. (LAC) MG 31, D130, vol. 6, folder 66.

25. On the Bandera assassination, see Serhii Plokhii, *The Man with the Poison Gun: A Cold War Spy Story* (New York, 2016).

26. On Canadian multicultural funding for Ukrainian diaspora nationalism, see Per A. Rudling, "Multiculturalism, Memory, and Ritualization: Ukrainian Nationalist Monuments in Edmonton, Alberta," *Nationalities Papers* 39, no. 55 (2011): 733–68.

27. Burds, *The Early Cold War,* 57.

28. Along with Hryn'okh, Lebed's closest collaborator was Evhen Stakhiv (1918–2014), a veteran of the OUN expeditionary groups during World War II, and later a leading figure of the OUN(z) in New York.

29. "PDDYNAMIC evolution, QRPLUMB," dated "late 1974," QRPLUMB, NARA, RG 263, entry ZZ-19. box 59, vol. 1, folder 1 of 2.

30. "Secret CA/PEO PROJECT DATA SHEET," 17 May 1971, QRPLUMB, NARA, RG 263, entry ZZ-19, box 59, vol. 2, folder 2 of 2.

31. "Memorandum for John H. Stein, Associate Deputy Director for Operations From: [redacted], Chief, Evaluations and Program Design Staff, Subject: Proposed Renewal of OPACY PDDYNAMIC," 19 May 1981," QRPLUMB, NARA, RG 263, entry ZZ-19, box 59, vol. 4.

32. "Memorandum for: The 303 Committee, Subject: Political, Propaganda ad Intelligence Activity Directed Against the Soviet Ukraine," p. 2, 4 December 1968, AERODYNAMIC, NARA, RG 263, entry ZZ-19, box 21, vol. 38, vol. 2 of 2.

33. "While Prolog reflects and encourages Ukrainian nationalism, it does not attempt in any way to provoke active separatist manifestations in the Ukrainian SSR," the CIA specified. "Memorandum for: The 303 Committee, Subject: Political, Propaganda ad Intelligence Activity Directed Against the Soviet Ukraine," p. 2, 4 December 1968, AERODYNAMIC, NARA, RG 263, entry ZZ-19, box 21, vol. 38, vol. 2 of 2.

34. Wulf Kansteiner, "Entertaining Catastrophe: The Reinvention of the Holocaust in the Television of the Federal Republic of Germany," *New German Critique* 90 (Fall 2003): 135–62, and Wulf Kansteiner, "Losing the War, Winning the Memory Battle: The Legacy of Nazism, World War II, and the Holocaust in the Federal Republic of Germany," in *The Politics of Memory in Postwar Europe,* ed. Richard Ned Lebow, Wulf Kansteiner, Claudio Fogy (Durham, NC, 2006), 124–25.

35. John-Paul Himka and Joanna Beata Michlic, "Introduction," in *Bringing the Dark Past to Light: The Reception of the Holocaust in Postcommuist Europe,* ed. John-Paul Himka and Joanna Beata Michlic (Lincoln, NE, 2013), 3; John-Paul Himka, "The Reception of the Holocaust in Postcommunist Ukraine," in Himka and Michlic, *Bringing the Dark Past to Light,* 648; John-Paul Himka, "Ukrainian Memories of the Holocaust: the Destruction of Jews as Reflected in Memoirs Collected in 1947," *Canadian Slavonic Papers / Revue canadienne des slavistes* 54, no. 3–4, (September–December 2012): 429.

36. Himka, "The Reception," 649. See also Johan Dietsch, *Making Sense of Suffering: Holocaust and Holodomor in Ukrainian Historical Culture* (Lund, 2006), 125.

37. John-Paul Himka, "Obstacles to the Integration of the Holocaust into Post-Communist East European Historical Narratives," *Canadian Slavonic Papers / Revue canadienne des slavistes* 50, no. 3–4 (September–December 2008): 361.

38. Per A. Rudling, *The OUN, the UPA and the Holocaust: A Study of the Manufacturing of Historical Myths = The Carl Beck Papers in Russian and East European Studies,* no. 2017 (Pittsburgh, 2011).

39. Lawrence Douglas, *The Right Wrong Man: John Demjanjuk and the Last Great Nazi War Crimes Trial* (Princeton, NJ, 2016); Myron B. Kuropas, "OSI: Still Untouchable," *The Ukrainian Weekly* no. 37, 14 September 2003, retrieved December 2013 from http://www.ukrweekly.com/old/archive/2003/370314.shtml.

40. On Linnas, see Jerome S. Legge, Jr. "The Karl Linnas Deportation Case, the Office of Special Investigations, and American Ethnic Politics," *Holocaust and Genocide Studies* 24, no. 1 (2010): 26–55.

41. On Artuković, see Tomislav Dulić, *Utopias of Nation: Local Mass Killing in Bosnia and Herzegovina, 1941–1942* (Uppsala, 2005), 81, 91, 221n19.

42. For reactions and commentaries from nationalist veterans linked to the OUN(m) and (b), respectively see, for instance, Zynovyi Knysh, *Vid'molovy: (Slovo v oboroni proty zhydivs'koi napasty na ukrainstiv i na narody skhidn'oi Evropy)* (Toronto, 1989), 73–80, and Petro Mirchuk, *Zustrichi i rozmovy v Izrailiu* (New York, 1982), 121.

43. Kevin Conley Ruffner, "Eagle and Swastika: CIA and Nazi War Criminals and Collaborators (U)," CIA Working Paper (Washington, DC, 2003), 26n58.

44. [redacted] "Memorandum for the Record. Subject: Justice Department Interest in QRPLUMB/2," 31 October 1991, Lebed Name File, NARA, RG 263, entry ZZ-18, box 16, folder 2 of 2; Ruffner, "Eagle and Swastika," 26n58.

45. "SUBJECT: GAO Report with Potential for Compromise of QRPLUMB Operation", p. 3, 7 October 1985, Lebed Name File, NARA, RG 263, entry ZZ-18, box 16, folder 2 of 2.

46. Roman Kupchinsky (1944–2010) was recruited to the AERODYNAMIC program by zpUHVR activist and CIA operative Evhen Stakhiv, a family friend, in 1964. After a year in Vietnam in 1968 he became a CIA operative, joining the zpUHVR inner circle in 1971, and Prolog as a full-time staffer in 1972, succeeding Lebed as director in 1977. After the CIA funding ceased, he worked for RFE/RL in 1990, setting up its Ukrainian bureau in Kyiv in 1994.

47. Ruffner, "Eagle and Swastika," 26n58.

48. "SUBJECT: GAO Report with Potential for Compromise of QRPLUMB Operation," p. 3, 7 October 1985, Lebed Name File, NARA, RG 263, entry ZZ-18, box 16, folder 2 of 2.

49. Author interview with Joe Conason, New York City, 15 April 2015.

50. Conason, "To Catch a Nazi," 17. Conason's contact was a temporary research fellow at Yad Vashem who shared materials from a small Ukrainian émigré paper in Germany that was critical of Lebed. I am thankful to Jeffrey Burds for providing this information.

51. Lebed's background in Zakopane was well-known to the US government. Lebed's CIC files refer to his collaboration with Nazi Germany. "Questionnaire submitted to Mr. Lebed in Connection with Clearing his Name with Immigration and Naturalization Services [8 April 1952]," Mykola Lebed Name file, NARA, RG 263, entry ZZ-18, box 80, folder 1 of 2. Lebed's Immigration and Naturalization Service file contains information from the FBI investigation on how Lebed attended a "terroristic school in a small Polish city of Krynitza" and explictly, how, "in Zakopane a Gestapo school for training diversionists is

created." See the 5 June 1953, and 28 February 1957 investigation reports and memoranda; NARA, RG 85, Records of the Federal Bureau of Investigation, Lebed, Mykola, box 5, folder 1 of 2. Thanks to Jared McBride for copying and sharing this folder.

52. Mykyta Kozakivs'kyi (1900–1961) was an OUN(b) activist, trained in Zakopane on the eve of Operation Barbarossa in June 1941. After the war he became disenchanted with the OUN. His recollections of the Zakopane school were published in émigré publications after his death. Mykyta Kosakivs'kyi, *Z nedavn'oho mynuloho* (London, 1965), 2; Mykyta Kosakivs'kyi, "Z nedavn'oho mynuloho," *Nashe Slovo,* Zbirnyk 5, (1977)/ *Our Word,* Review 5 (1977): 66–80, http://diaspo riana.org.ua/wp-content/uploads/books/8251/file.pdf.

53. Conason, "To Catch a Nazi," 19–20.

54. Ibid., 17–18, 21.

55. Marie Cortissoz, "City Man Collaborated with Nazis, Says Report," *The Herald Statesman,* 6 February 1986, URIA-HURI, Lebed Papers, box 1, Biographical material: Mykola Lebed, folder Lebed Archives, Newspaper clippings about Mykola Lebed and allegations of collaboration with Nazis (1986–1992).

56. Ralph Blumenthal, "CIA Said to Have Let Nazi into US," *The New York Times,* 6 February 1986. See also Ralph Blumenthal, "Nazi Hunter Says CIA Has Files on Man Accused of War Crimes," *The New York Times,* 17 September 1992, URIA-HURI, Lebed Papers, box 1.

57. Carolyn Weiner, "Innocent Until Proven Guilty," *The Jewish Chronicle,* 14 February 1986," URIA-HURI, Lebed Papers, box 1.

58 Marie Cortissoz, "City Man Collaborated with Nazis, Says Report," *The Herald Statesman,* 6 February 1986, URIA-HURI, Lebed Papers, box 1, folder Lebed Archives, Newspapers clippings about Mykola Lebed and allegations of collaboration with Nazis (1986–1992).

59. Michael B. Bociurkiw, "OUN Leaders Branded as Nazi: Sources say Allegations are Scurrilous," *The Ukrainian Weekly,* 9 February 1986, 10.

60. The Kupchinsky interview is in Michael B. Bociurkiw, "Prolog chief defends Lebed," *The Ukrainian Weekly,* February 16, 1986, 1, 4. Kupchinsky's assertion is false. Lebed led the SB OUN(b) from its foundation, and as OUN(b) leader he personally ordered terror against communists, Soviet symapthizers, and Melnykites. Iaroslav Antoniuk, *Diial'nist' SB OUN na Volyni* (Luts'k, 2007), 10; Petro J. Potichnyj, "The Struggle against the Agentura," in *Litopys Ukrains'koi Povstans'koi Armii, vol. 43, Struggle against Agentura: Protocols of Interrogation of the OUN SB in Ternopil Region 1946–1948. Book I,* ed. Petro J. Potichnyj (Toronto, 2006) http://www.litopysupa.com/main.php?pg=2&bookid=260 (Accessed November 2013); see also "Protokol zaiava protokol zaiavy Pavlyshyna L. S.," Lviv, 13 May 1986, p. 2. Yad Vashem Archives, RG 0.32, file 112. Thanks to Jeffrey Burds for bringing this document to my attention.

61. In reality, Lebed was less than forthcoming, and the CIA less interested in the Zakopane episode than when they brought him to the United States. In April 1952, Lebed told the CIA that he had left the Zakopane school immediately.

The affidavit, in which Lebed was asked to account for this episode was not even translated into English until 22 January 1986, strongly suggesting that it was never even read by any of his CIA contacts. "Questionnaire submitted to Mr. Lebed in connections with clearing his name with immigration and naturalization services," 8 April 1952, p. 36, and 55, Lebed Name File, NARA RG 263, ZZ-18, box 80, folder 1 of 2.

62. Conason, "To Catch a Nazi," 21.
63. Michael B. Bociurkiw, "Prolog chief defends Lebed," *The Ukrainian Weekly,* 16 February 1986, 1, 4. Kupchinsky's claims were, of course, completely false. In 1981, QRPLUMB received 80 percent of its funds from the CIA. "Memorandum for John H. Stein, Associate Deputy Director for Operations From: [redacted], Chief, Evaluations and Program Design Staff, Subject: Proposed Renewal of OPACY PDDYNAMIC," 19 May 1981," QRPLUMB, NARA, RG 263, entry ZZ-19, box 59, vol. 4. As the final CIA audit shows, subscriptions covered less than 5 percent of the QRPLUMB revenue. [Redacted], Inspector General 2 T 21 NHB, "Audit of Operational Activity QRPLUMB Newark Office Income Statement, 1 January 1989–30 September 1990, Exhibit B," 26 April 1991, p. 8, QRPLUMB, NARA, RG 263, entry ZZ-19, box 59, vol. 5; Sign. [redacted], Chief, Central Cover Staff, "Approval of 1989 OPACT QRPLUMB," 21 December 1988.
64. "Statement: In Protest against Defamation of Ukrainian Liberation Movement," *The Ukrainian Weekly,* 2 March 1986, 7, 11.
65. Taras Hunchak (b. 1932) immigrated to the United States in 1949 and was naturalized in 1954. BS Fordham, 1955; MA Fordham, 1958; Ph.D. Vienna, 1960; US Army Military Intelligence, 1956–1958; affiliated in various CIA projects from 1959; editor, *Suchasnist'* 1984–1991. "Memorandum for the Record, Subject: Report of Contact with AECASSOWARY/2 in Washington, 3–4 November 1960," 18 November 1960, p. 7, AERODYNAMIC, NARA, RG 263, Entry ZZ-19, box 23, vol. 45, folder: 1; "HUNCHAK Taras," 15 January 1961, AERODYNAMIC, NARA, RG 263, entry ZZ-19, box 13, vol. 20.
66. Taras Hunchak, *Moi spohady-stezhky zhyttia* (Kyiv, 2005), 67; Kamins'kyi, *Proloh,* 89.
67. Hunchak, *Moi spohady,* 16, 22.
68. Ibid., 72.
69. Taras Hunczak, unpublished letter to the editor of *The New York Times,* dated 10 February 1986. URIA-HURI Lebed Papers, box 1.
70. Taras Hunczak, "Nazi Charges are Absurd," *The Ukrainian Weekly,* 30 March 1986, Lebed Papers, URIA-HURI, box 1.
71. Sign. [redacted], Acting Chief, Political and Psychological Staff, SUBJECT: Recent Press Allegations Regarding QRPLUMB," QRPLUMB (Development and Plans, 1982-88), 18 February 1986, NARA, RG 263, entry ZZ-19, box 59, vol. 4.
72. Sign. [redacted], Acting Chief, Political and Psychological Staff, "New Public Inquiries Regarding QRPLUMB" 24 February 1986, ibid.
73. Mykola Lebed, "Letter to the Editor," *The Jewish Chronicle,* 14 March 1986, URIA-HURI, Lebed Papers, box 1.

74. Mykola Lebed, unpublished letter to the editor of *The New York Times*, dated 2 April 1986, URIA-HURI, Lebed Papers, box 1. Lebed supplied the CIA with a copy of the letter as it also appears in the CIA records. See Lebed Name File, NARA, RG 263, entry ZZ-18, box 80, folder 2 of 2.

75. "(draft response to the Village Voice article) For Nestor O[lesnycky]," Lebed Papers, URIA-HURI, Lebed Papers, box 1.

76. Ibid. That SS-Hauptsturmführer Hans Krüger would have informed Lebed about this on 22 January 1940 is highly unlikely, as the decision to attack the Soviet Union had not yet been made. See Gerd R. Ueberschär, "Hitlers Entschluß zum 'Lebensraum'-Krieg im Osten: Programmatisches Ziel oder militärstrategisches Kalkül?," in *Der deutsche Überfall auf die Sowjetunion: "Unternehmen Barbarossa" 1941*, ed. Gerd R. Ueberschär and Wolfram Wette, (Frankfurt am Main, 1991), 25. On Hans Krüger, see Dieter Pohl, "Hans Krüger—der 'König von Stanislau,'" in *Karrieren der Gewalt: Nationalsozialistische Täterbiographien*, ed. Klaus-Michael Mallmann (Darmstadt, 2004), 134–44. That Krüger would have informed Lebed about the upcoming invasion plans on January 22, 1941 is, however, a possibility, and would – if true – support the account Lebed initially gave Conason of being in Zakopane in the winter of 1940-41, rather than 1939-40. The OUN(b) enthusiastically endorsed the German invasion, and several OUN(b) units served in German uniform at the time. It is not plausible that Lebed would have left Zakopane out of disagreement with the Nazi invasion plans.

77. Sign. [redacted] PPS/SEO/SIB, "Update on Mykola Lebed's Situation. Memorandum for the Record" 25 March 1986, Lebed Name File, NARA, RG 263, entry ZZ-18, box 80, folder 2 of 2.

78. "Update on Mykola Lebed's Situation," Memorandum for Deputy Director for Operations from Acting Chief, Political and Psychological Staff, 10 April 1986, Lebed Name File, NARA, RG 263, entry ZZ-18, box 80, folder 2 of 2.

79. Sign. [redacted] PPS/SEO/SIB, "Update on Mykola Lebed's Situation, Memorandum for the record," 25 March 25, 1986, ibid.

80. Ibid.

81. Zakordonne predstavnytsvo Ukrains'koi Holovnoi Vyzvol'noi Rady, "Proty zneslavlennia ukrais'koho vyzvol'noho rukhy," *Suchasnist'* 4 (1986): 110–13.

82. The OUN(z), the smallest of the three OUN wings, was also the most moderate. It appeared out of a splinter group of the OUN(b), led by Zynovyi Matla (1910–1993) and Lev Rebet (1912–1957), who after 1943 rejected the Banderites' totalitarianism. From the early 1950s it was funded by the CIA.

83. Politychna rada Orhanizatsii ukrains'kykh natsionalistiv za kordonom, "Do kampanii zneslavliuvannia ukrains'koho imeny," *Suchasnist'* 9 (1986): 112.

84. "Zaiava ukrainskoi soloidarnosti," *America: Ukrainian Catholic Daily*, 25 April 1986, 1; "Zaiava ukrains'koi solidarnosty," *Ukrains'ki visti*, 20 April 1986, p. 1; "Zaiava ukrains'koi solidarnosty," *Ukrains'ke slovo*, 27 April 1986, URIA-HURI, Lebed Papers, box 1.

85. "Reestr stattei z presy v spravi M. Lebedia na 10 chervnia 1986," URIA-HURI, Lebed Papers, box 1.

86. "Reestr stattei z presy v spravi M. Lebedia na 3 kvitnia 1986," and "Reestr stattei z presy v spravi M. Lebedia na 10 chervnia 1986," URIA-HURI, Lebed Papers, box 1.
87. Sign. [redacted], C/PPS, "FY-88 Approval of Operational Activity – QRPLUMB," 11 December 1987, p. 6, QRPLUMB, NARA, RG 263, entry ZZ-19, box 59, vol. 4; Sign [Redacted] C/PPS, 14 November 1988, "FY-89 Approval of Operational Activity–QRPLUMB," p. 11, ibid.
88. [Redacted] "Memorandum for Deputy Director for Operations from Chief, Political and Psychological Staff. SUBJECT: Department of Justice Investigation of QRPLUMB/2," 6 January 1987, Lebed Name File, NARA, RG 263, entry ZZ-18, box 80, folder 2 of 2.
89. Kamins'kyi, *Proloh*, 149.
90. [redacted] "Memorandum for the Record. Subject: Justice Department Interest in QRPLUMB/2," 31 October 1991. Lebed Name File, NARA, RG 263, entry ZZ-18, box 80, folder 2 of 2.
91. Ibid.
92. W. O. Studeman to Elizabeth Holtzman, 10 August 1992, Lebed Name File, NARA, RG 263, entry ZZ-18, box 80, folder 2 of 2. The CIA claims notwithstanding, Mykola Lebed's CIA name file, released in 2005, contains several hundred pages; the files for AERODYNAMIC and successor programs constitute well over fifty boxes, with several hundred pages of material in each box.
93. In 1996, however, both the CIC and CIA began releasing files to Jeffrey Burds, confirming that Lebed had a CIA relationship. The same year, Harry Rositzke (1911–2002), who was in charge of running agents against the Soviet Union and Eastern Europe out of Munich between 1952–1954, confirmed to Burds that Lebed had worked with him in the CIA. These developments took place simultaneously as the CIA continued its official denial. Burds, *The Early Cold War*, 17, 56–57.
94. Kamins'kyi, *Proloh*, 148.
95. John Loftus, *America's Nazi Secret* (Waterville, OR, 2010).
96. The rationalization was also presented to the public by CIA operative Kupchinsky, cryptonym AECASSOWARY/57. "He was there for only five weeks and he left after he discovered it was a Gestapo police school," Kupchinsky said to *The Ukrainian Weekly*. Michael B. Bociurkiw, "Prolog Chief Defends Lebed," *The Ukrainian Weekly*, 16 February 1986, 1,4, which uncritically reproduced the story.

SELECT BIBLIOGRAPHY

Antoniuk, Iaroslav. *Diial'nist' SB OUN na Volyni*. Luts'k: Volyns'ka knyha, 2007.
Berkhoff, Karel C. *Harvest of Despair: Life and Death in Ukraine under Nazi Rule*. Cambridge, MA: The Belknap Press of Harvard University Press, 2004.

Bohunov, Serhii et al., ed. *Pol'shcha ta Ukraina u trydtsiatykh-sorokovykh rokakh XX stolittia: Nevidomy dokumenty z arkhiviv spetsial'nykh sluzhb, Tom 4, Poliaky i ukraintsi mizh dvoma totalitarnymy systemamy 1942–1945: Chastyna persha,* Warsaw: IPN, NAN Ukrainy, 2005.

Breitman, Richard, and Norman J.W. Goda. *Hitler's Shadow: Nazi War Criminals, U.S. Intelligence, and the Cold War.* Washington, DC: National Archives, 2010.

Breitman, Richard, Norman J.W. Goda, Timothy Naftali, and Robert Wolfe. *US Intelligence and the Nazis.* New York: Cambridge University Press, 2005.

Bruder, Franziska. *"Den ukrainischen Staat erkämpfen oder sterben!": Die Organisation Ukrainischer Nationalisten (OUN) 1929–1948.* Berlin: Metropol, 2007.

Burds, Dzheffri [Jeffrey]. *Shpionazh i natsionalizm: Pervyi gody 'kholodnoi voiny' na Zapadnoi Ukraine (1944–1948).* Moscow: Sovremennaia Istoriia, 2010.

Burds, Jeffrey. *The Early Cold War in Soviet West Ukraine, 1944–1948 = The Carl Beck Papers in Russian and East European Studies.* No. 1505. Pittsburgh: Center for Russian and East European Studies, University of Pittsburgh, 2001.

Carynnyk, Marco. "'A Knife in the Back of Our Revolution,' A Reply to Alexander J. Motyl's 'The Ukrainian Nationalist Movement and the Jews: Theoretical Reflections on Nationalism, Fascism, Rationality, Primordialism, and History,'" The website for The American Association for Polish-Jewish Studies. Retrieved on 31 January 2017 from http://aapjstudies.org/manager/external/ckfinder/us erfiles/files/Carynnyk%20Reply%20to%20Motyl%202%20.pdf.

Dean, Martin. *Collaboration in the Holocaust: Crimes of the Local Police in Belorussia and Ukraine, 1941–44.* New York: St. Martin's Press in association with the United States Holocaust Memorial Museum, 2000.

Douglas, Lawrence. *The Right Wrong Man: John Demjanjuk and the Last Great Nazi War Crimes Trial.* Princeton, NJ: Princeton University Press, 2016.

Dulić, Tomislav. *Utopias of Nation: Local Mass Killing in Bosnia and Herzegovina, 1941–1942.* Uppsala: Uppsala University Library, 2005.

Finder, Gabriel N., and Alexander V. Prusin. "Collaboration in Eastern Galicia: The Ukrainian Police and the Holocaust," *East European Jewish Affairs* 34, no. 2 (2004): 95–118.

Hammerschmidt, Peter. *Deckname Adler: Klaus Barbie und die westlichen Geheimdienste.* Frankfurt am Main: Fischer Verlag, 2014.

Himka, John-Paul. "Obstacles to the Integration of the Holocaust into Post-Communist East European Historical Narratives," *Canadian Slavonic Papers/Revue canadienne des slavistes* 50, no. 3–4 (2008): 359–72.

———. "Ukrainian Memories of the Holocaust: the Destruction of Jews as Reflected in Memoirs Collected in 1947," *Canadian Slavonic Papers/ Revue canadienne des slavistes* 44, no. 3–4 (2012): 427–42.

Himka, John-Paul, and Joanna Beata Michlic, eds. *Bringing the Dark Past to Light: The Reception of the Holocaust in Postcommunist Europe.* Lincoln, NE: University of Nebraska Press, 2013.

Hunchak, Taras. *Moi spohady-stezhky zhyttia.* Kyiv: Vydavnytstvo Dnipro, 2005.

Dietsch, Johan. *Making Sense of Suffering: Holocaust and Holodomor in Ukrainian Histori-cal Culture.* Lund: Lunds Universitet, 2006.

Kamins'kyi, Anatol. *Proloh u kholodnii viiny proty Moskvy: Prodovzhennia vyzvol'noi borot'bi iz-za kordonu.* Hadiach: Vydanytstvo "Hadiach," 2009.

Kansteiner, Wulf. "Entertaining Catastrophe: The Reinvention of the Holocaust in the Television of the Federal Republic of Germany," *New German Critique* 90 (Fall 2003): 135–62.

———. "Losing the War, Winning the Memory Battle: The Legacy of Nazism, World War II, and the Holocaust in the Federal Republic of Germany." In *The Politics of Memory in Postwar Europe,* ed. Richard Ned Lebow, Wulf Kansteiner, and Clau-dio Fogy, 102–46. Durham, NC: Duke University Press, 2006.

Knysh, Zynovyi. *Vid'molovy: (Slovo v oboroni proty zhydivs'koi napasty na ukrainstiv i na narody skhidn'oi Evropy).* Toronto: Vydavnytsvo "Novyi Shliakh," 1989.

Kosakivs'kyi, Mykyta. *Z nedavn'oho mynuloho.* London: Vydavnytstvo Nashe Slovo, 1965.

Kuzio, Taras. "U.S. Support for Ukraine's Liberation during the Cold War: A Study of Prolog Research and Publishing Corporation," *Communist and Post-Communist Studies* 45, no. 1–2 (2012): 51–64.

Legge, Jr., Jerome S. "The Karl Linnas Deportation Case, the Office of Special In-vestigations, and American Ethnic Politics," *Holocaust and Genocide Studies* 24, no. 1 (2010): 26–55.

Lingen, Kerstin von. *Allen Dulles, the OSS, and Nazi War Criminals: The Dynamics of Selective Prosecution.* New York: Cambridge University Press, 2013.

Loftus, John. *America's Nazi Secret.* Waterville, OR: Trine Day, 2010.

McBride, Jared. "'A Sea of Blood and Tears': Ethnic Diversity and Mass Violence in Nazi-Occupied Volhynia, Ukraine, 1941–1944," Ph.D. diss., UCLA, 2014.

———. "Peasants into Perpetrators: The OUN-UPA and the Ethnic Cleansing of Volynia, 1943–1944," *Slavic Review* 75, no. 3 (2016): 630–54.

Mirchuk, Petro. *Zustrichi i rozmovy v Izrailiu.* New York: Soiuz ukrains'kykh politviaz-niv, 1982.

Motyka, Grzegorz. *Ukraińska partyzantka 1942–1960: Działalność Organizacji Ukraiń-skich Nacjonalistów i Ukraińskiej Powstańczej Armii.* Warsaw: Oficyna wydawnicza Rytm, 2006.

O'Neill, Robin. *The Rabka Four: A Warning from History.* London: Spiderwise, 2011.

Panchenko, Oleksandr. *Mykola Lebed': zhyttia, diial'nist, derzhavno-pravivi poliady.* Ha-diach: Vydavnytsvo "Hadiach," 2001.

Plokhii, Serhii. *The Man with the Poison Gun: A Cold War Spy Story.* New York: Basic Books, 2016.

Pohl, Dieter. "Hans Krüger—der 'König von Stanislau.' In *Karrieren der Gewalt: Natio-nalsozialistische Täterbiographien,* ed. Klaus-Michael Mallmann, 134–44. Darmstadt: Primus, 2004.

Potichnyj, Petro J. ed. *Litopys Ukrains'koi Povstans'koi Armii.* v. 43: *Struggle against Agen-tura: Protocols of Interrogation of the OUN SB in Ternopil Region 1946–1948. Book I.* Toronto: Litopys UPA, 2006.

Rossoliński-Liebe, Grzegorz. "The 'Ukrainian National Revolution' of 1941: Discourse and Practice of a Fascist Movement," *Kritika* 12, no. 1 (2011): 83–114.

——. *Stepan Bandera: The Life and Afterlife of a Ukrainian Nationalist. Fascism, Genocide, and Cult.* Stuttgart: Ibidem-Verlag, 2014.

Rudling, Per A. *The OUN, the UPA and the Holocaust: A Study of the Manufacturing of Historical Myths = The Carl Beck Papers in Russian and East European Studies.* No. 2107. Pittsburgh: Center for Russian and East European Studies, University of Pittsburgh, 2011.

——. "Multiculturalism, Memory, and Ritualization: Ukrainian Nationalist Monuments in Edmonton, Alberta," *Nationalities Papers* 39, no. 55 (2011): 733–68.

Ruffner, Kevin Conley, "Eagle and Swastika: CIA and Nazi War Criminals and Collaborators. Retrieved 31 January 2017 from https://www.cia.gov/library/readingroom/docs/CIA%20AND%20NAZI%20WAR%20CRIM.%20AND%20COL.%20CHAP.%201-10,%20DRAFT%20WORKING%20PAPER_0001.pdf.

Ryan, Jr., Alan A. *Klaus Barbie and the United States Government: A Report to the Attorney General of the United States.* Washington, DC: US Department of Justice, 1983.

Serhiichuk, Volodymyr, ed. *OUN-UPA v roky viiny: novi dokumenty i materialy.* Kyiv: Dnipro, 1996.

——, ed. *Roman Shukhevych u dokumentakh radians'kykh organiv derzhavnoi bezpeky (1940–1950), Tom II.* Kyiv: PP Serhiichuk, M.I., 2007.

Siemaszko, Ewa. "Stan badań nad ludobójstwem dokonanym na ludności polskiej przez Organizację Nacjonalistów Ukraińskich i Ukraińską Powstańczą Armię." In *Prawda historyczna a prawda polityczna: Ludobójstwo na Kresach południowo-wschodnich Polski w latach 1939–1946,* ed. Bogusław Paź, 311–26. Wrocław: Wydawnictwo Uniwersytetu Wrocławskiego, 2011.

Snyder, Timothy. "The Causes of Ukrainian-Polish Ethnic Cleansing 1943." *Past and Present* 179 (2003): 197–234.

Struve, Kai. *Deutsche Herrschaft, ukrainischer Nationalismus, antijüdische Gewalt: Der Sommer 1941 in der Westukraine.* Oldenburg: De Gruyter, 2015.

Ueberschär, Gerd R. "Hitlers Entschluß zum 'Lebensraum'-Krieg im Osten: Programmatisches Ziel oder militärstrategisches Kalkül?" In *Der deutsche Überfall auf die Sowjetunion: "Unternehmen Barbarossa" 1941,* ed. Gerd R. Ueberschär and Wolfram Wette, 13–43. Frankfurt am Main: Fischer Verlag, 1991.

Chapter 7

Convicting the Cog
The Munich Trial of John Demjanjuk

Lawrence Douglas

One of the longest and strangest legal sagas to emerge from World War II began in 1975 when officials in the US Immigration and Naturalization Service received a tip that a Ford machinist living in Seven Hills, Ohio, a quiet suburb of Cleveland, had collaborated with the SS in Nazi genocide. John (Ivan) Demjanjuk was born in Ukraine in 1920 and had survived a childhood of privation before being drafted into the Soviet Red Army in the wake of the German invasion of the Soviet Union. Taken as a prisoner of war by the Germans in the spring of 1942, Demjanjuk was soon plucked from his prisoner of war (POW) camp and sent to a very different kind of camp, Ausbildungslager Trawniki der SS. Trawniki was an SS-run facility located in the outskirts of Lublin that trained "foreign units"—largely East European POWs deemed dependably antisemitic—to serve as death camp guards and perform other "auxiliary" duties in genocide.

After the war, Demjanjuk worked in several displaced persons (DP) camps in the US occupation zone of Germany before gaining entry to the United States in 1952. He settled in the Cleveland area where he worked for Ford in a unionized blue-collar job that supported a comfortable middle-class life for him and his family. He became a naturalized US citizen in 1958, officially changing his name from Ivan to John. But by the late 1970s, US prosecutors had come to identify Demjanjuk as a former Treblinka guard, and not just any guard. This was a guard whose legendary cruelty and wanton acts of sadism had earned him the sobriquet, Ivan *Grozny,* "Ivan the

Terrible." In the most highly publicized denaturalization proceeding in US history, Demjanjuk was stripped of his citizenship and extradited to Israel, where he was tried as Treblinka's Ivan *Grozny*.

In 1988, a special Jerusalem court, relying almost exclusively on the identifications supplied by a number of Treblinka survivors, convicted Demjanjuk and sentenced him to death. For the next several years, Demjanjuk idled in an Israeli prison as the appellate process ran its course. In the summer of 1993, the Israeli Supreme Court tossed out his conviction: newly gathered evidence from the unraveling Soviet Union made it clear that the Israelis had the wrong Ivan. Ivan the Terrible turned out to be an entirely different Ukrainian named Ivan Marchenko, who bore a small but not entirely negligible resemblance to Demjanjuk. A few months later, Demjanjuk returned to the United States, ending Israel's role in one of the most famous cases of mistaken identity in the annals of legal history.

But the overturning of the Israeli verdict hardly spelled the end of Demjanjuk's legal problems. Resettled with his family in suburban Cleveland and with his US citizenship restored, Demjanjuk became the subject of a fresh round of denaturalization proceedings. Although the evidence recovered from moldering KGB files had made it clear that Demjanjuk was not Treblinka's Ivan the Terrible, the material was less than exculpatory. Indeed, it rather conclusively indicated that Demjanjuk had served as a guard at Sobibór, an equally lethal Nazi death camp. In 2001, Demjanjuk earned the distinction of being the only person in US history to be stripped of his citizenship twice. Only now US officials could not find a country to which to deport him. Poland said no, as did Ukraine. Years passed.[1]

Finally, and rather unexpectedly, Germany, which had long resisted accepting alleged Nazi collaborators from the United States and which had essentially ceased trying former Nazis, agreed to take Demjanjuk. He arrived on German soil on 12 May 2009, and two years later to the day, a German court convicted the then 91-year-old defendant of being an accessory to the murder of 28,060 Jews during his time as a guard at Sobibór. Ten months later, on 17 March 2012, John Demjanjuk died in a Bavarian nursing home while his appeal was still pending. It brought to an end the most convoluted, lengthy, and bizarre criminal case to arise from the Holocaust.[2]

Yet for all its extraordinary twists and turns, the Demjanjuk case also places deeper, more persistent claims on our attention. Because Demjanjuk was tried twice in the United States (essentially for lying on immigration forms), once in Israel, and finally in Germany, his case provides a crucible in which we can study how three distinct domestic national legal systems—the American, the Israeli, and the German—sought to master the legal challenges posed by the destruction of Europe's Jews. In this chapter, I want to focus on the German system. In so doing, I hope to make clear the importance and distinctiveness of Demjanjuk's conviction in Munich in 2011.

THE *VERBRECHERSTAAT* AND THE ATROCITY PARADIGM

The law typically views criminal acts microscopically. Crimes are seen as deviant acts committed by individuals against other individuals—this is the standard model dutifully studied by law students around the globe. The state in this story is the bulwark of social order; it is the force that protects us from the mortal violence of strangers.[3]

Nazi crimes exploded this model and its assumption that private violence represents the most basic threat to the fabric of social life. Nazism revealed the terrible capacity of the state itself to turn reprobate, a phenomenon the German philosopher Karl Jaspers designated with the term *Verbrecherstaat,* the criminal state.[4] This idea—that the state, far from the locus and defender of law and order, was itself the source of the greatest acts of criminality—lay beyond the conventional model of criminal law. In his opening address at Nuremberg, chief US prosecutor Robert Jackson framed the legal challenge posed by the *Verbrecherstaat*: "Civilization asks whether law is so laggard as to be utterly helpless to deal with crimes of this magnitude by criminals of this order of importance."[5]

The Nuremberg trial offered a distinctive answer to this question. Nuremberg insisted that law was adequate to the task, but that the effort would require extraordinary legal innovations. Mastering the crimes of the *Verbrecherstaat* would require new jurisdictional principles, unorthodox evidentiary conventions, and most of all novel categories of wrong-doing sufficiently flexible and capacious to grasp crimes that spanned a continent, enlisted the participation of tens of thousands of perpetrators, and were supported by a complex organizational and logistical apparatus. The prosecution of the major Nazi war criminals before the International Military Tribunal (IMT) in Nuremberg marked a crucial first step toward submitting the crimes of the *Verbrecherstaat* to principled judgment.

As is well known, Nuremberg was not in the first instance a Holocaust trial; the main charge against the twenty-one defendants in the dock was that they had committed "crimes against peace"—that is, they had launched a war of aggression in violation of international law. Nonetheless, the trial was the first to confer judicial recognition on "crimes against humanity," and it was this incrimination that supplied the conduit through which much of the evidence of the Holocaust and other Nazi atrocities came before the IMT. US prosecutors built on this precedent in the twelve so-called "successor" trials staged by the US military, also at Nuremberg. Indeed, in these trials, US prosecutors shifted away from the IMT's primary focus on crimes against peace and now treated crimes against humanity as the Nazis' central offense.

Nazi atrocity prodded the legal imagination to recognize a second novel incrimination. In a book published in 1944 and bearing the sober title, *Axis Rule in Occupied Europe,* Raphael Lemkin, a Polish-Jewish advisor to the US War Department, coined a new term to describe the Nazis' treatment of Jews in occupied countries. Wedding an ancient Greek word for group (genos) to a Latin word for killing (cide), Lemkin's resulting neologism meant to describe something distinct from mass murder. For Lemkin, "genocide" sought to signify "a coordinated ... destruction of essential foundations of the life of ... groups, with the aim of annihilating the groups themselves."[6] At Nuremberg, genocide found use as a descriptive term, but within four years of its coining, on 9 December 1948, the United Nations General Assembly voted to recognize genocide as an independent crime in international law. Today genocide stands, in the words of William Schabas, as the "crime of crimes"–the most serious crime recognized by any legal code.[7]

These important legal innovations still did not address a more fundamental problem raised by atrocities of the *Verbrecherstaat.* In the classic model of retributive punishment that found its most enduring exposition in the works of Immanuel Kant, punishment is seen as *just* deserts. The purpose of punishment for Kant is not to rehabilitate or correct, but to restore the moral imbalance caused by the criminal's wrongful act.[8] Nazi atrocity introduced a radical disequilibrium to the Kantian equation. Writing at the time of the Nuremberg trial, Hannah Arendt famously observed, "For these crimes, no punishment is severe enough. It may well be essential to hang Göring, but it is totally inadequate."[9] Some years later, Adolf Eichmann prosecutor Gideon Hausner made much the same point. "It is not always possible," Hausner noted, "to apply a punishment which fits the enormity of the crime."[10]

The problem of the inadequacy of punishment was hardly a trivial matter; to the contrary, it raised a profound jurisprudential question. We can put the question in these terms: Incriminations such as "crimes against humanity" and "genocide" may have enabled prosecutions of perpetrators of Nazi atrocity, but if the Holocaust exposed the limits of the criminal law as a retributive scheme, then what purposes other than the inadequate logic of retribution did these trials serve?

In an earlier book, I argued that jurists sought a solution to this dilemma by reconfiguring the basic purpose of the atrocity trial.[11] In researching the records of Holocaust trials, I was struck by the fact that numerous prosecu-

tors defended the proceedings as "didactic" or "pedagogic" exercises. Eichmann prosecutor Hausner was perhaps most explicit in this regard, noting,
"I knew we needed more than a conviction; we needed a living record of a
gigantic human and national disaster."[12] But Hausner's words were hardly
anomalous; we find American prosecutors at Nuremberg, German prosecutors at the famous Frankfurt Auschwitz trial (1963–1965), and French prosecutors at the Klaus Barbie trial (1987), sounding many of the same chords.
While all these prosecutors saw the atrocity trial as serving the conventional
function of ascertaining guilt and assigning punishment, they also saw the
trial as means of teaching history and history lessons.

The atrocity trial as didactic exercise has not escaped criticism. Oddly
and disappointingly, the most influential criticism came from Hannah Arendt herself in her famous book, *Eichmann in Jerusalem*. There Arendt insisted, "the purpose of a trial is to render justice, and nothing else; even the
noblest of ulterior motives—'the making of a record of the Hitler regime
which would withstand the test of history'...—can only detract from the law's
main business: to weigh the charges against the accused, to render judgment, and to mete out due punishment."[13]

In making this argument, Arendt appeared to forget what she herself
had written about Nuremberg—that Nazi atrocities had so distorted the fabric of justice that no amount of "due punishment" would suffice to "render
justice." While Arendt was certainly correct that the primary responsibility
of any criminal trial is to fairly present and weigh the evidence against the
accused, her insistence that all other purposes are impermissible betrayed
an odd shortsightedness. Far from serving merely "ulterior motives," the
didactic trial represented a solution to the very problem that Arendt herself
first identified.

The atrocity trial as didactic exercise reached its purest and most successful elaboration in the Eichmann trial, where Holocaust history received
gripping expression in the form of survivor testimony.[14] Demjanjuk's "Ivan
the Terrible" trial in Jerusalem in 1987 and 1988, by contrast, represented
the collapse of the paradigm. The causes for the disastrous case of misiden-
tification were complex, but the calamitous trial made abundantly clear the
perils of didactic legality. In this case, the desire to teach history through the
lived memory of survivors led the Jerusalem court badly astray.[15]

Nonetheless, the didactic trial has been an important feature of what
I shall call the "atrocity paradigm"—the idea that special courts, processes,
and incriminations are required to respond to episodes of state-sponsored
mass atrocity such as the Holocaust. Many domestic national legal systems
embraced the atrocity paradigm. In 1950, Israel incorporated the international crime of "crimes against humanity" and a version of "genocide" into

its domestic legal code; and later used this law to try Eichmann. The French likewise incorporated Nuremberg's definition of crimes against humanity into French law, and used this law to try Klaus Barbie, the so-called Butcher of Lyon, and Maurice Papon, a former senior police official in the Vichy government and later French budget minister.[16]

Not all legal systems, however, embraced the atrocity paradigm. At Nuremberg, US jurists were the pioneering force behind the unprecedented trial of those responsible for Nazi aggression and atrocities. Yet by the 1970s, when US jurists began dealing with the problem of what Eric Lichtblau has called the "Nazis next door"—that is, former Nazis and Nazi collaborators who settled in the United States in the postwar years—this institutional memory of Nuremberg had, alas, faded. Domestic jurists worked from the assumption that domestic courts lacked jurisdiction over Nazi crimes, and that efforts to confer jurisdiction would violate bars against retroactivity; as a consequence, the very incriminations that Americans had pioneered at Nuremberg were unavailable to domestic prosecutors.

This did not leave US prosecutors altogether powerless. Former Nazis and Nazi collaborators who had acquired US citizenship could face civil charges, arising under immigration law. Section 340(a) of the US Immigration and Nationality Act of 1952 made it possible to initiate denaturalization proceedings in cases in which citizenship was "illegally procured or ... procured by concealment of a material fact or by willful misrepresentation."[17] And so those like Demjanjuk—persons alleged to have perpetrated or served as accessories to mass crimes—were simply handled as persons who had lied on immigration forms.

GERMANY AND THE REJECTION OF THE ATROCITY PARADIGM

But far more troubling and consequential than America's failure to adopt the atrocity paradigm was Germany's complete repudiation of it. Politically and culturally, Germany has emerged as the poster child for national self-reckoning, the land willing to bravely face down its monstrous past. Turkey and Japan have yet to accept responsibility for crimes of genocidal sweep, and Austria continues to indulge the myth of the "first victim" of Nazism. Germany, by contrast, has approached the difficult collective task known as *Vergangenheitsbewältigung*—confronting the past—with impressive thoroughness, its past atrocities the subject of countless memorials, symposia, films, and endless public discussions.

All the same, when it came to bringing Nazi perpetrators to justice, the Federal Republic's legal system amassed a pitifully thin record that stretched back to its founding days. In the years directly following the war, German courts in the Allied zones of occupation conducted over 4,600 trials of crimes committed during the Nazi period—a number that sounds impressive but obscures two crucial facts: first, that German courts until 1949 were operating under the watchful eye of Allied occupiers; and second, that the majority of these cases involved relatively trivial property crimes committed in the last months of the war, when Germany witnessed a collapse of public order.[18]

In the early years after the founding of the Federal Republic in 1949, trials involving Nazi atrocities came to a virtual standstill. So while Western German courts under Allied occupation handed down 1,800 convictions in 1948 for Nazi era crimes, in 1955 West German courts managed just twenty-one convictions.[19] East Germany demonstrated greater resolve in pursuing Nazi criminals, and yet the East's trials often amounted to little more than Stalinist show proceedings.

We should not be entirely surprised by the Federal Republic's record of disappointment. Postwar Germany [henceforth I will use "German" and "Germany" to refer specifically to the Federal Republic] was full of former Nazis. Many occupied leading positions in government and the judiciary. Few—even those who quickly adjusted to the new realities of a liberal democratic Germany—welcomed the aggressive prosecution of their former confederates. There is no denying, then, that the continuing influence of former Nazis contributed to Germany's repudiation of the atrocity paradigm and its distinctive approach to prosecuting Nazi crimes. But this is not to say that all the political, institutional, legal, and doctrinal roadblocks to successful prosecution were exclusively the handiwork of former Nazis. The story was often more complex. It is, for example, entirely understandable that Germany would reject the atrocity paradigm's reliance on special courts to address the juridical challenges posed by Nazi mass crimes. In Germany, the very term *Sondergerichte,* special courts, conjured images of special Nazi courts handing out arbitrary death sentences. So the German insistence on using ordinary courts to try former Nazis was entirely understandable.

The German refusal to use special law is, however, another matter altogether. We are all familiar with the idea that fundamental fairness bars the state from trying persons with retroactive criminal law. To convict someone for conduct that did not constitute a crime at the time it was committed violates basic principles of justice. That said, the atrocity paradigm has worked from the assumption that convicting Nazis of "crimes against humanity" or "genocide" does not represent a violation of the bar against retroactivity. Indeed, the 1950 European Convention on Human Rights, which recognized the bar against retroactivity as a fundamental norm, specifically carved out an exception for Nuremberg law. All European nations accepted this—except one. Germany alone insisted that trying Nazis for crimes against humanity or genocide would represent an impermissible—indeed, unconstitutional—violation of the bar against retroactivity.[20] We need not review how German jurists arrived at this highly problematic conclusion. But as a practical matter, it meant that the very incriminations designed to facilitate the prosecution of Nazi exterminators—crimes against humanity and genocide—were, for German prosecutors, off the table.

This raised a thorny question: what charges could be brought against those who had perpetrated or aided and abetted Nazi extermination? Given the posture of postwar German jurists, only an incrimination in place during the Third Reich could survive a challenge based on retroactive application. Theoretically speaking, German jurists might have concluded that even the most heinous Nazi atrocities violated no law in place at the time. Of course, such a result would have meant that no one involved in Nazi extermination could have been prosecuted in postwar Germany for anything, because however atrocious the actions, they did not constitute crimes under laws then operative. To conclude thusly would have been as shocking as it would have been untenable. It would have made an utter mockery of the postwar German judiciary's effort to legitimate itself as an instrument of the rule of law and would have grossly tainted Germany's status as a fledgling liberal democracy.

Fortunately, German jurists concluded they were not entirely powerless. After all, "murder" remained a crime on the books in the Third Reich, and German citizens were prosecuted and convicted of murder during the Nazi era. So presumably the then-operative murder statute could supply the basis for postwar trials. This seemed straightforward enough, and yet for the argument to work, one had to conclude that those who ordered, organized, and participated in Nazi genocide had violated German law in place at the time—a matter about which scholars and jurists have strongly disagreed. So, for example, noted historian Henry Friedlander insisted, "At no time was it 'legal' to kill Jews or gypsies; no law legalizing such killing was ever promulgated,"[21] while Gerhard Werle, a leading German scholar of human rights law, has argued, "According to the law of the Third Reich, genocide was authorized by law because it was provided legal cover by the will of the political leadership." "In the Third Reich," Werle notes, "the will of the Führer was recognized as a source of law."[22] It makes no sense, then, to claim that in ordering or approving acts of extermination, Hitler made himself a criminal under German law, as he was the very source of law. Werle insists that it is therefore "historically false and juridically a fiction" to believe that the legal standards of *damals* (back then) could supply a proper ground for [postwar] prosecutions."[23]

And yet it was precisely this juridical fiction that supplied the foundation for postwar German prosecutions of Nazi criminals. The consequences of this approach were far-reaching, both conceptually and practically. As a conceptual matter, all Nazi crimes, including acts of extermination and genocide, were to be treated as "ordinary crimes," no different, except perhaps in scope, from acts of ordinary murder.

But such ordinary crimes were subject to ordinary statutes of limitation. Not only, then, was statutory murder the most serious crime that any Nazi-era perpetrator could be charged with; after 1960, it was the *only* charge that could be brought against former Nazis, as the statute of limitations had expired for all other crimes committed during the Third Reich. Even murder was controlled by a twenty-year statute of limitations that would have expired in 1965. This statute was suspended thanks only to a series of stopgap measures taken by the German Bundestag, which, after exhaustive debate, was ultimately unwilling to face the international opprobrium and internal rancor that would have resulted from allowing a legal technicality to bar prosecution of all Nazi-era crimes.[24] And so, after years of debate, the statute of limitations for murders during the Nazi period was finally abolished in Germany in 1979.

But lifting the prescriptive period for statutory murder still did not solve the problems facing German prosecutors. On the contrary, the need to pigeonhole Nazi atrocity into the German law of murder continued to make for grave complications. For one thing, German law had long maintained a bewilderingly subjective standard of perpetration. This doctrine held that a person who engaged in the physical act of murder could only be considered a perpetrator (*Täter*) if he acted out of "inner conviction."[25] Those who satisfied this standard tended to be a select group of monsters, fanatics, and "bloodthirsty sadists"—sociopaths such as the real Ivan *Grozny*, who, according to the testimony of one survivor who had misidentified Demjanjuk in Jerusalem, had taken pleasure in cutting "off a piece of nose, a piece of ear ... Nobody had ordered him to do so. He did it all of his own accord."[26] *This* Ivan was the paradigmatic *Exzesstäter* (excess perpetrator), a beast whose cruelty and murderous zeal exceeded the logic of the order to exterminate.

By contrast, everyone else, that is, those who exterminated by order, were under German law mere accessories to the act of murder. Gustav Münzberger was an SS guard at Treblinka responsible for herding Jews into the gas chamber. In one clearly documented instance, Münzberger shot and killed a mother and her two children who could not fit into the packed chamber. Nonetheless, the court in the so-called Treblinka Trial in Düsseldorf (1964–1965) reasoned that Münzberger had not internalized the "will of the perpetrator" and so had acted as an accessory.[27] This jurisprudence effected, then, something of a double shift. Because the category of perpetrator came to be reserved for a select group of excess killers like Ivan *Grozny*, courts treated persons nonetheless deeply implicated in hands-on killing— those who shot Jews in mass graves and pushed them into gas chambers—as mere accessories. This category was filled with persons who had played an active and direct roll in acts of killing—that is, persons who might, or should, have been treated as murderers.

By contrast, those whom we might have expected to be treated as true accessories—"ordinary" members of killing units or guards at death camps— were treated as guilty of nothing at all. In cases involving these persons, evidence of specific, individual acts of killing, assumed to be required for a successful prosecution, was difficult to come by: the very efficiency of the exterminatory process guaranteed the absence of survivor-witnesses. And so while the majority of hands-on killers could only be convicted as accessories, the vastly larger group of death camp guards—for whom evidence of personal acts of killing were lacking—was never even prosecuted in the first place.

THE DEMJANJUK COURT'S BREAKTHROUGH

Demjanjuk's trial in Munich marked a historic break with this jurisprudence. By the time that Demjanjuk stood trial in Germany, prosecutors had gathered incontrovertible proof that the native Ukrainian had served as a guard at the Sobibór death camp during a five-and-a-half-month period in 1943. The only problem was that there was no evidence whatsoever about Demjanjuk's personal behavior or conduct during his tenure at the camp. Fewer than ten survivors of Sobibór remained alive by the trial's start; none could reliably identify Demjanjuk. Whether Demjanjuk had ever killed with his own hand, was, then, impossible to say. This, as I have noted, would have created an insuperable obstacle to prosecution under the model that controlled German prosecutions since at least the late 1960s.

But the prosecution in Munich succeeded in maneuvering around this obstacle. Relying on a theory first developed by Kirsten Goetze, who with her colleague Thomas Walther at the Central Office for the Investigation of Nazi Crimes in Ludwigsburg had prepared the preliminary investigation against Demjanjuk, German prosecutors offered an argument that had the simplicity of a syllogism:

> All Sobibór guards participated in the killing process.
> Demjanjuk was a Sobibór guard.
> *Therefore* Demjanjuk participated in the killing process.

The beauty of the argument lay in its insistence that the court could convict Demjanjuk as an accessory to murder even in the absence of evidence that Demjanjuk had killed with his own hand. The minor premise—that Demjanjuk had served as a Sobibór guard—was, as I have said, solidly established by documents, the authenticity of which could only be challenged by the most unhinged conspiracy theorist. Indeed, the most important of these documents, Demjanjuk's service ID from the Trawniki SS training camp, must now rank as one of the most exhaustively examined documents in legal history. The major premise—that all Sobibór guards participated in the killing process—was, by contrast, an aggregate historical claim that required a comprehensive historical study of Sobibór and of its Trawniki-trained guards.

The jurisprudential breakthrough achieved in Munich was made possible by a remarkable collaboration between jurists and historians, who turned the Munich proceeding into a trial by history. The trial essentially had no eyewitnesses. Two Sobibór survivors were called to testify, Thomas Blatt and Philip Bialowitz, but they limited their testimony to describing general conditions at the camp. By contrast, professional historians, most notably Dieter Pohl, who made several appearances before the court, supplied much of the critical information in support of the prosecution's theory of guilt. Pohl's testimony established, for example, that Sobibór was a death camp. This, of course, was hardly a novel insight. All the same, the distinction between hybrid camps such as Majdanek and Auschwitz, and pure death camps, such as Treblinka, Bełżec, and Sobibór, had often been blurred in the minds of jurists, both in the United States, in cases brought against alleged Nazi collaborators, and in Germany, in trials meant to assess the culpability of former guards. So, for example, of the 1.2 million persons, overwhelmingly Jews, sent to Auschwitz, about 100,000 Jews survived the initial selection and the work regimen. This is a death rate in excess of 90 percent; Auschwitz was a site of astonishing lethality. But compare this figure to the Nazis' three pure extermination facilities. About 1.5 million Jews were "resettled" to the killing centers of Treblinka, Bełżec, and Sobibór. No more than 120 lived, a death rate of 99.99 percent.[28]

As a second matter, Professor Pohl, relying on his own research and the work of others, most notably Peter Black of the US Holocaust Memorial Museum, attested that all guards at Sobibór were generalists. Sobibór was a small camp; its entire supervisory force consisted of no more than twenty or so SS men and 100 to 120 Trawniki-trained guards. (In addition, about six-hundred *Arbeitsjuden,* "work Jews," were forced to assist the process of destruction.) The Trawniki guard force was divided into three companies: the first was responsible for guarding the camp perimeter; the second guarded the work Jews; and the third was on standby. The companies rotated through these tasks in eight-hour cycles. When transports of Jews arrived, however, the entire bare-bones operation was mobilized. Some guards would have continued to man the guard towers while the rest were dispatched to the train ramp to manage the well-rehearsed process of destruction.[29] This point was crucial: if the defense had been able to demonstrate that some Trawniki men worked, say, exclusively as cooks, the prosecution's major premise would have been considerably weakened, as the indictment, as I have noted, turned not on what Demjanjuk personally did, but on the function he must have performed.[30] By establishing that Sobibór was a killing machine and that *all* guards participated in the machine's killing operation, Demjanjuk's complicity followed in lock step. At Sobibór, all Trawniki men served as accessories to murder because *that was their job.*

This theory of functional guilt represented a crucial prosecutorial break-through; still, it did not prove Demjanjuk's guilt. For even if the court accepted the prosecution's novel theory of criminal liability, it still had to answer per-haps the most vexing question raised by the case. Had Demjanjuk served at Sobibór voluntarily? Here again previous decisions by German courts had erected formidable obstacles for the prosecution. For decades, German courts in Nazi atrocity cases had been exceptionally receptive to the defense of "putative necessity." In contrast to a pure necessity defense, in which a defendant must show that he had no choice but to engage in the criminal act, a putative necessity defense requires that the accused show that he *believed* he lacked choice, and that this belief, even if erroneous, was reasonable under the circumstances. So for example, a major trial of Sobibór functionaries in Germany ended in 1966 with the outright acquittal of five of eleven former SS men on grounds of putative necessity. Among those acquitted was Erich Lachmann, who had served as head of the camp's Trawniki-trained guard force: Demjanjuk's own senior commanding officer had been acquitted of all charges decades before the underling was put on trial.[31]

But here again, the work of historians made possible a fresh legal reck-oning, as an extraordinary research effort was dedicated to exploring the question of duress. The results were astonishing. Historians failed to un-cover so much as a single instance in which a German officer or NCO had been executed or even severely punished for opting out of genocide.[32] *Not one.* And not because cases of opting out could not be found. People did opt out—not many, and surely not as many as one might have hoped, but enough to draw conclusions. It seems fair to say that opting out would not have been a promising career move. One faced being ostracized from the group, branded a coward, transferred to a position on the front, or even in the rare case tried before an SS court. (In cases that went before SS courts, the punishments were invariably minor.) None of these consequences would have been pleasant. Yet as one commentator has observed, "humiliation, damage to one's reputation, or unpleasant treatment by superiors" does not a defense of putative necessity make.[33]

As historians came to better understand SS culture and practices, German courts became far less receptive to the putative necessity defense of former members of the SS. Still, this material did not necessarily address the special case of the Trawniki-trained guards. After all, guards such as Demjanjuk had typically been taken as POWs before being selected to assist in genocide. As a result, German courts had for decades simply avoided trying non-German auxiliaries like Demjanjuk, assuming that all such cases remained vulnerable to a putative necessity defense.[34] Indeed, in a book published in 1988, Helga Grabitz, a leading German prosecutor and spouse of Wolfgang Scheffler, a prominent historian of the Nazi period, concluded that the Trawnikis served simply to "escape certain death from starvation, exposure or disease."[35] In the case of the Trawnikis, Grabitz argued, violations of the terms of their service were met with punishment out of all proportion. "Refusal of orders from the perspective [of the Trawnikis] was out of the question; given their special situation, they could have reckoned with their own shooting in case they resisted orders."[36] For Grabitz, all Trawnikis could legitimately raise putative—or outright—necessity claims.

In Munich, the prosecution argued that Grabitz had simply gotten it all wrong.[37] Nearly a quarter of a century had passed since the prosecutor published her conclusions, and in the interim historians had radically revised their understandings of the responsibilities, treatment, and activities of the Trawnikis. In an exhaustive study, Peter Black demonstrated that Trawnikis categorically ceased to be POWs once they entered the Trawniki camp. Trainees received uniforms and firearms, typically rifles captured from Russians, but sometimes German automatic rifles and pistols.[38] They were paid; during Demjanjuk's tenure at Sobibór, the Trawniki guards received an across-the-board wage increase. Trawniki-trained guards received regular days off during which they could enjoy ready access to tobacco, vodka, and women. They drew paid home leave.[39] They received free medical care in German military hospitals, and, if killed in the line of duty, were eligible for burial with honors.[40] Black even located cases of Trawnikis opting out of service. A guard named Victor Bogomolow successfully requested discharge on grounds that, "I'm not suited to guard service."[41] In short, Black's research demonstrated that the difference between the death camp inmates and the Trawnikis who guarded them was "stark and unequivocal."[42] In the case of Sobibór, no one could seriously maintain that the Trawniki *Wachmänner,* armed and outnumbering members of the SS by at least five to one, were no more than glorified prisoners. To the contrary, Trawniki-trained guards were valued and rewarded auxiliaries in genocide.

Which is not to say that the Trawnikis always rewarded the trust placed in them. They suffered from a wide range of disciplinary problems. Cases of drunkenness, corruption, sleeping on duty, theft, plundering, curfew violations, and unauthorized leave abounded. But most of all, they deserted. They deserted early and often. Black estimated that of the 5,000 Trawnikis, *at least* one-fifth—fully one thousand men—deserted their posts. This astonishingly high desertion rate may have had little to do with moral qualms about genocide. As the winds of war shifted, many Trawniki guards presumably came to reconsider the wisdom of collaborating with the SS. It is clear, for example, that the desertion rate jumped after the Germans' defeat at Stalingrad. Historians were also able to say something about the consequences of desertion. Trawnikis who fled with their weapons only to be caught faced draconian punishment from the SS: likely execution. Yet those who left their weapons behind and later were caught typically suffered far less severe punishment—indeed, were soon able to resume their guard duties.

Ultimately, the prosecution's case hinged on this point. For the prosecution, Demjanjuk had a moral and a *legal* obligation to desert.[43] The fact that Demjanjuk continued to work as a death camp guard while so many of his colleagues deserted showed that he had *chosen* to remain and that his choice had been voluntary. This, of course, was not the same as saying Demjanjuk would have elected to serve in a death camp under different circumstances. But once he found himself serving, he chose to stay put, and that choice, even if constrained by circumstance, was voluntary. Constrained choice, after all, is still altogether different than no choice whatsoever.

Perhaps Demjanjuk remained because he soberly calculated that his chances of surviving the war were greater if he assisted in genocide than if he struck off on his own. Perhaps he enjoyed the material comforts of being a camp guard despite the distasteful tasks he had to perform. Yet however one reconstructed his motives, the same conclusion emerged—given the range of available options, Demjanjuk voluntarily chose to continue to work as a guard in a death camp. Not all observers were convinced by this argument, though in crucial respects the defense made life easy for the prosecution. Demjanjuk's first line of defense from the time US investigators first learned of his activities back in 1975 was always to vehemently deny participation. He never backed off from his insistence that from spring 1942 until the war's end, he had remained a POW. In Munich, his lawyer, a towering attorney named Ulrich Busch, tried to launch an over-determined defense, insisting that his client never served as a guard, and even if he had, he still had to be acquitted. But the logic failed to parse. To launch a defense of putative necessity, one cannot argue, "I never served as a guard. But even if I had, I did so out of fear of life and limb."[44]

CONCLUSION

And so Demjanjuk was convicted, the first non-German auxiliary ever to be convicted in a German court, and the first to be convicted in the absence of any evidence of a specific act of killing. Armed with this belated precedent, German prosecutors promptly began investigating dozens of guards and low-level killers whom the old jurisprudential model had essentially shielded from legal scrutiny.[45] Perforce the investigations all involve old men; the youngest would have to be over ninety by the time the case went to trial. In December 2013, German prosecutors dropped charges against a former SS guard at Auschwitz-Birkenau named Hans Lipshis after Lipshis was diagnosed with dementia. In the summer of 2014, Germany sought the extradition of Johann Breyer, a US citizen by birth who was raised in Europe and later served in the SS, allegedly guarding the rail ramp at Auschwitz. The very day that a federal judge in Philadelphia upheld Germany's extradition request, word came that Breyer had died.[46]

And yet in 2015, a court in Lüneburg convicted Oskar Gröning, a former SS officer at Auschwitz, using precisely the theory pioneered in the Demjanjuk case.[47] A year later, in July 2016, a court in Detmold convicted Reinhold Hanning, a former SS sergeant at Auschwitz-Birkenau, again relying on the Demjanjuk theory. But even if these convictions remain the first and last applications of the Demjanjuk decision, the importance of the breakthrough in Munich remains undiminished. For the significance of this jurisprudential correction should not, I believe, be measured simply in terms of the prosecutions it sponsors or the convictions it secures; its importance lies in the renewal of judgment as a meaning-positing act.

In convicting Demjanjuk, the Munich court demonstrated the power of legal systems to modestly self-correct and to learn from past missteps, and it offered a powerful example of how criminal trials can deploy history in a responsible way to shift and re-center doctrine. Demjanjuk was rightly convicted not because he committed wanton murders but because he worked in a factory of death. To convict only in the presence of proof of viciousness is to treat the Holocaust as the product of sadists like Ivan the Terrible. Demjanjuk's Munich trial, by contrast, understood that Nazi genocide was not solely the work of sociopaths—it was the result of an exterminatory process. The irony, of course, is that a man who originally was pursued by prosecutors because of his alleged psychopathic cruelty ended up enabling a German court to finally comprehend the logic of factory-like genocide. When it comes to state-sponsored atrocities, guilt is not to be measured by acts of cruelty or nastiness; guilt follows *function*. Such was the simple and great insight of the court in Munich.

Lawrence Douglas is earned his J.D. from Yale University and is the James J. Grosfeld Professor of Law, Jurisprudence, and Social Thought at Amherst College. His scholarly books include *The Memory of Judgment: Making Law and History in the Trials of the Holocaust* (2005) and *The Right Wrong Man: John Demjanjuk and the Last Great Nazi War Crimes Trial* (2016), which was selected by the *New York Times* as an "Editor's Choice." He has co-edited fifteen books on contemporary legal issues.

NOTES

1. It should be noted that this schematic overview represents a simplification of an extremely complex backstory, which includes, for example, charges that American prosecutors failed to share with their Israeli colleagues early doubts about whether Demjanjuk was Ivan *Grozny*. For a more granular treatment see Lawrence Douglas *The Right Wrong Man: John Demjanjuk and the Last Great Nazi War Crimes Trial* (Princeton, NJ, 2016).
2. Again, readers interested in the fascinating twists and turns in the case should consult *The Right Wrong Man,* from which the present chapter is adapted.
3. The notion that the state represents the bulwark against acts of private violence found its most influential expression in Hobbes. See Thomas Hobbes, *Leviathan,* ed. Richard Tuck (New York, 1996).
4. "Für Völkermord gibts es keine Verjährung," *Der Spiegel,* 3 October 1965, http://www.spiegel.de/spiegel/print/d-25803766.html.
5. International Military Tribunal, *Trial of the Major War Criminals before the International Military Tribunal, Nuremberg, 14 November 1945–1 October 1946,* 42 vols. (Nuremberg, 1946), 2: 155.
6. Raphael Lemkin, *Axis Rule in Occupied Europe: Laws of Occupation, Analysis of Government, Proposals for Redress* (Washington, DC, 1944), 79.
7. See William A. Schabas, *Genocide in International Law* (New York, 2000).
8. See Immanuel Kant, "Justice and Punishment," trans. W. Hastie, in *Philosophical Perspectives on Punishment,* ed. Gertrude Ezorsky (Albany, NY, 1972), 102-106.
9. Hannah Arendt, *Hannah Arendt/Karl Jaspers Correspondence, 1926–1969* (New York, 1992), 39.
10. Hausner quoted in Lawrence Douglas, *The Memory of Judgment: Making Law and History in the Trials of the Holocaust* (New Haven, CT, 2001), 176.
11. See generally, Douglas, *The Memory of Judgment.*
12. Hausner quoted in Ibid., 106.

13. Hannah Arendt, *Eichmann in Jerusalem: A Report on the Banality of Evil* (New York, 1963), 223.

14. See Douglas, *The Memory of Judgment,* chapters 4-6.

15. Again, for a more textured account of the disastrous Jerusalem trial of Demjanjuk see Douglas, *The Right Wrong Man.*

16. See generally Richard J. Golsan, ed., *The Papon Affair: Memory and Justice on Trial* (London, 2000).

17. Immigration and Nationality Act of 1952, Pub. L. No. 414 §340(a), 66 Stat. 163, 260 (1952) (codified as amended at 8 USC §1451(a) (1982).

18. Adalbert Rückerl, *NS-Verbrechen vor Gericht: Versuch einer Vergangenheitsbewältigung* (Heidelberg, 1982), 111.

19. Ibid., 111.

20. See Lawrence Douglas, "Was damals Recht war: Nulla Poena and the Prosecution of Crimes against Humanity in Post-War Germany," in *Jus Post Bellum and Transitional Justice,* ed. Larry May and Elizabeth Edenberg (New York, 2013), 44-73.

21. Nathan Stoltzfus and Henry Friedlander eds., *Nazi Crimes and the Law* (New York, 2008), 22.

22. Gerhard Werle, *Auschwitz vor Gericht: Völkermord und bundesdeutsche Strafjustiz* (Munich, 1995), 35.

23. Ibid., 37.

24. See generally, Rolf Vogel, ed., *Ein Weg aus der Vergangenheit: Eine Dokumentation zur Verjährungsfrage und zu den NS-Prozessen* (Frankfurt am Main, 1969).

25. Kerstin Freudiger, *Die juristische Aufarbeitung von NS-Verbrechen* (Tübingen, 2002), 169.

26. Tom Teicholz, *The Trial of Ivan the Terrible: State of Israel vs. John Demjanjuk* (New York, 1990), 125, transcript changed.

27. Douglas, *The Right Wrong Man,* 188.

28. Timothy Snyder, *Bloodlands: Europe between Hitler and Stalin* (New York, 2010), 253–54. Three Jews survived Bełżec, and one of them, Chaim Hirszman, was murdered by right-wing antisemites on 19 March 1946, hours after testifying about the camp before the Jewish Historical District Commission in Lublin. Only thanks to the Jewish uprisings did Treblinka and Sobibór have as many survivors as they did.

29. LG München II, Urteil von 12.5.2011, Az.: 1 Ks 115 Js 12496/08, p. 1–227.

30. Among lawyers representing families of victims of Sobibór there was some disagreement about the importance of this evidence. Cornelius Nestler, the lead lawyer and a professor of criminal law, insisted that even if some guards had served exclusively as cooks, they still would have been guilty of supporting the overall killing process. Hardy Langer, another lawyer representing victims' families, by contrast, considered the evidence crucial. Kirsten Goetze, who pioneered the approach, agreed with Langer.

31. For the judgments see C. F. Rüter and Dick de Mildt, eds., *Justiz und NS-Verbrechen: Sammlung deutscher Strafurteile wegen nationalsozialistischer Tötungsverbre-*

chen 1945-2012, 49 vols., (Amsterdam, 1968-2012), XXV: Lfd. Nr. 641 und 642, LG Hagen vom 20.12.1966, 11 Ks 1/64; BGH vom 25.03.1971, 4 StR 47-48/69. Lfd. Nr. 642(a); for discussion of the reasons for acquittal based on putative necessity, see 227–30.

32. Christopher Browning, *Ordinary Men: Reserve Police Battalion 101 and the Final Solution in Poland,* reprint ed., (New York, 1998), 170.

33. Herbert Jäger, *Verbrechen unter totalitärer Herrschaft: Studien zur nationalsozialistischen Gewaltkriminalität* (Frankfurt am Main, 1982), 81.

34. Freudiger, *Die juristische Aufarbeitung,* 170; Heinrich Wefing, *Der Fall Demjanjuk: Der letzte große NS-Prozess* (Munich, 2011), 200.

35. Georg Bönisch et al., "Ein ganz gewöhnlicher Handlanger," *Der Spiegel,* 22 June 2009, http://www.spiegel.de/spiegel/print/d-65794351.html.

36. Helga Grabitz, *NS-Prozesse: Psychogramme der Beteiligten* (Heidelberg, 1985) 107–8.

37. Grabitz was not alone in reaching this conclusion. At trial, the court heard the testimony of Hans-Robert Richthof, the judge who presided over Karl Frenzel's retrial in 1985 (Frenzel had served in the SS at Sobibór). Richthof likewise expressed the belief that Trawnikis were in a "powerless" position. See "Ehemaliger Richter sagt im Verfahren gegen Demjanjuk aus," *T-Online,* 21 April 2010, http://www.t-online.de/regionales/id_41366780/ehemaliger-richter-sagt-im-verfahren-gegen-demjanjuk-aus.html.

38. Peter Black, "Foot Soldiers of the Final Solution: The Trawniki Training Camp and Operation Reinhard," *Holocaust and Genocide Studies* 25, no. 1 (2011): 12–13.

39. The Germans finally discontinued the leave policy after January 1944. Black, "Foot Soldiers," 14.

40. Black, "Foot Soldiers," 36–37; Angelika Benz, *Der Henkersknecht: Der Prozess gegen John (Iwan) Demjanuk in München* (Berlin, 2011), 68. According to Benz, only Trawnikis who were ethnic Germans were eligible for burial with honors; Black has shown that several such honors were extended to Trawnikis who were not ethnic Germans.

41. Black, "Foot Soldiers," 14, 15.

42. Ibid., 15.

43. The argument was not without its difficulties, as it raised vexing questions: when did the obligation to desert attach? On the very day that a *Wachmann* first became aware of his duties in the killing operation? What of the guards who deserted after months of service? Had they not acted voluntarily until their decision to flee?

44. For a more detailed discussion of the Demjanjuk's Munich defense, see Douglas, *The Right Wrong Man.*

45. Klaus Wiegrefe, "The Auschwitz Files: Why the Last SS Guards Will Go Unpunished," *Der Spiegel,* 28 August 2014, http://www.spiegel.de/international/germany/the-german-judiciary-failed-approach-to-auschwitz-and-holocaust-a-988082.html.

46. Eric Lichtblau, "Philadephia Man Accused in Nazi Case Dies," *The New York Times,* 23 July 2014, http://nyti.ms/1sUx0to.

47. Anklageschrift in der Strafsache gegen Oskar Gröning, LG Lüneburg. 27 Ks
     9/14, 1191 Js 98402/13. On file with author.

SELECT BIBLIOGRAPHY

Arendt, Hannah. *Eichmann in Jerusalem: A Report on the Banality of Evil,* rev. ed. New
     York: Viking, 1977.
Bankier, David and Dan Michman, ed. *Holocaust and Justice: Representation and Histo-
     riography of the Holocaust in Post-War Trials.* Jerusalem: Yad Vashem, 2010.
Benz, Angelika. *Der Henkersknecht: Der Prozess gegen John (Iwan) Demjanuk in München.*
     Berlin: Metropol Verlag, 2011.
——. *Handlager der SS: Die Rolle der Trawniki-Männer im Holocaust.* Berlin: Metropol
     Verlag, 2015.
Black, Peter. "Foot Soldiers of the Final Solution: The Trawniki Training Camp and
     Operation Reinhard." *Holocaust and Genocide Studies* 25, no. 1 (2011): 1–99.
Browning, Christopher. *Ordinary Men: Reserve Police Battalion 101 and the Final Solution
     in Poland,* reprint ed. New York: HarperCollins, 1998.
de Mildt, Dick. *In the Name of the People: Perpetrators of Genocide in the Reflection of their
     Post-War Prosecution in West Germany: The "Euthanasia" and "Aktion Reinhard" Cases.*
     The Hague: Martinus Nijhoff, 1996.
Douglas, Lawrence. *The Memory of Judgment: Making Law and History in the Trials of the
     Holocaust.* New Haven, CT: Yale University Press, 2001.
——. *The Right Wrong Man: John Demjanjuk and the Last Great Nazi War Crimes Trial.*
     Princeton, NJ: Princeton University Press, 2016.
——. "Was damals Recht war: Nulla Poena and the Prosecution of Crimes against
     Humanity in Post-War Germany." In *Jus Post Bellum and Transitional Justice,* ed.
     Larry May and Elizabeth Edenberg, 44–73. New York: Cambridge University
     Press, 2013.
Freudiger, Kerstin. *Die juristische Aufarbeitung von NS-Verbrechen.* Tübingen: Mohr
     Siebeck Verlag, 2002.
Grabitz, Helga. *NS-Prozesse: Psychogramme der Beteiligten.* Heidelberg: Juristischer Ver-
     lag, 1985.
Heberer, Patricia, and Jürgen Matthäus, eds. *Atrocities on Trial: Historical Perspectives
     on the Politics of Prosecuting War Crimes.* Lincoln, NE: University of Nebraska
     Press, 2008.
Henkys, Reinhard, ed. *Die nationalsozialistischen Gewaltverbrechen: Geschichte und Ge-
     richt.* Stuttgart: Kreuz-Verlag, 1964.
Himka, John-Paul, and Joanna Beata Michlic, eds. *Bringing the Dark Past to Light:
     The Reception of the Holocaust in Postcommunist Europe.* Lincoln, NE: University of
     Nebraska Press, 2013.
Hobbes, Thomas. *Leviathan,* edited by Richard Tuck. New York: Cambridge Univer-
     sity Press, 1996.

Jäger, Herbert. *Verbrechen unter totalitärer Herrschaft: Studien zur nationalsozialistischen Gewaltkriminalität.* Frankfurt am Main: Suhrkamp Verlag, 1982.

Kant, Immanuel. "Justice and Punishment," trans. W. Hastie. In *Philosophical Perspectives on Punishment,* ed. Gertrude Ezorsky, 102–106. Albany: State University of New York Press, 1972.

Lebow, Richard Ned, Wulf Kansteiner, and Claudio Fogy, eds. *The Politics of Memory in Postwar Europe.* Durham, NC: Duke University Press, 2006.

Pendas, Devin O. *The Frankfurt Auschwitz Trial, 1963–1965: Genocide, History, and the Limits of the Law.* New York: Cambridge University Press, 2005.

———. "Seeking Justice, Finding Law: Nazi Trials in Postwar Europe." *Journal of Modern History* 81, no. 2 (2009): 347–68.

Priemel, Kim C., and Alexa Stiller, eds. *Reassessing the Nuremberg Military Tribunals: Transitional Justice, Trial Narratives, and Historiography.* New York: Berghahn, 2012.

Schabas, William A. *Genocide in International Law.* New York: Cambridge University Press, 2000.

———. *Unimaginable Atrocities: Justice, Politics, and Rights at the War Crimes Tribunals.* New York: Oxford University Press, 2014.

Snyder, Timothy. *Bloodlands: Europe between Hitler and Stalin.* New York: Basic Books, 2010.

Stoltzfus, Nathan, and Henry Friedlander, eds. *Nazi Crimes and the Law.* New York: Cambridge University Press, 2008.

Teicholz, Tom. *The Trial of Ivan the Terrible: State of Israel vs. John Demjanjuk.* New York: St. Martin's, 1990.

Vollnhals, Clemens, and Jörg Osterloh, eds. *NS-Prozesse und deutsche Öffentlichkeit: Besatzungszeit, frühe Bundesrepublik und DDR.* Göttingen: Vandenhoeck & Ruprecht, 2012.

Wefing, Heinrich. *Der Fall Demjanjuk: Der letzte große NS-Prozess.* Munich: C.H. Beck, 2011.

Weinke, Annette. *Die Verfolgung von NS-Tätern im geteilten Deutschland: Vergangenheitsbewältigungen 1949–1969.* Paderborn: Ferdinand Schöningh, 2002.

Werle, Gerhard. *Auschwitz vor Gericht: Völkermord und bundesdeutsche Strafjustiz.* Munich: C.H. Beck, 1995.

Wittmann, Rebecca. *Beyond Justice: The Auschwitz Trial.* Cambridge, MA: Harvard University Press, 2005.

Part IV

Rethinking Approaches to Holocaust Restitution

Chapter 8

Reparations, Victims, and Trauma in the Wake of the Holocaust

Regula Ludi

What are reparations? How do they relate to the Holocaust? And what is their significance for societies' confrontation with the past? Some authors consider reparations a genuine response to the Holocaust and as such the source of a new political morality.[1] Others trace current claims to redress back to the ancient imperative to atone for wrongdoing.[2] Historically, however, both accounts are inaccurate. Reparations as victim-based remedies for past injustice do not have a long history nor were they an obvious reaction to Nazi crimes, or even more specifically, the Holocaust.[3] Instead they rest on the modern notion of citizenship as a web of rights and obligations; and they address problems that stem from the destructive potential of modernity.[4] As an innovation of the postwar period, they have unfolded in close interaction with changing Holocaust awareness and have spawned new ideas of past injustice.

Seen as just one among the many atrocities committed by the Nazi regime, the Jewish genocide did not loom large in the immediate postwar years. Grappling with its legacy was not a priority of Allied retribution. Few of its perpetrators had to face criminal prosecution. In the early 1950s, with the old elites' return to power and influence, convicted war criminals all over Europe benefited from amnesties and a political climate favorable to forgetting.[5] Similarly, Jewish survivors did not stand out among the masses of those who had suffered from war and persecution. Their claims and needs failed to constitute special entitlements and instead were lumped together with those of millions of war-damaged civilians, displaced persons (DPs), and disabled combatants. Often postwar authorities deliberately blurred dissimilarities between categories in order to facilitate reintegration of former forced laborers and POWs.[6] For a long period of time, any awareness of the distinctive nature of the Nazi genocide against the Jews was largely nonexistent outside the circles of survivors and specialized relief agencies.[7]

By the 1980s, however, an entirely new awareness of the Holocaust had taken hold in the West. Framed as the emblem of radical evil, the Jewish genocide became the "negative founding myth" of European unification; its memory assumed the quality of a moral universal and a source of human rights and democracy.[8] Parallel to these developments, the meaning of victimhood underwent a complete metamorphosis. From being a stigmatizing and disgraceful condition, it turned into a status ideally represented by the victim-cum-survivor as someone who "elicits honor, respect, fascination, and no small degree of awe."[9] Such a notion of victimhood endowed its bearers with the moral authority to give testimony of significant truths about extreme experiences. This semantic shift paralleled the advent of trauma as "one of the key interpretive categories of contemporary politics and culture," which is linked to recent "politics of regret" as a configuration of traumatic history modeled on the memory of the Holocaust, apology, and the right to reparation.[10]

The literature normally associates the origins of Holocaust awareness and the birth of the survivor as witness with the Eichmann trial of 1961. Extensive media coverage including broadcasts of dramatic witness testimonies guaranteed the trial international resonance.[11] Memory studies have also stressed the significance of popular culture productions, such as the miniseries *Holocaust,* released in 1978, for spreading a new interpretation of the Jewish genocide, one that specifically centers on the fate of the victims.[12] Those events take a prominent position in the explanation of the aforementioned cultural transformations. As spectacles in their own right, they eclipsed moments of more gradual change in perception, such as early efforts at reparations or the 1950s debates sparked by the politics of amnesty, which have often escaped scholarly attention in the context of Holocaust memory for methodological reasons and because their impact is more difficult to assess. Beginning in the mid-1950s, however, both issues gave survivors all over Europe many reasons for grievance. Frequent scandals revealed discontent concerning the ways authorities dealt with the past, and they contributed to changing public sensitivities by enhancing the visibility of Nazi victims.[13]

Yet the question of how reparations themselves shaped evolving ideas of typical Nazi injustice, new Holocaust awareness, and the emergence of Jews as the archetypal Nazi victims is largely unexplored, as these connections are generally taken for granted. Historians long ignored reparations as a rewarding field of research. In Germany, the first examinations only appeared in the late 1980s, in France and other European countries some years later.[14] Since that time, scholarship has rapidly expanded and recent publications have covered a wide range of topics.[15] Apart from the legal framework, this scholarship includes work on property restitution and compensation practices,[16] transnational entanglements of reparations politics, and the most recent restitution campaigns.[17] Though knowledge about postwar reparations in countries apart from Germany is still limited, comparative examinations give us an idea about European responses to mass victimization after World War II.[18] Some of these latter studies indicate that widely shared assumptions about the pioneering role of the Federal Republic of Germany lack justification. In fact, early calls for redress and new ideas of victim-based justice were a transnational phenomenon. New research also reveals a more complicated relationship between emerging ideas of past injustice, the assumption of responsibility, and Holocaust awareness than is generally presumed. This raises the question of how reparations came to be regarded as the seemingly natural response to the Jewish genocide. How did reparations intersect with the emergence of the victim-cum-survivor as a new subject position? And is there any connection between the late-twentieth century obsession with suffering and reparations as a strategy for Western societies to grapple with victimization and the pain of survivors?

Postwar remedies initially appeared as rewards for survivors who could claim special achievements; they honored sacrifices rather than indemnifying past injustice. What this implied for the notion of victimhood and emerging Holocaust awareness is the subject of the first part of this chapter. The second part raises some questions about interrelations between reparations and the new culture of trauma. As I argue, the legal framework of reparations presupposed a causal link between past events and survivors' current condition but also required claimants to provide evidence of such a connection. This provision created a demand for expertise and constituted incentives for the production of new knowledge on survivor pathology. As a consequence, reparations brought about new techniques and concepts for organizing the relationship between the past and the present and thus contributed to transforming dominant cultural notions of continuity and discontinuity.

REWARD OR REDRESS? THE FORMATIVE YEARS OF POSTWAR REPARATIONS IN EUROPE

At the end of World War II there existed no conclusive plans for satisfying the claims of Nazi victims. The demands of refugees, Jewish experts, and governments-in-exile remained vague, and Allied postwar planners generally ignored the needs of survivors in this regard. Given the absence of prior examples or blueprints, the transitional years marked a period of experiments. Postwar Europe constituted a laboratory in the realm of retribution as well as reparatory justice.[19] All over the continent, grappling with the impact of Nazi robbery and expropriation policies had priority.

Acting on the promises of governments-in-exile and resistance movements, the new authorities who came to power after liberation declared all wartime expropriation for political and racial reasons null and void. They also enforced special legislation for property restitution fairly quickly, often shortly after taking office. But their willingness to adopt such measures depended on practical constraints, such as the need to break the economic power of those who had enriched themselves and, if not deprived of their illicit gains, embodied a threat to political stability. Commitment to private ownership in Western societies required undoing abusive expropriation in order to restore legal confidence. And the return of confiscated property not only helped mitigate urgent social problems but brought swift clarification of disputed property rights, which was in itself essential to economic recovery. The daily reality of property restitution was mostly a question of political expediency.[20]

These factors explain why early restitution legislation did not distinguish between different categories of claims or identify Jews as a particularly deserving class of victims. In France, for instance, the new authorities' commitment to the principles of *laïcité* blinded their appreciation of the new social realities created by the expropriation of Jews. Only gradually did decision-makers come to acknowledge the unprecedented conditions created by the Nazi extermination policy and antisemitic expropriation. Such recognition was mostly the result of self-help initiatives and efforts by individual officials who were familiar with the obstacles Jewish survivors faced in filing their claims and who realized that conventional civil law provisions severely disadvantaged the aggrieved party. Their call for extraordinary measures eventually helped to ease procedures. Aryanization victims in France found a strong supporter in Emile Terroine who advocated speedy restitution of Jewish assets for reasons of national honor and to manifest the reestablishment of republican legality. In the spring of 1945, the provisional government passed exceptional legislation that simplified procedures for victims of Aryanization and shifted the burden of proof to the purchaser of expropriated assets.[21] In occupied Germany, US military authorities were the first to enact zonal legislation in November 1947. They acted after long and fruitless negotiation with their British, French, and Soviet partners over the thorny question of heirless assets whose owners had been murdered in the Holocaust, among other controversial issues. By recognizing the desire of Jewish organizations, the US military government set an important example with regard to awareness of Holocaust legacies: restitution legislation allowed for the creation of a Jewish successor organization entitled to collect heirless assets and Jewish community property in the US occupation zone.

Due to such interventions, heirless assets and Jewish community property over time came to epitomize the knotty issues that property restitution raised in a situation where most former owners had been murdered. The struggle with these predicaments found much opposition, particularly in postwar Germany where German judicial authorities were in charge of implementing restitution legislation. They often frustrated claimants by siding with the beneficiaries of Aryanization. But restitution in the longer run also established historical facts; courts accumulated documentary evidence, and procedures shed light on the specifics of antisemitic persecution.[22]

Similarly, there were no models at the end of the war for indemnifying living victims of political persecution. Generally, compensation programs of the late 1940s originated in previous efforts at rehabilitating destitute survivors. The liberation of German concentration camps had confronted the victorious powers with unparalleled misery. Overwhelmed by the hardships of newly freed prisoners, the new authorities realized that ordinary assistance provided for average civilian war victims would not meet the needs of concentration camp survivors. They subsequently introduced additional benefits and special services to mitigate the pain suffered by the victims of the Nazis. But these measures spawned expectations and further upset survivors. Former political prisoners and resistance fighters considered pure welfare payments that grouped them with civilian war victims—orphans and widows—degrading. They instead demanded gestures that would signal appreciation for their personal sacrifices in the struggle against the oppressor. Gradually, such practices crystallized a right to reparations and constituted Nazi victims as a distinct class of claimants.

In 1948, France was one of the first European states to introduce reparations legislation; some of its innovations subsequently became important models for other countries. Covering a wide range of injuries, French legislation provided benefits for those who had suffered abuses at the hands of the Nazis or Vichy collaborators. It sought to benefit a variety of potential claimants, such as resistance fighters, political prisoners, and victims of racial persecution. Including Jewish victims in the compensation program was anything but natural; parallel legislation in other countries, for instance in the Netherlands, limited entitlements to former resisters who had been brutalized by the Nazis for their action against the occupier and ignored the claims of supposedly "passive" victims.[23]

Differentiation between the "active" and the "passive" was not unknown in France either. Most proponents of the new legislation were former resisters insisting on special honors for those who had made personal sacrifices during the dark years of war and collaboration. For most members of the National Assembly, such distinction appeared natural. Even supporters of a uniform status did not fundamentally question that the French Republic ought to respect differences and honor patriotic sacrifices. But at the same time they had reservations about a merit-based concept of reparations, since it would turn compensation payments into rewards for special services. In the end these concerns did not prevail, and French legislation indeed introduced different ranks, which constituted former resistance fighters as a claimant aristocracy entitled to higher pensions and other privileges. As a consequence, reparations became a key battlefield in the struggle over the symbolic capital of wartime patriotism. Procedures set high hurdles for those who yearned for recognition as a resistance member and had a strong anticommunist bias. As a result, the allocation of compensation payments developed into a race for the highest prize, with countless scandals overshadowing the examination of claims.

French reparations practices were in no way unique. Most European countries offered remedies to Nazi victims that differed from need-based assistance and correspondingly entailed the legal requirement that injuries be attributable to specific acts of persecution. This involved meticulous examination of claims, which identified deserving victims as individuals who had suffered wrongs. Reparations thus recognized a set of harms as past injustice. Almost everywhere, even in the four occupation zones of defeated Germany, it was former political prisoners who succeeded in shaping the fledgling reparations systems according to their desires and established pronounced victim hierarchies. Wherever their priorities prevailed, benefits assumed the character of awards for special merits. Designed to constitute a new status, reparations served antifascists' claim to power and bolstered their political ambitions at a moment when former concentration camp prisoners generally still had a highly ambiguous reputation. Survivors suffered lingering prejudices based on the vicious legacy of Nazi defamation or were accused of having escaped death because of their allegedly ruthless behavior toward fellow prisoners.[24] Compensation procedures involving painstaking examination of claims thus proved helpful in defending the integrity of eligible victims. Such scrutiny authenticated their stories and officially confirmed that their suffering was undeserved. For antifascist activists, stratification according to an active-passive dichotomy had the additional advantage of neutralizing the emasculating weakness associated with victimization. Jews in turn, if eligible, were generally classified as "passive" victims and subsequently found themselves in the lower ranks of the pecking order. In some places, regulations even required them to provide evidence of their moral strength and uncompromising attitude in the face of their tormentors.[25]

In the 1950s, most European countries upheld special privileges for "active" victims. Only the Federal Republic of Germany introduced a new standard when designing federal compensation legislation in the mid-1950s. In the climate of fierce anticommunism, West German compensation agencies, while exhibiting more consideration for "passive" victims, started to intensify their hostility toward antifascist activists who were suspected of communist sympathies. Defenseless exposure to Nazi atrocities no longer epitomized mortifying weakness but became proof of political innocence. Moreover, under the Argus-eyed observation of the Claims Conference and other Jewish organizations, compensation agencies in the Federal Republic felt growing international pressure to deliver on the commitment their government had made in the 1952 Luxembourg Agreement. Apart from monetary payments to the Israeli government and the Claims Conference, this agreement included the West German promise to improve the situation of Jewish claimants and lower hurdles for recognition of collective persecution. It permitted the Claims Conference to act as the watchdog of Jewish rights in West German compensation procedures and monitor the allocation of benefits to Holocaust survivors. This opened a direct avenue for Jewish complaints to impact German legislation. Their desires subsequently found their way into amended federal legislation of the late 1950s and the 1960s that helped to ease previous territorial restrictions on compensation—East Bloc nations were initially excluded—and other eligibility requirements. As a result, Jews increasingly embodied the ideal, even archetypal victims of Nazism.

As German compensation agencies shifted their emphasis from valuing bravery to verifying innocence, they transformed the very meaning of officially recognized victimhood. At the same time, notorious delays of decisions and the rejections of specific claims left many survivors in a legal limbo. At the end of 1955, compensation agencies had received more than 1.2 million claims that fell into five major categories (deprivation of liberty, health damages, death of breadwinner, loss of income, and other material damages not covered by property restitution). For each category claimants were required to fill out separate forms and provide special documentary evidence, eyewitness testimony, and expert opinions. In the same year, that is ten years after the fall of the Third Reich and more than five years after the introduction of compensation legislation in most areas of West Germany, a tiny minority of those claims had been brought to a conclusion—for most categories the figures were below 15 percent. Even "ordinary" cases, such as those of Jewish émigrés who had lost their jobs, been excluded from their professions, deprived of their income, and robbed of their property before being driven into exile in the 1930s, could easily take ten years or more to be settled. Prospects for a favorable decision were particularly bleak for absent claimants such as Jewish DPs and émigrés from whom half of all claims originated. Without the help of lawyers, they got lost in the tangle of special regulations, decrees, and provisions that turned German compensation practice into arcanum. And not unlike French compensation agencies, German officials handed down decisions that were simply incomprehensible because they ignored the most basic historical facts and produced highly distorted representations of the victims' ordeal. One claimant was outraged to learn that an official report made his detention appear as a "summer vacation" and thus trivialized the constant threat of deportation to which he was exposed as a Jew.[26]

These problems had adverse consequences for survivors' material situation but even more so for their moral standing. Beginning in the 1950s, grievances about the slow pace of compensation procedures, about pedantic official examinations of claims, and about biased decisions grew louder. Not only in Germany did victim associations see parallels between the malfunctions of the administration of reparations and concurrent lenience toward perpetrators. These complaints had transnational repercussions. By the mid-1950s, they carried strong resonance with the international media and gave compensation practice a bad name. Subsequently, claimants who threatened to publicize examples of official obstruction could regularly count on more expeditious and generous settlements. Drawing attention to the broken biographies and personal tragedies behind the victims' stories, media reports invited readers to empathize, particularly with Jewish survivors. In the late 1950s, a convergence of developments stemming from reparations practice thus helped prepare the ground for the advent of the survivor as witness and new Holocaust awareness centering on the horrors of Nazi extermination policy.

At the same time, compensation demands on Germany from other West European governments invigorated transnational debate and compelled the West German government to settle the claims of survivors from formerly occupied and neutral countries in the West.[27] Ensuing reparations diplomacy helped harmonize international standards. Antifascist victim hierarchies gradually lost their justification, even in countries where resistance movements had a strong political lobby and could count on public approval. In France, for instance, several amendments in the 1960s and 1970s raised benefits for the lower class of claimants and slowly reconciled entitlement categories. This reflected and contributed to a semantic shift in the meaning of reparations, as past injustice and suffering gradually replaced sacrifices as the chief reference.

Step by step, the reparations practice and discourse of the 1950s and 1960s impacted cultural sensitivies in Western Europe. Reports about the scandalous handling of claims presented survivors as the authentic authors of their stories, in contrast to the representations issued by state compensation agencies, which appeared distorted and disrespectful toward the claimants. In a dialectic manner, this discrepancy bespoke the significance of reparations for establishing the truth of past injustice via victims' testimonies. Moreover, by linking suffering to rights, reparations entailed a discourse about the past that permitted eligible claimants to frame their injuries in the moral and legal vocabulary of injustice. From the victims' perspective—though not for those who faced rejection—this was an important improvement. It helped break the previous association of victimhood with shame, which had long silenced survivors. Instead, reparations practice created a new space and gave birth to a new language to talk about painful experiences to a degree not possible earlier.

THE TRAUMA OF REPARATIONS

In the early 1980s, a new term began haunting German reparations. Compensation agencies faced the accusation of "retraumatizing" claimants. Critics complained that bureaucratic routine and the requirement for survivors to produce evidence even for the most obvious facts made victims revive previous experiences of exclusion and abuse. Historians and journalists weighed in to support such allegations.[28] The media disclosed confidential expert opinions by official medical examiners who consistently denied any connection between past atrocities claimants had witnessed and the disorders they later experienced. Grievances about reparations coincided with the ongoing battles during the 1980s over the adequate memorialization of the Nazi era, such as the highly publicized controversies about Bitburg and the *Historikerstreit*.[29] Survivors' complaints, therefore, fell on fertile ground. The Green Party in West Germany, the new voice of parliamentary opposition in the Federal Republic, was quick to take up the issue. It orchestrated a campaign in favor of the belated recognition of "forgotten victims." These efforts marked a turning point in the history of *Wiedergutmachung*.

In contrast to the scholarly and political memory wars of the 1980s, however, the sudden appearance of new language in the context of reparations went largely unnoticed. Obviously, the charge of retraumatization appeared plausible and by then did not require further explanation. It went without saying that claimants exposed to a retraumatizing experience must have been traumatized in the first place, thus implying Nazi atrocities, and especially the Holocaust, had a traumatic impact. But such association, as obvious as it appears today, was rather new at the time.[30] How then to explain the sudden emergence of such notions? And what was the significance of reparations for linking the extreme event of the Holocaust with trauma, which had not been available as an explanatory category in previous decades?

There are no easy answers to these questions. In its current meaning, trauma has become a "major signifier of our age," according to Didier Fassin and Richard Rechtman, and its vocabulary has rapidly spread around the globe via humanitarian aid and relief organizations. Accordingly, it also constitutes "one of the dominant modes of representing our relationship with the past."[31] Trauma thus conceptualizes a specific manner of interpreting temporality; it implies that horrendous events in the past, though bygone and absent, are still present, and if not adequately grappled with, continue to torment those involved, often in a compulsive and highly disturbing manner. But still, the term is elusive and vague enough to capture and entwine different phenomena. It signifies disasters as well as the "wounds" inflicted on those affected; it refers to psychic disorders experienced by individuals but in a metaphorical sense also applies to collectives.[32]

The semantic shift of trauma from its originally purely physical denotation to the psychological realm dates from the late nineteenth century. This change paralleled the rapid rise in industrial accidents and the introduction of compensation payments for work-related disabilities. Thus trauma in its modern sense was not a purely medical category but informed by political considerations and a medico-legal discourse that entangled diagnosis, therapy, and legal institutions.[33] Accordingly, its meaning oscillated in correspondence with the dominant legal constraints, medical nosology, and prevailing theories about the origins of mental disorders, which in the course of the early twentieth century increasingly denied the impact of external events on individuals' psychic condition after a certain age, regardless of their epistemological foundation. This opinion came to dominate medical diagnosis up until the first postwar decades.

The decision of the American Psychiatric Association to integrate the clinical picture of post-traumatic stress disorder in the 1980 edition of the *Diagnostic and Statistical Manual of Mental Disorders* thus marked a "scientific revolution."[34] It codified a new diagnosis and attributed symptoms frequently observed in persons exposed to violence, such as flashbacks, nightmares, anxieties, depression, and other psychic and physical disorders, to external events. Such recognition encouraged new therapeutic approaches. It spawned a "trauma industry" in psychotherapy and marked the breakthrough of contemporary trauma culture via the dissemination of a new model of suffering in the mass media.[35] In the last few decades trauma also achieved a much wider metaphorical meaning. This shift entailed a new sense of traumatic history associated with Nazi extermination policy as a "limit event," according to Dominick LaCapra.[36]

However, according to Ruth Leys, the new theories that took shape in the 1970s and eventuated in the new diagnostic pattern mostly ignored the findings of Holocaust-related survivor pathology, then still an isolated field of study.[37] Most scholarship on the emergence of new notions of trauma neglects the significance of social practices that occasioned incremental changes in cultural attitudes, such as the daily routine of claiming and allocating compensation payments, new ways of contemplating the impact of past events, and new techniques of knowledge production involved in such practices.[38] Yet by presupposing connections between past harm and the victims' later condition, reparations presented a key arena where discourses about past injustice and medical diagnosis intersected. Moreover, the administration of claims created a demand for expertise in determining whether disabilities were attributable to specific damaging events. Given the huge number of unprecedented injuries, medical diagnoses had to grapple with unknown disorders and find adequate explanations for recurring patterns of symptoms. Examining those practices could actually offer a key to understanding how the association of external events with mental disorders suddenly appeared natural and acquired facticity.[39] This connection promises a new avenue for inquiring into the advent of trauma and the explanatory power that the concept of trauma has since obtained.

Until the early 1960s, many compensation agencies, and German reparations in particular, subscribed to the interwar opinion according to which no disaster whatsoever could lead to lasting mental disorders in healthy adults. Survivors who complained about depression, anxiety, insomnia, lack of energy, nightmares, and so on, were regularly denied disability pensions. Medical experts argued that such symptoms originated in psychological weakness that predated the event of persecution. Or they believed that patients suffered from "claim neurosis," a concept that had emerged in response to the rising number of claims for industrial accidents at the turn of the century. The term implied that the prospect of receiving benefits delayed patients' recovery or promoted the manifestation of respective symptoms.[40] In adopting those doctrines, compensation agencies denied a causal link between claimants' diseases and acts of persecution. As a consequence, thousands of survivors, including Holocaust victims who had witnessed their families murdered and suffered dehumanizing abuses, faced rejection of their claims for health damages.

Medical experts in other European countries were more inclined to question previous doctrine than were their German colleagues. There the preparation of reparations legislation provided important incentives for physicians and psychiatrists to carry out systematic examinations. Researchers familiar with the conditions in concentrations camps from their own experience often played a pioneering role. The findings of these first systematic studies informed institutional arrangements. In France, for instance, a decree of 1953 introduced a medical guideline for fixing disability pensions for Nazi victims. It relied on the scientific work and recommendations of an expert committee among whose members were several survivors. One of the decree's most important innovations was the "presumption of origin," a concept stipulating that certain symptoms including psychic disorders diagnosed in concentration camp survivors be automatically attributed to abuses.[41]

Similar studies as those carried out in France followed in other formerly occupied countries, mainly in Norway, Denmark, Holland, and Poland. Beginning in the mid-1950s, a series of international conferences most of which were organized by victim associations provided a forum for dialogue and transnational exchange of research that contributed to solidifying a new clinical picture.[42] The first of these meetings took place in 1954 in Copenhagen. Its papers appeared in several languages and indicated their authors' intense confrontation with the wider implications of mass victimization. As the editor Max Michel stressed, medical experts were confronted with unprecedented problems because "the totality of the intention to systematically exterminate whole races and peoples" distinguished Nazi atrocities from other human-made catastrophes and left those who happened to escape death permanently scarred.[43]

Though different terms were in use, such as "pathologie des déportés," "asthénie psychique des déportés," "concentration camp syndrome," and others, specialists of survivor pathology generally agreed on the nosology. It encompassed many of the complaints that later comprised the clinical picture of posttraumatic stress disorder. But the experts had not yet developed a consistent etiology of the described syndrome. They differed as to whether symptoms primarily resulted from psychological shocks or rather stemmed from physical injuries and brain damage caused by malnutrition and untreated infections. As a tendency, however, psychological explanation prevailed. Protagonists of the new doctrine emphasized that the horror of Nazi atrocities constituted experiences for which no parallels existed, particularly for the victims of racial persecution. They stressed that for those affected, complete dehumanization and deprivation of rights had been such a blow as to induce irretrievable change in their personality. And they underlined the collective nature of such experiences by stressing that Nazi extermination policy had targeted the "historical-social existence" of Jews and other victims of racial persecution with the attempt to destroy the past, present, and future of racially defined groups.[44] Such atrocities fundamentally questioned any known context of meaning, these psychiatrists argued, and for those affected shattered any sense of a person's self and identity.[45]

Clinical pictures resting on the medical histories of claimants also accounted for another recurrent pattern, which constituted one of the main obstacles for the recognition of health damages. Medical doctors frequently observed that patients developed the first symptoms only months, even years after their seemingly full recovery after liberation from the camps. The French studies of the late 1940s were the first to discover such a latency period. But until the early 1960s, the temporary absence of symptoms was understood as evidence for the lack of a causal link between the events of persecution and the disorders claimants later experienced. Particularly in Germany, it generally justified rejection of claims.

Research by American psychiatrists who acted as medical experts for German compensation procedures yielded similar results. The Austrian-born Kurt R. Eissler, an analyst in New York writing expert opinions for Jewish survivors represented by the United Restitution Organization, observed that former Nazi victims guarded their personal concentration camp experiences "almost like secrets" and were extremely reluctant to impart their recollections to outsiders, an instance he explained with the unprecedented nature of their ordeal, feelings of guilt, and the agonizing uncertainty about the circumstances of their family members' death.[46] Beginning in the 1960s, the concept of "survivor syndrome," which mainly centered on feelings of guilt that the US psychiatrist William Niederland had discovered in many of his patients, would achieve wider resonance. Together with new German findings, Niederland's publications and terminology helped promote a change in course. Amended German legislation in 1965 adopted a presumption of origin clause for all former concentration camp prisoners comparable to the French provisions of 1953. This marked a clear break with previous German practice.[47] The paradigm shift in the medical doctrine amounted to the legal reversal of the burden of proof. For claimants it involved a procedural alleviation. But it also entailed new constraints by pathologizing the impact of past injustice and redefining Nazi victims as persons who were psychically impaired.[48] A survivor was not merely someone who had suffered a grave injustice and escaped death, but a traumatized individual who deserved to be treated with care and respect. Official recognition of claimants' pain had wider implications. It underlined a tendency to immunize survivors and their testimony against disbelief and criticism. As such, it was also a step in the direction of sanctifying victimhood.

In brief, reparations stimulated a transnational medical debate that challenged the period's dominant doctrines. In the course of the late 1950s, a consistent clinical picture solidified. Its etiology placed the main emphasis on the psychic shock patients had suffered because of their entirely defenseless exposure to uncontrollable and inconceivable brutality. In many respects, such descriptions bore a resemblance to later definitions of post-traumatic stress syndrome. More importantly, however, the routine of reparations practice as a daily activity and the involved persons' efforts to make sense of previously unknown troubles prepared the ground for new interpretation of extreme events and their lasting impact on survivors and societies. As Jolande Withuis emphasizes in a recent study on survivor pathology, physicians and psychiatrists acted as gatekeepers.[49] In their role as experts, they increasingly monopolized defining the relationship between the past and the present. In eroding previous concepts, their theories made room for a new understanding of temporality, which materialized in thousands of decisions about compensation claims that directly affected people's lives and had wider public repercussions by creating social facts.

But reparations not only transformed practices, attitudes, and how we interpret the relationship between the past and the present. They also provided specific conditions for medical research. The requirement of expertise stimulated specialized studies of survivor pathology. By defining Nazi victims and typical Nazi injustice, compensation legislation, on the other hand, constituted a relatively homogenous group sharing similar experiences in the past and forming a sample for study whose members experienced "uniform" symptoms, as sympathetic specialists did not cease to emphasize.[50] Their huge numbers allowed medical research to identify clusters of disorders and develop cognitive tools that made it possible to describe a consistent pattern and classify pathogenic factors. In a nutshell, reparations provided a precondition for knowledge production that resulted in the definition of new objects of study and new scientific concepts while uniting the resulting medical categories with moral norms and entitlements.

CONCLUSION

There is a normative way of judging the achievements of postwar reparations. Its standard has long dominated historical interpretation. Accordingly, historical scholarship emphasized the many shortcomings of compensation practices. It revealed that legislation disenfranchised whole groups of victims and based entitlements on the perpetrators' motives, such as antisemitism or repression of political opposition. Research has shown that subsequent notions of past injustice relied on criminal intent rather than the fact of harm. It has also demonstrated how the administration of claims further narrowed the group of eligible survivors through biased procedures. Even within recognized categories, some groups, such as the Roma and Sinti, faced prejudices stemming from entrenched attitudes. This made it virtually impossible for them to prove that their victimization was undeserved. Unsurprisingly, such mechanisms of exclusion and discrimination caused indignation when gauged by new Holocaust awareness and changing interpretation of Nazi atrocities in the 1980s and 1990s.

With the passage of time, however, other aspects of reparations have come into focus. Growing distance from the events has allowed us to ask different questions and to look at what reparations did and how reparations have changed our wider dealing with the past. As I argue in this chapter, mechanisms of redress were a postwar innovation that vested victims with a new language to articulate their experiences as past injustices. The binary code of the law guaranteed clarity between right and wrong and thus permitted moral condemnation of the harms in unambiguous terms. As a performative act, reparations issued public judgment and established new facts. By discriminating between deserving and undeserving victims, they constituted victimhood as an exclusive status that enfranchised its bearers. Painful examination of claims was not only vexatious and annoying for the claimants but also certified the authenticity of the victims' experiences and encouraged the transformation of their recollections into testimonies. If eligible for redress, survivors no longer had to shy away from telling their stories in public, which was conducive to popularizing victim-based representations of Nazi injustice.

In the longer run, reparations thus contributed to changing awareness of extreme events and the significance of their legacy for individuals and society as a whole. Institutional provisions acknowledged the lasting impact past abuses had on survivors. Such arrangements stimulated a discourse about the nature of that impact—not least through the requirement of specialized expertise to establish causal links—and triggered a paradigm shift in medical doctrine. Subsequently, the daily routine of compensation practice established social facts by issuing decisions that recognized such association of psychic disorders with past victimization. It did so long before this association found its canonization in the concept of post-traumatic stress disorder. In other words, incremental changes reconfiguring the relationship between past and present within the medico-legal framework of remedies for Nazi victims prepared the ground for the advent of trauma as a truth in its own right.

As "an additional way of testifying to the reality of persecution" and a symbolic resource for victims in support of their claims, trauma today shapes societies' responses to disasters.[51] But current trauma culture has little in common with the initial achievements of reparations, that is, categorical distinction between past injustice and any kind of pain resulting from the pure accident of being in the wrong place at the wrong time. Instead, prevalent inclination to articulate harms in the therapeutic language of healing blurs such distinction. And cultural obsession with suffering also shifts responses to victimization from the legal to the humanitarian realm, from recognizing victims' rights to the potentially condescending attitudes of compassion. This seems to be the price for changing notions about the relationship between past events and present suffering. What this implies for the victims and dominant ideas of victimhood must remain the subject of future research.

Regula Ludi received her Ph.D. in history at the University of Berne. She teaches at the University of Fribourg and has held fellowships at Harvard University, the University of California at Los Angeles, and the United States Holocaust Memorial Museum. She is the author of *Reparations for Nazi Victims in Postwar Europe* (New York, 2012).

NOTES

1. Elazar Barkan, *The Guilt of Nations: Restitution and Negotiating Historical Injustices* (New York, 2000); John Torpey, *Making Whole What Has Been Smashed: On Reparations Politics* (Cambridge, MA, 2006).
2. Some of the transitional justice literature assumes a long lineage of reparations. See Ruti G. Teitel, *Transitional Justice* (New York, 2000), tracing redress back to the Old Testament; Jon Elster, *Closing the Books: Transitional Justice in Historical Perspective* (New York, 2004).
3. In the following, I use *reparations* as the generic term for any kind of righting of past wrongs through victim-based approaches, *restitution* to signify the return of assets to their original owners, and *compensation* to denote the material and symbolic indemnification of past abuses. For the international law terminology, see Pablo de Greiff, ed. *The Handbook of Reparations* (New York, 2006).
4. Postwar reparations were modeled on interwar pension systems for veterans and war victims as the first systematic efforts to mitigate the impact of modern warfare through institutions of the welfare state.
5. See Tony Judt, *Postwar: A History of Europe Since 1945* (New York, 2005).
6. Most pronounced in France, see Pieter Lagrou, *The Legacy of Nazi Occupation: Patriotic Memory and National Recovery in Western Europe, 1945–1965* (New York, 2000).
7. On the activity of survivors, see the contributions in David Cesarani, ed. *After the Holocaust: Challenging the Myth of Silence* (London, 2012). On new international

practices, see Gerard Daniel Cohen, *In War's Wake: Europe's Displaced Persons in the Postwar Order* (New York, 2012).

8. Peter Novick, *The Holocaust and Collective Memory: The American Experience* (London, 2000). On the negative founding myth, see Claus Leggewie, *Der Kampf um die europäische Erinnerung: Ein Schlachtfeld wird besichtigt* (Munich, 2011); Aleida Assmann, "The Holocaust—a Global Memory? Extensions and Limits of New Memory Community," in *Memory in a Global Age: Discourses, Practices and Trajectories,* ed. Aleida Assmann and Sebastian Conrad (Basingstoke, 2010). Also Jeffrey C. Alexander, "On the Social Construction of Moral Universals: The 'Holocaust' from War Crime to Trauma Drama," *European Journal of Social Theory* 5, no. 1 (2002): 5–58.

9. Alvin Rosenfeld, "The Americanization of the Holocaust," in *Thinking about the Holocaust: After Half a Century,* ed. Alvin Rosenfeld (Bloomington, IN, 1997), 137. Critically, Ian Buruma, "The Joys and Perils of Victimhood," *The New York Review of Books* 46, no. 6 (1999): 4–9.

10. Jeffrey K. Olick, *The Politics of Regret: On Collective Memory and Historical Responsibility* (New York, 2007), esp. 121–38. Critically also Wulf Kansteiner, "Genealogy of a Category Mistake: A Critical Intellectual History of the Cultural Trauma Metaphor," *Rethinking History: The Journal of Theory and Practice* 8, no. 2 (2006): 193.

11. Annette Wieviorka, *L'ère du témoin* (Paris, 1998); David Cesarani, *After Eichmann: Collective Memory and the Holocaust Since 1961* (London, 2005); Lawrence Douglas, *The Memory of Judgment: Making Law and History in the Trials of the Holocaust* (New Haven, CT, 2001).

12. Wulf Kansteiner, *In Pursuit of German Memory: History, Television, and Politics after Auschwitz* (Athens, OH, 2006), 109–53.

13. On the impact of French and German reparations scandals, see Regula Ludi, *Reparations for Nazi Victims in Postwar Europe* (New York, 2012), 39–44, 105–9, 29.

14. Christian Pross, *Wiedergutmachung: Der Kleinkrieg gegen die Opfer* (Frankfurt am Main, 1988). On France, see Annette Wieviorka, *Déportation et génocide: Entre la mémoire et l'oubli* (Paris, 1992), 141–58. On Austria, Brigitte Bailer-Galanda, *Wiedergutmachung kein Thema: Österreich und die Opfer des Nationalsozialismus* (Vienna, 1993).

15. Constantin Goschler, *Schuld und Schulden: Die Politik der Wiedergutmachung für NS-Verfolgte seit 1945* (Göttingen, 2005).

16. On property restitution in Germany, see Jürgen Lillteicher, *Raub, Recht und Restitution: Die Rückerstattung jüdischen Eigentums in der frühen Bundesrepublik* (Göttingen, 2007). For a recent examination of local compensation practice, see Julia Volmer-Naumann, *Bürokratische Bewältigung: Entschädigung für nationalsozialistisch Verfolgte im Regierungsbezirk Münster* (Essen, 2012).

17. For an excellent overview, see Michael R. Marrus, *Some Measure of Justice: The Holocaust Era Restitution Campaign of the 1990s* (Madison, WI, 2009). Also José Brunner, Constantin Goschler, and Norbert Frei, eds., *Die Globalisierung der Wiedergutmachung. Politik, Moral, Moralpolitik* (Göttingen, 2013).

18. See, for example, Dieter Stiefel, ed. *Die politische Ökonomie des Holocaust: Zur wirtschaftlichen Logik von Verfolgung und "Wiedergutmachung"* (Vienna, 2001). From a comparative perspective, Jolande Withuis and Annet Mooij, eds., *The Politics of War Trauma: The Aftermath of World War II in Eleven European Countries* (Amsterdam, 2010).

19. For a comparative survey, see István Deák, Jan T. Gross, and Tony Judt, eds., *The Politics of Retribution in Europe: World War II and Its Aftermath* (Princeton, NJ, 2000).

20. Lillteicher, *Raub, Recht und Restitution.* From a comparative perspective, Martin Dean, Constantin Goschler, and Philipp Ther, eds., *Robbery and Restitution: The Conflict over Jewish Property in Europe* (New York, 2007).

21. On self-help initiatives, Antoine Prost, Rémi Skoutelsky, and Sonia Etienne, *Aryanisation économique et restitutions* (Paris, 2000); Olivier Lalieu, "La création des associations d'anciens déportés," in *La France de 1945: Résistances, retours, renaissances,* ed. Christiane Franck (Caen, 1996); Cordula Lissner, *Den Fluchtweg zurückgehen: Remigration nach Nordrhein und Wetsfalen 1945–1955* (Essen, 2006), 80–87. The following is mostly based on Ludi, *Reparations for Nazi Victims in Postwar Europe.*

22. Ayaka Takei, "The 'Gemeinde Problem'. The Jewish Restitution Successor Organization and the Postwar Jewish Communities in Germany 1947–1954," *Holocaust and Genocide Studies* 16, no. 2 (2002): 266–88; Ludi, *Reparations for Nazi Victims in Postwar Europe,* 87–92.

23. Jolande Withuis and Annet Mooij, "From Totalitarianism to Trauma: A Paradigm Change in the Netherlands," in Withuis and Mooij, *The Politics of War Trauma,* 191–215; Paola Bertilotti, "La notion de déporté en Italie de 1945 à nos jours: Droit, politiques de la mémoire et mémoires concurrentes," in *Qu'est-ce qu'un déporté? Histoire et mémoires des déportations de la Seconde Guerre mondiale,* ed. Tal Bruttmann, Laurent Joly, and Annette Wieviorka (Paris, 2009), 377–402.

24. Many of those allegations originated in the antagonism between different categories of concentration camp prisoners that the SS had systematically exploited as a means of control and led to high-profile trials in the immediate postwar period. See Wolfgang Sofsky, *The Order of Terror: The Concentration Camp,* trans. William Templer (Princeton, NJ, 1997); Olivier Lalieu, *La zone grise? La Résistance française à Buchenwald* (Paris, 2005).

25. Regula Ludi, "Antifaschistische Kämpfer und Opfer des Faschismus nach dem Zweiten Weltkrieg: Überlegungen zur historischen Semantik des Opferbegriffs," *Themenportal Europäische Geschichte* (2012), http://www.europa.clio-on line.de/2012/Article=536. On gendered symbolism in antifascist discourse, see Anson Rabinbach, "Antifascism," in *Europe Since 1914: Encyclopedia of the Age of War and Reconstruction,* ed. John Merriman and Jay Winter (Detroit, MI, 2006), 106–13.

26. Ludi, *Reparations for Nazi Victims in Postwar Europe,* 115–16, 131.

27. See the contributions in Hans Günter Hockerts, Claudia Moisel, and Tobias Winstel, eds., *Grenzen der Wiedergutmachung: Die Entschädigung für NS-Verfolgte in*

42. Jolande Withuis, "The Management of Victimhood: Long Term Health Damage from Asthenia to PTSD," in Withuis and Mooij, *The Politics of War Trauma,* 191–215. For a list of international conferences, see Helmut Paul, "Internationale Erfahrungen mit psychischen Spädschäden," in *Psychische Spätschäden nach politischer Verfolgung,* ed. Helmut Paul and Hans-Joachim Herberg (Basel, 1963).
43. Max Michel, ed. *Gesundheitsschäden durch Verfolgung und Gefangenschaft und ihre Spätfolgen* (Frankfurt am Main, 1955), 12.
44. Walter Ritter von Baeyer, Heinz Häfner, and Karl Peter Kisker, *Psychiatrie der Verfolgten: Psychopathologische und gutachtliche Erfahrungen an den Opfern der nationalsozialistischen Verfolgung und vergleichbarer Extrembelastung* (Berlin, 1964), 103.
45. The theory of an irreversible personality change caused by external shocks originated from the German psychiatrist Ulrich Venzlaff. See also Svenja Goltermann, "Kausalitätsfragen: Psychisches Leid und psychiatrisches Wissen in der Entschädigung," in *Die Praxis der Wiedergutmachung: Geschichte, Erfahrung und Wirkung in Deutschland und Israel,* ed. Norbert Frei, José Brunner, and Constantin Goschler (Göttingen, 2009), 427–51.
46. Kurt R. Eissler, "Die Ermordung von wievielen seiner Kinder muss ein Mensch symptomfrei ertragen können, um einen normale Konstitution zu haben?" *Psyche: Zeitschrift für Psychoanalyse und ihre Anwendungen* 17 (1963), 241–91.
47. On Niederland, see Ruth Leys, *From Guilt to Shame: Auschwitz and After* (Princeton, NJ, 2007), 38–48; Pross, *Wiedergutmachung,* 122. See also Wenda Focke, *William G. Niederland. Psychiater der Verfolgten: Seine Zeit–sein Leben–sein Werk. Ein Porträt* (Würzburg, 1992).
48. In France, survivors refused to adopt the syndrome and new identity outside reparations procedures, see Nathalie Zajde, *Guérir de la Shoah* (Paris, 2005), 244.
49. Withuis, "The Management of Victimhood," 302.
50. von Baeyer, Häfner, and Kisker, *Psychiatrie der Verfolgten,* 99.
51. Fassin and Rechtman, *The Empire of Trauma,* 10.

SELECT BIBLIOGRAPHY

Alexander, Jeffrey C. "On the Social Construction of Moral Universals: The 'Holocaust' from War Crime to Trauma Drama." *European Journal of Social Theory* 5, no. 1 (2002): 5–58.

Assmann, Aleida. "The Holocaust—a Global Memory? Extensions and Limits of New Memory Community." In *Memory in a Global Age: Discourses, Practices and Trajectories,* ed. Aleida Assmann and Sebastian Conrad, 97–117. London: Palgrave Macmillan, 2010.

Bailer-Galanda, Brigitte. *Wiedergutmachung kein Thema: Österreich und die Opfer des Nationalsozialismus.* Vienna: Löcker, 1993.

Barkan, Elazar. *The Guilt of Nations: Restitution and Negotiating Historical Injustices.* New York: Norton, 2000.

Baumann, Stefanie Michaela. *Menschenversuche und Wiedergutmachung: Der lange Streit um Entschädigung und Anerkennung der Opfer nationalsozialistischer Humanexperimente.* Munich: Oldenbourg Verlag, 2009.

Bertilotti, Paola. "La notion de déporté en Italie de 1945 à nos jours: Droit, politiques de la mémoire et mémoires concurrentes." In *Qu'est-ce qu'un déporté? Histoire et mémoires des déportations de la Seconde Guerre mondiale,* ed. Tal Bruttmann, Laurent Joly, and Annette Wieviorka, 377–402. Paris: CNRS Editions, 2009.

Brancaccio, Maria Teresa. "From 'Deportation Pathology' to 'Traumatismes Psychiques de Guerre': Trauma and Reparation in Postwar France (1940s–1990s)." In *The Politics of War Trauma: The Aftermath of World War II in Eleven European Countries,* ed. Jolande Withuis and Annet Mooij, 79–105. Amsterdam: Aksant, 2010.

Brunner, José. "Trauma in Jerusalem? Zur Polyphonie der Opferstimmen im Eichmann-Prozess." In *Zeugenschaft des Holocaust: Zwischen Trauma, Tradierung und Ermittlung,* ed. Michael Elm and Gottfried Kössler, 92–115. Frankfurt am Main: Campus Verlag, 2007.

———. "Gesetze, Gutachter, Geld–Das Trauma als Paradigma das Holocausts." In *Holocaust und Trauma: Kritische Perspektiven zur Entstehung und Wirkung eines Paradigmas,* ed. José Brunner and Nathalie Zajde, 40–71. Göttingen: Wallstein Verlag, 2011.

———. *Die Politik des Traumas: Gewalterfahrungen und psychisches Leid in den USA, in Deutschland und im Israel/Palästina-Konflikt.* Frankfurt am Main: Suhrkamp Verlag, 2014.

Brunner, José, Constantin Goschler, and Norbert Frei, eds. *Die Globalisierung der Wiedergutmachung: Politik, Moral, Moralpolitik.* Göttingen: Wallstein Verlag, 2013.

Buruma, Ian. "The Joys and Perils of Victimhood." *The New York Review of Books* 46, no. 6 (1999): 4–9.

Cesarani, David, ed. *After Eichmann: Collective Memory and the Holocaust Since 1961.* London: Routledge, 2005.

———. ed. *After the Holocaust: Challenging the Myth of Silence.* London: Routledge, 2012.

Cohen, Gerard Daniel. *In War's Wake: Europe's Displaced Persons in the Postwar Order.* New York: Oxford University Press, 2012.

de Greiff, Pablo, ed. *The Handbook of Reparations.* New York: Oxford University Press, 2006.

Deák, István, Jan T. Gross, and Tony Judt, eds. *The Politics of Retribution in Europe: World War II and Its Aftermath.* Princeton, NJ: Princeton University Press, 2000.

Dean, Martin, Constantin Goschler, and Philipp Ther, eds. *Robbery and Restitution: The Conflict over Jewish Property in Europe.* New York: Berghahn, 2007.

Douglas, Lawrence. *The Memory of Judgment: Making Law and History in the Trials of the Holocaust.* New Haven, CT: Yale University Press, 2001.

Eissler, Kurt R.. "Die Ermordung von wievielen seiner Kinder muss ein Mensch symptomfrei ertragen können, um einen normale Konstitution zu haben?" *Psyche: Zeitschrift für Psychoanalyse und ihre Anwendungen* 17 (1963): 241–91.

Elster, Jon. *Closing the Books: Transitional Justice in Historical Perspective.* New York: Cambridge University Press, 2004.

Fassin, Didier, and Richard Rechtman. *The Empire of Trauma: An Inquiry into the Condition of Victimhood.* Princeton, NJ: Princeton University Press, 2009.

Fischer-Hübner, Helga, and Hermann Fischer-Hübner. *Die Kehrseite der "Wiedergutmachung": Das Leiden von NS-Verfolgten in den Entschädigungsverfahren.* Gerlingen: Bleicher Verlag, 1990.

Focke, Wenda, *William G. Niederland. Psychiater der Verfolgten: Seine Zeit–sein Leben–sein Werk. Ein Porträt.* Würzburg: Königshausen & Neumann, 1992.

Frahm, Klaus, Detlef Garbe, Bertina Schulze-Mittendorf, Udo Sierck, and Gaby Zürn, eds. *Verachtet – verfolgt – vernichtet: Zu den "vergessenen" Opfern des NS-Regimes.* Hamburg: VSA-Verlag, 1986.

Goltermann, Svenja. "Kausalitätsfragen: Psychisches Leid und psychiatrisches Wissen in der Entschädigung." In *Die Praxis der Wiedergutmachung: Geschichte, Erfahrung und Wirkung in Deutschland und Israel,* ed. Norbert Frei, José Brunner, and Constantin Goschler, 427–51. Göttingen: Wallstein Verlag, 2009.

Goschler, Constantin. *Schuld und Schulden: Die Politik der Wiedergutmachung für NS-Verfolgte seit 1945.* Göttingen: Wallstein Verlag, 2005.

Herbst, Ludolf, and Constantin Goschler, eds. *Wiedergutmachung in der Bundesrepublik Deutschland.* Munich: Oldenbourg Verlag, 1989.

Hockerts, Hans Günter, Claudia Moisel, and Tobias Winstel, eds. *Grenzen der Wiedergutmachung: Die Entschädigung für NS-Verfolgte in West- und Osteuropa 1945–2000.* Göttingen: Wallstein Verlag, 2006.

Judt, Tony. *Postwar: A History of Europe Since 1945.* New York: Penguin, 2005.

Kansteiner, Wulf. "Genealogy of a Category Mistake: A Critical Intellectual History of the Cultural Trauma Metaphor." *Rethinking History: The Journal of Theory and Practice* 8, no. 2 (2006): 193–221.

——. *In Pursuit of German Memory: History, Television, and Politics after Auschwitz.* Athens, OH: Ohio University Press, 2006.

——. "Losing the War, Winning the Memory Battle: The Legacy of Nazism, World War II, and the Holocaust in the Federal Republic of Germany." In *The Politics of Memory in Postwar Europe,* ed. Richard Ned Lebow, Wulf Kansteiner, and Claudio Fogu, 102–46. Durham, NC: Duke University Press, 2006.

LaCapra, Dominick. *Writing History, Writing Trauma.* Baltimore, MD: Johns Hopkins University Press, 2014.

Lagrou, Pieter. *The Legacy of Nazi Occupation: Patriotic Memory and National Recovery in Western Europe, 1945–1965.* New York: Cambridge University Press, 2000.

Lalieu, Olivier. "La création des associations d'anciens déportés." In *La France de 1945: Résistances, retours, renaissances,* ed. Christiane Franck, 193–203. Caen: Presses Universitaires de Caen, 1996.

Lalieu, Olivier. *La zone grise? La Résistance française à Buchenwald.* Paris: Tallandier, 2005.

Leggewie, Claus. *Der Kampf um die europäische Erinnerung: Ein Schlachtfeld wird besichtigt.* Munich: C.H. Beck, 2011.

Leys, Ruth. *Trauma: A Genealogy*. Chicago: University of Chicago Press, 2000.

———. *From Guilt to Shame: Auschwitz and After*. Princeton, NJ: Princeton University Press, 2007.

Lillteicher, Jürgen. *Raub, Recht und Restitution: Die Rückerstattung jüdischen Eigentums in der frühen Bundesrepublik*. Göttingen: Wallstein Verlag, 2007.

Lissner, Cordula. *Den Fluchtweg zurückgehen: Remigration nach Nordrhein und Westfalen 1945–1955*. Essen: Klartext Verlag, 2006.

Ludi, Regula. "Antifaschistische Kämpfer und Opfer des Faschismus nach dem Zweiten Weltkrieg: Überlegungen zur historischen Semantik des Opferbegriffs." In *Themenportal Europäische Geschichte*, 2012. http://www.europa.clio-on line.de/2012/Article=536.

———. *Reparations for Nazi Victims in Postwar Europe*. New York: Cambridge University Press, 2012.

Marrus, Michael R. *Some Measure of Justice: The Holocaust Era Restitution Campaign of the 1990s*. Madison, WI: University of Wisconsin Press, 2009.

Micale, Mark S., and Paul Lerner, ed. *Traumatic Pasts: History, Psychiatry, and Trauma in the Modern Age, 1870–1930*. New York: Cambridge University Press, 2001.

Michel, Max, ed. *Gesundheitsschäden durch Verfolgung und Gefangenschaft und ihre Spätfolgen*. Frankfurt am Main: Röderberger-Verlag, 1955.

Novick, Peter. *The Holocaust and Collective Memory: The American Experience*. London: Bloomsbury, 2000.

Olick, Jeffrey K. *The Politics of Regret: On Collective Memory and Historical Responsibility*. New York: Routledge, 2007.

Paul, Helmut. "Internationale Erfahrungen mit psychischen Spädschäden." In *Psychische Spätschäden nach politischer Verfolgung*, ed. Helmut Paul and Hans Joachim Herberg, 37–48. Basel: Karger, 1963.

Pross, Christian. *Wiedergutmachung: Der Kleinkrieg gegen die Opfer*. Frankfurt am Main: Athenäum Verlag, 1988.

Prost, Antoine, Rémi Skoutelsky, and Sonia Etienne. *Aryanisation économique et restitutions*. Paris: La Documentation française, 2000.

Rabinbach, Anson. "Antifascism." In *Europe Since 1914: Encyclopedia of the Age of War and Reconstruction*, ed. John Merriman and Jay Winter, 106–13. Detroit, MI: Thomson Gale, 2006.

Rosenfeld, Alvin. "The Americanization of the Holocaust." In *Thinking about the Holocaust: After Half a Century*, ed. Alvin Rosenfeld, 119–50. Bloomington, IN: Indiana University Press, 1997.

Rothe, Anne. *Popular Trauma Culture: Selling the Pain of Others in the Mass Media*. New Brunswick, NJ: Rutgers University Press, 2011.

Sofsky, Wolfgang. *The Order of Terror: The Concentration Camp*, trans. William Templer. Princeton, NJ: Princeton University Press, 1997.

Stiefel, Dieter, ed. *Die politische Ökonomie des Holocaust: Zur wirtschaftlichen Logik von Verfolgung und "Wiedergutmachung."* Vienna: Verlag für Geschichte und Politik, 2001.

Takei, Ayaka. "The 'Gemeinde Problem': The Jewish Restitution Successor Organization and the Postwar Jewish Communities in Germany 1947–1954." *Holocaust and Genocide Studies* 16, no. 2 (2002): 266–88.

Teitel, Ruti G. *Transitional Justice.* New York: Oxford University Press, 2000.

Torpey, John. *Making Whole What Has Been Smashed: On Reparations Politics.* Cambridge, MA: Harvard University Press, 2006.

Volmer-Naumann, Julia. *Bürokratische Bewältigung: Entschädigung für nationalsozialistisch Verfolgte im Regierungsbezirk Münster.* Essen: Klartext Verlag, 2011.

von Baeyer, Walter Ritter, Heinz Häfner, and Karl Peter Kisker. *Psychiatrie der Verfolgten: Psychopathologische und gutachtliche Erfahrungen an den Opfern der nationalsozialistischen Verfolgung und vergleichbarer Extrembelastung.* Berlin: Springer Verlag, 1964.

Wieviorka, Annette. *Déportation et génocide: Entre la mémoire et l'oubli.* Paris: Plon, 1992.

———. *L'ère du témoin.* Paris: Plon, 1998.

Withuis, Jolande. "The Management of Victimhood: Long Term Health Damage from Asthenia to PTSD." In *The Politics of War Trauma: The Aftermath of World War II in Eleven European Countries,* ed. Jolande Withuis and Annet Mooij, 287–322. Amsterdam: Aksant, 2011.

Withuis, Jolande, and Annet Mooij. "From Totalitarianism to Trauma: A Paradigm Change in the Netherlands." In *The Politics of War Trauma: The Aftermath of World War II in Eleven European Countries,* ed. Jolande Withuis and Annet Mooij, 191–215. Amsterdam: Aksant, 2010.

Withuis, Jolande, and Annet Mooij, eds. *The Politics of War Trauma: The Aftermath of World War II in Eleven European Countries.* Amsterdam: Aksant, 2010.

Young, Allan. *The Harmony of Illusions: Inventing Post-traumatic Stress Disorder.* Princeton, NJ: Princeton University Press, 1995.

Zajde, Nathalie. *Guérir de la Shoah.* Paris: Odile Jacob, 2005.

Chapter 9

Achieving a Measure of Justice and Writing Holocaust History

Through US Restitution Litigation

Michael J. Bazyler

INTRODUCTION

In a volume devoted to the subject of Holocaust justice and its meaning, it is appropriate to examine the role of law, and the efforts of lawyers, in achieving a modicum of justice in the aftermath of the Holocaust. Many of the other chapters in this volume focus on postwar criminal justice. This chapter focuses on economic justice: the parallel endeavor to disgorge from the German perpetrators and other thieves and successors the massive wealth stolen from the Jews of Europe between 1933 and 1945.[1] Part and parcel of every genocide is also mass theft, and the Holocaust is no exception. What is exceptional is that much of the effort made for Holocaust restitution did not begin until the 1990s, more than half a century after the end of World War II.[2] Adding to this exceptionality is that the arena where the modern campaign over restitution took place was not Europe, where the Holocaust took place, but the United States. More specifically, ground zero for Holocaust restitution was the US courthouse. There, alleged thieves and successors were sued under both international law and US law for monetary losses amounting to billions of dollars.[3]

This chapter provides an overview and analysis of Holocaust economic justice achieved in the United States through litigation. My theme is threefold: (1) Holocaust restitution litigation that began in the 1990s has been a positive development, most significantly by compensating still-living Holocaust survivors for losses that heretofore remained unresolved; (2) contemporary restitution efforts are very much ongoing in the twenty-first century; and (3) the litigation has an efficacy from the standpoint of a legal scholar that Holocaust historians overlook. In this regard, I confront the charge from some historians that US lawyers litigating Holocaust-related claims have distorted history. As I show, the degree to which these civil suits over monetary claims may have distorted Holocaust history is only a short-term issue. Further, whatever distortion has taken place is significantly outweighed by the contribution made by this litigation to Holocaust historiography. Holocaust historians aim to give us an accurate history of the events between 1933 and 1945. Lawyers today litigating thievery that took place during the Holocaust and its aftermath have made (and will continue to make) positive contributions to that historiography.

HOLOCAUST RESTITUTION LITIGATION IN THE 1990S

Holocaust restitution has two broad periods. The first was the immediate postwar era from 1945 to 1957. In the immediate aftermath of Germany's unconditional surrender in 1945, the Allies attempted to recover and return assets stolen by the Nazis throughout Europe, including those once held by Jews.[4] With the return of (West) German sovereignty in 1949, Chancellor Konrad Adenauer aimed to normalize relations with the West, and restitution was part of this effort. Under the Luxembourg Agreement signed with Israel in September 1952, the Federal Republic of Germany agreed to pay Israel 3 billion Deutschmarks over the next fourteen years. Israel used a large portion of the reparations to purchase goods and services from West Germany and to aid in the settlement of new immigrants in Israel, the largest group being Holocaust survivors. Representatives of twenty-three Jewish organizations met in 1951 and formed the Conference on Jewish Material Claims against Germany (popularly known as the Claims Conference), which represents the Jewish world to Germany. The Claims Conference still administers allocations from Germany to individual survivors and is the heir to heirless Holocaust property in Germany. Since 1952, more than 500,000 survivors have received compensation from Germany, totaling approximately $60 billion.[5]

The contemporary Holocaust restitution campaign began with three class action lawsuits filed in 1996 in US courts against Swiss banks. At issue was the banks' failure to return assets deposited by Jews during the Hitler era, and the banks' trade with Nazi Germany in looted assets, including gold. In 1998, the Swiss banks settled for $1.25 billion.[6] The restitution campaign then proceeded with suits brought in the US against European insurance companies for their failure to honor Holocaust-era insurance policies. Holocaust survivors then filed class action suits, also in the United States, against German companies for profiting from slave labor. French and Austrian banks were also sued for persecuting their Jewish customers. Finally, museums, galleries, and private collectors were sued for the return of art looted by the Nazis from Jewish families that came into the hands of these persons and entities after the war.

Why the United States? Previous efforts at restitution, including diplomacy, individual pleas by Holocaust survivors and Jewish organizations, and even suits in foreign courts, had not brought satisfactory results. The US system of civil litigation, however, made the United States the world's only forum in which Holocaust claims could be heard. The US legal culture allowed lawyers to take on high-risk cases with a low probability of success in order to test the limits of the law. Foreign citizens could file suit in the United States for human rights abuses committed elsewhere, and US courts recognized their own jurisdiction concerning Holocaust claims over defendants that did business in the United States. US law also recognizes class action lawsuits. US lawyers and their foreign co-counsel, furthermore, could take cases on a contingency basis, thereby giving Holocaust claimants topnotch legal representation when confronting Wall Street law firms, hired by European and American corporate giants as defense counsel. Other factors helped, including fixed and affordable court filing fees for civil lawsuits; the ability to have a jury trial in civil litigation; and the existence of an independent judiciary uninfluenced by the political branches of government. The great British jurist Lord Denning recognized US courts as the most desirable forum for transnational litigation when he wryly observed in an English court opinion, "As a moth is drawn to the light, so is a litigant drawn to the United States. If he can only get his case into their courts, he stands to win a fortune."[7]

Litigating the financial crimes of the Holocaust in US courthouses captured the public imagination in the 1990s. Holocaust consciousness in the United States was at an all-time high, particularly thanks to the opening of the United States Holocaust Memorial Museum in Washington, DC, in 1993. The US media further spotlighted the restitution problem by writing or even screening stories on the theft of Jewish property. Jewish organizations such as the World Jewish Congress added determined voices to the restitution effort, particularly during the longtime tenure of billionaire businessman Edgar Bronfman (1979–2007) as WJC president. US public officials, including members of Congress, raised issues of Nazi plunder. Some even threatened sanctions against European companies involved in the theft and slave labor as a lever to move the companies to deal with these claims. Senator Alfonse D'Amato (R-NY, 1981–1999) who headed the Senate Banking Committee, held public hearings in 1997 on the failure by Swiss banks to return deposits European Jews made with the banks on the eve of World War II. State financial officials in California and New York in 1998 threatened to pull out their public investment funds from the banks.[8] When European insurance companies declined to disclose full information on policies they issued to Jews in Europe prior to the war, California enacted the Holocaust Victim Insurance Relief Act (HVIRA), a law forcing the companies to reveal such data as a condition to doing business in the state.[9] In 2003, the United States Supreme Court in a 5–4 decision declared HVIRA unconstitutional on the grounds that the California law unduly encroached on the exclusive power by the federal government to engage in foreign affairs.[10] By that time, however, the insurance companies had created the International Commission on Holocaust-era Insurance Claims, a body whose sole purpose was to pay out on unpaid policies issued to Jews prior to the war.[11]

On the other hand, restitution in the 1990s was incomplete. In that decade, there were three international conferences focusing on Holocaust economic justice. The London Gold Conference in 1997 worked to return the assets of the Tripartite Gold Commission (TGC).[12] About 5.5 tons of gold stolen by the Nazis, worth some $60 million, remained to be distributed. Upon recommendation of TGC officials, countries holding this gold agreed to contribute their portions of the remaining assets to assist with the needs of still-living Holocaust survivors.[13] The Washington Art Conference in 1998 adopted the "Washington Principles on Nazi Confiscated Art," a unified set of standards by which art looted by the Nazis would be returned to its prewar Jewish owners or their heirs. But the guidelines have not been as successful as initially envisioned.[14] The Stockholm Holocaust Conference in 1999 focused on Holocaust education, establishing the International Task Force (ITF) on Holocaust Education, Remembrance, and Research, an intergovernmental body of thirty-one member states. The ITF is voluntary, however, with a requirement for unanimity and with no power of enforcement.

Two more conferences in the 2000s also had mixed results. The Vilnius International Forum on Holocaust-Era Looted Cultural Assets in 2000 attempted to measure progress concerning Nazi-looted art since the Washington Conference two years earlier. In the Vilnius Declaration, the attending

governments recognized "the massive and unprecedented looting and con-
fiscations of art and other cultural property owned by Jewish individuals,
communities and others, and the need to reach just and fair solutions to
the return of such art and cultural property." The conference reaffirmed
the Washington Principles and proposed further actions for the restitution
of Nazi-looted cultural property. The impact of the Vilnius Forum on the
return of art and other confiscated Jewish objects can be evaluated as negligible at best.

In June 2009, the Czech Republic, during its one-year term at the head of
the European Union, initiated an international conference on Holocaust-era
assets. Forty-seven countries participated. To head the US delegation, the
Obama White House appointed Stuart Eizenstat as "Special Advisor on
Holocaust Issues to the Secretary of State."[15] Eizenstat had been the chief
architect of the global Holocaust-restitution settlements of the 1990s during
the Clinton presidency, and of course he knew Secretary of State Hillary
Clinton well. His appointment signaled that the new administration, more
than that of George W. Bush, would take seriously what Eizenstat called
the "unfinished business of World War II."[16] On the final day of the conference, the delegates issued the so-called Terezín Declaration at the very site
of the former transit ghetto. It called for the establishment within one year
of Guidelines and Best Practices for the Restitution and Compensation of
Immovable (Real) Property.[17] The Guidelines were in place by June 2010,
but as their preamble makes clear, they are "legally non-binding but morally
important."[18] Unlike with the Washington Principles and the Vilnius Forum,
the state signatories to the Terezín Declaration created a body, the European Shoah Legacy Institute (ESLI), to monitor the implementation of the
provisions of the Terezín Declaration and its Guidelines.[19]

In 2017, ESLI issued The Holocaust (Shoah) Immovable Property Restitution Study, the first-ever comprehensive compilation of all significant
legislation passed since 1945 by the 47 states that participated in the 2009
Prague Conference.[20] The Study found that most Western European states
have complied or substantially complied with the precepts of the Terezín
Declaration. The situation was bleaker for Eastern Europe. The significant
outlier is Poland, the only post-communist East European state in the European Union to have failed to enact a law covering Holocaust-era private
property restitution. In April 2011, Polish President Bronisław Komorowski
called the failure by the Polish parliament to pass a restitution law "a dis-
grace for Poland."[21] In 2014, fifteen members of the British Parliament sent
a letter to the Polish prime minister lamenting Poland's "failure to fulfill—or
even recognize—its responsibility to victims."[22] In late 2015, elections in Po-

land brought to power the nationalist Law and Justice Party, marking the death knell, at least for the moment, of any serious efforts at restitution of real property owned by Jews in prewar Poland.[23] With a prewar Jewish population of 3.3 million, the largest in Europe, the issue looms large. Ninety percent of Polish Jews did not survive the war, with most land and buildings owned by individual Jews or Jewish communal institutions never returned to survivors or heirs. The impending demise of any still-living survivors means that soon only heirs will remain to continue the fight for Holocaust restitution in Poland.[24]

LEGAL EFFORTS IN THE TWENTY-FIRST CENTURY

The past decade or so of international conferences has not been completely without results, however. A number of foundations have been established in Central and Western Europe; educational initiatives have undertaken new efforts on the subject of the Holocaust and genocide; and historical commissions have been created to investigate the conduct of states during the Shoah, with government reports exposing for the first time the extent of local collaboration of the non-Jewish population in Nazi-occupied Europe with the murder of the Jews and theft of their property.[25] Multinationals, who had done business with the Nazis and then were sued decades later in US courts, hired prominent historians to produce studies that revealed for the first time the companies' wartime complicity. We know now much more about how commerce was conducted by German and other companies in occupied Europe because of these studies, written more than half a century after the end of the war.

And the Holocaust continues to be litigated. Criminal cases in Germany have included that of John Demjanjuk in 2011, and even more recently, the trial in Lüneburg of Oskar Gröning, the 93-year-old "bookkeeper of Auschwitz" in 2014.[26] Among Gröning's duties was the counting of money and other possessions of Jews arriving at Auschwitz, and the subsequent shipping of the loot back to Germany. Gröning claimed never to have participated in the selection process or any acts of killing, just theft. In past years, the prosecution's inability to prove base motives or actual involvement would have resulted in an acquittal under German law. Yet in Gröning's trial, the prosecutors argued that the sorting of banknotes taken from the trainloads of arriving Jews by definition made Gröning an accomplice to the mass murder, since he was part of the machinery of death. After a three-month trial, Gröning was convicted as an accessory to murder and sentenced to four years' imprisonment.[27]

Trains and the Holocaust

The Gröning case is significant not only for its importance regarding new interpretations of the German statute concerning homicide. Symbolically, it also focused on the destruction process through the use of railroads, which themselves have been the recent focus of restitution suits in the United States. Trains have long been a ubiquitous symbol of the Holocaust. The great Holocaust historian Raul Hilberg once noted that, though "railways [cannot] be regarded as anything more than physical equipment," they became in German hands "a live organism which acted in concert with Germany's military, industry, and SS to make German history"[28] and marked "the end of the Jewish people in Europe."[29] Simone Gigliotti writes: "[T]he use of trains for death camp transports was a critical enabler of the Nazis' genocidal ambition. Without the involvement of trains, the murderous pace of killing in the camps would be undeniably diminished, as would be the number of Jewish victims who now perpetually rest in the figure of six million."[30] Alfred Mierzejewski notes that it took no more than 2,000 trains to perpetuate the Holocaust.[31] In 2016, Yad Vashem launched a database that documents about 1,100 of these transports, searchable by train (or other modes of transportation) or the victim's name.[32]

In 2008, the German state railway company Deutsche Bahn staged, after initial refusal, a traveling exhibition at railroad stations in Germany called *Sonderzüge in den Tod* (Special trains to death). Based on the 2006 French exhibition *Enfants juifs déportés de France* (Exhibition of Jewish children deported from France), compiled by prominent French lawyer and Holocaust survivor Serge Klarsfeld, it commemorated deportations by rail while highlighting the role of the German state railway company.[33]

Hungarian Train Litigation

Four Holocaust restitution suits litigated in US courts—all of which focus on railroads during the Holocaust—help to illustrate the current state of the Holocaust restitution movement. The so-called Hungarian Gold Train case involved the robbery of Hungarian Jews by the Germans and their Hungarian allies beginning in the spring of 1944 as a prelude to the deportation to Auschwitz of some 440,000 Hungarian Jews.[34] As the Soviets closed in on Budapest, Hungarian officials loaded confiscated movable Jewish property onto a special train, which eventually made its way to Austria, where it fell under the control of US occupation authorities. The cargo on the so-called Gold Train included some jewelry, but mostly comprised household items

ranging from candlesticks to furniture to rugs. Regardless, the train carried
a legend of great wealth. In 2001, Hungarian Jewish survivors filed a class
action lawsuit against the United States in federal court in Southern Florida.
They claimed that US troops looted the train and that the US government
later failed to return the remaining captured booty to the proper owners. In
2005, the suit was settled for $26 million, with the money to be used to aid
Hungarian survivors worldwide.[35]

The settlement did not reflect accurate history. The US Army in fact
took no valuable loot from the train upon its capture, only items used by
the occupation forces such as typewriters, rugs, cutlery, and linens. The remaining items were transferred in 1948 to the International Refugee Organization (IRO), which then sold the property at an auction with the proceeds
applied primarily for the benefit of Jewish victims. None of these proceeds
were kept by the United States. The Israeli historian Ronald Zweig, in his
book on the Gold Train, finds that the legend about the fabulous wealth on
the train is a myth.[36] Yet the myth continues, partly thanks to the Gold Train
case. The 2014 novel *Love and Treasure* by best-selling author Ayelet Waldman
weaves a fictional tale around the supposed riches of the Hungarian Gold
Train.[37]

The Hungarian Gold Train settlement with the US government led to
the filing of similar suits, this time against Hungary and Hungarian entities
for theft. Hungarian survivors in 2010 filed two class action lawsuits in federal courts in Illinois. The first named the Hungarian State Railways as the
defendant.[38] The other named five banks, all of which did business in the
United States.[39] The defendants in both cases were accused of stealing cash,
art, and other assets from Hungarian Jews following the German occupation of Hungary in March 1944. In January 2015, the United States Court of
Appeals for the Seventh Circuit affirmed the earlier dismissal of both cases
in Federal District Court based on plaintiffs' failure to exhaust legal remedies in Hungary.[40] But as of this writing the case is not over. As the Seventh
Circuit explained: "Nevertheless, while the doors of United States courts are
closed to these claims for now, they are not locked forever. All dismissals are
without prejudice. If plaintiffs find that future attempts to pursue remedies
in Hungary are frustrated unreasonably or arbitrarily, a United States court
could once again hear these claims."[41]

In January 2016, the US Court of Appeals for the District of Columbia
demonstrated that US courts are still ready to hear civil suits arising from
crimes of the Holocaust. On appeal, the court revived a separate suit filed
by another group of Hungarian survivors against the Hungarian State Railway in the United States District Court for the District of Columbia.[42] In a
unanimous opinion written by Judge Sri Srinivasan, a three-judge panel of

the appeals court rejected the lower court's ruling that a 1947 treaty between Hungary and the Allied powers prevented the survivors from filing suits in US courts. The appeals court held that the survivors could sue the railway for stripping Hungarian Jews of their property in 1944 when transporting them to Auschwitz. According to the opinion, US courts have jurisdiction because the suit fell within the international takings exception, 28 U.S.C.§1605(a)(3), to sovereign immunity found in the Foreign Sovereign Immunities Act (FSIA). The FSIA is the federal law that since 1977 has exclusively governed litigation against foreign states and their entities in US courts.[43] Section 1605(a)(3), the international takings exception of the FSIA, denies immunity to states and their entities when the suit is for property taken in violation of international law. Here, the court found the necessary predicate to the suit: the property theft arose out of genocide, the supreme crime under international law.[44] As Judge Srinivasan explained: "In our view, the alleged takings did more than effectuate genocide or serve as a means of carrying out genocide. Rather, we see the expropriations as themselves genocide. It follows necessarily that the takings were 'in violation of international law.'"[45] The Court's conclusion: "The text of §1605(a)(3) ... applies foursquare to genocidal takings committed by a state against its [own] nationals."[46]

Because of the peculiar language of the international takings exception, applying only to expropriation of property in violation of international law (and not to international law violations that result in personal injury or even death), the only claims left standing were those limited to the Hungarian railway's theft of property from Hungarian Jews.[47] As the court explained: "[J]urisdiction exists as to those of the plaintiffs' claims that directly implicate rights in property."[48] The fourteen plaintiff Holocaust survivors in the Washington, DC, litigation are in their eighties and it is not entirely clear if they will live to see a resolution of their suit. Hungary retains the opportunity to convince the trial judge to whom the case will return to dismiss the lawsuit on other jurisdictional grounds, and also on the basis of the statute of limitations. The District of Columbia Circuit Appeals Court also gave the trial judge the option of placing the plaintiffs' claims against the railroad on hold and ordering the plaintiffs to exhaust any potential remedies in Hungary, as did the Seventh Circuit.

French Train Litigation

The litigation against the Hungarian railway arising from its transportation of Hungarian Jews to Auschwitz did not arise in a vacuum. It emerged from the earlier suits against European corporations for their thievery of

Jewish assets and use of Jews as slaves. Specifically, the Hungarian railway cases followed a similar set of suits filed more than a decade earlier against the French national railway for its transportation of French and foreign Jews to Auschwitz and other camps in German-occupied Poland. Litigation against the Société Nationale des Chemins de fer Français (SNCF), began in the year 2000 in federal court in New York's Eastern District.[49] Raymonde Abrams and his fellow plaintiffs sued SNCF for its role in transporting approximately 76,000 Jews to Auschwitz beginning in the summer of 1942. SNCF has never denied that it transported Jewish deportees to their deaths. But it has refused to pay compensation, stating that it acted under duress applied by the German occupation authorities. In 2011, the suit was finally dismissed when the United States Supreme Court declined to review a lower court's ruling that the case fell outside of US legal jurisdiction.[50] Specifically, the lower courts held that because SNCF was a state-owned enterprise, it possessed sovereign immunity from suit in US courts.[51] Unlike the DC federal appeals court's decision in 2016 against the Hungarian state-owned national railway, the courts reviewing the litigation against the French state-owned railway held that none of the FSIA exceptions to sovereign immunity applied. But all was not lost.

Soon afterwards, SNCF's subsidiary in the United States, Keolis North America, bid on commuter rail contracts in Maryland.[52] Leo Bretholz was an Austrian Jewish survivor who fled Vienna after the German takeover in 1938. After living in the Netherlands, Belgium, and France, Bretholz was interned by the French government at the Rivesaltes detention camp in 1942 before he was sent to the transit camp at Drancy and then to Auschwitz. He escaped from the moving train and survived for the remainder of the war in a series of forced labor details. After the war he settled near Baltimore, Maryland, eventually writing a book about his experiences.[53] In 2011, he emerged as the voice for the claimants, becoming the star witness in congressional hearings on the proposed Holocaust Rail Justice Act, which would have allowed Holocaust-era suits against SNCF in US district courts.[54]

Bretholz died at age 93 in March 2014. In December, a deal was reached between the United States and France, in which the French government agreed to pay $60 million to non-French survivors (and for those deceased, to their heirs) who were deported on French trains. A formal accord was signed the same month. According to Ambassador Stuart Eizenstat, the chief US negotiator and architect of many of the Holocaust restitution settlements: "It's an extremely just and quite remarkable program given that 70 years after the fact that they are trying to compensate people. There are thousands of people who because they are not French never got a nickel who will now be dividing $60 million."[55] French survivors were expressly excluded from the deal on the grounds that they had previously received compensation from the French government under a reparations program that began in 1948. US lawyers vowed to fight on by "look[ing] for ways to block transportation contracts for the SNCF" in the United States.[56]

Nazi-Looted Art Litigation

An additional category carrying new developments is that of art. Art looted by the Nazis and discovered to have been in prominent collections, museums, and in private hands for the last half century began to be returned to their rightful owners and heirs at the end of the 1990s. In 2006, after six years of litigation in the United States, including a victory before the United States Supreme Court in 2004,[57] Maria Altmann, an elderly survivor from Austria, recovered from the Austrian National Gallery five artworks by Gustav Klimt stolen from her family by the Nazis. Altmann and her fellow heirs sold one of the works, *Portrait of Adele Bloch-Bauer I,* to the Neue Gallerie in New York for a reported $135 million, at that time the highest price ever paid for a single work of art. The four other Klimts were later sold through auctions for a total of $192 million.[58]

A decade later, Holocaust art restitution continues, albeit with fits and starts. On 20 January 2015, the US Supreme Court declined to hear the appeal by the defendant museum in *Von Saher v. Norton Simon Museum,* a case brought by relatives of Jacques Goudstikker, a Jewish art dealer in Amsterdam who fled after the German invasion in 1940.[59] Goudstikker's heirs are contesting the museum's possession of two life-size companion paintings, *Adam* and *Eve,* painted in 1530 by Lucas Cranach the Elder and currently valued together at around $24 million.[60] During the war, the two paintings became part of stolen booty in the personal collection of Nazi leader Hermann Göring. Restored to the Netherlands after the war, the Norton Simon Museum in California purchased the paintings in 1971 from a private collector. The collector bought them earlier from the Dutch government. The museum insisted that it had good title to the paintings, and a US district court agreed. Marei von Saher has appealed to the Ninth Circuit.[61] If the case ever goes to trial, it will be a rare instance of a Nazi-looted art case actually being decided on the merits in court.[62]

The restitution of the vast amount of art and other cultural objects stolen by the Nazis continues to be a live issue in the twenty-first century. Thousands of works of art looted by the Nazis have yet to be located.[63] In May 2015, Henri Matisse's *Femme Assise* was returned to the family of Paul Rosenberg in New York by the German government.[64] The painting had belonged to Paul Rosenberg, one of the world's leading modern art dealers, whose collection the Nazis looted. It was discovered in 2012 in the hoard of 1,200 paintings in the Munich apartment of Cornelius Gurlitt, the reclusive son of a wartime art dealer Hildebrand Gurlitt, who sold stolen artworks on behalf of the Nazis. German prosecutors seized the paintings as part of a tax investigation, but kept the discovery secret until journalists revealed it a year later. Gurlitt died in 2014, having "donated" the paintings to a Swiss museum. The German government is holding the collection until it determines how each painting came into Gurlitt's possession.[65]

CONTENTIOUS RESULTS

The contemporary restitution campaign has been a success in many ways. Most remarkable is that US courts, more than fifty years after the events, have undertaken cases concerning World War II. In the history of US litigation, no class of cases had ever appeared in which so much time had elapsed between the acts in question and the filing of the lawsuit. The results, in terms of monetary settlements, are impressive as well. Ambassador J. Christian Kennedy, the then-US State Department Special Envoy for Holocaust Issues, summed up in 2007:

> A combination of court settlements and other U.S.-facilitated agreements resulted in over $8 billion for Holocaust victims and their heirs from Swiss banks, German companies, Austrian companies, and French banks, as well as several large European insurance companies. Most of these agreements were concluded with the participation of European governments and the U.S. Government. As of today, nearly all of the $8 billion from these agreements has been either distributed to survivors and heirs or otherwise obligated for continuing programs to support needy survivors or promote Holocaust education and remembrance.[66]

But the results are not only monetary. As a result of the litigation, the shrouded role of German and other European companies during the Nazi era has also been partially revealed. Many of the firms that were sued, now multinational entities, opened their archives to Holocaust historians who have written very fine assessments on their wartime history.[67] The lawsuits have also led many European states to reevaluate their wartime history by creating historical commissions to research their archives and thereafter to issue statements of contrition for their wartime behavior. The Holocaust restitution movement, therefore, yielded not only money; it also yielded new history.

Restitution suits have had their limits. All suits have ended with out-of-court settlements, and thus the victims of the Holocaust or their heirs filing these suits never got their "day in court," in order to represent their experiences publicly, as for instance was the case with witnesses in the 1961 trial of Adolf Eichmann. Some of the restitution suits also ended in complete defeat.[68] However, even when European defendants won by successfully convincing a US judge to dismiss the suit on technical grounds such as lack of jurisdiction or because the suit was time-barred, the corporate defendants in some instances did not walk away from the negotiating table, but continued many rounds of negotiation.[69] And bitter discourse followed disappointing results. Legal victories by defendants, for instance, did not end attempts by US politicians from pushing for compensation, nor has it kept Holocaust survivors and activists from reminding US consumers that the European products they were buying–whether cars, computers, medical equipment, aspirin, or insurance–were from companies implicated in the worst crimes in human history.

Even seemingly large settlements were in fact small when divided on the individual level. Former prisoners who had worked as slave laborers could expect a one-time payment of approximately $7,500. Survivors of gruesome medical experiments at Auschwitz received less than $10,000 as total compensation for their suffering.[70] Count Otto Lambsdorff, the German government representative to the slave labor negotiations, testifying before the US Congress, defended the settlement figures: "I wish I had greater funds available for distribution," he said, "but 10 billion marks is what we got and what was agreed upon by all the participating parties after long and arduous negotiations."[71] We can call these payments "symbolic justice." As explained by Eva Kor, an identical twin experimented upon at Auschwitz by the infamous Dr. Joseph Mengele: "Even though this is a small amount of money, it is a big help to those survivors who are in need of assistance. And more importantly, this shows that Germany has recognized what was done to the victims and has not forgotten their suffering."[72]

Monetizing the Holocaust?

Money is a most difficult issue in principle, because arguments over monetary compensation seem to reduce the Holocaust to a crime that can be compensated. It also potentially casts Holocaust survivors with the antisemitic trope of the money-seeking Jew. Some critics have complained, hyperbolically, of a "Holocaust industry."[73] Serious scholars have been more nuanced. Professor Michael Marrus of the University of Toronto, in his excellent and measured assessment of the restitution campaign of the 1990s, likens compensation negotiations to Otto von Bismarck's quip regarding the process by which sausage is made: It is best not to look.[74] Literary critic Leon Wieseltier urged his mother, when discussing an offer made by Germany to make restitution payments to Holocaust survivors, to "spit at it."[75] Elie Wiesel spoke of feeling "reluctant to define the greatest tragedy in Jewish history in terms of money."[76] Anthropologist Susan Slyomovics of UCLA notes that her mother and grandmother, survivors of three German concentration camps, disagreed whether to accept money from the Germans.[77]

Matters have been made all the more contentious by some of the lead actors in the restitution drama, namely US trial attorneys. Even representatives of Jewish organizations like the World Jewish Congress, which played a leading role in the restitution campaign, criticized the attorneys who filed class action Holocaust restitution lawsuits.[78] Yet, at the Berlin ceremony in July 2000 to conclude the US-German settlement of the Holocaust claims against Germany, Ambassador Stuart Eizenstat demurred.

> We must be frank. It was the American lawyers, through the lawsuits they brought in U.S. courts, who placed the long-forgotten wrongs by German companies during the Nazi era on the international agenda. It was their research and their work which highlighted these old injustices and forced us to confront them. Without question, we would not be here without them.[79]

To Marrus, Eizenstat "was exceptionally generous to the [legal] representatives of the Holocaust survivors, given what we have already seen of his harsh view of the matter."[80]

Distorting Holocaust History?

Yet the main issue might be the ways in which the restitution cases have affected historical understanding of the Holocaust itself. Marrus's concern in evaluating the process, he says, "involves its implications for the history of the destruction of the European Jews."[81] He has been especially critical of the SNCF litigation. Pursuing a state entity for crimes of the occupation period sixty years after the fact, he argues,

> [M]akes no sense—particularly in light of a lengthy process by which the French state has solemnly assumed, both rhetorically and materially, its part of the responsibility for the Holocaust in France ... I can appreciate [the victims'] nightmarish frustration, their sense of insufficiency about reparation and restitution, and their anger at mistakes and snubs that have been made along the way. But

as Michel Zaoui, former counsel for the civil parties in the [Maurice] Papon case commented ... "At a certain point, one has to say: 'That's enough!'" For many observers, the S.N.C.F. case may well have been that point.[82]

Marrus further explains how allegations made in the legal filings in US courts mischaracterize the thievery; how they named as defendants entities whose wrongdoing was not actually clear; and how they placed all blame on a certain defendant or group, when guilt was more widely shared. And by shining a spotlight only on defendants who did business in the United States (which subjected them to US courts) and who had deep pockets, the litigators provided a false picture of history.[83] Thus the Holocaust becomes "misshapen to fit the idiom of the law."[84] The late historian Gerald Feldman said in 1999 that the briefs in some class action cases "make me feel that our worst history students have decided to take up the law."[85]

Tel Aviv University law professor Leora Bilsky disagrees with both Marrus and Feldman.[86] Bilsky explains:

> The recent shift in legal treatment of the Holocaust from criminal to civil litigation, with the Holocaust restitution lawsuits brought before American federal courts in the 1990s, has only exacerbated historians' critique of the law. In contrast, [I] argue ... that the restitution litigation represents a new and fruitful model for the relation of law to historical inquiry. In this model, the judge [presiding over a Holocaust restitution lawsuit] plays a facilitative and supervisory role vis-à-vis the historian, encouraging the production of broad and contextualized historical narratives.[87]

Bilsky sees much potential for the enhancement of Holocaust historiography through the civil restitution lawsuit. As she explains:

> [A] closer look at the restitution litigation reveals that it provides new possibilities for the relationship between law and history. In particular, by avoiding the individualistic bias of criminal law and focusing on the organization, the civil class action enabled the emergence of data and narratives regarding the involvement of business corporations in the Nazi crimes.[88]

In her mind, a civil suit arising out of the Holocaust can yield better history than its well-known counterpart, the Holocaust criminal trial.[89]

> Furthermore, I would like to suggest that settlement represents an opportunity rather than a danger to the clarification of history. As a result of settlement, we witness not the disappearance of narrative but a renewed division of the judicial and historical functions. Contrary to didactic criminal trials, where the historical and legal functions of judging are blended in the judgment, here the

judge takes on a facilitative role, providing incentives to the parties to cooperate and supervising and shaping the historical research undertaken by nonlegal actors. The privatization and decentralization of the litigation means, however, that these new narratives are not to be found in the judgment of a court but are produced in various locations and times alongside the litigation.[90]

Using the Swiss banks settlement as a model, Bilsky shows how the class action civil litigation led to the $1.25 billion settlement in 1998 and then to a decade-long claims distribution process overseen by New York federal judge Edward R. Korman—yielding both money and memory.[91] Bilsky concludes that "[the Holocaust restitution civil] litigation alter[ed] the relationship between law and historical research, not only by uncovering precious data for historical research, but also by enabling the emergence of new historical narratives concerning corporate involvement in the Holocaust."[92] In the same vein, Count Otto Graf Lambsdorff, chief negotiator for the German government and German industry observed: "[R]estitution enhances memory."[93]

The legal profession has been involved in the historiography of the Holocaust from the start. The contribution began as the war drew to a close. In a memorandum to President Roosevelt in January 1945, Secretary of War Henry Stimson and Secretary of State Edward Stettinius observed that "[The] ... judicial method ... will make available for all mankind to study in the future years an authentic record of Nazi crimes and criminality."[94] After the war, prosecutors for the International Military Tribunal at Nuremberg sifted through tens of thousands of captured German records that set out the methodology for Germany's war of aggression, its war crimes, and its crimes against humanity to present their case before the tribunal's judges. At the time, the revelations were overwhelming. Justice Robert Jackson, the US Chief of Counsel for the prosecution of Nazi war criminals, was stunned: "I did not think men would ever be so foolish as to put in writing some of the things the Germans did. The stupidity of it and the brutality of it would simply appall you."[95] In the midst of controversies in 1946 regarding the trial's legality, Charles E. Wyzanski, a federal judge on the US District Court for Massachusetts, noted: "[I]f it had not been for the trial and the diligent efforts of the staff of able lawyers and investigators, acting promptly and in response to the necessities of legal technique, the important documents in which the defendants convicted themselves might never have been uncovered."[96] For Wyzanski, the trial had "given historians much of the data which the world will require for proper evaluation of the causes and events of World War II."[97] Robert M.W. Kempner, a junior prosecutor at Nuremberg, called the Nuremberg trials "the greatest history seminar ever held in the history of the world."[98] Sir Hartley Shawcross, the chief British prosecutor, hoped that the Nuremberg trial would "provide ... an authoritative and impartial record to which future historians may turn for truth."[99]

Indeed, the first great historical treatment of the Nazi Final Solution, Raul Hilberg's *The Destruction of the European Jews* (1961), was based on the documents unearthed by the prosecution at Nuremberg. As Hilberg later recollected, "What I found inside was absolutely extraordinary ... It took but one glance at all these documents to realize that their contents could not be read by one individual in a lifetime."[100] Countless scholars have followed Hilberg's paper trail to research and write histories of that era. Contemporary civil lawyers and their staffs continue the historical work. In the course of the litigation and during the post-settlement claims distribution, they have uncovered critical materials that can make a significant contribution to the historiography of the Holocaust. The best example is the mounds of documents generated by lawyers and claimants painstakingly seeking for the last fifteen years (2000–2015) to match claimants to the Swiss dormant accounts in the $1.25 billion Swiss bank settlement.[101] Each of the almost 3,000 awards for documented claims issued by the court-supervised Swiss Claims Resolution Tribunal in Zurich presents a different story of how the Jews of Europe were robbed of their wealth, most often through some legal machinations with the Swiss banks.[102] These awards and the documents supporting them provide current and future generations of Holocaust historians with raw data to study for years to come.[103] University of Connecticut law professor Leonard Orland, in his study of the Swiss Banks Settlement, observes: "A particularly noteworthy aspect of this case is the detailed, scholarly, and humane documentation of the experiences of Holocaust victims under the Nazi regime."[104]

Last, the accusation that the legal process distorts history, particularly that of the Holocaust, is one that we have heard before. Lawrence Douglas and Donald Bloxham have shown how postwar criminal trials of Nazi perpetrators, beginning with Nuremberg, presented a distorted picture of the character and breadth of the Holocaust.[105] A major reason was the need to prove Nazi criminality within an existing rigid legal framework; what Douglas calls "legal filters."[106] Moreover, "the historical and political realities in which courts—both domestic and international—operate serve to shape, and arguably misshape history and memory in the courtroom."[107] Looking at current-day prosecutions for genocide, crimes against humanity, and war crimes, Douglas sees a continuing need to "find the proper procedures to serve the interests of history and memory in the courtroom."[108] Douglas, of course, is speaking about the criminal process. But since the Holocaust has now entered the civil law legal arena, the same may be said for the Holocaust restitution suits which, as can be seen by the current train and art litigation, are still with us.

CONCLUSION

Two decades after it began, civil litigation in the United States for Holocaust economic justice is ongoing. Even the impending death of the last Holocaust survivor by the next decade will not necessarily end efforts at Holocaust restitution. Under US law, a thief cannot transfer good title, even to an unwary good faith purchaser.[109] As long, therefore, as any formerly Jewish-owned land, business, art, or other personal property has not been restituted to its prewar owner or heir, a chance remains that a US-based lawsuit can succeed in returning that property to the proper owner—or compensation in lieu of actual return. While some historians may have misgivings about litigators doing historical research, experience as far as back as Nuremberg demonstrates that the mining of Holocaust-era documents by lawyers and their staffs, whether in a criminal trial or a civil proceeding, can yield important truths that add to our understanding of the Holocaust.

Michael J. Bazyler is a professor of law and the 1939 Society Scholar in Holocaust and Human Rights Studies at the Fowler School of Law of Chapman University. He is the author of several books, most recently *Holocaust, Genocide, and the Law: A Quest for Justice in a Post-Holocaust World* (2016), which was awarded the National Jewish Book Award in Holocaust studies, as well as *Forgotten Trials of the Holocaust* (2013) with Frank Tuerkheimer.

NOTES

1. For an excellent overview see Peter Hayes, "Plunder and Restitution," in Peter Hayes and John K. Roth, eds. *The Oxford Handbook of Holocaust Studies* (New York, 2010), 540–59.
2. I use the term *Holocaust restitution* to designate both the actual return of properties (real and personal) and financial compensation. The term thus encompasses payments made to Jews who toiled as slaves and non-Jews as forced laborers for Nazi Germany; Jewish and non-Jewish victims of Nazi Germany's medical experiments; Jewish survivors of Nazi concentration camps, in ghettoes and in hiding; payments made on unpaid insurance policies and confiscated and dormant bank accounts; compensation or return of Nazi-looted art; and other instances where money was paid to victims or heirs of mass atrocities in Europe during World War II. For further discussion of the terminology of *restitution*

and the related term *reparations* see Pablo de Greiff, ed., *The Oxford Handbook of Reparations* (New York, 2006); Regula Ludi, *Reparations for Nazi Victims in Postwar Europe* (New York, 2012); Susan Slyomovics, *How to Accept German Reparations* (Philadelphia, 2014).

3. For monographs on the subject, see Michael J. Bazyler, *Holocaust Justice: The Battle for Restitution in America's Courts* (New York, 2003); Stuart E. Eizenstat, *Imperfect Justice: Looted Assets, Slave Labor, and the Unfinished Business of World War II* (New York, 2003); Michael R. Marrus, *Some Measure of Justice: The Holocaust Restitution Campaign of the 1990s* (Madison, WI, 2009); Michael J. Bazyler and Roger P. Alford, eds., *Holocaust Restitution: Perspectives on the Litigation and Its Legacy* (New York, 2006). For significant journal articles, see, e.g., Michael Thad Allen, "The Limit of Lex Americana: The Holocaust Restitution Litigation as a Cul-de-Sac of International Human Rights Law," *Widener Law Review* 17, no.1 (2011): 1–68; Leora Bilsky, Rodger D. Citron, and Natalie R. Davidson, "From *Kiobel* Back to Structural Reform: The Hidden Legacy of Holocaust Restitution Litigation," *Stanford Journal of Complex Litigation* 2, no. 1 (2014): 139–84.

4. For discussion, see Benjamin B. Ferencz, *Less Than Slaves: Jewish Forced Labor and the Quest for Compensation* (Bloomington, IN, 1979) (Ferencz was a Nuremberg prosecutor and later headed Jewish restitution efforts in occupied Germany). For restitution of Nazi-looted art in the postwar era, see Robert M. Edsel with Bret Witter, *The Monuments Men: Allied Heroes, Nazi Thieves and the Greatest Treasure Hunt in History* (New York, 2010); Lynn H. Nicholas, *The Rape of Europa: The Fate of Europe's Treasures in the Third Reich and the Second World War* (New York, 1995).

5. Gideon Taylor, "Where Morality Meets Money," in Bazyler and Alford, *Holocaust Restitution,* 163. Taylor was executive vice-president and chief operating officer of the Claims Conference. The German Foreign Office reports that, as of 2013, some 32,000 lifetime pensions were still being paid to Jewish survivors, totaling €270 million. Germany, Auswärtiges Amt, Compensation for National Socialist Injustice, retrieved August 2017 from http://www.auswaertiges-amt.de/EN/Aussenpolitik/Themen/InternatRecht/Entschaedigung_node.html.

6. For discussion of the Swiss Banks Settlement, see, e.g., Leonard Orland, *A Final Accounting: Holocaust Survivors and Swiss Banks* (Durham, NC, 2010), Michael J. Bazyler, "www.swissbankclaims.com: The Legality and Morality of the Holocaust-Era Settlement with the Swiss Banks," *Fordham International Law Journal* 25, no. 6, (2001): S64.

7. Smith Kline & French Labs, Ltd. v. Bloch [1983], 2 All E.R. 72, 74 (Eng.).

8. See Bazyler, *Holocaust Justice,* 21–29.

9. Ibid., 128.

10. American Insurance Ass'n. v. Garamendi, 539 U.S. 396 (2003).

11. For discussion of the International Commission on Holocaust-era Insurance Claims from three perspectives, see Bazyler and Alford, *Holocaust Restitution,* 239–67.

12. The TGC, formally titled the Tripartite Commission for the Restitution of Monetary Gold, was created in 1946 by the United States, the United Kingdom,

and France to return monetary gold stolen by the Nazis from the central banks of occupied Europe. Fifty years later, the TGC was still holding on to some of the gold. It was disbanded in 1998. See Final Report, Tripartite Commission for the Restitution of Monetary Gold, Brussels (13 September 1998), retrieved August 2017 from http://www.state.gov/s/l/65668.htm

13. Bazyler, *Holocaust Justice,* 12.

14. In 2011, the Holocaust Art Restitution Project, in a report titled *Revisiting the Washington Conference Principles on Nazi-Confiscated Art–13 Years Later,* examined each of the Principles and judged their impact with such terms as "completely ineffectual," "utter failure," and "unadulterated sham." See Holocaust Art Restitution Project, *Revisiting the Washington Conference Principles on Nazi-Confiscated Art–13 Years Later, Plundered Art,* 25 June 2011, retrieved August 2017 from http://plundered-art.blogspot.com/2011/06/revisiting-washington-conference.html.

15. Office of the Spokesman, "Secretary Clinton Appoints Stuart E. Eizenstat as Head of U.S. Delegation to the Prague Holocaust Era Assets Conference, June 26–30, 2009," US Department of State, 19 May 2009, retrieved August 2017 from https://2009-2017.state.gov/r/pa/prs/ps/2009/05/123653.htm. Eizenstat was later named Special Adviser for Holocaust Issues. See Office of the Spokesperson, "Stuart E. Eizenstat Named Special Adviser to the Secretary on Holocaust Issues, US Department of State, 18 December 2013, retrieved August 2017 from https://2009-2017.state.gov/r/pa/prs/ps/2013/218904.htm.

16. See Eizenstat, *Imperfect Justice.*

17. Guidelines and Best Practices for the Restitution and Compensation of Immovable (Real) Property Confiscated or Otherwise Wrongfully Seized by the Nazis, Fascists and Their Collaborators during the Holocaust (Shoah) Era between 1933–1945, Including the Period of World War II, June 9, 2010, retrieved August 2017 from http://shoahlegacy.org/wp-content/uploads/2014/06/guidelines_and_best_practices_for_the_restitution_and_compensation_of_immovable_property_09062010.pdf.

18. Ibid.

19. See European Shoah Legacy Institute, retrieved August 2017 from http://shoahlegacy.org.

20. See http://shoahlegacy.org. The author is the lead author of the ESLI Study.

21. "Jewish Property Restitution Still Thorn in Polish-Israel Relations," Radio Poland, 11 April 2013.

22. "British Lawmakers Press Poland on Holocaust Restitution," *Jewish Telegraphic Agency Bulletin,* 24 February 2014.

23. See Joanna Berendt, "Polish Court Limits World War II-Era Restitution Claims in Warsaw," *The New York Times,* 27 July 2016, ("The conservative Law and Justice Party, which swept to power in October, has taken a hard-line view, declaring that restitution legislation is not necessary because the past is the past.").

24. See Lydia Tomkiw, "Holocaust Survivor Stories in 2015: In Poland, The Fight To Get Their Property Back," *International Business Times,* 14 November 2015. For successful accounts of Polish restitution efforts, see, e.g., Ofer Aderet, "The Polish Hipster Who Found Out He's Jewish—And Reclaimed Warsaw Build-

ing," *Haaretz*, 3 April, 2016; Jill Singer, "Australian Jew's Fight Against the Catholic Church of Poland," *The Australian*, 7 May 2016.

25. See, e.g., Independent Commission of Experts Switzerland–Second World War, *Switzerland, National Socialism and the Second World War: Final Report* (Zurich, 2011), commonly known as the Bergier Report, after its chairman, Jean-François Bergier; International Commission on the Holocaust in Romania, *Final Report of the International Commission on the Holocaust in Romania* (Bucharest, 2004), the commission chaired by Elie Wiesel, who was born in Romania.

26. See Matthias Geyer, "An SS Officer Remembers: The Bookkeeper from Auschwitz," *Der Spiegel*, 9 May 2005.

27. Alison Smale, "Oskar Gröning, Ex-SS Soldier at Auschwitz, Gets Four-Year Sentence," *The New York Times*, 15 July 2015.

28. Raul Hilberg, "German Railroads/Jewish Souls" *Society* 35, no. 2 (Jan/Feb. 1998), 162, reprinted in *The Nazi Holocaust: Historical Articles on the Destruction of the European Jews*, ed. Michael R. Marrus (Chicago, 1989), 3:520.

29. Raul Hilberg, *The Politics of Memory: The Journey of a Holocaust Historian* (Chicago 2002), 40.

30. Simone Gigliotti, ed., *The Train Journey: Transit, Captivity, and Witnessing the Holocaust* (New York, 2010), 36.

31. Alfred C. Mierzejewski, "A Public Enterprise in the Service of Mass Murder: The Deutsche Reichsbahn and the Holocaust," *Holocaust and Genocide Studies* 15, no. 1 (2001): 35–36.

32. Transports to Extinction: Shoah (Holocaust) Deportation Database, retrieved August 2017 from http://db.yadvashem.org/deportation/search.html?language=en. See also Isabel Kershner, "Mapping the Holocaust: How Jews Were Taken to their Final Destinations," *The New York Times*, 5 May 2016.

33. "Train Transports to the Death Camps: Deutsche Reichsbahn's Deportations," DB Museum, retrieved December 2016 from http://www.dbmuseum.de/museum_en/service/veroeffentlichungen/8209310/sonderzuege_in_den_tod.html.

34. Full account in Ronald W. Zweig, *The Gold Train: The Destruction of the Jews and the Looting of Hungary* (New York, 2003). See also Gábor Kádár and Zoltán Vagi, *Self-Financing Genocide: The Gold Train, the Becher Case and the Wealth of Hungarian Jews* (Budapest, 2004).

35. For a summary of the case, see The Hungarian Gold Train Settlement, retrieved August 2017 from http://www.hungariangoldtrain.org/index_en.php.

36. Zweig, *The Gold Train*.

37. Ayelet Waldman, *Love and Treasure* (New York, 2014).

38. Victims of the Hungarian Holocaust v. Hungarian State Railways, 798 F. Supp. 2d 934 (N.D. Ill. 2011).

39. Holocaust Victims of Bank Theft v. Magyar Nemzeti Bank, 807 F. Supp. 2d 699 (N.D. Ill. 2011). The five banks were Magyar Nemzeti Bank, Erste Group Bank, MKB Bayerische Landesbank, OTP Bank, and Credit Anstalt Bank.

40. Fischer v. Magyar Allamvasutak Zrt., 777 F.3d 847 (7th Cir. 2015), *cert denied sub. nom.* Fischer v. Magyar Ialamvasutak Zrt., 135 S. Ct. 2817 (2015). Earlier opinions by the Seventh Circuit in this litigation can be found at Abelesz v. OTP

Bank, 692. F.3d 638 (7th Cir. 2012), Abelesz v. Magyar Nemzeti Bank, 692 F.3d 661 (7th Cir., 2012), and Abelesz v. Erste Group Bank AG, 695 F.3d 655 (7th Cir. 2012).

41. Fischer v. Magyar Allamvasutak Zrt., 777 F.3d at 852.

42. Simon v. Republic of Hungary, 812 F.3d 127 (D.C. Cir. 2016).

43. 28 U.S.C.§§ 1330, 1605 *et. seq.* Section 1605(a)(3) reads: "(a)A foreign state shall not be immune from the jurisdiction of courts of the United States or of the States in any case—(3) in which rights in property taken in violation of international law are in issue and that property or any property exchanged for such property is present in the United States in connection with a commercial activity carried on in the United States by the foreign state; or that property or any property exchanged for such property is owned or operated by an agency or instrumentality of the foreign state and that agency or instrumentality is engaged in a commercial activity in the United States."

44. See William A. Schabas, *Genocide in International Law: The Crime of Crimes,* 2nd ed. (New York, 2009), 11.

45. Simon v. Republic of Hungary, 812 F.3d at 142–44. In another part of the opinion, the court explained: "The systematic, 'wholesale plunder of Jewish property' at issue here, however, aimed to deprive Hungarian Jews of the resources needed to survive as a people. Expropriations undertaken for the purpose of bringing about a protected group's physical destruction qualify as genocide." The court also referenced the Genocide Convention's definition of genocide as including "(c) Deliberately inflicting on the group conditions of life calculated to bring about its physical destruction in whole or in part."

46. Ibid., 145.

47. As the Washington, DC, appeals court explained, quoting the Hungarian railways decision from the Seventh Circuit: "We recognize one seeming anomaly, also noted by the Seventh Circuit in addressing parallel claims arising from the Hungarian Holocaust: that the FSIA scheme, as we construe it, enables the plaintiffs to 'seek compensation for taken property but not for taken lives.' Abelesz, 692 F.3d at 677. But that is a byproduct of the particular way in which Congress fashioned each of the various FSIA exceptions … There is no reason to assume that, in every discrete context in which those exceptions might be applied (such as claims arising from genocide), there would be perfect coherence in outcome across all of the exceptions." Ibid, 146.

48. Ibid., 140.

49. Abrams v. Société Nationale des Chemins de fer Français, 175 F. Supp. 2d 423 (E.D.N.Y. 2001), vacated, 332 F.3d 173 (2d Cir. 2003), cert. granted, judgment vacated, 542 U.S. 901 (2004), and aff'd, 389 F.3d 61 (2d Cir. 2004).

50. Freund v. Société Nationale des Chemins de fer Français, 132 S. Ct. 96 (2011).

51. Freund v. Republic of France, 592 F. Supp. 2d 540 (S.D.N.Y. 2008), aff'd sub nom. Freund v. Société Nationale des Chemins de fer Français, 391 F. App'x 939 (2nd Cir. 2010).

52. Keolis North America currently operates the Virginia Railway Express commuter trains.

53. Leo Bretholtz with Michael Olesker, *Leap Into Darkness: Seven Years on the Run in Wartime Europe* (New York, 1999).

54. "Leo Bretholtz, 93, Dies; Escaped Train to Auschwitz," *The New York Times,* 29 March 2014.

55. Doreen Carvajal, "French Holocaust Survivors Promise to Fight Exclusion from New Reparations," *The New York Times,* 8 December 2014. Roughly two-thirds of the Jews deported from France between 1942 and 1944 were East European Jews who were not French citizens. See Renée Poznanski, *Jews in France During World War II* (Hanover, NH, 2002).

56. Carvajal, "French Holocaust."

57. Republic of Austria v. Altmann, 541 U.S. 677 (2004).

58. Sophie Lillie and Georg Gaugusch, *Portrait of Adele Bloch Bauer* (New York, 2009); Anne-Marie O'Connor, *The Lady in Gold: The Extraordinary Tale of Gustav Klimt's Masterpiece, Portrait of Adele Bloch-Bauer* (New York, 2012). Maria Altmann's story and legal saga were dramatized in the Hollywood film, *The Woman in Gold* (2015). Usually omitted from the Bloch-Bauer narrative was that Maria Altmann and her heirs received an additional $47 million from the Swiss Claims Resolution Tribunal operating under the supervision of a US federal court. These awards arose from an unidentified Swiss bank's participation in the Nazi confiscation of their shares in the Bloch-Bauer sugar factory, formally known as Österreichische Zuckerindustrie AG Syndicate (ÖZAG). For amounts see Swiss Bank Claims, "Swiss Banks Settlement Fund Distribution Statistics as of December 31, 2015 (Amounts Approved and Paid by the Court)," Holocaust Victim Assets Litigation, Case No. CV 96-4849, retrieved August 2017 from http://www.swissbankclaims.com/Documents/Distribution%20Stats.pdf. For the decisions see http://www.crt-ii.org/_awards/_apdfs/Oesterreichische_Zuckerindustrie_2.pdf. See also Burt Neuborne, "A Tale of Two Cities: Administering the Holocaust Settlement in Brooklyn and Berlin," in Bazyler and Alford, *Holocaust Restitution,* 71–72.

59. Von Saher v. Norton Simon Museum of Art at Pasadena, 754 F.3d 712 (9th Cir. 2014), cert. denied sub nom. Norton Simon Museum of Art at Pasadena v. von Sher, 135 S. Ct. 1158 (2015) (mem.).

60. Laura Gilbert, "Supreme Court Rejects Norton Simon's Appeal in Looted Art Case," *The Art Newspaper,* 20 January 2015.

61. Von Saher v. Norton Simon Museum of Art at Pasadena, No. CV 07-2866 (C.D. Cal. Aug. 9, 2016) (minute order granting defendants' motion for summary judgment and order denying plaintiff's motion for summary judgment). Von Saher v. Norton Simon Museum of Art at Pasadena, appeal docketed, No. 16-56308 (9th Cir. 2016).

62. Leila Amineddoleh, "The Norton Simon Museum's Multi-Million-Dollar Nazi Restitution Case of Two Paintings by Cranach the Elder, Explained," *Artsy,* 4 April 2016, retrieved August 2017 from https://www.artsy.net/article/artsy-editorial-the-norton-simon-museum-s-multi-million-dollar-nazi-restitution-case-explained.

63. Elizabeth Campbell Karsgodt, "Why Are Museums Holding On to Art Looted by the Nazis," *Newsweek,* 10 May 2015. The number of works looted during the Holocaust era and not returned to rightful owners is unknown, and estimates vary. See Jonathan Petropoulus, "Art Looting During the Third Reich: An Overview with Recommendations for Further Research," in *Proceedings of the Washington Conference on Holocaust-Era Assets* (1999), 441–48, estimating that the Nazis looted approximately 150,000 art objects in Western Europe and about 500,000 works in Eastern Europe, but cautioning that these numbers are "imprecise and even speculative." Petropoulus adds that "[t]here is similar lack of precision with respect to the number of artworks still considered missing … There is still much research to be done."

64. Mellissa Eddy, "Matisse from Gurlitt Collection Is Returned to Jewish Art Dealer's Heirs," *The New York Times,* 15 May 2015.

65. Two monographs have already been written on the Gurlitt controversy. See Susan Ronald, *Hitler's Art Thief: Hildebrand Gurlitt, the Nazis, and the Looting of Europe's Treasures* (New York, 2015); Catherine Hickley, *The Munich Art Hoard: Hitler's Dealer and His Secret Legacy* (New York, 2015).

66. *America's Role in Addressing Outstanding Holocaust Issues: Hearing Before the Subcomm. on Europe of the H. Comm. on Foreign Affairs,* 110th Cong. 8 (2007) (statement of J. Christian Kennedy, Special Envoy for Holocaust Issues) (United States House of Representatives, 3 October 2007), retrieved August 2017 from http://archives .republicans.foreignaffairs.house.gov/110/38141.pdf.

67. See, e.g., Harold James, *The Deutsche Bank and the Nazi Economic War Against the Jews: The Expropriation of Jewish-Owned Property* (New York, 2001); Christopher Simpson, *War Crimes of the Deutsche Bank and the Dresdner Bank: Office of the Military Government (U.S.) Reports* (New York, 2002); Peter Hayes, *From Cooperation to Complicity: Degussa in the Third Reich* (New York, 2004); Gerald Feldman, *Allianz and the German Insurance Business, 1933–1945* (New York, 2006); Henry Ashby Turner, *General Motors and the Nazis: The Struggle for Control of Opel, Europe's Biggest Carmaker* (New Haven, CT, 2006). See also Joachim Scholtyseck, *Der Aufstieg Der Quandts: Eine Deutsche Unternehmerdynastie* (Munich, 2011), the BMW-commissioned study of the Quandt family, founders and still controlling shareholders of BMW, and its dealings with the Nazis. In March 2016, during its centennial celebration, BMW formally apologized for its Nazi past. See Ray Massey, "German Car Giant BMW Apologizes for its Wartime Past, Admitting Its 'Profound Regret' for Supplying Nazis with Vehicles and Using Slave Labourers," *Daily Mail,* 7 March 2016.

68. This included class action suits filed in New Jersey federal court against Ford Motor Company and its German subsidiary Ford Werke (Iwanowa v. Ford Motor Co., 67 F. Supp. 2d 424 [D.N.J. 1999]) and four separate suits filed against German companies Degussa and Siemens (Burger-Fischer v. Degussa AG, 65 F. Supp. 2d 248 [D.N.J. 1999]). All were dismissed on technical grounds in September 1999. Ford and the German companies (and other German companies that were sued) continued to negotiate though winning the first round

of litigation. A final settlement was reached in December 1999. See Bazyler, *Holocaust Justice,* 59–109

69. This is in contrast to the suits filed against Japanese companies for their use of slave labor during World War II in the Pacific theater. These suits were dismissed on the grounds that the 1951 Peace Treaty between the Allies and Japan extinguished the claims. Unlike their German counterparts, the Japanese companies were unwilling to negotiate once they achieved legal victory. In 2015 Mitsubishi Materials Corporation apologized for its use of American POWs as slave laborers, becoming the first Japanese company to express remorse publicly for both its wartime behavior and for not apologizing sooner. The apology was not accompanied by any financial settlement. See Abby Phillip, "Mitsubishi Apologizes for Using American POWs as Slaves During WWII," *The Washington Post,* 20 July 2015.

70. Bazyler, *Holocaust Justice,* 101–2. Not all of the individual payments were small. For example, the average award issued under the Swiss Banks Settlement to Holocaust survivors or heirs for deposited assets was approximately $184,000. See "Swiss Banks Settlement Fund Distribution Statistics as of December 31, 2015, (Amounts Approved and Paid by the Court)," *Holocaust Victim Assets Litigation,* Case No. CV 96-4849, retrieved August 2017 from http://www.swissbank claims.com/Documents/Distribution%20Stats.pdf.

71. *Hearing before the H. Committee on Banking and Financial Services,* 106th Cong. 6 (9 February 2000) (statement of Otto Graf Lambsdorff, Special Rep. of the German Chancellor).

72. Conference on Jewish Material Claims against Germany, retrieved December 2016 from http://www.claimscon.org/ ?url=medex/payment2 (statement by Eva Kor).

73. See, e.g., Norman G. Finkelstein, *The Holocaust Industry: Reflections on the Exploitation of Jewish Suffering* (New York, 2000).

74. Michael R. Marrus, *Some Measure of Justice,* 10.

75. Ibid., 3.

76. Elie Wiesel, "Foreword" to Eizenstat, *Imperfect Justice,* ix.

77. Slyomovics, *How to Accept German Reparations,* 3.

78. See, e.g., Stewart Ain, "'Fee Grabbing' Lawyers Rebuked in Swiss Case," *The New York Jewish Week,* 25 November 1999; Eric Fettmann, "Money is the Least of It—Will Time and Greedy Lawyers Obscure the Holocaust's Horror," *New York Post,* 8 December 1999.

79. Stuart E. Eizenstat, Deputy Secretary of the Treasury and Special Representative of the President and Secretary of State for Holocaust Issues, Remarks at the 12th and Concluding Plenary on the German Foundation Berlin, Germany, 17 July 2000. Eizenstat is currently a lawyer with the prestigious Covington & Burling law firm.

80. Marrus, *Some Measure of Justice,* 30. Marrus was referring to earlier statements made by Eizenstat criticizing the plaintiffs' lawyers. Ibid., 28–29.

81. Ibid., 91.

82. Michael R. Marrus, "The Case of the French Railways and the Deportation of the Jews in 1944," in *Holocaust and Justice: Representation & Historiography of the Holocaust in Post-War Trials,* ed. David Bankier and Dan Michman, eds. (Jerusalem, 2010), 264.

83. Marrus, *Some Measure of Justice,* 90.

84. Ibid., 92.

85. Quoted in Ibid., 99.

86. Leora Bilsky, "The Judge and the Historian: Transnational Holocaust Litigation as a New Model," *History and Memory* 24, no. 2 (Fall/Winter 2012): 117–56. Bilsky summarizes well the objections made by some historians to the bringing of Holocaust history into an US civil suit—especially of the class action variety—whose primary aim is monetary restitution: "[C]ivil litigation, and in particular the amounts at stake in settlement, create incentives for the parties to present partisan versions of history that are not likely to be corrected absent a court judgment. Furthermore, the class structure of the lawsuit and the goal of monetary compensation raise the specter of commodification and the loss of personal narratives, as victims are turned into anonymous members of a group whose entitlements are calculated with the help of statistics. Finally, the focus on corporations with deep pockets appears to distort the historical understanding of responsibility for the Nazi crimes by shifting attention from the state and direct perpetrators to a few indirect perpetrators." Ibid., 123.

87. Ibid., 117.

88. Ibid., 123.

89. For examples of how Holocaust criminal trials can contribute to the historiography of the Holocaust, see, e.g., Michael J. Bazyler and Frank M. Tuerkheimer, *Forgotten Trials of the Holocaust* (New York, 2014).

90. Bilsky, "The Judge and the Historian," 123.

91. Ibid. Bilsky quotes Burt Neuborne, New York University School of Law professor and chief settlement counsel in the Swiss banks settlement and one of the lead plaintiffs' lawyers in the class action litigation against German industry, who contends that one of the goals of the Holocaust restitution litigation was to "'speak to history—to build a historical record that could never be denied.'" Ibid, 129, quoting Neuborne, "Preliminary Reflections on Aspects of Holocaust-Era Litigation in American Courts," *Washington University Law Quarterly* 80, no. 2 (2002): 830.

92. Bilsky, "The Judge and the Historian," 119.

93. "Transcripts: The Evolution and Objectives of the Holocaust Restitution Initiatives," *Fordham International Law Journal* 25 (2001): 145. Lambsdorff explains: "[T]he debate, the memory, the dealing with Holocaust affairs in Germany became more and more lively. Companies are looking into their archives. Companies have asked academics, professors, to write reports, to find out what happened within the companies." Ibid., 167–68.

94. Memorandum to Roosevelt, 22 January 1945, quoted in Lawrence Douglas, *The Memory of Judgment: Making Law and History in the Trials of the Holocaust* (New Haven, CT, 2001), 18.

95. Norbert Ehrenfreund, *The Nuremberg Legacy: How the Nazi War Crimes Trials Changed the Course of History* (New York, 2007), 35, quoting Justice Jackson from Minutes of Conference Session, 13 July 1945.

96. Charles E. Wyzanski, Jr. "Nuremberg in Retrospect," *Atlantic Monthly* (December 1946): 57.

97. Ibid. Seventy years later, historian Eric D. Weitz made a similar point about the contribution to historiography made by the UN international criminal tribunals for the former Yugoslavia and Rwanda: "[T]he Hague Tribunal and its sister, the Arusha Tribunal—convened for the Rwandan genocide— … have accumulated vast stores of documentary evidence on two of the most tragic events of the waning 20th century. Their archives will prove as vital as the Nuremberg Tribunal documents as scholars, politicians, servicemen and women and regular citizens try to make sense of these horrific events." Eric D. Weitz, "America Should Prioritize International Justice," *CNN*, 15 April 2016.

98. Quoted in Douglas, *The Memory of Judgment* (New Haven, 2005), 2.

99. Ibid., 2.

100. Hilberg, *The Politics of Memory*, 71.

101. The Swiss Banks Settlement claims process returned nearly $720 million to depositors and their heirs. More than $1.284 billion in total has been paid out under the settlement, which included classes of compensation that arose from claims under several classes including bank deposits, slave labor, mistreatment of refugees, and looting. See http://www.swissbankclaims.com/Documents/Dis tribution%20Stats.pdf, retrieved August 2017 from www.swissbankclaims.com, the website of the federal court-supervised Swiss Banks Settlement..

102. The Swiss Banks Settlement awards are broken down as follows: The Court-supervised deposited assets class claims process issued 2,950 awards, paying out to Holocaust victims and their heirs $615.5 million. These awards were based upon documentation available in the files of the Swiss banks or from other sources. Another 12,301 in awards, in the amount of $7,250 each and for a total of $86 million, was paid to claimants whose claims were determined plausible by the court-supervised Swiss Claims Resolution Tribunal in Zurich, but for whom evidence of an actual prewar Swiss bank account was not available due to the banks' destruction of records and the passage of decades. Finally, $18 million was paid to claimants for an earlier process begun prior to the settlement in August 1998. See www.swissbankclaims.com for all figures.

103. The Final Report from Special Master Judah Gribetz and Deputy Special Master Shari C. Reig to Judge Edward R. Korman on the Swiss Banks Settlement Distribution Process (to be posted at swissbankclaims.com) is expected to yield additional information on the over fifteen-year and over $1.25 billion settlement distribution process of Swiss bank funds to Holocaust survivors and heirs conducted under the US justice system.

104. Orland, *A Final Accounting: Holocaust Survivors and Swiss Banks*, xvi.

105. Donald Bloxham, *Genocide on Trial: War Crimes Trials and the Formation of Holocaust History and Memory* (New York, 2001); Lawrence Douglas, *The Memory of Judgment*. Bilsky summarizes: "Since the Nuremberg trials, the relationship between the

legal process and historical research has been the subject of much scrutiny, leading to a consensus that courts produce distorted and poor historical accounts of the causes of mass atrocity. The critique voiced by historians has found support in two very different schools of legal thought. Proponents of legal liberalism warn that courts' attempts to write history compromises the rights of the defendant, while the law and society movement points to the law's inability to reflect history's complexity." Bilsky, "The Judge and the Historian," 122.

106. Lawrence Douglas, "The Didactic Trial: Filtering History and Memory into the Courtroom," in Bankier and Michman, *Holocaust and Justice,* 15–18.
107. Ibid., 15.
108. Ibid., 16.
109. As put by New York art law attorney Howard N. Spiegler: "Underlying any claim for the recovery of Nazi-looted art in the United States is a single, fundamental rule … no one, not even a good faith purchaser, can obtain good title to stolen property. This simple truth is accepted and applied as a fundamental tenet of property law in the United States." Bazyler, *Holocaust Justice,* 212, quoting Howard N. Spiegler, "Recovering Nazi-Stolen Art: Report from the Front Lines," *Connecticut Journal of International Law* 16 (2001): 299. The principle is expressed in the legal maxim *nemo dat quod non habet* ("no one gives what he doesn't have"), often shortened as the *nemo dat* rule. Bazyler, *Holocaust Justice,* 212. See also Bryan A. Garner, ed., *Black's Law Dictionary,* 10th ed. (St. Paul, MN, 2014), 1,933.

SELECT BIBLIOGRAPHY

Allen, Michael Thad. "The Limits of Lex Americana: The Holocaust Restitution Litigation as a Cul-de-Sac of International Human-Rights Law." *Widener Law Review* 17, no.1 (2011): 1–68.
Bazyler, Michael J. "www.swissbankclaims.com: The Legality and Morality of the Holocaust-Era Settlement with the Swiss Banks." *Fordham International Law Journal* 25, no. 6 (2001): S64–S106.
——. *Holocaust Justice: The Battle for Restitution in America's Courts.* New York: New York University Press, 2003.
Bazyler, Michael J., and Frank M. Tuerkheimer. *Forgotten Trials of the Holocaust.* New York: New York University Press, 2014.
Bazyler, Michael J., and Roger P. Alford, eds. *Holocaust Restitution: Perspectives on the Litigation and Its Legacy.* New York: New York University Press, 2006.
Bilsky, Leora. "The Judge and the Historian: Transnational Holocaust Litigation as a New Model." *History and Memory* 24, no. 2 (Fall/Winter 2012): 117–56.
Bilsky, Leora, Rodger D. Citron, and Natalie R. Davidson. "From *Kiobel* Back to Structural Reform: The Hidden Legacy of Holocaust Restitution Litigation." *Stanford Journal of Complex Litigation* 2, no.1 (2014): 139–84.
Bloxham, Donald. *Genocide on Trial: War Crimes Trials and the Formation of Holocaust History and Memory.* New York: Oxford University Press, 2001.

Bretholtz, Leo, with Michael Olesker. *Leap Into Darkness: Seven Years on the Run in Wartime Europe.* New York: First Anchor Books Edition, 1999.

de Greiff, Pablo, ed. *The Handbook of Reparations.* New York: Oxford University Press, 2006.

Douglas, Lawrence. *The Memory of Judgment: Making Law and History in the Trials of the Holocaust.* New Haven, CT: Yale University Press, 2001.

———. "The Didactic Trial: Filtering History and Memory into the Courtroom." In *Holocaust and Justice: Representation and Historiography of the Holocaust in Post-War Trials,* ed. David Bankier and Dan Michman, 11–22. Jerusalem: Yad Vashem, 2010.

Edsel, Robert M., with Bret Witter, *The Monuments Men: Allied Heroes, Nazi Thieves, and the Greatest Treasure Hunt in History.* New York: Hachette, 2010.

Ehrenfreund, Norbert. *The Nuremberg Legacy: How the Nazi War Crimes Trials Changed the Court of History.* New York: St. Martin's, 2007.

Eizenstat, Stuart E. *Imperfect Justice: Looted Assets, Slave Labor, and the Unfinished Business of World War II.* New York: Public Affairs. 2003.

Feldman, Gerald D. *Allianz and the German Insurance Business, 1933–1945.* New York: Cambridge University Press, 2001.

Ferencz, Benjamin B. *Less Than Slaves: Jewish Forced Labor and the Quest for Compensation.* Cambridge, MA: Harvard University Press, 1979.

Gigliotti, Simone, ed., *The Train Journey: Transit, Captivity, and Witnessing in the Holocaust.* New York: Berghahn, 2010.

Hayes, Peter. *From Cooperation to Complicity: Degussa in the Third Reich.* New York: Cambridge University Press, 2004.

———. "Plunder and Restitution." In *The Oxford Handbook of Holocaust Studies,* ed. Peter Hayes and John K. Roth, 540–59. New York: Oxford University Press, 2010.

Hickley, Catherine. *The Munich Art Hoard: Hitler's Dealer and His Secret Legacy.* London: Thames & Hudson, 2015.

Hilberg, Raul. *The Politics of Memory: The Journey of a Holocaust Historian.* Chicago: Ivan R. Dee, 1996.

———. "German Railroads/Jewish Souls." *Society* 35, no. 2 (Jan./Feb. 1998): 162–74.

Independent Commission of Experts Switzerland–Second World War, *Switzerland, National Socialism and the Second World War: Final Report.* Zürich: Pendo, 2002.

International Commission on the Holocaust in Romania, *Final Report of the International Commission on the Holocaust in Romania.* Bucharest, 2004. Retrieved 17 April 2017 from https://www.ushmm.org/research/scholarly-presentations/symposia/holocaust-in-romania/romania-facing-its-past.

James, Harold. *The Deutsche Bank and the Nazi Economic War against the Jews: The Expropriation of Jewish-Owned Property.* New York: Cambridge University Press, 2001.

Kádár, Gábor, and Zoltán Vági, *Self-Financing Genocide: The Gold Train, the Becher Case and the Wealth of Hungarian Jews.* Budapest: Central European University Press, 2004.

Lillie, Sophie, and Georg Gaugusch. *Portrait of Adele Bloch-Bauer.* New York: Neue Galerie, 2006.

Ludi, Regula. *Reparations for Nazi Victims in Postwar Europe.* New York: Cambridge University Press, 2012.

Marrus, Michael R. *Some Measure of Justice: The Holocaust Restitution Campaign of the 1990s.* Madison, WI: University of Wisconsin Press, 2009.

——. "The Case of the French Railways and the Deportation of Jews in 1944." In *Holocaust and Justice: Representation and Historiography of the Holocaust in Post-War Trials,* ed. David Bankier and Dan Michman, 245–64. Jerusalem: Yad Vashem, 2010.

Mierzejewski, Alfred C. "A Public Enterprise in the Service of Mass Murder: The Deutsche Reichsbahn and the Holocaust." *Holocaust and Genocide Studies* 15, no. 1 (2001): 33–46.

Neuborne, Burt. "Preliminary Reflections on Aspects of Holocaust-Era Litigation in American Courts." *Washington University Law Quarterly* 80, no. 3 (2002): 795–834.

Nicholas, Lynn H. *The Rape of Europa: The Fate of Europe's Treasures in the Third Reich and the Second World War.* New York: Vintage, 1995.

O'Connor, Anne-Marie. *The Lady in Gold: The Extraordinary Tale of Gustav Klimt's Masterpiece, Portrait of Adele Bloch-Bauer.* New York: Knopf, 2012.

Orland, Leonard. *A Final Accounting: Holocaust Survivors and Swiss Banks.* Durham, NC: Carolina Academic Press, 2010.

Petropoulos, Jonathan. "Art Looting During the Third Reich: An Overview with Recommendations for Further Research." In *Proceedings of the Washington Conference on Holocaust-Era Assets,* ed. J.D. Bindenagel, 441–48. Washington, DC: Department of State, 1999.

Poznanski, Renée. *Jews in France during World War II,* trans. by Nathan Bracher. Hanover, NH: University Press of New England for Brandeis University Press in association with the United States Holocaust Memorial Museum, 2001.

Ronald, Susan. *Hitler's Art Thief: Hildebrand Gurlitt, the Nazis, and the Looting of Europe's Treasures.* New York: St. Martin's, 2015.

Schabas, William A. *Genocide in International Law: The Crime of Crimes.* 2nd ed. New York: Cambridge University Press, 2009.

Simpson, Christopher, ed., *War Crimes of the Deutsche Bank and the Dresdner Bank: Office of Military Government (U.S.) Reports.* New York: Holmes & Meier, 2002.

Slyomovics, Susan. *How to Accept German Reparations.* Philadelphia: University of Pennsylvania Press, 2014.

Taylor, Gideon. "Where Morality Meets Money." In *Holocaust Restitution: Perspectives on the Litigation and Its Legacy,* ed. Michael J. Bazyler and Roger P. Alford, 163–69. New York: New York University Press, 2006.

"Transcripts: The Evolution and Objectives of the Holocaust Restitution Initiatives." *Fordham International Law Journal* 25 (2001): S145–S176.

Turner, Henry Ashby, Jr. *General Motors and the Nazis: The Struggle for Control of Opel, Europe's Biggest Carmaker.* New Haven, CT: Yale University Press, 2005.

Waldman, Ayelet. *Love and Treasure.* New York: Knopf, 2014.

Zweig, Ronald W. *The Gold Train: The Destruction of the Jews and the Looting of Hungary.* New York: Morrow, 2003.

Chapter 10

The Fortunate Possessor
The Case of Gustav Klimt's *Beethoven Frieze*

Sophie Lillie

Gustav Klimt's *Beethoven Frieze,* a monumental fresco illustrating Beethoven's Ninth Symphony,[1] is to remain in Austria—this was the decision handed down by Austria's restitution panel in March 2015. The frieze was once the property of Erich Lederer, whose family's art collection had been seized by the Nazis, and whose heirs now petitioned for its return. Concluding its investigation of the case, the restitution panel rejected any notion that the *Beethoven Frieze* had been misappropriated, and instead voted unanimously to keep Gustav Klimt's famous fin-de-siècle masterpiece in the country.[2]

The Lederer claim made international headlines. Austria had not witnessed a restitution case of this magnitude since the investigation into the provenance of five works by Gustav Klimt from the Ferdinand Bloch-Bauer collection. Austria's restitution panel had famously thrown out that case in 1999, prompting Bloch-Bauer's niece Maria Altmann of Los Angeles, to challenge the decision before a US court.[3]

First steps toward Austrian art restitution date to 1997, when a *New York Times* article alleged that two paintings on loan to the Museum of Modern Art (MoMA)—Egon Schiele's *Dead City III* and his *Portrait of Wally*—had been looted from their rightful owners after the Nazis' annexation of Austria in 1938.[4] Manhattan's district attorney duly issued a subpoena to prevent the paintings' return to Vienna until all questions of ownership had been settled. With the media spotlight focused so squarely on Austria's restitution record, the Austrian government was forced to take immediate action.

In November 1998, Austria adopted an Art Restitution Act to govern the restitution of art looted during the Nazi era from its federal museums.[5] This bill was to apply to works acquired during the Nazi era itself, as well as works that Holocaust survivors had been pressured to donate to the Austrian state after World War II. Since 1998, Austria has earned international recognition for the return of thousands of individual objects, ranging from precious old master oils to objects of everyday life. While books, photographs, and silverware have accounted for the great volume of restitutions, Austria's reputation has hinged upon the return by Austrian museums between 2000 and 2011 of twelve Klimt paintings.[6] These works alone come to an estimated cumulative value of over $450 million.

When it was first made public in October 2013, the Lederers' petition for the restitution of the *Beethoven Frieze* sent shock waves through the Austrian media. Although the country had come to support restitution in the decade since the MoMA-Schiele scandal, the limits of political and popular support were clearly evident in this case. As it stood to lose yet another iconic work, Austria replicated many of the mistakes it had made in the handling of the Bloch-Bauer case, opting for business as usual rather than mediation to settle the dispute.

HISTORY OF THE FRIEZE

The *Beethoven Frieze*—which is 7 feet high and spans some 112 feet in length—was created in 1902 for the Secession, the hub of Vienna's art nouveau movement. In a sequence of allegorical murals illustrating Beethoven's Ninth Symphony, it depicts the universal longing for happiness; the hero who fights to secure it; the hostile forces that oppose him; the solace of poetry, represented by a choir of heavenly angels; and finally, the salvation of man—as personified by the iconic embrace of lovers (a motif that Klimt later paraphrased in his best-known work, *The Kiss*).[7] Klimt initially conceived of the frieze as a temporary work to be shown in the main gallery space at the Secession's fourteenth exhibition. This show grouped works by twenty-one contemporary artists around a single work: Max Klinger's statue of the composer Ludwig van Beethoven.[8] The objective was that the arts—architecture, painting, sculpture, and music—be united in the spirit of the *Gesamtkunstwerk* or total work of art. The exhibition drew a record number of 60,000 visitors.

When the exhibition closed, all of its works were completely dismantled, and many of the auxiliary works were destroyed. Klimt's *Beethoven Frieze* stayed in place, so as to be included in the Klimt one-man show that the Secession was to mount the following year.[9] Plans were that it be taken down

Figure 10.1. Gustav Klimt, *Beethoven Frieze*. Original installation at the Secession's fourteenth exhibition, 1902. By Moritz Nähr, with permission from the Austrian National Library

immediately thereafter. Carl Reinighaus, the owner of a beer brewery and a major patron of the Secession, is said to have stopped the destruction of the *Beethoven Frieze* at the last minute.[10] According to one story, Reininghaus happened to be present just as workmen began chipping the frieze off the wall. He ordered that the frieze be carefully dismantled, mounted on timber, separated into seven segments, and placed in storage, all at his expense. About twelve years later, in 1915, Reininghaus sold the *Beethoven Frieze* to fellow philanthropist and art collector August Lederer.[11] The sale was mediated through the young Egon Schiele, who purportedly received 1,000 kronen as an introductory commission.

August Lederer's acquisition of the *Beethoven Frieze*, like Reininghaus's earlier, was one of prestige: a deferral gesture of acknowledging and endorsing Klimt's *oeuvre*, and of preserving a key work for the long term. There was no tangible personal benefit because of its size. The frieze could not be exhibited privately and only burdened the owner with annual storage costs. In fact, Reininghaus is reported to have said that he had paid for storage long enough and now it was Lederer's turn to foot the bill.[12]

THE LEDERER COLLECTION

August Lederer (1857–1936) was the president and managing director of the
Raaber Spiritusfabrik und Raffinerie, a spirits factory in the small Hungarian town of Győr. His wife was Szerena Pulitzer (1867–1943), the youngest
of four daughters of a wealthy entrepreneur originally from Makó, a small
town close to the Romanian border. The Lederers lived in the imperial capital of Vienna, in a townhouse at Bartensteingasse 8, which also housed the
burgeoning family businesses. They belonged to Vienna's tiny segment of
the super-rich who conspicuously consumed culture as one of many luxury
commodities.

The couple had begun collecting at the turn of the century and continued to do so over almost three decades.[13] In 1921, their collection was
officially recognized as a cultural landmark of Vienna.[14] Among its highlights were Italian Renaissance works such as the fifteenth-century *Madonna
dell'Umiltà* by Gherardo Starnina, now at the Cleveland Museum of Art;[15]
and *Saint Luke* by Simone Martini, now at the Getty Museum in Los Angeles.[16] Most famously of all, the Lederers owned the largest privately-owned
collection of works by Gustav Klimt.

Szerena had been introduced to Klimt through her uncle, the famous
otologist Adam Politzer (1835–1920), who in the 1860s had hired Gustav's
younger brother Ernst Klimt for medical illustrations.[17] One of the best in-
dicators of Szerena's early association with Klimt is the prominent inclusion
of her portrait, at age twenty-one, in Klimt's painting *Auditorium of the Old
Burgtheater*,[18] depicting the interior of the old imperial theater shortly before
it was torn down in 1888.

Paintings from all of Klimt's major periods were exhibited at the Lederers' apartment. One of the most prized works was the *supraporte* (overdoor)
panel *Schubert at the Piano*,[19] which the art critic Hermann Bahr extolled as
"the most beautiful painting ever painted by an Austrian."[20] Other iconic
works included *Farm Garden with Crucifix*,[21] *Garden Path with Chickens*,[22] and
Girl Friends.[23] Moreover, the Lederer collection comprised three generations
of family portraits: Klimt's 1899 portrait of Szerena Lederer,[24] now at the
Metropolitan Museum of Art in New York; the portrait of her daughter,
Elisabeth Bachofen-Echt,[25] now at the Neue Galerie New York; and the portrait of Szerena's mother, Charlotte Pulitzer,[26] the whereabouts of which are
unknown. More prestigious still than these commissioned portraits were
three monumental works that the Lederers had acquired with the intention
of supporting Klimt both financially and morally. They were the *Beethoven
Frieze,* and two of three panels originally made by Klimt for the University of
Vienna depicting the faculties *Philosophy* and *Jurisprudence*. [27]

Figure 10.2. Szerena Lederer in her apartment, about 1930. By Martin W. Gerlach, with permission from the Austrian National Library

KLIMT'S PREWAR COLLECTORS

Gustav Klimt's rise to prominence was owed to state commissions as a *Historienmaler,* a painter of historical scenes. The young graduate of Vienna's Academy of Fine Arts was engaged to embellish the grand imperial institutions of the city's Ringstrasse, the great representative boulevard planned by

Emperor Franz Joseph. In 1894, this culminated in Klimt's commission for three panels for the great hall of the University of Vienna, depicting the faculties of Philosophy, Jurisprudence, and Medicine. Klimt's highly evocative treatment of the subject caused ripples of controversy that quickly erupted into scandal. He was derided for what was described as his "dark, obscure symbolism," and accused of pornography. In the words of one of his most ferocious opponents, university professor Friedrich Jodl, Klimt's critics were not opposed to "naked or free art, but to ugly art."[28]

Overnight, Klimt became the rebellious superstar of Vienna's fledgling avant-garde. Philanthropists like journalist Berta Zuckerkandl (1864–1945) and her husband, the physician Emil Zuckerkandl (1849–1910), rallied support for the artist among their social circle of intellectuals and entrepreneurs.[29] In 1897, the iron and steel magnate Karl Wittgenstein (1847–1913)–the father of philosopher Ludwig Wittgenstein–financed the Secession's landmark building.[30] August and Szerena Lederer followed suit by providing Klimt with the funds to repay his advance honorarium of 30,000 kronen. One indication of Klimt's reliance on these very families are the portraits of his patrons' wives and daughters–such as those of Amalie Zuckerkandl, Margaret Stonborough-Wittgenstein, and Szerena Lederer.

Private patrons made Klimt uniquely independent. Klimt never again received a state commission, and he was denied a coveted professorship at the Academy. The artist's notoriously slow working style–which is reflected in the rather small number of paintings executed during his lifetime–only heightened demand. Within a few short years, and most certainly by the time of his death in 1918, Klimt had become the most highly-priced Austrian artist of his generation.

DISPOSSESSION BY THE NAZIS

Germany's annexation of Austria in March 1938 brutally ended the great era of private collection. In just seven years, the Nazis' barbaric acts of dispossession and persecution destroyed the tradition of private patronage and collecting.

Szerena Lederer fled from Vienna to Budapest just after the *Anschluss* in March 1938. That fall, Vienna's new municipal authorities ordered that the most valuable objects in the Lederer collection be impounded to prevent their being exported.[31] Two more security orders were issued shortly thereafter.[32] In 1939, dozens of Lederer works were placed in the so-called *Zentraldepot,* a central storage facility for looted artwork administered by Vienna's Kunsthistorisches Museum, the museum of fine art. The Lederer works were subsequently inventoried, photographed, and entered into the "Reich List"—a central registry of cultural treasures in the German Reich.[33]

All leading cultural institutions eagerly submitted wish lists for the Lederer works they hoped to secure. Vienna's Kunsthistorisches Museum vied for its share of the loot, as did the Belvedere (the museum dedicated to nineteenth- and twentieth-century Austrian art) and the Albertina (Vienna's museum of graphic arts).[34] The right of first choice, however, was reserved for the so-called "Führermuseum," the monumental museum that Hitler planned to build in the Upper Austrian town of Linz.[35]

Klimt is often assumed to have been among those artists whom the Nazis labeled "degenerate," but this was not the case. Klimt's work continued to be exhibited and traded throughout the Nazi era. In fact, an unprecedented number of Klimt paintings changed hands during those years, as major works from private, Jewish-owned collections were seized by the Nazis and tossed on the market for well below value.[36] Among those works were paintings from Klimt's best-known and most distinguished prewar patrons such as the Lederers, the Bloch-Bauers, and the Zuckerkandls—all of whom suffered dispossession and persecution as Jews.

The infamous climax of the Nazis' embrace of Klimt was a major retrospective in 1943, commemorating the eightieth anniversary of the artist's birth.[37] This show was held under the patronage of the Reichsstaathalter of Vienna, Baldur von Schirach, and curated by the Nazi-appointed director of the Belvedere, Bruno Grimschitz. Its venue was, again, the Secession—but with one significant modification. The Nazis had renamed the building "Ausstellungshaus Friedrichstrasse," literally meaning exhibition space on Friedrichstrasse—a neutral title to de-emphasize its secessionist, revolutionary beginnings.

The 1943 Klimt show was symptomatic of the Nazis' culture and war propaganda effort.[38] Staged at the height of Germany's "total war," its aim was to bolster morale by demonstrating cultural greatness and instilling civic pride. Coinciding with Germany's crushing defeat at Stalingrad, the show drew a record number of 24,000 visitors in just one month.[39]

The show assembled fifty paintings and forty-eight works on paper, and two sections of the *Beethoven Frieze*. No less than a third of the exhibited paintings originated in looted Viennese collections. Twelve were Lederer works: *Philosophy, Farm Garden with Crucifix, Jurisprudence, Music, Schubert at the Piano, Golden Apple Tree,* two *Beethoven Frieze* panels, the portrait of Charlotte Pulitzer, *Wally, Leda, Girl Friends,* and *Garden Path with Chickens.*[40] A generous selection of Klimt drawings was culled from three Lederer portfolios.[41] Two paintings were those of Szerena's sister, Jenny Steiner, including the splendid portrait of Mäda Primavesi, now at the Metropolitan Museum of Art.[42]

Another four were Bloch-Bauer works.[43] The origin of Jewish portraits was concealed: the catalogue referred to Charlotte Pulitzer anonymously as a "portrait of an old lady" and Adele Bloch-Bauer's two likenesses as a "portrait of a lady on gold ground" and a "lady standing."

When the 1943 show was taken down, works from the Lederer collection were hauled off to Schloss Immendorf, a castle in Lower Austria close to the Czech border. Immendorf was one of many rural storage facilities that the Nazis used to spirit artwork away from the capital, ostensibly to protect it from air raids. Coinciding with Germany's capitulation in May 1945, retreating Nazi storm troopers set a devastating fire, to prevent the artwork stored there from being discovered by the approaching Red Army.[44] Most of the Lederer Klimts were thus willfully destroyed.

One of the very few Lederer works to be saved was the *Beethoven Frieze*, which, because of its size, had been stored not at Immendorf but at Schloss Thürnthal, a Baroque castle on the banks of the Danube River, about fifty miles west of Vienna. From 1939, the premises of Schloss Thürnthal were used to store artwork looted by the Nazis, eventually to include objects seized in occupied France by the Einsatzstab Reichsleiter Alfred Rosenberg. The Jewish owner of the Thürnthal estate, Guido Bunzel, as well as his wife and daughter, were murdered at Maly Trostinec, the extermination camp near Minsk, in 1942.[45]

POSTWAR RESTITUTION

Szerena Lederer died in Budapest in 1943—a timely death just one year before the Nazi occupation of Hungary. Her eldest son Erich, who had fled to Geneva, first returned to Vienna in December 1945.[46] Erich Lederer found that little remained of his family's once formidable fortune. Some Lederer works were recovered by the US Monuments, Fine Arts, and Archives Branch (also known as the "Monuments Men") in the salt mines of Altaussee. The *Beethoven Frieze* was discovered at Thürnthal by the Soviet army. Two of Klimt's family portraits—those of Szerena and her daughter Elisabeth—resurfaced at the state auction house, Dorotheum, in 1948.[47] Erich Lederer soon learned that his title to these works was only theoretical in nature.

Erich Lederer faced two obstacles to restitution. The first was the dire state of the Lederers' businesses, which had been thoroughly ravaged by the Nazis. Owing to crushing fines imposed during the Nazi era, Erich Lederer now faced bankruptcy. During the course of settlement proceedings, he was forced to surrender all of his industrial interests, as well as the family's substantial real estate holdings.[48] He recovered what remained of his family's

Figure 10.3. Erich Lederer with his wife Elisabeth, about 1936. Private Collection

art, with the understanding that the sale proceeds would be used to satisfy company creditors, and to cover court costs.[49] The second obstacle was the need to obtain export licenses from the Austrian authorities, which would permit him to ship restituted artworks to his new home in Switzerland.

The export of artworks was governed by the Austrian Art Preservation Act of 1923, a national heritage protection law prohibiting the movement of objects of historical, artistic, or cultural value.[50] By exercising strategic export embargoes, the state effectively locked within the country many precious works that it was due to restitute. It was the general practice that restrictions would be waived only if selected items were to be donated to public collections as a quid pro quo. Never was this practice more extortive than in the case of Nazi refugees who were effectively barred from recovering their belongings unless they acquiesced to making substantial gifts to the country from which they had fled. Thus between 1948 and its reopening in 1954, the Belvedere doubled its Klimt holdings through works that it had acquired as a direct or secondary effect of Nazi looting. The most infamous of these onerous export settlements was the bequest in 1948 of five Klimt paintings from the Bloch-Bauer collection—now the subject of a major Hollywood movie, *Woman in Gold* (2015).

In the Lederers' case, the most difficult negotiations surrounded the *Beethoven Frieze*. While Austria was quick to place a unilateral export ban on the frieze, it did not pursue its acquisition—possibly because of the prohibitive costs of its storage and restoration. Instead, monuments officials picked and chose the best of the Lederers' other works. Vienna's Kunsthistorisches Museum received Gentile Bellini's *Cardinal Bessarion with Two Members of the Scuola della Carità with the Bessarion Reliquary*—a magnificent piece, now at the National Gallery in London.[51] A handsome selection of watercolors, including works by Egon Schiele[52] and Moritz von Schwind[53] were gifted to the Albertina; Vienna's municipal museum received a Franz Alt watercolor of St. Stephan's Cathedral.[54]

The state exerted enormous pressure on Erich Lederer to assume liability for the *Beethoven Frieze* and to pay for its upkeep, while at the same time denying the owner any rights over its whereabouts. This confrontation was tried in multiple court cases over several decades, and ultimately before Austria's Supreme Court.[55] During this time, the frieze languished in storage at Schloss Thürnthal until 1956, when it was transferred, without Erich Lederer's knowledge, to Stift Altenburg, a Benedictine monastery in Lower Austria. Here, the *Beethoven Frieze* was kept in appallingly inadequate conditions. Finally, in 1961, it was moved to a former stable on the grounds of the Belvedere.[56] By the late 1960s, it seemed that the frieze would deteriorate beyond repair, but the stalemate remained firmly in place. Erich Lederer was held responsible for the frieze's upkeep, but was not permitted to export or sell it. Austrian officials, meanwhile, eagerly sought a legal loophole that would grant the state not only access but title to the frieze.

Figure 10.4. The *Beethoven Frieze* at Stift Altenburg in the 1950s. Private Collection

The extant documents show that in 1967, Austria's Attorney General devised a devious plan: the Monuments Office was to restore the frieze, without notifying Erich Lederer or securing his permission. As the owner, Erich Lederer would be held liable for all costs. In the event that he was unable to reimburse the state—and of course, Erich Lederer's inability to cover these costs was the authorities' surreptitious objective—the Austrian state would impound the *Beethoven Frieze* as the only tangible domestic security. A public auction would be held, to allow the state to acquire the *Beethoven Frieze*. Officials confidently predicted a bargain price, since the export embargo discouraged international interest.[57] Having waged an unsuccessful legal battle over the terms of the frieze's upkeep, Erich Lederer now faced not only the export ban but the very real threat of dispossession.

In 1970, Erich Lederer's friend Karl Kahane, a leading industrialist in postwar Austria and a close confidant of the newly-elected Federal Chancellor Bruno Kreisky, attempted to settle the dispute. Another far less likely advocate was Hans Aurenhammer, the director of the Belvedere, who cautiously tried behind the scenes to rally support for acquisition of the *Beethoven Frieze*. In Aurenhammer's view, Erich Lederer had been continuously fobbed off with frivolous propositions, and had not received what he called a single "serious" bid from Austria.[58] While acknowledging that the frieze's value lay in the realm of $1 million, Aurenhammer urged Bruno Kreisky not to be guided by monetary concerns, but to consider only the ideal value of the *Beethoven Frieze* to Austria.[59]

After two decades of agonizing negotiations, the elderly Erich Lederer was ultimately defeated. In 1972, he conceded to the frieze's sale to the Austrian state for the sum of 15 million schillings—about half of the $1 million evaluation given by Aurenhammer. It was not before 1985—the year of Erich Lederer's death—that the frieze was first shown at the exhibition *Dream and Reality,* a landmark show that popularized the concept of "*fin-de-siècle* Vienna."[60] It was thereafter mounted in the basement of the Secession, where it remains to this day, as an extended loan from the Belvedere to the artist's association.[61]

THE AMENDED ART RESTITUTION ACT
VERSUS THE COURT OF PUBLIC OPINION

The *Beethoven Frieze's* questionable provenance was first addressed in the wake of the MoMA-Schiele scandal in 1998. One of two hundred works featured in a parliamentary inquiry by Austria's Green Party, it then served as a key example to illustrate the urgent necessity of introducing legislation to remedy the inadequacies of Austrian restitution.[62] Pursuant to the Art Restitution Act that emerged from that inquiry, Austria's restitution panel in 1999 voted to return a number of Lederer works, including Bellini's *Cardinal Bessarion* and six Schiele watercolors.[63] But the same panel declined to consider the restitution of the *Beethoven Frieze*. Because it had been sold rather than gifted to the state, the frieze did not fulfill the requirements of the law.

This state of affairs changed in 2009 when the Art Restitution Act was amended, owing to the fact that previous practice had shown the 1998 version to be too restrictive.[64] In its amended version, the law now applies to any artwork seized on the territory of the German Reich between 1933 and 1945, where previously it had applied only to works seized in Austria following the *Anschluss* in 1938. Another pivotal improvement was that the new bill extends to *all* artworks subject to post-1945 export negotiations—to include not only works donated to the Austrian state, but also works which owners were pressured to sell to the state to forgo an export ban. In such cases, claimants must reimburse the state for any compensation received.

In late 2013, one of Erich Lederer's heirs submitted a renewed petition for the *Beethoven Frieze*.[65] This move was announced at a highly-publicized media event hosted by two of the family's attorneys and two university professors who spoke out in favor of the Lederer claim.[66] The daily newspaper *Der Standard* viciously criticized the affair: it disparagingly referred to the press conference panel as "four men in suits," and contrasted the attorneys' brazen demeanor with the old-world charm of the late Maria Altmann. In the newspaper's retelling, the mild-mannered heiress of the Bloch-Bauer fortune had "fought like a lioness" but had remained thoroughly "graceful" and "loveable" throughout. Her modest composure, it was implied, made Maria Altmann more deserving of restitution, while the bold assertion of her younger counterpart was considered unseemly.[67]

The stakes were indeed high. It is no exaggeration to say that the *Beethoven Frieze* had kept the Secession financially afloat for the past three decades, with ticket sales providing a reported two-thirds of the Secession's annual budget.[68] The Secession was thus quick to lash out at the Lederer heirs and to denounce the claim as "devastating."[69]

Employing rhetoric of moral outrage, the Secession branded the claim a threat to the very fabric of Austrian restitution. Sanctimoniously, it predicted that if the state were indeed to accommodate Erich Lederer's heirs,

Figure 10.5. The *Beethoven Frieze* in the Secession, October 2013, shortly after the Lederer heirs' petition for restitution. Photo by Roland Schlager, with permission from APA Picture Desk

there would be no alternative but to abolish the restitution law to prevent similar abuses in the future. The Secession further questioned the moral position of what it referred to as "far-flung relatives" to submit restitution claims. Persons who did not share "the fate of persecution and exile" were not equipped to challenge the deal struck by Chancellor Kreisky and Erich Lederer—which the Secession alluded to as a consensual agreement between Jewish émigrés.[70]

In the media, the Lederer heirs were stigmatized as greedy and keen to cash in on the misfortune of a distant Jewish relative. That judgment was, and is, typical of the backlash experienced by many claimants.[71] Opponents of restitution insinuate that the true catalyst of Holocaust-era claims is not the vindication of atrocities but the art market—an anxious perception that is fueled by antisemitic stereotypes of avarice and self-enrichment. The Lederer heirs were further accused of "double dipping," of spuriously seeking a second round of compensation—although this was precisely what the law had set out to do: to provide restitution even where compensation had been previously paid.

The Art Restitution Act, moreover, does not restrict claims to the nearest of kin, contrary to immediate postwar restitution decrees. Since its inception, the Restitution Act has strictly followed Austrian inheritance laws, accepting the order of succession as admitted to probate. One need not be Jewish to qualify. Instances of restitution to immediate descendants are exceedingly rare—unsurprisingly so, given the many decades that have elapsed between the provision of a legal framework and the crime it was intended to remedy. Many of Austria's most highly profiled returns—including those made to the Bloch-Bauer heirs—were made to what the Secession would refer to as "far-flung relatives," to persons not related by blood, to institutions, and to charitable organizations.

The Secession's suggestion that the postwar export deal was a parity agreement between peer partners was at best naïve. Erich Lederer fought tooth and nail to recover the frieze and he was forced to suffer the protracted dispute over decades. He was sophisticated, self-confident, and determined not to be short-changed. But the state stood strong, triumphing as the *beatus possidens*—the fortunate possessor who prevails over the actual owner in an ownership dispute. Now witnesses, each claiming close friendship with Lederer, volunteered themselves to the media. Elisabeth Leopold, the widow of Austrian collector Rudolf Leopold and an outspoken restitution skeptic, jumped at the opportunity of trivializing Erich's plight. According to Leopold, Lederer had received a fair price for the badly damaged frieze.[72] The art dealer John Sailer, himself an émigré, likewise stressed how satisfied Erich Lederer had been with the settlement.[73] Although neither Erich

Lederer's subjective well-being nor the purchase price were relevant to the legal inquiry, these notions weighed far more heavily in the court of public opinion than the objective facts.

NEGOTIATING HISTORY

Austria, unlike Germany, never made monetary compensation payments to Holocaust victims. The 1943 Moscow Declaration acknowledged Austria as the first victim of Nazi aggression, removing any taint of complicity in Nazi crimes. It was not until 1991—in the wake of the scandal over the war record of presidential candidate Kurt Waldheim—that Austria first publicly acknowledged its shared moral responsibility for the Holocaust, and went on to establish, in 1995, a National Fund for Nazi victims.

When the Austrian Restitution Act was initially passed in 1998, it was intended as a "quick fix"—as is often the case in the face of scandal—to address the need for damage control. Most likely, politicians reckoned there would be two or three "show" restitutions, after which life would return to normal. But as a young generation of museum staff delved into the history of their institutions, they uncovered documents of extortion and shame. Provenance research showed how deeply implicated Austria's museums and the art trade was in the dispossession of Austrian Jews, and how deeply affected Austrian society remains to this day. Confronting the past, acknowledging institutional responsibility, declassifying archival holdings—these were all facets of a process driven by the generation of grandchildren of Austrian perpetrators. Present-day restitution efforts are so distanced in time that they are more therapeutic than cathartic in nature; they have created a positive momentum of their own, breathing life into the concept of *Wiedergutmachung*—the undoing of historical wrongs.

The historic turning point in accepting and indeed embracing art restitution came with *Maria Altmann v. Republic of Austria.* The heiress to the famous collection once owned by her uncle, Ferdinand Bloch-Bauer, had turned to the US courts after failing to have her case heard in Austria. In 2004, the United States Supreme Court affirmed the earlier judgment of the Ninth Circuit Court of Appeals, asserting that jurisdiction over the dispute was based on the Foreign Sovereign Immunities Act.[74] As a result, both parties agreed to arbitration in Austria. In early 2006, a panel of three Austrian arbitrators finally ruled in Altmann's favor. Praise of Austria's handling of the case was thus undeserved, since the Altmann victory was spearheaded by the American legal system. But more so than any other case, it sparked a public domestic debate that eroded the endemic "blockade of empathy"[75] and ended Austria's disimpassioned view of the experience of Nazi victims. In 2006, billboards across Vienna bid Gustav Klimt's portrait of Adele Bloch-Bauer a wistful goodbye.[76]

Indeed, restitution hinges on the concept of national patrimony—a concept that the *Beethoven Frieze* illustrates more emphatically than any other work, since it is literally anchored into the walls of the Secession and cannot be easily moved—so much so that we have come to think of it as an integral part of the very fabric of fin-de-siècle Viennese culture, rather than as the private property of one family. Postwar Austria prided itself on its rich cultural history but erased the memory of the rightful owners of those works it had acquired, directly or indirectly, as a result of Nazi spoliation. Masterpieces such as Adele's golden portrait were publicly presented as icons of a shared cultural identity. But the processes leading to the expropriation of these works were glossed over, just as Austria glossed over its own role in and responsibility for the Nazis' atrocities. It is only now—as a result of provenance research—that prewar patrons are receiving the attention they deserve. Today, we acknowledge the role of individuals who served as catalysts in the building of cultural identity and modernity; we are reinvesting art with its own history.

Like so many restitution cases, the debate over the *Beethoven Frieze* is not about Nazi-era spoliation, but over Austria's handling of restitution claims after the war ended. But unlike its predecessors, the *Beethoven Frieze* dispute is focused on the 1960s and 1970s rather on the immediate postwar period. Its protagonists were not Nazi thugs, but respected public servants of Austria's Second Republic—a predicament that exposed the lingering effects of the Holocaust to the very present.

BUSINESS AS USUAL

While Austria's dismissal of the claim for the *Beethoven Frieze* in March 2015 was a predictable outcome, its reasoning was curious. The panel denied any connection between the export embargo and the state's acquisition of the frieze; moreover, it submitted that the state had not vetoed, but only discouraged the export of the frieze. The London-based *Art Newspaper* called this a distinction "worthy of Kafka."[77]

In fact, the *Beethoven Frieze* decision highlights all of the shortcomings of the Art Restitution Act. The act is not a law in the common-sense meaning of the word: it provides a framework to allow Austria to deaccession looted artwork from its federal collections, but it does not afford Holocaust victims a legal right to restitution. When all goes well, the process is a bureaucratic and inexpensive one; claimants (for lack of a better word) may humbly accept decisions in their favor. But when a negative ruling is handed down, the outcome is devastating: the Art Restitution Act provides no legal recourse to appeal the verdict.

There is no parity of forces in Austria's restitution process. The law does not include heirs as party to the proceedings, nor does it invite them to give testimony of their view of events. The panel's deliberations are made *in camera,* and claimants are barred from reviewing the research reports on which the panel's decisions are based. The notion that a team of well-meaning individuals—mostly historians and not lawyers—might operate without procedural checks and balances is not only patronizing, but a violation of the fundamental right to a fair trial before an impartial tribunal. Equally disturbing is the inherent conflict of interest. By appointing a panel of Austrian experts to determine whether the country is to return objects owned by its federal museums, Austria presides over cases in which it is itself an interested party.

Since the announcement that the *Beethoven Frieze* would remain in Austria, public outrage has given way to indifference. *The Beethoven Frieze* will be filed as but one of hundreds of restitution cases reviewed since 1999. Visitors to the Secession will not be reminded through a plaque or any other signage of Erich Lederer's decades-long and bitter legal battle, nor of the ways and means by which he was strong-armed into selling the last vestige of his parents' collection. The last word thus belongs to Austria's restitution panel. It claimed that the state had enforced the export ban without a purchasing motive, implying that Erich Lederer's lack of alternative to selling the frieze was a matter of fact but not morally questionable. Although it conceded that Erich had been "shabbily" treated by postwar Austria, the panel took the position that the frieze's sale in 1972 had removed any stain of previous extortion.

Austria thus compromised its leadership role by passing equivocal judgment instead of deciding the case on its merits alone. The verdict bowed to a political and popular consensus biased against the restitution of a priceless masterpiece, proving that the country's professed commitment to restitution was at best ambivalent. According to a scathing commentary by art critic Olga Kronsteiner, Austria's restitution panel demonstrated "admirable ambiguity" as it struggled to justify a very questionable verdict.[78]

Sophie Lillie holds a Ph.D. in contemporary history. She is an independent scholar in the field of provenance regarding Holocaust-era art. Her publications include *Was einmal war: Handbuch der enteigneten Kunstsammlung Wiens* (2003), the definitive history of some 150 Nazi-plundered Jewish collections of Vienna and, with Georg Gaugusch, *Portrait of Adele Bloch-Bauer* (2005), which explores the odyssey of the famous 1901 painting by Gustav Klimt.

NOTES

1. Fritz Novotny and Johannes Dobai, *Gustav Klimt* (Salzburg, 1967), no. 127. Belvedere, Vienna, inventory no. 5987; on permanent loan to the Vereinigung bildender KünstlerInnen Wiener Secession.

2. Restitution Decision, 6 March 2015, retrieved 21 August 2015 from www.provenienzforschung.gv.at/wp-content/uploads/2015/03/Lederer_Erich_2015-03-06 .pdf.

3. For an overview of the Bloch-Bauer case, see Sophie Lillie and Georg Gaugusch, *Portrait of Adele Bloch-Bauer* (New York, 2006); Anne-Marie O'Connor, *The Lady in Gold: The Extraordinary Tale of Gustav Klimt's Masterpiece, Portrait of Adele Bloch-Bauer* (New York, 2012). The story is also the subject of a recent movie, *Woman in Gold* (2015), starring Helen Mirren and Ryan Reynolds.

4. Judith H. Dobryznski, "The Zealous Collector—A Special Report: A Singular Passion for Amassing Art, One Way or Another," *New York Times,* 24 December 1997.

5. Federal Law of 4 December 1998, regarding the Return of Artworks from Austrian Federal Museums and Public Collections (Federal Law Gazette BGBl. 181/I/1998).

6. Chronologically, the returned paintings were: *Country House on Lake Attersee, Apple Tree II, Lady with Hat and Feather Boa, Farm House with Birch Trees,* a 1898 portrait of a lady, *Adele Bloch-Bauer I* and *II, Birch Forest, Apple Tree I,* and *Houses at Unterach on Lake Attersee.* All of these were restituted between 2000 and 2006 from the Belvedere pursuant to the 1998 Art Restitution Act. At the non-federal level, in 2009 and 2011 respectively, the Lentos Museum in Linz returned *Portrait of Ria Munk III,* and the Museum der Moderne returned *Litzlberg on Lake Attersee.*

7. For a detailed discussion of the *Beethoven Frieze,* see, e.g., Peter Vergo, "Gustav Klimt's Beethoven Frieze," *The Burlington Magazine,* 115, no. 839 (February 1973): 108–13; Marian Bisanz-Prakken, *Der Beethovenfries: Geschichte, Funktion, Bedeutung* (Salzburg, 1977); Stephan Koja, ed., *Der Beethoven Fries und die Kontroverse um die Freiheit der Kunst* (Munich, 2006).

8. *Klinger Beethoven,* XIV (fourteenth) exh. Secession, Vienna, April 15–June 27, 1902. On the Beethoven exhibition, see *Die Wiener Secession: Die Vereinigung bildender Künstler 1897–1985* (Vienna, 1986), 35–38.

9. *Ver Sacrum Gustav Klimt.* XVIII (eighteenth) exh. Secession, Vienna. 14 November–6 January 1903.

10. Carl Reininghaus (1857–1929), industrialist and major collector of Austrian modernist art, particularly by Egon Schiele and Ferdinand Hodler. On the

Reininghaus collection, see Tobias G. Natter, *Die Welt von Klimt, Schiele und Kokoschka: Sammler und Mäzene* (Cologne, 2003), 165–77.

11. Gustav Nebehay, *Gustav Klimt, Egon Schiele und die Familie Lederer* (Bern, 1987), 35–38.
12. Nebehay, *Familie Lederer,* 35–38.
13. On the Lederer collection, see Nebehay, *Familie Lederer*; Tobias G. Natter and Gerbert Frodl, *Klimt und die Frauen,* exhibition catalogue, Österreichische Galerie, Vienna, 20 September 2000–7 January 2001 (Cologne, 2000), 88–91; Natter, *Sammler und Mäzene,* 111–39; Sophie Lillie, *Was einmal war: Handbuch der enteigneten Kunstsammlungen Wiens* (Vienna, 2003), 656–71; Sophie Lillie, "The Golden Age of Klimt: The Artist's Great Patrons: Lederer, Zuckerkandl and Bloch-Bauer," in *Gustav Klimt: The Ronald S. Lauder and Serge Sabarsky Collections,* exhibition catalogue, Neue Galerie New York, 18 October 2007–30 June 2008, 55–89; Monika Sommer and Alexandra Steiner-Strauss, *Gustav Klimt in Wien* (Vienna, 2012), 141–45; Sophie Lillie, "Klimt's Women Collectors: The Pulitzer Sisters Szerena Lederer, Jenny Steiner and Aranka Munk" (Ph.D. diss., University of Vienna, 2014).
14. Bundesdenkmalamt [hereafter BDA], Vienna, Export Materials, notary file no. 1788/21, August Lederer; BDA, box 68, no. 55/26, Vermögensabgabe.
15. Cleveland Museum of Art, ID no. 1985.8.
16. J. Paul Getty Museum, Los Angeles, object no. 82.PB.72.
17. Lillie, "Klimt's Women Collectors," 125–39.
18. Novotny and Dobai, *Gustav Klimt,* no. 44. Wien Museum, inventory no. 31318. The painting also includes portrait vignettes of Szerena's sister Aranka Munk with husband Alexander; her sister Irma Politzer with husband Zsigmond; and Irma and Zsigmond's sister-in-law Tinka Politzer. Zsigmond's brothers Adam Politzer and Gusztáv Politzer (Tinka's husband) are depicted in the theater stalls below. See Sophie Lillie and Georg Gaugusch, "Die Gründer-Zeit im Bild: Gustav Klimts Zuschauerraum im alten Burgtheater," in *Klimt: Die Sammlung des Wien Museums,* exhibition catalogue, Wien Museum, 15 May–15 September 2012, 112–23.
19. Novotny and Dobai, *Gustav Klimt,* no. 101. Destroyed at Schloss Immendorf, May 1945.
20. Hermann Bahr, "Die vierte Ausstellung: Klimt, Engelhart, Andri, Fräulein Ries," in *Secession* (Vienna, 1900), 122–27, reprinted in Hermann Bahr, *Secession,* ed. Claus Pias (Weimar, 2007).
21. Novotny and Dobai, *Gustav Klimt,* no. 174. Destroyed at Schloss Immendorf, May 1945.
22. Ibid., no. 215. Destroyed at Schloss Immendorf, May 1945.
23. Ibid., no. 201. Destroyed at Schloss Immendorf, May 1945.
24. Ibid., no. 103. Metropolitan Museum of Art, inventory no. 1980.412.
25. Ibid., no. 188. Private collection, New York.
26. Ibid., no. 190. Current whereabouts unknown.
27. Ibid., nos. 105, 128. Destroyed at Schloss Immendorf, 1945.

28. "Die Agitation gegen Klimt's 'Philosophie,'" *Neue Freie Presse,* 26 March 1900.

29. Berta Zuckerkandl's diaries published as Österreich intim: Erinnerungen 1892–*1942,* ed. Reinhard Federmann (Frankfurt am Main, 1970; reprint, Vienna, 2013); Theresia Klugsberger and Ruth Pleyer, eds., *Berta Zuckerkandl–Flucht! Von Bourges nach Algier im Sommer 1940* (Vienna, 2013).

30. On the Wittgenstein collection, see Natter and Frodl, *Klimt und die Frauen,* 108–110; Natter, *Sammler und Mäzene,* 38–53; Lillie, *Was einmal war,* 1332–39.

31. BDA, Restitution Materials, box 9, file 1a, fol. 179f. Notice no. MA 2/9148/38, 26 November 1938.

32. Wiener Stadt- und Landesarchiv [herafter WStLA], MA 350, box A1/3: Allgemeine Registratur 1939 (nos. 651–1065), no. MA 50/1029/39, Elisabeth Bachofen-Echt. notice no. MA50/1220/38, 7 December 1938; BDA, Restitution Materials, box 9, file 1a, fol. 156f. Notice no. MA50/26/39, 4 January 1939.

33. BDA, Restitution Materials, box 9, file 1, fols. 28–44. Reich List Serena Lederer [1939].

34. BDA, Restitution Materials, box 9, file 1, fols. 60–91. Inventory of museums and public offices interested in the distribution of seized artworks.

35. On the "Führermuseum," see Birgit Schwarz, *Hitler's Museum: Die Fotoalben Gemäldegalerie Linz: Dokumente zum "Führermuseum"* (Vienna, 2004).

36. Sophie Lillie, "Commodities versus Connoisseurship: A Short Price History of Gustav Klimt Sales during the Nazi Era," in *Markt und Macht: Der Kunsthandel im 'Dritten Reich',* ed. Uwe Fleckner, Thomas W. Gaehtgens and Christian Huemer (Berlin, 2017), 293–321.

37. *Gustav Klimt,* exhibition catalogue, Ausstellungshaus Friedrichstrasse (formerly the Secession), Vienna, 7 February–7 March 1943.

38. For a detailed discussion of the show, see Sophie Lillie, "Die Gustav Klimt-Ausstellung von 1943," in *Das Wiener Künstlerhaus,* ed. Peter Bogner, Richard Kurdiovsky, and Johannes Stoll (Vienna, 2015), 335–41.

39. Künstlerhaus Archive, Jahresbericht, 1943.

40. *Klimt 1943,* exhibition catalogue, nos. 6, 7, 9, 20, 22, 25, 39, 46, 49, 51, 52, 56, 61.

41. BDA, Restitution Materials, box 9, file 2: Sammlung Lederer 1940–1946 (I), fol. 88. Grimschitz to IfD, 26 January 1943; BDA, Restitution Materials, box 9, file 2, fol. 99, receipt Grimschitz, 26 January 1943. ÖG Archive, no. 398/42, Klimt-Ausstellung in der Secession. Receipts of the Institute für Denkmalpflege, 26 and 28 January and 16 March 1943.

42. *Klimt 1943,* exhibition catalogue, nos. 26, 50.

43. *Klimt 1943,* exhibition catalogue, nos. 10, 38, 55, 62.

44. "Der Brand aus Immendorf," *Der Turm* 1, no. 2 (September 1945): 40.

45. Central Database of Shoah Victims' Names, Yad Vashem, Jerusalem.

46. WStLA, municipal registration of residence, Erich Lederer.

47. Dorotheum, Vienna, 18–20 March 1948, lot nos. 75, 76, pl. 28, 29.

48. Landesgericht für Zivilrechtssachen [hereafter LGfZRS], nos. 49 S 8/46, August Lederer; 49 S 13/46, Serena Lederer; 49 S 11/46, Erich Lederer. These files have not been preserved.

49. Österreichisches Staatsarchiv, Archiv der Republik, Bundesministerium für Vermögenssicherung und Wirtschaftsplanung, no. 104.871/14-6/50. Transcript of LGfZRS, no. S 8/46, application for bankruptcy settlement, 12 December 1949.

50. Austrian Federal Law of 25 January 1923 amending the Law of 5 December 1918, State Law Gazette (StGBl. 90/1918), Prohibiting the Export or Sale of Objects of Historical, Artistic or Cultural Value (BGBl. 80/1923).

51. National Gallery, London, inventory no. NG6590.

52. Albertina, inventory nos. 31.102–107. See Jane Kallir, *Egon Schiele: Complete Works,* rev. ed. (New York, 1998), nos. D768, D1638, D1654, D1769, D2020, and D2123.

53. Albertina, inventory nos. 31.108–110. Of these three works, *Queen of the Night,* now at the Getty Museum, object no. 2009.55; *Three Boys Save the Despairing Pamina from Suicide,* Metropolitan Museum of Art, accession no. 2003.518.

54. Wien Museum, inventory no. 95.822.

55. Bezirksgericht Kirchberg am Wagram, no. 1Nc 72/52, Republic of Austria v. Erich Lederer; Kreisgericht (Regional Court) Krems, no. 1 Nc 72/52, R 264/53; Oberster Gerichtshof (Supreme Court), no. 2 Ob 548/53.

56. "Die Reisen des Beethovenfrieses, erzählt von Erich Lederer," in Nebehay, *Familie Lederer,* 39–41.

57. Bruno Kreisky-Archiv, Vienna, File Lederer–Beethovenfries. Finanzprokuratur, no. 32599/67. Memorandum responding to BMU no. 96.970-II/2/67, 11 July 1967.

58. Bruno Kreisky-Archiv, File Lederer–Beethovenfries. [Hans Aurenhammer], Memorandum for Federal Chancellor Bruno Kreisky, 21 February 1972.

59. Ibid.

60. *Traum und Wirklichkeit,* exh. cat., Historisches Museum der Stadt Wien, 28 March–6 October 1985.

61. Margarethe Szeless, "Der Beethovenfries—Provenienz- und Ausstellungsgeschichte," 49–67, in: Secession, ed., *Gustav Klimt: Beethovenfries* (Vienna, 2002).

62. Austrian Parliament, XX (twentieth) legislative period, 15 April 1998, 115th session, inquiry no. 4031-NR/1998.

63. Restitution Decision, 10 May 1999, retrieved August 2015 from www.provenienzforschung.gv.at/wp-content/uploads/2006/04/Lederer.pdf.

64. Federal Law regarding the Restitution of Art objects and Other Moveable Assets from Austrian Federal Museums and Collections or other Federal Property (BGBl. 117/2009).

65. Lanter Rechsanwälte, press release, 17 October 2013, retrieved March 2014 from www.ots.at/presseaussendung/ OTS_20131017_OTS0118/erben-fordern-ruckgabe-des-beethovenfries-von-gustav-klimt-durch-die-republik-oesterreich. Claim supported by legal statements by David J. Rowland and Patricia Hertling, 10 September 2013, and Georg Graf, 13 September 2013, in author's private archive. See also the Noll, Keider Rechtsanwalts GmbH press release,

18 October 2013, retrieved March 2014 from www.ots.at/presseaussendung/ OTS_20131018_OTS0169/beethovenfries, and unpublished opinion statement by the author, 15 September 2013.

66. The press conference was hosted by Swiss attorney Marc Weber and his Austrian colleague Stefan Nenning; the two other panel members were university professors Georg Graf and Robert Jan van Pelt.

67. Thomas Trenkler, "Ein Fries mit vier Männern im Anzug," *Der Standard,* 18 October 2013.

68. Olga Kronsteiner, "Ringen um den 'Goldesel'," *Der Standard,* 21 February 2015.

69. Press release, apa/KI II 20131118-APA0325-1, 18 November 2013, author's private archive.

70. Schönherr Law Offices, Opinion Statement, 13 November 2013, retrieved 11 March 2014 from www.secession.at. Its authors are Christian Hauer, attorney at law and board member of the Friends of the Secession, and historian Oliver Rathkolb.

71. Sophie Lillie, "The Backlash against Claimants," lecture delivered at Holocaust-Era Assets Conference, hosted by the Czech Presidency of the European Union, Prague, 28 June 2009.

72. Dagmar Kaindl et al., "Der Restitutionsfall des Jahres," *News,* 8 January 2015.

73. Thomas Trenkler, "Lederer wollte, dass Beethovenfries in Österreich bleibt," *Der Standard,* 3 November 2013.

74. Supreme Court, Republic of Austria vs. Altmann, no. 03–13, 541 US 677 (2004), https://supreme.justia.com/cases/federal/us/541/677/. United States Court of Appeals, Ninth Circuit, Altmann vs. Republic of Austria, nos. 01–56003, 01–56398 (2002), retrieved March 2016 from http://caselaw.findlaw.com/us-9th-circuit/1464064.html.

75. A very fitting term borrowed from German scholar Aleida Assmann.

76. Austria's largest outdoor advertising company Gewista was responsible for this campaign, titled "Ciao Adele."

77. David D'Arcy, "Austrian Amnesia over How it Treated Victims of Nazi Looting," *The Art Newspaper,* 1 April 2015.

78. Olga Kronsteiner, "Vorbildhafte Schwammigkeit," *Der Standard,* 6 March 2015.

SELECT BIBLIOGRAPHY

Bahr, Hermann. *Secession,* ed. Claus Pias. Weimar: Bauhaus Universitätsverlag, 2007.

Bisanz-Prakken, Marian. *Der Beethovenfries: Geschichte, Funktion, Bedeutung.* Salzburg: Residenz Verlag, 1977.

D'Arcy, David. "Austrian Amnesia over How it Treated Victims of Nazi Looting." *The Art Newspaper,* 1 April 2015.

Dobryznski, Judith H. "The Zealous Collector—A Special Report: A Singular Passion for Amassing Art, One Way or Another." *The New York Times,* 24 December 1997.

Lillie, Sophie, and Georg Gaugusch, Georg. *Portrait of Adele Bloch-Bauer.* New York: Neue Galerie, 2006.

Kaindl, Dagmar, et al. "Der Restitutionsfall des Jahres." *News,* 8 January 2015.

Klugsberger, Theresia, and Ruth Pleyer, eds. *Berta Zuckerkandl–Flucht! Von Bourges nach Algier im Sommer 1940.* Vienna: Czernin Verlag, 2013.

Koja, Stephan, ed. *Der* Beethoven Fries *und die Kontroverse um die Freiheit der Kunst.* Munich: Prestel Verlag, 2006.

Kronsteiner, Olga. "Vorbildhafte Schwammigkeit." *Der Standard,* 6 March 2015.

Lillie, Sophie. *Feindliche Gewalten: Das Ringen um Gustav Klimts Beethovenfries.* Vienna: Czernin Verlag, 2017.

———. *Was einmal war: Handbuch der enteigneten Kunstsammlungen Wiens.* Vienna: Czernin Verlag, 2003.

———. "Klimt's Women Collectors: The Pulitzer Sisters Szerena Lederer, Jenny Steiner and Aranka Munk." Ph.D diss., University of Vienna, 2014.

———. "Die Gustav Klimt-Ausstellung von 1943." In *Das Wiener Künstlerhaus,* ed. Peter Bogner, Richard Kurdiovsky, and Johannes Stoll, 335–41. Vienna: Verlag Lehner, 2015.

Natter, Tobias G. *Die Welt von Klimt, Schiele und Kokoschka: Sammler und Mäzene.* Cologne: DuMont, 2003.

Nebehay, Gustav. *Gustav Klimt, Egon Schiele und die Familie Lederer.* Bern: Galerie Kornfeld, 1987.

O'Connor, Anne-Marie. *The Lady in Gold: The Extraordinary Tale of Gustav Klimt's Masterpiece, Portrait of Adele Bloch-Bauer.* New York: Knopf, 2012.

Schwarz, Birgit. *Hitlers Museum: Die Fotoalben Gemäldegalerie Linz: Dokumente zum "Führermuseum."* Vienna: Böhlau Verlag, 2004.

Sommer, Monika, and Alexandra Steiner-Strauss. *Gustav Klimt in Wien.* Vienna: Metroverlag, 2012.

Supreme Court, Republic of Austria vs. Altmann, no. 03–13, 541 US 677 (2004), https://supreme.justia.com/cases/federal/us/541/677/.

Szeless, Margarethe. "Der Beethovenfries—Provenienz- und Ausstellungsgeschichte." In *Gustav Klimt: Beethovenfries,* ed. Secession, 49–67. Vienna: Secession, 2002.

Trenkler, Thomas. "Ein Fries mit vier Männern im Anzug," *Der Standard,* 18 October 2013.

———. "Lederer wollte, dass Beethovenfries in Österreich bleibt," *Der Standard,* 3 November 2013.

United States Court of Appeals, Ninth Circuit, Altmann vs. Republic of Austria, nos. 01–56003, 01–56398 (2002). Retrieved 20 January 2015 from http://caselaw.findlaw.com/us-9th-circuit/1464064.html.

Vergo, Peter. "Gustav Klimt's Beethoven Frieze." *The Burlington Magazine* 115, no. 839 (February 1973): 108–113.

Part V

Return to Nuremberg

Chapter 11

Judging from Without

German Clergy, Public Pressure, and Postwar Justice

JonDavid K. Wyneken

The cover of the 7 May 1945 edition of *Life* magazine featured a cover photo and caption appropriate for the issue, which appeared just hours before the end of World War II in Europe. Simply titled "The German People," the cover shows three disheveled men with expressions that combine exhaustion, fear, anger, and resignation. The photo is one of ambivalence, uncertainty, and curiosity about the fate of Germany's people in light of what Nazism had wreaked upon Europe. The issue's main editorial echoed these sentiments. It wondered if Allied occupation policies would be as successful in rebuilding and reshaping Germany as Allied armies had been in conquering it. In particular, the editorial emphasized that the world would care most about how Nazi war criminals would be tried and punished. "[T]he law and the procedural nature of justice to be meted out to war criminals," it said, "has yet to be spelled out for the public."[1]

Once the details had been released and the trial process began in late 1945 with the International Military Tribunal (IMT) at Nuremberg, many international organizations and individual observers quickly registered what would eventually become strong and consistent critiques of the entire postwar criminal prosecution process. Eventually the critique included all of the US trials conducted at Nuremberg and at the former Nazi concentration camp at Dachau. Many critics brought pressure to bear on Allied policymakers to change the war crimes prosecution program or discard it entirely.

Such arguments were often expressed publicly and heatedly in intertwined moral, political, spiritual, legal, and ethical terms. The extensive correspondence between Allied policymakers and their critics, as well as the public's attention to these debates, both inside Germany and among observers in the West, illustrates that this pressure put those charged with formulating and conducting war crimes prosecution on the defensive as they worked hard to defend the foundational and moral precepts of the trials to the world. After all, the staying power of the judgments reached and precedents created in these trials depended in large part on the public's willingness to accept the trials themselves as morally, politically, and legally valid. External pressure put the war crimes process itself on trial, and the discourse brought no clear consensus about the trials' validity during the formative years of postwar justice. Exploring the ways in which public pressure—defined here as the general public's perceptions of the trials and their subsequent private and public statements to Allied decision-makers denouncing and calling for an end to the trial program—can better frame examinations of the trials themselves and can help develop new avenues for research and writing on Holocaust justice.

My thinking on the issue originated from research on the German churches during the occupation period (1945–1952).[2] The Protestant and Catholic churches' public statements and activities helped shape negative international public opinions about Allied trials. The churches sought to shield the German public from Allied scrutiny about the recent past under the Nazis, to advocate a vehemently anti-communist stance against the Soviets and their occupation of eastern Germany, and to create—consciously or not—what scholars have deemed a "usable" past for Germans where they could be seen more as victims than perpetrators.[3] Challenging the trials was a way to reshape historical understanding of the war itself, and therefore the types of lessons that might be derived from it. The churches thus urged the Allies to end the trials as quickly as possible and to reduce or overturn the punishments for those convicted. An extraordinary amount of information on the trials is in the records of the US, British, and French occupation zones and particularly in the records concerning religious affairs.[4] Likewise, a great number of relevant records are in the personal papers of prominent German Catholic and Protestant leaders in all three zones. These papers, held at ecclesiastical archives in Munich (Michael Cardinal von Faulhaber), Freiburg im Breisgau (Archbishop Conrad Gröber), Stuttgart (Evangelical Bishop Theophil Wurm), and elsewhere contain file after file of critical letters, written articles, defendant dossiers, and correspondence with the highest ranking Allied officials in Germany, with their home governments, and with influential religious figures around the world. Dominant in these materials are fundamental disagreements with and criticisms of the war crimes trials.

The German churches used their international contacts—many of them developed clandestinely as channels of resistance while living under the Third Reich—to publicize their criticisms in international newspapers and magazines, among individual congregations, and in the halls of government.[5] Public statements and private correspondence by church figures with established (if not wholly deserved) reputations for resistance against the Nazis—and therefore with legitimate bona fides among Christians—furthered this effort to leverage notions of Christian morality and charges of "victor's justice" against the Allied war crimes prosecution effort. Their attacks on the trials helped shape early postwar views of Nazism's origins, life, and crimes. And, in an effort to protect themselves from Allied examination, to prevent Germans from being blamed collectively for Nazism, and out of a desire to restore the centrality of Christian faith to German life, the churches also added to the myths that most Germans were unaware of Nazi crimes, such as the tale that only SS (Schutzstaffel) soldiers and high-level Nazi leaders had committed acts of murder and that the churches had been stalwart resisters against Nazism since its inception. Though the churches' efforts failed to end or undercut the trials or overturn any convictions and sentences, they nevertheless helped establish and frame the dissent against the precepts, conduct, and outcome of the trials themselves. They contributed to a number of the moral, ethical, legal, and political debates that have continued to the present day about war crimes prosecution.[6] This fact on its own suggests that one such avenue for writing about Holocaust justice is to examine the effect religious bodies have had on trials and on how postwar international justice has been understood.

Opposition to the trials among church leaders became evident in the earliest days of the occupation. In October 1945, Michael Cardinal von Faulhaber of Munich surprised visiting US officials with his concerns that the upcoming IMT in Nuremberg would ignore established legal precedents, would conclude that all Germans were guilty for the crimes of Nazism, and would make Germans the scapegoats for the war out of a spirit of revenge.[7] A year later when the IMT's verdicts were about to be handed down, Faulhaber's sentiments had become well enough known that Dr. Alfred Seidl, the defense attorney for former General Governor Hans Frank, petitioned the cardinal to call publicly on the Allies to show leniency to Frank or to stay his expected execution in light of Frank's proclamation in the dock that he become a "believing Christian."[8] Faulhaber followed through, forwarding the request to Pope Pius XII, who on the eve of the rulings issued a statement to the court that was broadcast over Vatican radio for Catholics around the world to hear.[9] Though the petition was unsuccessful and Frank was hanged for his crimes, the highest Catholic authority was now on record as having grave misgivings about the intent and effect of the Nuremberg proceedings. The pontiff made no secret his frustration—echoed by many others in Catholic and Protestant leadership—with Soviet participation in the IMT, and he spoke forcefully for a conception of war crimes prosecution that would include examining Allied wartime activities.[10] Such a stance could only be taken as a serious development by the Western Allies and food for thought for Catholics who were trying to form their opinions about the trials and the recent past.

German Catholic and Protestant leaders added to Pius XII's challenge by openly denouncing the IMT verdicts in letters, in the press, and in the pulpit. The archbishop of Cologne, Josef Frings, deplored publicly in the Catholic press the Allies' refusal to prosecute "the crimes [that] had occurred elsewhere [by the Allies], that deserve investigation." By this Frings clearly meant the aerial bombardment of German cities, the behavior of Soviet troops as they occupied German territory, and the expulsion of millions of Germans from the eastern areas of Germany officially ceded to Poland at the Potsdam Conference in July 1945.[11] Frings argued that if these transgressions were not investigated and prosecuted, then the idea that justice could be objective would be rejected throughout Germany.[12] The archbishop of Freiburg, Conrad Gröber, went even further in a strongly worded letter to French occupation officials, blasting the IMT as a "big spectacle" that had alienated the majority of Germans and had created "a new proletariat ... poisoned by bitterness and the desire for vengeance." Gröber called on the Western Allies to forgive their former enemies in the interest of preventing "liberal democracy [from] progressively becoming the source of new evils and dangers." He asserted that in making such criticisms the churches met their "duties to perform for this Fatherland ... the holy church has not only the right but the duty to ... safeguard natural rights and Christian moral law."[13]

Protestant leaders also made their opinions known. The Evangelical Bishop of Stuttgart Theophil Wurm, also the first president of the new postwar unified Protestant church, publicly called on the IMT judges to consider "the momentous sentence which will go down in the annals of history and from which far-reaching consequences are to be expected not only for the German people but also for the community of nations." Wurm warned the tribunal that "it would be most dreadful if, through the judgment passed at Nuremberg, the opinion should be strengthened that there is no longer justice on earth but that rather right is dictated by might." Only an equivalency of application of the laws to the whole world could constitute justice:

"The Nuremberg sentence[s] will only master the deterioration of justice if the will and the strength become apparent to punish crimes against humanity everywhere in the past, present, and future wherever, by whomever, and against whomever they are committed. It is only under these conditions that the court is in a position to pass judgment in the name of humanity."[14] Notably, US intelligence officials closely tracked Wurm's public statement and others like it in the wake of the IMT verdicts.[15]

In anticipation of subsequent trials throughout the western zones, with particular focus on the US-led trials at Nuremberg and Dachau, the churches stepped up their efforts to bring private and public pressure to bear on the Allies' war crimes prosecution processes. Beginning in 1947 Wurm wrote numerous petitions and letters critical of the trials to US occupation leaders. He also wrote to prominent foreign dignitaries like Archbishop of Canterbury Geoffrey Fisher, Anglican Bishop of Chichester George Bell, and even King George VI of England. He advocated leniency or exoneration for specific defendants in British war crimes cases such as Field Marshall Erich von Manstein—who would eventually be convicted by a British court-martial in Hamburg in 1949—and the former ambassador to Rome Eberhard von Mackensen whose 1946 conviction for war crimes committed in Italy Wurm called "an obvious injustice."[16] Wurm also engaged in a public defense and appeal for clemency on behalf of Konstantin von Neurath, the former Nazi foreign minister and Reichsprotektor of Bohemia and Moravia. Sentenced to fifteen years in Spandau prison, von Neurath had intervened personally with Hitler to have Wurm released from house arrest in 1934.[17] Wurm seemed to want to return the favor. He appealed to George Bell for aid, arguing that von Neurath had "never worked actively for nationalsocialism [*sic*] and handed in his resignation as soon as he recognized Hitler's aggressive intentions." Von Neurath, Wurm continued, used his position "to cover many an injustice with his name," and eventually "drew back because he could no longer bear the responsibilities of this position."[18] Wurm did not succeed in securing von Neurath's release, but he continued to petition the Allies regularly on von Neurath's behalf until his eventual release on humanitarian grounds in 1954.

Wurm also argued, as did many others, that Allied war crimes trials were based on ex post facto law in the sense that the defendants' actions were consistent with German law under the Nazis. Wurm believed that defendants were prosecuted for "politically wrong decisions" that were mistakenly "placed on the same level as criminal offenses." To Wurm, this did not serve "a constructive effect in a moral and cultural sense." The bishop concluded that "it is not right to judge the words and actions of people with such attitudes only according to their conformity with nationalsocialist [*sic*] principles."[19] US offiicals countered that these interpretations, if applied in Germany, would preclude the Western Allies' ability to hold anyone accountable for the crimes committed against all of Europe by the Nazis.[20] Wurm, however, continued to insist that the legal precept of nulla poena sine lege be recognized in the trials, though to the Americans accepting this precept as Wurm defined it meant that no trials could be held at all.

Beginning in 1947, Wurm increased pressure on Allied officials by writing dozens of letters and publishing them in newspapers in Germany and abroad. The military governor of the US occupation zone, Lieutenant General Lucius Clay, and the deputy prosecutor for the post-IMT trials in Nuremberg, Robert Kempner, were most often the targets of this campaign. Kempner came to believe—not without reason—that Wurm disliked him partly for his Jewish background. Kempner had been removed from law practice by the Nazis in 1934 and fled to the United States. He subsequently defined Nazism as inherently criminal and asserted that the majority of Germans, including many in the German churches, supported it.[21] In attacking both men, Wurm once again dismissed the IMT and its successor trials as "victor's justice" masquerading as universally accepted international law.[22] To Wurm, the trials served more political ends than judicial ones. He cited the Soviet participation in the IMT despite Moscow's direct role in conducting the "aggressive war" against Poland for which many of the IMT defendants had been tried and convicted. By failing in their "moral" duty to keep the Soviets off of the IMT, Wurm argued, the Western Allies had "bowed to the compulsion of the political situation just as the diplomats and generals during Hitler's regime, just as numberless German professors, officials, and industrialists, and men in the streets did."[23] Wurm also argued that "aggressive war" had been conducted by nations other than Germany, including Great Britain's war against the South African Boers and the United States' conquest of Spanish-held territories. None of those nations, he said, had been held accountable. The reference to the Boer War, in fact, hearkened back to its use by the Nazis as a major piece of anti-British propaganda and underscores the deep degree to which it had apparently influenced Wurm.[24] In the meantime, he pointed out that "no one judges victorious generals and successful statesmen."[25] The Allied refusal to consider their own crimes convinced Wurm that power, not justice, truly motivated the trials. This, he argued, only "further undermined the already shaken confidence in the impartial nature of these Tribunals."[26]

US officials rejected these arguments and denied Wurm's charges that the trials were slanted toward the prosecution and that defendants had been "arbitrarily selected" for prosecution. To Clay, the convictions at Nuremberg had been based on such overwhelming evidence of guilt that prosecutors had no need to force confessions.[27] Clay and Kempner further denied Wurm's charges of abuse of prisoners and prosecutorial misconduct at Nuremberg and Dachau.[28] On several occasions both invited Wurm to Nuremberg to visit one of the trials (which Wurm did once) and examine the prosecution's evidence (which Wurm never did).[29]

Matters came to a head in March 1948 when Wurm and Kempner each published their correspondence with the other in various newspapers inside and outside Germany. This added fuel to the ongoing public debate on both sides of the Atlantic about the legitimacy of the trials, rooted in the efforts of a recognized religious authority. The catalyst for this escalation in rhetoric came when Clay and Kempner warned Wurm that his "indictment of a court, established for a high purpose, on such evidence by leaders of spiritual life in Germany cannot help but be adverse to its purpose." Wurm then denied Clay's charge that he was the "vanguard of a national group" out to discredit the trials. He instead cited "an inner sense of duty," and hoped that "responsible men amongst those who have fought against and overcome this Reich wish to act differently [than the Nazis had]."[30]

The controversy from 1946 through 1949 surrounding the Malmédy trial merged with this public feud and led to some remarkable examples of how outside pressure can affect trials in unexpected ways. The trial concerned the massacre of some eighty US Army POWs by members of the 1st SS Panzer Division during the German winter offensive of December 1944. Seventy-three Waffen-SS members stood trial at Dachau in mid-1946, with forty-three sentenced to death. Recent scholarship suggests that many of the Dachau trials, and the Malmédy trial in particular, were conducted poorly; it gives credence to the widespread claims at the time that defendants were subjected to various abuses, both physical and psychological, during interrogations and even during proceedings.[31] At the time, these claims were considered sensational by many, but they nevertheless triggered another round of vehement debate in Germany and in the United States about the morality and legitimacy of war crimes prosecution more broadly. And they gave vocal and well-known critics like Theophil Wurm an ideal platform from which to highlight their moral opposition and advance their arguments against the Allied effort.

In May 1948, Dachau trial defense lawyer Willis M. Everett appealed to the United States Supreme Court for a writ of habeas corpus on behalf of the forty-three former Waffen-SS soldiers who had been sentenced to death.[32] Following this public bombshell, German defense lawyers from the Dachau trials including the aforementioned Alfred Seidl, sent their case dossiers directly to Wurm, asking him for aid in making their arguments public. Wurm's Nachlass contain dozens of such dossiers, all of them strongly advocating leniency or outright acquittal.[33] Wurm got information and statements into newspapers like *Neue Zeitung, Flensburger Tageblatt, Zeit,* and the *Chicago Tribune.*[34] He also released to the international press a detailed statement outlining his own longstanding arguments against the trials in the US occupation zone. By June, Wurm noted with satisfaction that Everett's evidence—with Wurm's help—had by then been seen by President Harry S. Truman, Secretary of State George Marshall, Pope Pius XII, Michael Cardinal von Faulhaber, and Red Cross headquarters in Switzerland.[35]

In July 1948, US Secretary of the Army Kenneth Royall established the Simpson Commission to investigate the conduct of the Malmédy trial and others conducted at Dachau. Its report, which critiqued the US pretrial investigations of German defendants, was published in September. During the Simpson Commission's investigation, Wurm circumvented Clay's authority and sent a series of angry letters. As Truman was expected to be defeated in the November 1948 presidential election, Wurm contacted figures on both sides of the American political divide. Letters thus went to Truman and Secretaries Marshall and Royall, but also to Republican Senator Arthur H. Vandenburg of Michigan (then chair of the Senate Foreign Relations Committee) and John Foster Dulles—Republican foreign policy strategist, member of the US delegation to the UN General Assembly, and member of the Federal Council of Churches—who many expected to be the next secretary of state under Thomas Dewey.[36] In one of his letters to Dulles, Wurm asserted that true justice could only be achieved if the United States managed to "drive Hitler's spirit completely out of their own country and if law and justice can be meted out for no one's benefit and no one's harm, but solely in the interests of the matter itself."[37]

At the same time, Wurm managed to place more letters in German and US newspapers. He equated US trial practices with those of the Nazis, saying that "the worst effect of totalitarianism is the destruction of legal conceptions, legal security, and equality of law." Wurm asserted that "as early as 1933 the highest court in Germany was not in a position to unmask the farce of the trial of the Reichstag fire," and that the murders committed on the Night of the Long Knives went unpunished. This failure, argued Wurm, "caused the deterioration of law to spread; it reached its culmination in the treatment of the mentally diseased, of the Jews and of those circles which were opposed to the nationalsocialist [*sic*] system."[38] Other German church leaders like Frings, Catholic Auxiliary Bishop of Munich Johannes Neuhäusler, and Evangelical Bishop Hans Meisier of Bavaria sent frantic cables and letters to Truman and Clay clamoring for executions being scheduled at the US war crimes enclosure at Landsberg prison to be cancelled and for any death sentences from the Malmédy cases to be treated similarly.[39] Wurm became convinced that he had helped shift "public opinion on both sides of the Atlantic" against the trials.[40]

Wurm's confidence came partly from his use of political back channels since spring 1948. Wurm had begun a correspondence George Dix, a Madison Avenue lawyer and staunch critic of the US occupation. Dix had close personal and political connections with Republican Senators William Langer of North Dakota and Joseph McCarthy of Wisconsin. These two powerful senators, both ardent anti-communists like Dix and Wurm and each representing states with large German populations, were openly hostile toward the Truman administration, were longstanding critics of the New Deal, and blasted America's postwar foreign policy as weak against communism. After the Simpson Commission recommended staying only some executions of Germans convicted at the Dachau trials, Langer and McCarthy spearheaded an effort to launch a broader Senate investigation of the Dachau trials.[41] Wurm's correspondence with Dix helped shape the arguments and provided some of the rhetoric employed by Langer and McCarthy on the Senate floor. Among other things, Dix shared Wurm's deep antipathy for Kempner, who at the time was working on the US Military Tribunal's "Ministries Trial" at Nuremberg. Together they sought to discredit the prosecutor publicly. In June, Dix traveled to Germany and met with Protestant officials to discuss Kempner and exchange information through Oberkirchenrat Rudolf Weeber, a high-level colleague of Wurm's in the Protestant leadership.[42] In October 1948 Dix asked Weeber and Wurm, on behalf of Senator Langer, "to obtain whatever information" he could about Kempner.

An acquaintance told Dix that Rudolf Diels, the chief of the Gestapo in 1933 and 1934, had worked together with Kempner prior to 1933 in the Prussian Ministry for Home Affairs. Dix even suggested that Diels had helped Kempner emigrate from Germany in 1935.[43] According to Dix, a German journalist had further reported that Kempner had employed Diels after the war in the collection of war crimes evidence against Nuremberg defendants. If this were true, Dix argued, then "politically much can be made of the fact that Kempner is willing to work with anybody, even Gestapo men."[44] Dix wondered if Diels had long been a communist agent, even during the Nazi years. Either way, Dix argued, such information could destroy Kempner's reputation and thus discredit the entire war crimes enterprise. Dix asked to be notified of any "similar cases of employment by Kempner of notorious former Nazis or Communists" that could be passed on to US senators. Wurm and Weeber quietly continued their own investigation into Kempner's alleged connections with communists.[45]

Wurm and Dix were raising once again the old Nazi canard that the Jews were in league with communism, as two prominent anti-communist US senators assisted them in recasting the trials as undercutting the US position vis-à-vis the Soviet Union in the deepening Cold War, which by now had entered a new phase with the Berlin Blockade. And it was not without effect. The Evangelical Bishop of Oslo, Eivind Berggrav, after he was cross-examined by Kempner during the 1948 Ministries Trial concerning defendant Ernst von Weizsäcker—former state secretary in the German Foreign Ministry and afterwards Hitler's ambassador to the Vatican—publicly described Kempner as "a most Gestapo-like man," and added that "the honor of America [was] at stake." In March 1949, "the wide publicity which was given to the public controversy between Bishop Wurm and the Public Prosecutor at the Nuernberg [*sic*] trials, Mr. Kempner" led the popular US theologian Reinhold Niebuhr, writing in *Christianity and Crisis,* to label Kempner's behavior as "questionable." Niebuhr lamented "the fact that it is so difficult to gain public attention for the moral problems of these trials" and that the power behind them was "wielded in places so remote from the home base that the light of public opinion does not play upon our policy." Niebuhr's article was distributed widely among churches in Germany, and the entire OMGUS (Office of Military Government, US) Religious Branch office, according to one of its officials, agreed strongly with the critiques expressed by Wurm, Berggrav, and Niebuhr.[46] Their office's conclusion was that the strong criticism by the churches had "had the effect of further undermining public confidence in the objectivity of international justice." Prominent British publications like *The Economist* and the London-based *Church Times* added their open agreement with the criticisms made by the German Evangelical and Catholic churches against the war crimes process.[47]

Wurm's multi-pronged campaign and his relationship with key officials in Allied countries grew deeper in 1949. Samuel Cavert of the Federal Council of Churches of Christ in America released official statements of concern about the trials and asked US politicians to investigate the German churches' charges. At one point, Cavert arranged a meeting with the US Attorney General Thomas Campbell Clark to lobby him personally.[48] John O'Donnell, well-known journalist at the *New York Daily News,* utilized materials that he acknowledged came from Wurm and Dix to write critical articles that were then syndicated nationwide. The vocal US lobbying group, the National Council for the Prevention of War (NCPW), also worked closely with the churches and with Senators Langer and McCarthy. The NCPW's long-time leader, Frederick J. Libby, kept Wurm apprised of sentiments among sympathetic individuals and organizations in the United States and often sent material to German newspapers.[49] Wurm reciprocated by providing Dix and Libby with the names of German defense lawyers with whom to consult,[50] along with statements from the law schools at Tübingen and Heidelberg that challenged the legality of the trials.[51] In March 1949, Wurm passed over copies of at least ten different dossiers from the defense attorneys of the Malmédy trial. Langer had them translated from German by the Library of Congress.[52] Weeber and Wurm also composed extensive memorandums outlining their protests against the war crimes trials, including one titled "The Continuation of the War in the Court Rooms," for the NCPW, Dix, Langer, and McCarthy to use in influencing public opinion in the United States.[53]

Did the extensive efforts by Wurm and other German church leaders bear fruit? Ultimately, they did not succeed in upsetting the Malmédy or other Dachau cases as such. In October 1949, the Senate subcommittee created by Langer's and McCarthy's Senate Resolution the previous January, led by Republican Senator Raymond Baldwin of Connecticut, found that allegations of physical abuse at Dachau were unfounded, that mock trials had not been widespread, and that other accounts of misconduct were exceptions rather than the rule in US war crimes trials. The report further suggested that there was "a plan [by] certain groups in Germany to revive the nationalist spirit in Germany through discrediting the US military government, and to profit by attacks on the latter," and it recommended that US authorities investigate the matter. Wurm took this as a threat against him and other church leaders.[54] Naturally, he was determined to have the last word, even with the formation of the Federal Republic of Germany, the end of Allied military government there, and the formation of Allied high commissions to supervise the new state. In cooperation with the NCPW, Wurm published an article in the international press condemning the Baldwin findings and accusing the subcommittee of "sidetracking" the key charges against the trials in order to condemn those—namely himself and other clergy specifically—who criticized the occupation. He also continued to condemn US-led trials. At the time, several leading German perpetrators condemned at Nuremberg still awaited execution. These included Oswald Pohl, the former chief of the SS Economic and Administrative Main Office (WVHA), Otto Ohlendorf, a former SS-Gruppenführer and former leader of Einsatzgruppe D in the Soviet Union, and three other Einsatzgruppen officers. With the help of defense attorneys like Alfred Seidl, Wurm challenged the convictions.[55] Republican congressman Orland K. Armstrong of Missouri, a longtime critic of US occupation policy, filed an ultimately unsuccessful writ of habeas corpus with the US Supreme Court on behalf of the condemned.[56] In the end, US High Commissioner John J. McCloy declined to stay the executions (carried out on 7 June 1951), though McCloy acknowledged to Wurm that he had given the elderly bishop's feelings and arguments serious consideration.[57]

In the end, occupation officials felt compelled to respond regularly to the charges leveled by the churches, publicly when necessary. They recognized a threat to the public belief in the legitimacy of the trials, which, if lost, could prevent the trials from having long-lasting impact on international law, global peace, and the ways in which the history of World War II would be understood for generations. Despite these efforts, though, the number of new trials in the 1950s decreased, while increasing numbers of convicted criminals were released before the end of their sentences. The churches' criticisms of the trial processes from their very beginnings helped undercut their legitimacy and public support for them. Interestingly, the German public's shock at the revelations of the 1958 Einsatzgruppen trial in Ulm, as if such deeds had not been brought to light in earlier trials, in part can be traced back to the churches' attacks on the morality and motives of earlier trials, and of war crimes prosecution more broadly.[58]

For this reason, further exploration of how the churches' dissent was discussed and debated internally among occupation officials provides valuable insights into the contours of the postwar trials during the first decade after the war. In addition, the churches' criticisms forced the Western Allies to sharpen their own conceptions and aims for the trials, as well as the language they used to describe and defend them for posterity. Determining the degree to which "iron sharpened iron" in such contexts may also provide new avenues through which to view how dissent from multiple sources and directions can affect the conduct of war crimes trials in any time or place. Exploring public pressure is a way to ensure that the cultural, political, and moral contexts of such trials are not forgotten in research. Such trials do not happen in a historical vacuum, immune from influence by global events, cultural biases, social expectations, or the clash of individual personalities. Nor should it be forgotten that those involved in such trials, whether as prosecutors, defendants, defense attorneys, judges, or observers, are human beings with their own aims and vulnerabilities. Indeed, further studies into individuals like Robert Kempner that seek to trace the origins of their legal thought, their personal experiences and beliefs, their biases and temperament, and how these all worked within the pressure-packed framework of war crimes trials, could tell us much about what such people prioritized and why. This contextualizes those involved in the trials and, indeed, the trials themselves. This then can provide a better platform on which to examine the larger legal, philosophical, and political ideals that often are themselves put on trial by outside observers, not only by the deliberations and debates in the courtroom.

The examination of public pressure can also help researchers track how the perceptions of trials, over time, can build myths and false narratives that do not conform to the historical and legal records of the trials themselves. The churches' charges against the trials, incomplete and cloaked in strong moral and religious language, helped produce myths about the trials, about the Nazi past, and about the Holocaust. These myths found common currency throughout the world and proved necessary for many scholars to work to refute. Such myths, once entrenched, have proven difficult to dislodge from popular consciousness, classrooms, popular media, and political discourse. Studies that challenge such notions like Ronald Smelser and Edward J. Davies' examination of the myths of the Eastern Front in US popular culture are ideal models for how public pressure and perception can be studied to reach sound fact-based counterarguments to popular historical myths.[59]

In order to maximize its potential and benefit, studies of Holocaust justice should be open to examining all of the factors and issues that the Holocaust itself brought forth so painfully—the role of politics and ideology, expressions in art and literature, notions of universal law and order, religious and philosophical shortcomings and correctives, the roles of bystanders and observers, and the need for new precedents to be set in the laws and morality of nations and in their diplomatic relations. Public pressure, as nebulous and challenging to track definitively as it can be, nevertheless brings into the discussions of Holocaust justice the beliefs, attitudes, emotions, and ideas of the people who, over time, will help decide the degree to which the rulings and lessons of war crimes trials are internalized, accepted, remembered, and promulgated in the present and future. As living memory of the trials and the crimes they prosecuted disappears steadily, their legacies will have to continue to be explained and defended with the same—if not more—urgency than ever before, from multiple directions and sources beyond only scholars, academic publishing houses, and university seminars. This suggests that the inverse of the public pressure against the trials will play a significant role moving forward in keeping the trials relevant in a world increasingly removed from the time frame in which they occurred. Journalists, filmmakers, politicians, religious and secular organizations, foundations, and social media entities all have their part to play in creating relevant, cohesive, historically sound narratives that inform and enhance applicability of the trials' past to the problems of the present. For these reasons, such voices—whether they are from the German churches in the past attacking the trials, or from the numerous sources today that can either defend them or discard them—should neither be ignored nor dismissed as inconsequential.

JonDavid K. Wyneken received his Ph.D. in history from Ohio University. He is an adjunct professor of history at Seattle Pacific University. His publications include "Remembering the Architecture of Death: Teaching the History and Psychology of the Holocaust," in *The Holocaust: Memories and History,* ed. Victoria Khiterer et al. (2014); "The Western Allies, German Churches, and the Emerging Cold War in Germany, 1948–1952," in *Religion and the Cold War: A Global Perspective,* ed. Philip Muehlenbeck (2012); and "Memory as Diplomatic Leverage: Evangelical Bishop Theophil Wurm and War Crimes Trials, 1948–1952," *Kirchliche Zeitgeschichte* 19, no. 2 (2006).

NOTES

1. "The End of the War in Europe: Coming at a Gas-Engine Clip, It Outmatches Our Ability to Think About the Peace," *Life,* 7 May 1945, 30.
2. JonDavid K. Wyneken, "Driving Out the Demons: German Churches, the Western Allies, and the Internationalization of Memory of Nazism, 1945–1952," (Ph.D. diss., Ohio University, 2007).
3. The literature on the notions of "usable pasts" and German victimization is best summarized in Robert G. Moeller, *War Stories: The Search for a Usable Past in the Federal Republic of Germany* (Berkeley, CA, 2003); Bill Niven, ed., *Germans as Victims: Remembering the Past in Contemporary Germany* (London, 2006); Mary Nolan, "Air Wars, Memory Wars," *Central European History,* 38, no. 1 (March 2005): 7–40.
4. Held respectively at the National Archives and Records Administration in College Park, MD, [hereafter NARA]; The National Archives in Kew; and the Centre des Archives diplomatiques de La Corneuve.
5. Victoria Barnett, *For the Soul of the People: Protestant Protest Against Hitler* (New York, 1992); Matthew Hockenos, *A Church Divided: German Protestants Confront the Nazi Past* (Bloomington, IN, 2004); Peter Hoffmann, *The History of the German Resistance, 1933–1945* (Montreal, 1996); Michael Phayer, *The Catholic Church and the Holocaust, 1930–1965* (Bloomington, IN, 2000); Mary M. Solberg, ed., *A Church Undone: Documents from the German Christian Faith Movement, 1932–1940* (Minneapolis, MN, 2015); Gordon C. Zahn, *German Catholics and Hitler's Wars: A Study in Social Control* (Notre Dame, IN, 1988).
6. Ernst Klee, *Persilscheine und falsche Pässe: Wie die Kirchen den Nazis halfen* (Frankfurt am Main, 1991); Katharina von Kellenbach, *The Mark of Cain: Guilt and Denial in the Post-War Lives of Nazi Perpetrators* (New York, 2013); Hilary Earl, *The Nuremberg SS-Einsatzgruppen Trial: Atrocity, Law, and History* (New York, 2009); Richard Merritt, *Democracy Imposed: US Occupation Policy and the German Public, 1945–1949* (New Haven, CT, 1995); Norbert Frei, *Adenauer's Germany and the Nazi Past: The Politics of Amnesty and Integration* (New York, 2002); Gerald Steinacher, *Nazis on the Run: How Hitler's Henchmen Fled Justice* (New York, 2011).

7. "Protokoll über die am 4 Oktober 1945 stattgefundene Unterredung v. 2 amerikan. Offizieren aus dem hauptquartier des Gen. Eisenhower mit Sr. Eminenz," Erzbistumsarchiv München und Freising [hereafter EBA-M], Faulhaber Nachlass [FN] Bestandsnummer [BN] 7501, 2.

8. Robert E. Conot, *Justice at Nuremberg* (New York, 1983), 78–81, 501–7. Alfred Seidl became a notorious defender of and apologist for Nazi war criminals long after the IMT. See Norman J.W. Goda, *Tales from Spandau: Nazi Criminals and the Cold War* (New York, 2008), 64–65, 230–31, 234–35.

9. Seidl to Faulhaber, 5 October 1946, EBA-M, FN, BN 8504; Aufzeichnung Faulhabers, Betreff: Dr. Hans Frank, Schlussformel, October 17, 1946, in *Akten Kardinal Michael von Faulhaber*, vol. III: *1945–1952* (Mainz, 2003), 215–18.

10. See Robert A. Graham, *The Vatican and Communism in World War II: What Really Happened?* (San Francisco, 1996); Phayer, *The Catholic Church and the Holocaust*, 41–66, 159–83.

11. For the most recent research on the Allied bombing campaigns against Germany, see Richard Overy, *The Bombers and the Bombed: Allied Air War Over Germany, 1940–1945* (New York, 2013). For recent summations of the nature of the Soviet advance into Germany, see Richard Bessel, *Germany, 1945: From War to Peace* (London, 2009), 10–66; Richard J. Evans, *The Third Reich at War* (New York, 2009), 435–505; and Ian Kershaw, *The End: Germany 1944–45* (New York, 2012), 167–206. On the Soviet occupation of Germany after 1945, see Norman M. Naimark, *The Russians in Germany: A History of the Soviet Zone of Occupation, 1945–1949* (Cambridge, MA, 1995). For recent research on the expulsion of Germans, see R.M. Douglas, *Orderly and Humane: The Expulsion of the Germans after the Second World War* (New Haven, CT, 2012); also Timothy Snyder, *Bloodlands: Europe Between Hitler and Stalin* (New York, 2010), 313–37.

12. *Das Oberbild,* 16 October 1946, 3–4, EBA-M, FN, BN 8504.

13. Archeveque Conrad Gröber à le Gouvernement Militaire, 1947, Erzbistumsarchiv Freiburg im Breisgau [hereafter cited as EBA-F], GN, Signatur Nb8 / 66.

14. Landesbischof Wurm to Lord Justice G. Lawrence, Nuremberg, 16 September 1946, Landeskirchliches Archiv Stuttgart [hereafter LAS], Wurm Nachlass [WN], BN D1, 272.

15. OMG-B[avaria] Intelligence Branch, "Das Nuremberger Echo," *Suddeutsche Zeitung,* 8 October 1946, NARA, Record Group [RG] 260, Box 180, Records of Intelligence Division, Folder #13/41-4.4.

16. Quote from Letter from Wurm to George Bell, Anglican Bishop of Chichester, 10 May 1947, LAS, WN, BN D1, 235; Anglican Bishop of Chichester George Bell to Wurm, 5 May 1947, LAS, WN, BN D1, 235; Wurm to Ambassador Robert Murphy, American Military Government, Berlin, 19 January 1947, LAS, WN, BN D1, 272.

17. Goda, *Tales From Spandau,* 76–77.

18. Landesbischof Wurm to the Lordbishop of Chichester, 5 January 1947, LAS, WN, BN D1, 276.

19. Kempner to Wurm, 12 May 1948, LAS, WN, BN D1, 289. Wurm's initial letter is not in the correspondence. Kempner, however, quoted passages from it.

20. Lucius Clay to Bishop Theophil Wurm, 19 June 1948, LAS, WN, BN D1, 289.

21. See Robert M.W. Kempner, "The Enemy Alien Problem in the Present War," *The American Journal of International Law* 34, no. 3 (July 1940), 443–58; Robert M.W. Kempner, "The German National Registration System as Means of Police Control of Population," *Journal of Criminal Law and Criminology* 36, no. 5 (January/February 1946): 362–87. See Robert M.W. Kempner, "The Nuremberg Trials as Sources of Recent German Political and Historical Materials," *The American Political Science Review* 44, no. 2 (June 1950): 447–59; "Hitler and Rosenberg's Secret Plans for the Annihilation of the Christian Churches after the War," EBA-M, FN, BN 8515. For more on Kempner, see Gerhard Niederstucke and Thomas F. Schneider, *Robert M.W. Kempner (17.10.1899–15.8.1993): Reden zum Kempner-Gedenken in Berlin und Osnabrück aus Anlass seines 100. Geburtstages* (Osnabrück, 2000); Thomas Schneider and Robert M.W. Kempner, *Robert M.W. Kempner: Bibliographie* (Osnabrück, 1987).

22. Wurm was not unique among German Protestant leaders in this belief. See Ronald Webster, "Opposing 'Victor's Justice': German Protestant Churchmen and Convicted War Criminals in Western Europe after 1945," *Holocaust and Genocide Studies* 15, no. 1 (Spring 2001): 47–69.

23. Wurm to Kempner, 29 January 1948, LAS, WN, BN D1, 289.

24. For more on use of the Boer War in Nazi propaganda, see Gerwin Strobl, *The Germanic Isle: Nazi Perceptions of Britain* (New York, 2000).

25. Wurm to Kempner, 19 February 1948, LAS, WN, BN D1, 289.

26. Abschrift, Die Ev. Landeskirche in Wuerttemberg, Ev.-luth. Kirche in Bayern r.d.Rh., Vereinigte Evgl. Prot. Landeskirche Badens, Evgl. Kirche in Hessen-Nassau to Clay, 20 May 1948, LAS, WN, BN D1, 289

27. Clay to Wurm, 19 June 1948, LAS, WN, BN D1, 289.

28. Kempner to Wurm, 16 March 1948, LAS, WN, BN D1, 289.

29. Lucius Clay to Bishop Theophil Wurm, 19 June 1948, LAS, WN, BN D1, 289.

30. Wurm to Kempner, 5 June 1948, LAS, WN, BN D1, 290. Wurm's public response to Kempner's statements came a few weeks earlier. See "Rede des Herrn Landesbischofs im 4. Ev. Landeskirchentag vom 20. Mai 1948," LAS, WN, BN D1, 289.

31. Newer interpretations and evidence are explored in Tomaz Jardim's chapter in this volume and in his *The Mauthausen Trial* (Cambridge, MA, 2012); a larger examination of the Malmédy case and trial can be found in Steven Remy, *The Malmédy Massacre: The War Crimes Controversy* (Cambridge, MA, 2017).

32. Copy of Petition for Writ of Habeas Corpus, to the US Supreme Court, petition by Willis M. Everett, Jr., on behalf of Valentin Bersin, et al. (including Sepp Dietrich, etc.) vs. Harry Truman, James Forrestal (US Secretary of Defense), Kenneth Royall (Secretary of the Army), General Omar Bradley (US Army Chief of Staff), and Thomas Clark (US Attorney General) over conduct of the

Malmédy defendants trial at Dachau, 11 May 1948, LAS, WN, BN D1, 291. For background and detail on Everett and the Malmédy trial, see James J. Weingartner, *A Peculiar Crusade: Willis M. Everett and the Malmédy Massacre* (New York, 2000); Remy, *The Malmédy Massacre.*

33. For example, see "Memorandum: Dachau, August 26, 1947" and other dossiers in LAS, WN, BN D1, 292.

34. Report, "Kriegsverbrecher-Gefängnis I (War Criminal Prison I)," Landsberg, April 1948, LAS, WN, BN D1, 289.

35. Landesbischof D. Wurm to Dr. Robert M.W. Kempner, Nuremberg, 5 June 1948, LAS, WN, BN D1, 290.

36. Rat der Evangelischen Kirche in Deutschland, Der Vorsitzende, (Landesbischofs Wurm, Meiser, Wustemann [Hessen-Kassel], Bender [Baden], Kirchenpraesident D. Niemoeller, D.D., D.D. Hessen, Vice Chairman of the Council of the Evangelical Church in Germany, to the Honorable George C. Marshall, Secretary of State Department, Washington, DC, to the Honorable Kenneth C. Royall, Secretary of the Army, Washington, DC, and to the Honorable Senator Arthur H. Vandenbergh, President of the US Senate and Chairman of the Foreign Relations Committee US Senate Office Building, Washington, DC, August 1948, LAS, WN, BN D1, 272.

37. Wurm to John Foster Dulles, 18 October 1948, LAS, WN, BN D1, 272.

38. Wurm statement, "Nuremberg and Dachau," October 1948, LAS, WN, BN D1, 297.

39. Oberkommando der Europäischen Streitskräfte, Amt des Oberkommandanten, 30 November 1948; Weeber an Herrn Landesbischof D. Meiser, December18, 1948, LAS, WN, BN D1, 292; "Statement by Bishop D. Wurm and Bishop Dr. Neuhäusler on the War Crimes Trials at Dachau," (ca. Fall 1948), LAS, WN, BN D1, 292.

40. Wurm statement, "Nuremberg and Dachau," October 1948, LAS, WN, BN D1, 297.

41. For detailed background on McCarthy's and Langer's involvement in the Malmédy investigations, see Thomas C. Reeves, *The Life and Times of Joe McCarthy: A Biography* (New York, 1982), 161–85.

42. Dix to Weeber, October 19, 1948, LAS, WN, BN D1, 291.

43. Dix to Weeber, January 14, 1949, LAS, WN, BN D1, 291.

44. Dix to Weeber, 19 October 1948, LAS, WN, BN D1, 291. Diels had been appointed head of the Gestapo in April 1933 by his mentor Hermann Göring. Diels had led the interrogation of the accused Reichstag arsonist Marinus van der Lubbe in February 1933 and managed to barely survive the 1934 "Night of the Long Knives" purge of the SA (Sturmabteilungen, Storm Troopers) by Heinrich Himmler and the SS (Schutzstaffel). He later was arrested as part of the roundup following the 20 July 1944 attempted assassination of Hitler. After the war, Diels provided a prosecution affidavit against Göring, but was also called to the stand by his mentor's defense team.

45. Dix to Weeber, 29 October 1948, LAS, WN, BN D1, 291.

46. Monthly Report, Religious Affairs, 3 March 1949, Concordia Historical Institute, St. Louis, MO [hereafter CHI], NL Arndt, box 1, Folder: Reports–Semi-Monthly, Religious Affairs.
47. Monthly Report, Religious Affairs, November 1948, CHI, NL Arndt, box 1, Folder: Reports–Semi-Monthly, Religious Affairs.
48. Memorandum of Conference with the Attorney General of the US on the Trial of German War Criminals (ca. February 1949), LAS, WN, BN D1, 293.
49. James Finucane [associate secretary, NCPW] to Wurm, 8 November 1949, LAS, WN BN D1, 303.
50. Oberkirchenrat to Frederick J. Libby, 11 February 1949, LAS, WN, BN D1, 293.
51. Weeber to Dix, 10 February 1948; Weeber to Libby, 11 February 1948, LAS, WN, BN D1, 293.
52. Dix to Weeber, 31 March 1949, LAS, WN, BN D1, 293.
53. "Memorandum Concerning the War Crimes Trials by Oberkirchenrat Dr. Weeber, Stuttgart, February 26, 1949," LAS, WN, BN D1, 293.
54. "The Demands of Justice: A Churchman's Critique of the Malmédy War Crimes Investigation," by Bishop D. Wurm (ret.), Stuttgart, Germany, 26 October 1949 [Distributed by National Council for Prevention of War, Washington, D.C.], LAS, WN, BN D1, 318.
55. Pohl to Wurm, 17 August 1948, LAS, WN, BN D1, 306, 5. See also Wurm to the High Commissioner John J. McCloy, 27 January 1950, LAS, WN, BN, D1, 295. For more on Pohl and his trial, see Michael Thad Allen, *The Business of Genocide: The SS, Slave Labor, and the Concentration Camps* (Chapel Hill, 2002); Thomas Alan Schwartz, "John J. McCloy and the Landsberg Cases," in *American Policy and the Reconstruction of West Germany, 1945–1955,* ed. Jeffry Diefendorf, Axel Frohn, and Hermann-Josef Rupieper (New York, 2004), 433–53.
56. From the office of O.K. Armstrong (R., Mo.), 22 February 1951, LAS, WN, BN D1, 295.
57. McCloy to Wurm, 14 February 1951, LAS, WN, BN D1, 306, 5.
58. On the Ulm trial, Patrick Tobin, "Crossroads at Ulm: Postwar West Germany and the 1958 Ulm *Einsatzkommando* Trial," Ph.D. diss., University of North Carolina at Chapel Hill, 2013.
59. Ronald Smelser and Edward J. Davies II, *The Myth of the Eastern Front: The Nazi-Soviet War in Popular Culture* (New York, 2007).

SELECT BIBLIOGRAPHY

Archives

Centre des Archives diplomatiques de La Corneuve.
Concordia Historical Institute, St Louis, MO.
Erzbistumsarchiv Freiburg im Breisgau
Erzbistumsarchiv München und Freising

Landeskirchliches Archiv Stuttgart
The National Archives, Kew, London.
National Archives and Records Administration, College Park, MD.

Secondary Sources

Akten Kardinal Michael von Faulhaber. Vol. III: *1945–1952.* Mainz: Matthias Grünewald, 2003.

Allen, Michael Thad. *The Business of Genocide: The SS, Slave Labor, and the Concentration Camps.* Chapel Hill, NC: University of North Carolina Press, 2002.

Barnett, Victoria. *For the Soul of the People: Protestant Protest against Hitler.* New York: Oxford University Press, 1992.

Bessel, Richard. *Germany, 1945: From War to Peace.* New York: HarperCollins, 2009.

Evans, Richard J. *The Third Reich at War.* New York: Penguin, 2009.

Conot, Robert E. *Justice at Nuremberg.* New York: Carroll and Graf, 1983.

Douglas, R.M. *Orderly and Humane: The Expulsion of the Germans after the Second World War.* New Haven, CT: Yale University Press, 2012.

Goda, Norman J.W. *Tales from Spandau: Nazi Criminals and the Cold War.* New York: Cambridge University Press, 2007.

Graham, Robert A. *The Vatican and Communism in World War II: What Really Happened?* San Francisco, CA: Ignatius, 1996.

Hockenos, Matthew. *A Church Divided: German Protestants Confront the Nazi Past.* Bloomington, IN: University of Indiana Press, 2004.

Hoffmann, Peter. *The History of the German Resistance, 1933–1945.* Montreal: McGill-Queens, 1996.

Jardim, Tomaz. "Rough Justice and the American Approach to War Crimes Prosecution: Dachau, Guantanamo Bay, and the Nuremberg Exception." Paper presented at Writing Retribution–Holocaust Justice and its Meaning: An International Conference, University of Florida, 21–22 February 2015.

Kempner, Robert M.W. "The Enemy Alien Problem in the Present War." *The American Journal of International Law* 34, no. 3 (July 1940): 443–58.

———. "The German National Registration System as Means of Police Control of Population." *Journal of Criminal Law and Criminology (1931–1951)* 36, no. 5 (January/February 1946): 362–87.

———. "The Nuremberg Trials as Sources of Recent German Political and Historical Materials." *The American Political Science Review* 44, no. 2 (June 1950): 447–59.

Kershaw, Ian. *The End: The Defiance and Destruction of Hitler's Germany 1944–45.* New York: Penguin, 2012.

Moeller, Robert G. *War Stories: The Search for a Usable Past in the Federal Republic of Germany.* Berkeley, CA: University of California Press, 2003.

Naimark, Norman M. *The Russians in Germany: A History of the Soviet Zone of Occupation, 1945–1949.* Cambridge, MA: Belknap Press of Harvard University Press, 1995.

Niederstucke, Gerhard, and Thomas F. Schneider, eds. *Robert M.W. Kempner (17.10.1899–15.8.1993): Reden zum Kempner-Gedenken in Berlin und Osnabrück aus Anlass seines 100. Geburtstages.* Osnabrück: Rasch, 2000.

Niven, Bill, ed. *Germans as Victims: Remembering the Past in Contemporary Germany*. London: Palgrave, 2006.

Nolan, Mary. "Air Wars, Memory Wars." *Central European History* 38, no. 1 (March 2005): 7–40.

Overy, Richard. *The Bombers and the Bombed: Allied Air War over Germany, 1940–1945*. New York: Penguin, 2013.

Phayer, Michael. *The Catholic Church and the Holocaust, 1930–1965*. Bloomington, IN: University of Indiana Press, 2000.

Reeves, Thomas C. *The Life and Times of Joe McCarthy: A Biography*. New York: Stein and Day, 1982.

Schneider, Thomas and Robert M.W. Kempner. *Robert M.W. Kempner: Bibliographie*. Osnabrück: Universität Osnabrück, 1987.

Schwartz, Thomas Alan. "John J. McCloy and the Landsberg Cases." In *American Policy and the Reconstruction of West Germany, 1945–1955*, ed. Jeffry Diefendorf, Axel Frohn, and Hermann-Josef Rupieper, 433–53. New York: Cambridge University Press, 2004.

Smelser, Ronald and Edward J. Davies II. *The Myth of the Eastern Front: The Nazi-Soviet War in Popular Culture*. New York: Cambridge University Press, 2007.

Snyder, Timothy. *Bloodlands: Europe between Hitler and Stalin*. New York: Basic Books, 2010.

Solberg, Mary M., ed. *A Church Undone: Documents from the German Christian Faith Movement, 1932–1940*. Minneapolis, MN: Fortress, 2015.

Webster, Ronald. "Opposing 'Victor's Justice': German Protestant Churchmen and Convicted War Criminals in Western Europe after 1945." *Holocaust and Genocide Studies* 15, no. 1 (2001): 47–69.

Weingartner, James J. *A Peculiar Crusade: Willis M. Everett and the Malmédy Massacre*. New York: New York University Press, 2000.

———. *Americans, Germans, and War Crimes Justice: Law, Memory, and the "Good War."* Santa Barbara, CA: Praeger, 2011.

Wyneken, JonDavid K. "Driving Out the Demons: German Churches, the Western Allies, and the Internationalization of Memory of Nazism, 1945–1952." Ph.D. diss., Ohio University, 2007.

Zahn, Gordon C. *German Catholics and Hitler's Wars: A Study in Social Control*. Notre Dame, IN: University of Notre Dame Press, 1988.

Chapter 12

Rough Justice and the US Approach to War Crimes Prosecution

Dachau, Guantanamo Bay, and the Nuremberg Exception

Tomaz Jardim

On 13 November 2001, US President George W. Bush signed an executive order establishing military commission courts to prosecute those suspected of complicity in the 9/11 terrorist attacks. The subsequent legal proceedings at Guantanamo Bay, Cuba, have come under immense scrutiny, often founded on claims that the rough justice meted out by US Army prosecutors represents a betrayal of US judicial commitments as established by the Nuremberg trials that followed World War II. Yet while the trials that have occurred at Guantanamo Bay may goad the conscience, the argument that they represent a radical departure from past practice rests upon a fundamentally flawed perception of the US postwar trial program. Indeed, there appears to exist a selective and collective amnesia about the United States' legal past with regard to war crimes prosecution.

Though the International Military Tribunal (IMT) at Nuremberg is rightly heralded for its vital contributions to international and war crimes law, it sat in judgment of only twenty-two of the nearly 1,900 war crimes suspects that the United States brought to justice for Nazi atrocities. The vast majority of those tried by the United States—some 1,672 defendants—appeared before military commission courts akin to those at Guantanamo Bay. This latter program, headquartered on the grounds of the former concentration camp Dachau, was typified by rapid trials, lax rules of evidence and procedure, persistent claims of violence and other forms of abuse in pursuit of confessions and, finally, by mass executions. Only through the substantial reintegration of the Dachau trials into the US legal memory does it become clear that while the Nuremberg trials had no domestic precedent or successor, the military commission courts at Guantanamo Bay are largely in keeping with how the United States has traditionally chosen to deal with war crimes suspects.

Just as the shock and audacity of the attacks of 11 September 2001 spurred the establishment of military commission courts at Guantanamo Bay, the outrage generated by the US encounter with Nazi atrocity, in particular at the liberated concentration camps, spurred the creation of the military courts at Dachau. The well-established desire of officials within the Bush administration to launch a trial program that would leave wide latitude for prosecutors while depriving defendants of legal protections that might inhibit their convictions made the IMT, with its emphasis on due process of law, an unappealing and impractical model. The rough justice of the military commission court system on the other hand, which had numerous precedents in the United States dating back to the Mexican-American War and which had achieved mass convictions following World War II, was a more appealing foundation on which to build.[1]

Indeed the Nuremberg model, established to try the Nazi leadership, would have been an odd fit for the generally low-ranking terror suspects— described by one military prosecutor as "the butcher, the baker, the candlestick maker"—at Guantanamo Bay.[2] Instead, an exploration of the military commission courts at Dachau, expressly created to try rank-and-file Nazi perpetrators, illustrates that the tribunals at Guantanamo Bay bear a far greater resemblance to the courts used by the United States to adjudicate the vast majority of Nazi war crimes cases than is commonly recognized. Establishing and interrogating this resemblance reveals both the exceptional nature of the IMT and the largely consistent US approach to war crimes prosecution based on the ever-evolving military commission system throughout US history.

On 1 November 1943, the United States, alongside its major wartime allies, issued the Moscow Declaration, establishing even before the war's end two distinct paths along which Nazi perpetrators would be brought to justice. The first path, reserved for the highest-ranking members of the Nazi state, would lead to Nuremberg, following a future "joint decision of the Governments of the Allies."[3] This joint decision came in August 1945 when representatives of the American, British, Soviet, and French governments met in London and hammered out a charter to govern a cooperative international trial for the senior surviving figures of the Third Reich. The innovation of the London Charter was its introduction of two new legal charges, "crimes against peace" and "crimes against humanity," aimed at prosecuting the war of aggression that began with the invasion of Poland in 1939 as well as Nazi mass atrocities, even those carried out against Germany's own Jewish subjects. These novel charges, alongside "conspiracy" and the more traditional charge of "war crimes," would be used to try twenty-two defendants before the International Tribunal at Nuremberg, as well as 185 additional defendants at twelve subsequent Nuremberg proceedings conducted unilaterally by the United States. These charges would also be employed by the International Tribunal for the Far East, which prosecuted twenty-eight Japanese government officials and military leaders for their conduct of the war in the Pacific. These internationally governed trials, which placed significant emphasis on due process of law and were guided by this new set of legal charges, were reserved, therefore, for a small minority of those ultimately brought to justice at the war's end for war crimes and other atrocities.

The second path established by the Moscow Declaration, intended for the vast majority of perpetrators, would lead to the establishment of the military commission courts at Dachau (as well as courts belonging to the other occupying powers) in order to fulfill the Declaration's promise that common war criminals would be "brought back to the scene of their crimes and judged on the spot by the peoples whom they have outraged."[4] As a result, the US Army began operating military commission courts in Germany even before the Allied governments had adopted the London Charter to govern the trials at Nuremberg.[5] Over time, the US Army opened no fewer than 3,887 cases and held 462 commission court trials before the end of 1947.[6] These trials, held largely at Dachau, therefore constitute by far the largest war crimes program ever undertaken in history. These proceedings include 226 trials against 646 defendants accused of crimes against US servicemen, and resulted in 199 death sentences. The proceedings also include 232 trials involving 1,030 defendants accused of mass atrocities in the German concentration camps, and resulted in an additional 233 death sentences.[7] Not surprisingly, the military commissions that followed World War II, despite scandals that later emerged, provided an attractive precedent for those who searched for an efficient method of rapidly convicting terror suspects in the wake of 9/11.

The astounding prosecutorial efficiency of the military commission court system based at Dachau was achieved through recourse to lax rules of procedure and evidence that eventually threatened to cast the entire program into disrepute. According to US Army guidelines published in 1945, military commissions were to adopt "simple and expeditious procedures designed to accomplish substantial justice without technicality."[8] To this end, the rules of evidence common to US domestic courts and courts-martial were explicitly rejected, replaced instead by the simple principle that the court could accept any evidence "having probative value to the reasonable man," including hearsay and unsworn testimony of witnesses not present at trial.[9] Dachau prosecutors were able to make frequent use of testimony from those with only second-hand knowledge of the crimes in question. At the US trials of German concentration camp personnel, for instance, the court often heard testimony concerning camp rumor, or stories that constituted what was referred to as the "common knowledge" of the inmates.[10] Witnesses were paid and housed in return for their testimony, leading Army authorities eventually to label some as "professional witnesses" for the suspiciously large number of trials at which they provided testimony.[11] More dubious still, convictions at Dachau were often won through the introduction of signed confessions of the accused—confessions that many defendants insisted had been extracted from them through violence, threats, or various forms of deception.[12]

The courts that rapidly dispensed justice at Dachau were not made up of legally trained judges, but rather seven to nine senior officers considered "men of stature in their professions."[13] Only one member of the court was required to have legal training and even then the rule was not absolute.[14] Verdict and sentence would be the result of a mere majority vote, with a two-thirds majority required for a sentence of death. There was no mechanism for appeal, but instead a review of each judgment by the Deputy Judge Advocate for War Crimes—the same person who had appointed the court as well as the US prosecution and defense teams. Defendants were at times tried in large groups of many dozens. The trial of personnel from Mauthausen concentration camp, for instance, brought sixty-one men into the dock and yet lasted only thirty-six days in court, providing each defendant an average of four hours of court time before all were declared guilty, and fifty-eight sentenced to death.[15] That the military commission system at Dachau was streamlined for expedient judgment is illustrated by the fact that Chief Prosecutor William Denson, responsible for all of the largest concentration camp trials at Dachau, returned to the United States in 1947 with a 100 percent rate of conviction for the 177 defendants he tried.[16]

No case at Dachau prefigured the rough justice of the military commissions to be re-established at Guantanamo Bay, nor the stinging criticism their rules and procedures would attract, more than the trial of seventy-three members of SS-Kampfgruppe Peiper for the slaughter of disarmed US servicemen at Malmédy in December 1944. Following an eight-week trial and subsequent deliberation that devoted only a few minutes to each defendant, the Dachau court found all but one of the seventy-three defendants guilty and sentenced forty-three to death.[17] Their US defense counsel Colonel Willis M. Everett argued that the defendants had not had a fair trial, and insisted that the confessions signed by his clients had been acquired through physical abuse, mock trials, stool pigeons, or phony priests. Though his ensuing 1948 petition to the US Supreme Court failed, the judges' 4–4 vote prompted both the US Army and the US Military Governor of Germany, Lucius Clay, to investigate these allegations and to review 127 other death sentences handed down by the Dachau courts.

While the results of these investigations were mixed, Clay's Administration of Justice Review Board reported in March 1949 that mock trials had occurred, during which prisoners forced to wear black hoods were brought before fake judges in order to gain confessions. The board found further evidence that interrogators had threatened harm to the families of the accused, and "did use some physical force on a recalcitrant suspect."[18] Worse still were comments made to the press by Judge Edward L. van Roden, a member of an earlier legal review of Dachau trial sentencing launched in 1948 by the US Army and led by Texas Supreme Court Justice Gordon Simpson. In February 1949, van Roden reported that he had seen evidence that beatings and mock-trials were in fact commonplace, and that such activities had caused "permanent and irreparable damage" to "the prestige of America and American justice." Military authorities at Dachau, van Roden insisted, had "abused the powers of victory and prostituted justice to vengeance."[19] A subsequent Senate subcommittee investigation, while partly exonerating the US military trial program, heard explosive charges of torture and abuse, leading Republican Senator Joseph McCarthy to accuse US Army personnel of using "Gestapo tactics" in pursuit of their cases.[20] All remaining executions of war crimes convicts were halted.

Some sixty-five years following the scandal created by the Malmédy trial and the Dachau trial program more broadly, reports of the torture of war crimes suspects and a prosecution program far too rough to produce true justice again echo through the US Senate and reverberate in the press. When compared to Nuremberg, Guantanamo indeed appears as a dramatic departure from US legal principle. Yet the existence of the Dachau trial program, as well as its scope, nature, and genealogical relationship to Guantanamo Bay, illustrate that this popular comparison is an odd one to make. Like Nuremberg prosecutor Benjamin Ferencz once explained when asked to compare the IMT to the Dachau trials, comparing the IMT to Guantanamo Bay is akin to comparing "apples and trucks."[21] Conversely, the seldom-made comparison between Guantanamo Bay and the previous incarnation of military justice at Dachau is far more fruitful and reveals deep continuities that fundamentally challenge the popular and often triumphalist postwar US legal legacy typified by Nuremberg.

Military Commission Order No. 1, issued by the US Department of Defense in 2002, established courts at Guantanamo Bay that strongly resemble those at Dachau, in part through the adoption of various rules and principles of World War II-era military commissions virtually word-for-word.[22] The courts at Guantanamo, as at Dachau, are made up of military officers, only one of whom requires legal training. Stricter than at Dachau, the rules for the Guantanamo courts stipulate that a two-thirds majority vote among the judges is required for conviction, and a unanimous vote in instances where the defendant may be sentenced to death. As at Dachau, there is no appeals procedure, but instead a review of each trial by the appointing authority. The controversial rules of evidence at Guantanamo are virtually identical to those drawn up by the US Army during World War II. Any evidence is admissible by the court that "would have probative value to the reasonable person," only slightly modernized from the Dachau-era rule regarding "probative value to the reasonable man."[23] In sharp contrast to Nuremberg and its emphasis on documentary evidence, the past and present tribunals governed by these rules have permitted the extensive use of hearsay, as well as testimony provided by witnesses not present in court or available for cross-examination.

Most troubling at both Dachau and Guantanamo have been allegations of torture and abuse in the service of gaining confessions. While the Malmédy investigation revealed the use of mock trials and executions, and deprivation and violence against recalcitrant subjects, such behavior was not limited to that case. Instead, accusations of abuse rippled through many of the major trials at Dachau. Benjamin Ferencz, who interrogated numerous suspects to be tried by the US Army for concentration camp crimes, insisted he had had no qualms both threatening and humiliating his subjects in pursuit of a confession. "Tell me the truth or I'll kill you," he explained, "that seemed to make a big impression."[24] While the 2014 US Senate Intelligence Committee report on torture makes it clear that abuse of a more systematic and perverse nature has come to define the treatment of suspects captured during the "War on Terror," the phenomenon is not new nor exceptional but by degree.[25]

Indeed, US authorities went to great lengths to ensure that the war crimes suspects held both at Dachau and Guantanamo Bay had no recourse to the protections offered by the Geneva Conventions. The 1929 Convention Relative to the Treatment of Prisoners of War declares that "no coercion may be used on prisoners to secure information," and that prisoners under interrogation could not be "threatened, insulted, or exposed to unpleasant or disadvantageous treatment of any kind whatsoever." In addition, this convention states that a prisoner of war could only be brought to trial "by the same courts and according to the same procedure as in the case of persons belonging to the armed forces of the detaining Power."[26] In line with a 1945 US Supreme Court ruling, however, US military authorities instructed those working at Dachau that involvement in war crimes nullified an individual's right to receive the benefits associated with prisoner of war status. The 15,000 internees held by the US Army in Germany at war's end were instead labeled only "unlawful belligerents."[27] In February 2002, a memo issued by George W. Bush similarly instructed US forces to consider the protections of the Geneva Convention as void for al-Qaeda or Taliban fighters captured in Afghanistan, as neither organization was a "High Contracting Party to Geneva."[28] Officials in the Pentagon fortified this position through reference to *Ex Parte Quirin*, the case of eight Nazi saboteurs caught on US soil in 1942 and brought before a military commission by executive order of the president.[29] The US Supreme Court had ruled the defendants ineligible for Geneva protection because they were caught engaged in acts of war without uniform. The eight would-be saboteurs, as well as those captured during the "War on Terror," instead were labeled "unlawful combatants" and were left without Geneva protection.[30]

Since 2002 and the issuing of Military Commission Order No. 1, a series of US Supreme Court rulings critical of proceedings at Guantanamo Bay have spurred revisions to the rules and procedures governing America's military commission courts. In 2006, the Court ruled in *Hamdan v. Rumsfeld* that detainees could not be deprived of the rights enshrined in the Geneva Convention, but must instead be treated humanely and protected from torture, cruelty, and outrages upon personal dignity.[31] In 2008, the Supreme Court went further, determining that all detainees at Guantanamo Bay, including those labeled as unlawful enemy combatants, had the right to file habeas corpus petitions to federal courts in order to challenge their detention.[32] Nonetheless, the courts at Guantanamo Bay remain highly controversial, given their on-going use of hearsay evidence and evidence obtained through "enhanced interrogation techniques," the restricted access of defendants to the evidence against them, and the fact that even those who serve out their sentences are not guaranteed release from captivity.

Given the nature of the justice meted out at Guantanamo Bay, it is not surprising that this latest incarnation of US military commission courts has come in for withering criticism. What is surprising is how poorly understood the deep continuities in the US approach to war crimes prosecution are. Otherwise informed critics appear unaware that the vast majority of

Nazi war criminals were tried at Dachau, or are unwilling to look beyond
the triumphalist narrative that sees Nuremberg, with its emphasis on full
due process of law, as the centerpiece of the US response to Nazi criminality. Richard Dicker, director of Human Rights Watch's International Justice
Program, writes in *The Guardian* that "U.S. military commissions revoke for
al-Qaeda suspects the standard of justice extended to Nazi war criminals,"
in contrast to the past commitment to "the uncharted path of international
prosecution for monstrous crimes."[33] In a *New York Times* op-ed, international lawyer and professor Guénaël Mettraux recommends "a Nuremberg"
for those at Guantanamo Bay, that "would bring the nation back within the
tradition of law and justice that it so forcefully defended six decades ago."[34]

Tim McCormack, the Red Cross Professor of International Law at the
University of Melbourne, has an equally myopic view of the US legal past.
Seemingly oblivious to the nature or sheer existence of the Dachau trials,
he writes, "In 1945, the [Truman] administration was committed to legal
principle ... Now the [Bush] administration is determined to proceed with
the pretence of running a 'court' with non-legally trained judges, no requirement for written reasons for the judgement, no independent appeal process,
no limitations on the admission of evidence."[35] In a similar fashion, Norbert
Ehrenfreund's *The Nuremberg Legacy: How the Nazi War Crimes Trials Changed
the Course of History,* which includes no reference to the Dachau trials, concludes that Nuremberg convinced the world "that the United States was the
guardian of the highest ideals of justice." "America," he warns, "must take
back that legacy and save it from being lost."[36] Even former Nuremberg prosecutor Henry King, Jr. dramatically simplified the United States' legal past
in his 2007 criticism of Guantanamo Bay, seeming to forget that the legal
procedures and safeguards at Nuremberg were reserved for a privileged few.
"The United States has always stood for fairness," he lamented. "We were
the ones who started war crimes tribunals and we're the architects. I don't
think we should turn our backs on that architecture."[37]

The failure to integrate the Dachau trials substantially into the legal
memory of World War II therefore has not been without consequence. In
scholarship on the Third Reich and postwar justice, the early historiographical preference for top-down models of the Nazi state and Nazi criminality
may help to explain the near exclusive focus on Nuremberg, where only
figures of authority faced trial. It is important to note that the press did not
share this disinterest, but instead paid substantial attention to the Dachau
trials as they occurred, with coverage that rivaled that generated by Nuremberg. A quick search through the *New York Times,* for instance, reveals more
than two hundred stories on the various trials at Dachau between 1945 and
1948. While scholarly interest in these trials has since grown, studies of US

postwar justice that acknowledge the importance of the program at Dachau seldom dedicate to it a fraction of the space reserved for the IMT. The end result is a popular and skewed perception of the US postwar legal legacy that makes the tribunals at Guantanamo Bay (or the refusal to join the International Criminal Court, for that matter) difficult to comprehend as anything other than a deep violation of US judicial ideals. A new scholarly emphasis, which correctly sees the Dachau trial program as the central pillar of the US response to Nazi criminality and Nuremberg as a rich and laudable exception to common practice, will also view the commission courts at Guantanamo Bay as largely in keeping with the well-trodden but lamentable path the United States traditionally has chosen to deal with war criminals in its custody.

Tomaz Jardim received his Ph.D. in history from the University of Toronto and is an associate professor of history at Ryerson University in Toronto. He is the author of *The Mauthausen Trial: American Military Justice in Germany* (2012). He is currently working on a book exploring the trials of Ilse Koch, known notoriously as "The Bitch of Buchenwald."

NOTES

1. For a comprehensive look at military commission courts throughout US history, see Peter Maguire, *Law and War* (New York, 2001).
2. Jess Bravin, *The Terror Courts–Rough Justice at Guantanamo Bay* (New Haven, CT, 2013), 128.
3. Winston Churchill, Franklin Roosevelt, and Joseph Stalin, "Moscow Declaration, November 1, 1943," in Michael Marrus, ed., *The Nuremberg War Crimes Trial 1945–46: A Documentary History* (Boston, 1997), 20–21.
4. Ibid.
5. In addition to establishing military courts in Germany, the United States also created military tribunals in the Pacific theater for the prosecution of Japanese war crimes suspects. The trial of General Tomoyuki Yamashita for war crimes committed during the occupation of the Philippines proved particularly controversial, with the court sentencing the defendant to death for atrocities committed by soldiers under his command in the Philippines, but not according to his orders, nor with his knowledge. The court, which relied to a substantial degree on hearsay evidence, nonetheless declared that it had been Yamashita's responsibility as commander to prevent his troops for committing atrocities in the heat of battle. See Allan A. Ryan, *Yamashita's Ghost* (Lawrence, KS, 2012)
6. Lt. Col. C.E. Straight, *Report of the Deputy Judge Advocate for War Crimes, European Command, June 1944 to July 1948,* National Archives and Records Administra-

tion, College Park, MD [hereafter NARA] Record Group [RG] 549, Records of the US Army, Europe, General Admin., box 13, p. 160.

7. Lisa Yavnai, "U.S. Army War Crimes Trials in Germany, 1945–1947," in *Atrocities on Trial,* ed. Patricia Heberer and Jürgen Matthäus (Lincoln, NE, 2008), 56–62.

8. *JCS 1023/10–Directive on the Identification and Apprehension of Persons Suspected of War Crimes or Other Offenses and Trial of Certain Offenders, July 8, 1945,* NARA, RG 549, General Admin., box 1.

9. Straight, *Report of the Deputy Judge Advocate for War Crimes,* 162.

10. Tomaz Jardim, *The Mauthausen Trial–American Military Justice in Germany* (Cambridge, MA, 2012), 126–27.

11. Straight, *Report of the Deputy Judge Advocate for War Crimes,* 188.

12. See for instance Jardim, *The Mauthausen Trial,* 162–67.

13. *Rules of Procedure in Military Government Courts, June, 1945.* Reproduced in Holger Lessing, *Der Erste Dachauer Prozess, 1945–1946* (Baden-Baden, 1993), Appendix 5.

14. The tribunal that tried Justus Gerstenberg for the killing of a US airman, for instance, contained no defense attorney. Nonetheless, the reviewing authority found that this did not constitute an injustice to the accused, allowing for his subsequent execution. Straight, *Report of the Deputy Judge Advocate for War Crimes,* 57; Jardim, *The Mauthausen Trial,* 38.

15. See Jardim, *The Mauthausen Trial.*

16. William Dowdell Denson, *Justice in Germany: Memories of the Chief Prosecutor* (Mineola, NY, 1995), 3.

17. See James J. Weingartner, *Crossroads of Death: The Story of the Malmédy Massacre and Trial* (Berkeley, CA, 1979).

18. Headquarters European Command, *Final Report of Proceedings of Administration of Justice Review Board, February 14, 1949,* NARA, RG 549, General Admin., box 13.

19. Frank M. Buscher, *The U.S. War Crimes Trial Program in Germany, 1946–1955* (New York, 1989), 41.

20. Ibid., 32.

21. Benjamin Ferencz, Interview by Tomaz Jardim, 11 April 2006.

22. Department of Defense, *Military Commission Order No. 1, 26 March 2002,* retrieved January 2015 from http://www.defense.gov/news/Mar2002/d20020321ord.pdf.

23. Ibid.

24. Benjamin Ferencz, Interview by Tomaz Jardim, 11 April 2006.

25. Senate Select Committee on Intelligence, Committee Study of the Central Intelligence Agency's Detention and Interrogation Program, retrieved January 2015 from http://www.intelligence.senate.gov/study2014/sscistudy1.pdf.

26. Convention Relative to the Treatment of Prisoners of War, Geneva, 29 July 1929, retrieved January 2015 from http://avalon.law.yale.edu/20th_century/geneva02.asp#art3.

27. Straight, *Report of the Deputy Judge Advocate for War Crimes,* 54; Jardim, *Mauthausen Trial,* 117–18.

28. George W. Bush, Memorandum for the Vice President et al., Subject: Humane Treatment of Taliban and al-Qaeda Detainees, Washington, DC, 7 February 2002, retrieved January 2015 from http://www.pegc.us/archive/White_House/ bush_memo_20020207_ed.pdf.
29. See Louis Fischer, *Nazi Saboteurs on Trial: A Military Tribunal and American Law* (Lawrence, KS, 2005).
30. Bravin, *The Terror Courts,* 34–35.
31. Supreme Court of the United States: Hamdan v. Rumsfeld, Secretary of Defense, et al., retrieved May 2015 from https://www.law.cornell.edu/supct/html/ 05-184.ZS.html.
32. Supreme Court of the United States, Boumediene et al. v. Bush, President of the United States, et al., retrieved May 2015 from https://www.law.cornell.edu/ supct/html/06-1195.ZS.html.
33. Richard Dicker, "Guantanamo's Perversion of Justice," *The Guardian,* 3 September 2012.
34. Guenael Mettraux, "A Nuremberg for Guantanamo," *New York Times,* 30 August 2009, A27.
35. Tim McCormack, "Nuremberg's Lessons for Guantanamo," *The Age* [Melbourne, Australia], 22 November 2005, retrieved January 2015 from http:// www.theage.com.au/news/opinion/nurembergs-lessons-for-guantanamo/2005/ 11/21/1132421599765.html
36. Norbert Ehrenfreund, *The Nuremberg Legacy: How the Nazi War Crimes Trials Changed the Course of History* (New York, 2007), 207.
37. Jane Sutton, "Nuremberg Prosecutor Says Guantanamo Trials Unfair," *Reuters,* 11 June 2007.

SELECT BIBLIOGRAPHY

Bravin, Jess. *The Terror Courts–Rough Justice at Guantanamo Bay.* New Haven, CT: Yale University Press, 2013.
Brenner, Marie. "Taking on Guantanamo." *Vanity Fair* 559 (March 2007). Retrieved 4 August 2017 from https://www.vanityfair.com/news/2007/03/guanta namo200703.
Buscher, Frank M. *The U.S. War Crimes Trial Program in Germany, 1946–1955.* Westport, CT: Praeger, 1989.
Bush, George W. *Memorandum for the Vice President et al., Subject: Humane Treatment of Taliban and al-Qaeda Detainees, Washington, DC, February 7, 2002.* Retrieved 15 May 2015 from http://www.pegc.us/archive/White_House/bush_memo_20 020207_ed.pdf.
Davis, Morris D. "The Guantanamo I Know." *The New York Times,* 26 June 2007: A21.
Denson, William Dowdell. *Justice in Germany: Memories of the Chief Prosecutor.* Mineola, NY: Meltzer et al., 1995.

Department of Defense. *Military Commission Order No. 1, March 26, 2002.* Retrieved 30 January 2015 from http://www.defense.gov/news/Mar2002/d20020321ord.pdf.

Dicker, Richard. "Guantanamo's Perversion of Justice." *The Guardian,* 3 September 2012. Retrieved 19 August 2017 from https://www.theguardian.com/com mentisfree/2012/sep/03/guantanamo-perversion-justice.

Douglas, Lawrence. "A Kangaroo in Obama's Court." *Harpers,* October 2013. Retrieved 19 August 2017 from https://harpers.org/archive/2013/10/a-kangaroo-in-obamas-court/ (9 pages).

Ehrenfreund, Norbert. *The Nuremberg Legacy: How the Nazi War Crimes Trials Changed the Course of History.* New York: St. Martins, 2007.

Final Report of Proceedings of Administration of Justice Review Board, February 14, 1949. National Archives and Records Administration, College Park, MD, RG 549, Records of the US Army, Europe, General Admin., box 13.

Fischer, Louis. *Nazi Saboteurs on Trial: A Military Tribunal and American Law.* Lawrence, KS: University Press of Kansas, 2005.

Goldsmith, Jack. "The Shadow of Nuremberg." *The New York Times,* 20 January 2012: BR8.

Jardim, Tomaz. *The Mauthausen Trial–American Military Justice in Germany.* Cambridge, MA: Harvard University Press, 2012.

Maguire, Peter. *Law and War,* rev. ed.. New York: Columbia University Press, 2010.

Marrus, Michael, ed. *The Nuremberg War Crimes Trial 1945–46: A Documentary History.* Boston: Bedford/St. Martins, 1997.

McCormack, Tim. "Nuremberg's Lessons for Guantanamo," *The Age* [Melbourne, Australia], 22 November 2005. Retrieved 19 August 2017 from http://www.theage.com.au/news/opinion/nurembergs-lessons-for-guantanamo/2005/11/21/1132421599765.html.

Mettraux, Guenael. "A Nuremberg for Guantanamo," *The New York Times,* 20 August 20: A27.

Rose, David. "Guantanamo Bay on Trial." *Vanity Fair* 521 (January 2004). Retrieved 4 August 2017 from https://www.vanityfair.com/news/2004/01/guanta namo200401.

Ryan, Allan A. *Yamashita's Ghost.* Lawrence, KS: University of Kansas, 2012.

Sadat, Leila Nadya. "Shattering the Nuremberg Consensus: US Rendition Policy and International Criminal Law." *Yale Journal of International Affairs* (Winter 2008): 65–77.

Senate Select Committee on Intelligence. *Committee Study of the Central Intelligence Agency's Detention and Interrogation Program.* Retrieved 30 January 2015 from http://www.intelligence.senate.gov/study2014/sscistudy1.pdf.

Smith, Charles Anthony. *The Rise and Fall of War Crimes Trials–From Charles I to Bush II.* New York: Cambridge University Press, 2012.

Smith, Clive Stafford. *Bad Men: Guantanamo Bay and the Secret Prisons.* London: Phoenix, 2007.

Straight, Lt. Col. C.E. *Report of the Deputy Judge Advocate for War Crimes, European Command, June 1944 to July 1948.* National Archives and Records Administration,

College Park, MD, Record Group 549, Records of the US Army, Europe, General Admin., Box 13.

Supreme Court of the United States. Hamdan v. Rumsfeld, Secretary of Defense, et al. Retrieved 15 May 2015 from https://www.law.cornell.edu/supct/html/05-184 .ZS.html.

Supreme Court of the United States. Boumediene et al. v. Bush, President of the United States, et al. Retrieved 15 May 2015 from https://www.law.cornell.edu/ supct/html/06-1195.ZS.html.

Sutton, Jane. "Nuremberg Prosecutor Says Guantanamo Trials Unfair." *Reuters,* 11 June 2007. Retrieved 19 August 2017 from http://www.reuters.com/article/ us-guantanamo-nuremberg-idUSN6B38479920070611.

Tenove, Chris. "A Tribute Paid to Reason." *The Walrus* (November 2005). Retrieved 4 August 2017 from https://thewalrus.ca/2005-11-politics/.

Wala, Raha. "From Guantanamo to Nuremberg and Back: An Analysis of Conspiracy to Commit War Crimes Under International Humanitarian Law." *Georgetown Journal of International Law* 41, no. 3 (2010): 683–709.

Weingartner, James J. *Crossroads of Death.* Berkeley, CA: University of California Press, 1979.

Yavnai, Lisa. "U.S. Army War Crimes Trials in Germany, 1945–1947." In *Atrocities on Trial,* ed. Patricia Heberer and Jürgen Matthäus, 49–71. Lincoln, NE: University of Nebraska Press, 2008.

Zolo, Danilo. *Victors' Justice: From Nuremberg to Baghdad.* New York: Verso, 2009.

Index

Page numbers in *italic* indicate figures and tables.

Pronicheva, Dina, 72, 143
purification and purification rituals:
    antisemitism and, 52, 53;
    cleansing in, 50–51, 52, 53, 57,
    64n20; for the community and,
    49–51, 55–56, 57; culpability and,
    50–51; ecology of, 59–61; for the
    individual and, 49–50; language
    and metaphors for, 52–53, 59–61;
    of memory, 60–61; postwar trials
    as, 61, 62–63; retribution and, 49,
    57; rituals described and, 61–62;
    in Soviet Union, 53; of toxic
    ideologies, 61; transitional justice
    and, 49, 61–62

Rahm, Karl, 75, 83, 84, 85, 93n26
Raphaelson, Paul, 83, 95n52
Rauff, Walter, 100, 101, 109, 110, 111
Rechtman, Richard, 220
Reininghaus, Carl, 267, 282n10
reparations: about, 6, 10, 15n31,
    211–14, 224–26, 226nn2–4; active-
    passive victim dichotomy and,
    216; in Czechoslovakia, 77, 94n40;
    past and present relationship and,
    213, 220, 224, 225; for resisters,
    77, 94n40, 215–16, 218; survivor
    pathology and, 213, 221–24,
    230n45; transnational character
    of, 213, 218, 222, 224; trauma and,
    212, 213, 219–24, 225–26; victim
    as survivor and, 212, 213, 217–18;
    victimhood and, 212, 213, 216,
    223, 225, 226
restitution: about, 10, 226n3;
    conferences on, 238–39, 253n12,
    254n14; Holocaust restitution
    and, 235, 252n2; postwar trial
    scholarship and, 6, 15n31;
    property restitution and, 213,
    214–15, 217, 239–40; talionic
    restitution and, 57, 58. *See also* art
    and cultural objects restitution

restitution litigation in 1990s, US, 2, 6,
    10, 235–37, 238, 247–48
restitution litigation in twenty-
    first century, US: about, 236,
    240, 241, 252; art and cultural
    objects and, 238–39, 240–44,
    242, 245–46, 247, 252, 258n63,
    261n101, 262n109, 279; attorneys
    and, 6, 248; against companies,
    246, 247, 258nn67–68, 259n69;
    compensation payments and,
    247–48, 259n70; French railroads
    and, 244–45, 248–49, 256n52,
    257n55; Holocaust historiography
    and, 236, 246, 248–52, 260n86,
    260n91, 261nn101–3; Hungarian
    railroads and, 241–43, 256n43,
    256n45, 256n47; legal scholarship
    and, 6, 236, 248, 249–50, 260n86,
    261n106; out-of-court settlements
    and, 247; for slave laborers, 237,
    238, 247, 259n69, 261n101; Swiss
    banks settlements and, 246, 250,
    251, 259n70, 260n91, 261nn101–3;
    symbolic indemnification and,
    247–48
Rogat, Yosal, 34
Rosenberg, Paul, 245–46
Royall, Kenneth, 298
Růžička, Otakar, 80, 81, 82, 83–84, 85,
    93n27

Sailer, John, 278
Schabas, William A., 191
Schiele, Egon, 265, 266, 267, 274, 276,
    282n10
Schlingensiepen, Hermann, 48, 54
Schmid, Anton, 38–39
Scholem, Gershom, 28
Schwarz, Erika, 96n84
Schwarzbard, Sholem, 71–72
Seidl, Alfred, 293, 297, 301, 305n8
Seidl, Siegfried, 73, 81
Sekanina, Ivan, 85, 96n75